It's a Setup

It's a Setup

Fathering from the Social and Economic Margins

TIMOTHY BLACK AND SKY KEYES

OXFORD
UNIVERSITY PRESS

Oxford University Press is a department of the University of Oxford. It furthers
the University's objective of excellence in research, scholarship, and education
by publishing worldwide. Oxford is a registered trade mark of Oxford University
Press in the UK and certain other countries.

Published in the United States of America by Oxford University Press
198 Madison Avenue, New York, NY 10016, United States of America.

Library of Congress Cataloging-in-Publication Data
Names: Black, Timothy, author. | Keyes, Sky, author.
Title: It's a setup : fathering from the social and economic margins /
Timothy Black, Sky Keyes.
Description: New York, NY : Oxford University Press, 2021. |
Includes bibliographical references and index.
Identifiers: LCCN 2020023818 (print) | LCCN 2020023819 (ebook) |
ISBN 9780190062217 (hardback) | ISBN 9780190062224 (paperback) |
ISBN 9780190062248 (epub)
Subjects: LCSH: Fathers—United States—Social conditions—Case studies. |
Fathers—United States—Economic conditions—Case studies. |
Fathers—United States—Interviews. | Fatherhood—Social aspects—United States. |
Fatherhood—Economic aspects—United States. | Marginality, Social—United States.
Classification: LCC HQ756 .B553 2020 (print) | LCC HQ756 (ebook) |
DDC 306.874/2—dc23
LC record available at https://lccn.loc.gov/2020023818
LC ebook record available at https://lccn.loc.gov/2020023819

DOI: 10.1093/ oso/ 9780190062217.001.0001

1 3 5 7 9 8 6 4 2

Paperback printed by LSC Communications, United States of America
Hardback printed by Bridgeport National Bindery, Inc., United States of America

For Kaléa:
papa loves you very much,
Sky

And Greg:
the most amazing father I know,
Tim

Contents

Illustrations

Figures

Tables

Preface

It started with a knock on my office door. Standing there was a tall, thin man with a serious face. He took a seat and explained that he had been sent there by the university's academic counselor who worked with "nontraditional" students. After answering a few of her questions and sharing a little of his personal story, she told him, "You should go talk to Tim Black." His name was Sky.

Our conversation began on that fall day in 2007, thirteen years ago, and this book—in addition to deep friendship—is the consequence. Sky was 24 years old, was working in a Whole Foods warehouse, had deep familiarity with the streets, and because of his involvement in *Socialist Action* had read more broadly than most of my students graduating with bachelor's degrees. He spoke eloquently about issues concerning Colombia and South Africa, local union-organizing efforts, as well as a recent federal raid on the Latin Kings. Our conversation meandered from global issues to issues closer to home—to street gangs, prisons, and the drug trade. We talked for hours and, as we did, it became clear to me that Sky was what Antonio Gramsci had called an "organic intellectual." Sky had taken only one college course.

Working at the warehouse, he had saved his money to take more college courses, but he had been hoodwinked by the common view that taking courses from a private university would provide him with a better education. He was enrolled in two classes at the time and was gravely disappointed with his experience. I encouraged him to enroll in a public university where he would get more for his money. In the meantime, I hired him to work for me at the research center I directed at the university.

I was starting a new project when I met Sky and was hiring interviewers who had street experience and the skills to relate to socially and economically marginalized fathers. The two-year study began in 2008. Sky and one other extraordinary field researcher, who worked on the study for its duration, Matthew "Sagacity" Walker, assisted me in writing the final report, which we presented at the State Legislative Office Building in Hartford in 2010.

The journey toward writing a book manuscript began shortly after we finished our report. But our own lives would fill with drama as our analyses of
the transcripts deepened. I sold Sky a car, which he drove to California to be
closer to his family. He settled in Oakland, rented a room he could afford, and
walked through neighborhoods each day to and from the BART (subway)
in which he was identity checked by youth patrolling the borders. Although
an outsider, Sky had the skills and life experiences to negotiate these situations and receive the green light. He rode the BART each day, applying to
jobs, with the heaviness of nothingness closing in on all sides. We talked each
week and the growing stint of unemployment increased his weariness. His
eyes followed the can collectors during the day, while he walked the streets
late at night to test his mettle and draw closer to a familiar past. Club patrons
smiled at this handsome man as they left city ATMs; he smiled back, staring
at their wad of cash and glittering jewelry. Sky was living the chapter we were
writing at the time—the chapter about jobs and marginalization. Through it
all, we kept reading and analyzing transcripts, drafting chapters, and talking.
Always talking.

A former student reached out to me who was living in the Bay Area, and
I told her about Sky. She helped him find part-time work as a counselor with
the Progress Foundation in their Acute Diversion Unit. This was all Sky
needed; once inside the network of social services working with distressed
populations, his life skills were recognized. Soon, he started working as a case
manager in the Tenderloin district of San Francisco, where he was assigned
a caseload of clients struggling with drug addictions, mental health issues,
and homelessness. Educational requirements were waived and promotions
occurred as his uncanny ability to connect with his clients was recognized.
Soon he became trusted by his coworkers to represent them in their union
negotiations. Meanwhile, squeezed by the housing crisis in the Bay Area, he
moved into an SRO (single-room occupancy) dwelling in the Mission district in San Francisco. He now lived in the same environment in which he
worked. I could see the bare, dreary walls of the apartment where Sky resided
when we Skyped (no pun intended) each week, while Sky would tell me
stories about overdosed neighbors being carried out that week on stretchers.
While we continued reading and writing each week, it almost seemed as if
Sky was living our book.

I emailed sociologist Loïc Wacquant and told him about Sky to see if there
was some way to get him more intellectual nourishment. Loïc set him up with
one of his graduate students who was doing an ethnography involving SROs in

the city. They met several times, and I was sure that Sky was holding his own, even though he had virtually no college experience. In 2014, the American Sociological Association annual meeting was in San Francisco, and I walked the Tenderloin several times with Sky. Stories leaped from the sidewalks and corners where we walked and talked, and I observed head nods between men lying on the sidewalk and Sky as we passed. He was not just a case manager; he was an engaged case manager, in the fullest sense of the term.

Meanwhile, my own life was disrupted when I took a new position at Case Western Reserve University in Cleveland in 2012. I assumed positions in the social justice institute and the sociology department, including leadership roles in both. We kept Skyping through it all. Mary Patrice Erdmans and I published our book on teen mothers in 2015, using overlapping data, while Sky and I kept our project moving forward in fits and spurts. In 2017, Sky met a woman and moved out of his roach-infested apartment and in with her in a student-infested neighborhood in Berkeley. Ironically, his romantic partner was a Puerto Rican woman from Springfield, Massachusetts, where I had done fieldwork for more than two decades—the basis of my first book, *When a Heart Turns Rock Solid*.[1] I did not know her . . . and yet I did. We kept Skyping.

In 2018, as the first draft of our manuscript was nearing its end, Sky shared with me that his partner was pregnant. Sky was going to be a *father*, and each week he talked about his trepidations concerning fatherhood. Above all, he did not want to be the father his father had been, and the pregnancy had opened up a rush of memories about his father, leaving his stomach churning and his future refracted by the past. Once again, in an eerie way, Sky was living the book.

Sky's journey informed his interpretive sensibilities as it had when I first met him, and, as such, he dug deep into the thousands of pages of transcripts. My career of relating to marginalized men did not stop when I arrived in Cleveland. There, I immediately got "on the ground" in an alternative incarceration facility and began developing relationships with dispossessed men, most of whom were fathers. Accumulations of experiences and voices over 25 years echoed through my own consciousness as we reviewed and discussed our work.

This book reflects our intense relationship and the fusion of our lives and perspectives. Through it all, we shared ideas and experiences, learned from one another, and watched one another grow and age weekly on our computer screens. And through it all, we attempted to understand, as deeply as we could, the experiences of fatherhood among the most disadvantaged groups in our society.

Tim Black
Cleveland, Ohio
2020

Sitting where I am now in life—engaged to my partner, father of an amazing two-year-old, working in management at a nonprofit for families—it seems like a lifetime ago from when I walked into Tim's office in 2007. At that time, you could just as easily find me around activists, my warehouse coworkers, or "street entrepreneurs." The first two college classes I was taking were boring to me, and I was hungry to engage in research, to dive deeper.

Working on the team for the Nurturing Families Network (NFN) Study was one of the greatest experiences of my life. Conducting the interviews, discussing them with the team, writing the reports, presenting our findings—it was incredible. I connected deeply with the material; this could be me or my friends.

After the study wrapped up, Tim and I kept exploring it, along with two other studies that, together, spanned a decade. We saw there was enough material there to discuss marginalized fathers in a way that wasn't done enough—with real context. The funny thing is, neither of us has a great relationship with our fathers, to say the least, so we were very cautious at first. Ultimately, it's the material itself that convinced us. We agreed it was worth putting together, even though the subject of struggling fathers can cause a kneejerk reaction in conversation. There has to be a way to talk about struggling fathers, we believed, without minimizing women's struggles.

The project that Tim and I took on—that became this book—began with us endlessly pouring over transcripts and interviewers' notes. We linked up every week via videochat, discussing quotes, lifestories, and families. I moved to the Bay Area and Tim moved to Cleveland, but we kept the project moving forward.

Over the years my life has changed a lot, and not in a smooth and painless way. Sometimes working on the book was difficult to manage; other times it felt like the only worthwhile thing I was doing. We always kept pushing the ball forward, meeting weekly over videochat. I think Tim became my unofficial therapist during a couple of those meetings, when life had me stressed out, and that's just how it goes sometimes. Wherever I was at, my relationship with the material, with the work, with the fathers and mothers who had shared their lives and viewpoints, always took on new meaning for me. Not the least of which was when I became a father myself. The pressure of parental expectations and responsibilities that I had read and wrote so much about was now a part of my life.

We present this work to you with the humblest respect to the parents out there like those in our book, whose economic position and condition is evermore precarious in the new economy.

Sky Keyes
Berkeley, California
2020

Acknowledgments

Foremost, we are deeply appreciative of the fathers and mothers who contributed to our study. We are grateful for their time and their willingness to discuss difficult issues with us. We have done our best to represent them as men and women parenting on the social and economic margins, and we hope that our book honors their participation in the study, centers their voices, and encourages others to take notice of their daily struggles and the consequences of structural violence.

Because this research includes three different studies across a decade, we have many people to thank. At the top of our list are Karen Foley Schain, the former director of the Child Trust Fund, and Dr. John Leventhal, professor of Pediatrics at Yale Medical School, for their leadership and collaboration in research for over 15 years; co-principal investigators, Mary Patrice Erdmans and Stephen Markson; and field researcher extraordinaires, Ronald Albert and Mathew "Sagacity" Walker. Others who contributed to the research include Emmanuel Adero, Erik Beach, Meredith Clay Damboise, Madelyn Figueroa, Patrick Hynes, Lisa Jones, Kevin Lamkins, Lauren Lo Bue, Juhen Navarro, Victor Pacheco, Wesley Santiago, Omar Vazquez, Scott Virgin, and Christine Wooley.

We benefited immensely from critical feedback provided by several scholars, including Mary Patrice Erdmans, Michael Lewis, John O'Connor, George Gonos, Dale Dannefer, and Susan Hinze. Steve Killpack, coordinator of the Healthy Fathering Collaborative in Greater Cleveland, also read the entire manuscript and provided valuable commentary. In addition, Michael Slone dedicated extensive time to reviewing and preparing the manuscript. We also appreciate the work of James Cook, our editor at Oxford University Press, and Emily MacKenzie who shepherded us through the publication process and kept it moving at all times.

We want to thank the Children's Trust Fund, now a division of the Connecticut Department of Social Services, for funding the Couples Study and the NFN Study. The Children's Trust Fund's contributions included funds provided by the Community-Based Child Abuse Prevention Program from the U.S. Department of Health and Human Services, Administration of Children and Families, Children's Bureau. We also want to thank the Department of Social Services for funding the Father Initiative Study and Patricia Coker-Wilson, Dawn Homer-Bouthiette, and Anthony Judkins for their support of the research.

Sky would personally like to give thanks to his mother Diana, his sisters—Sunshine, Rainbow, Starrose, Gretchen, and Susanna—his Aunt Karen, his brother Nightsnow, Kumar Viswanathan, Charles Solomon, Daryl Dawkins, Matthew Lehet, Gustavo Morales, Pete Garcia, Ryan Murphy, Alexander Bunaev, Basilio Reyes, Scott Walsh, Tyeshon Johnson, Jose Biggie Ortiz, Joey and Brent Cunningham, Brande Brown, Anthony Patton, Hilmar, and G. Their support during this 10-year effort was crucial.

Finally, we want to express our deep gratitude to our life partners, Mary Erdmans and Yanina Rivera, for their support, patience, and compromises across life transitions and years of Sunday morning video-communication meetings. We also want to recognize the addition to Sky and Yanina's family, Kaléa, whose curiosity about the computer camera on Sunday morning always reminded us of the true importance of fatherhood. We love and appreciate you three deeply.

1

Introduction

As we move through the early 21st century, we see images of engaged fathers: fathers cooking dinner, walking hand in hand with children to the bus stop, pushing baby carriages, braiding hair, and holding babies. These images of black, brown, and white fathers can be found in magazines, on billboards, across computer screens, on televisions, and in films.

But not always.

In 2013, New York City initiated a shaming campaign directed at teen mothers and their unwed partners. Frowning, crying, and pensive babies, mostly black and brown, were shown on posters plastered in public places throughout the city, saying to mothers: "Honestly, Mom, chances are he won't stay with you. What happens to me?" And to fathers: "Dad, you'll be paying to support me for the next 20 years." Or perhaps to both, "If you finish high school, get a job, and get married before having children, you have a 98 percent chance of not being in poverty."[1]

These are different images of fatherhood. The former projects the responsible, involved father; the latter, the irresponsible, absent father. These are today's salient categories representing and defining fatherhood: responsible and involved versus irresponsible and absent.

The conceptions, representations, and expectations of fatherhood are fluid—they change across time, are embedded within social class and different racial and ethnic histories, expressed within biographies and interpersonal relationships, located within status hierarchies, and situated within varying practices of masculinity. Fatherhood is not so simple, and certainly not as simple as the binary construction of the involved or uninvolved father would have us believe. Moreover, the public images of fatherhood represent contested terrain—which image is being represented, valued, and affirmed and which is being devalued or even demonized. Which narrative dominates and why?

The engaged and nurturing father has gained cultural traction in a short period of time—arguably in less than one or, at most, two generations. On September 25, 1954, iconic illustrator Norman Rockwell's *Breaking Home*

It's a Setup. Timothy Black and Sky Keyes, Oxford University Press (2021). © Timothy Black and Sky Keyes.
DOI: 10.1093/oso/9780190062217.003.0001

Ties appeared on the front page of *The Saturday Evening Post*. The painting showed a father and his son, waiting for the train that will take the son away to college. The father, dressed in denim with a cigarette hanging from his mouth, looks forlorn as he bends away from his son and stares off in the distance. His fresh-faced son, awkwardly wearing a tie and jacket, with a stack of books in front of him, looks in the other direction for the train. Discomfort emanates, silence permeates, while masculinity insinuates. Affection is apparent, but painfully avoided.

Rockwell's portrayal of fathers, however, was not so simple. He also painted a father feeding his infant, reading to his daughter, and affectionately greeting his wife and children as he arrived home from work. However, these fathers wore ties, suggesting a social class difference in emotional expression and father involvement. Still, the fathers in these illustrations were almost always dressed in their work clothes, taking care of children in and around work schedules. Whether wrapped up in work outside of the home or emotionally removed from children through the distant, detached miens of masculinity, father involvement was expressed differently across social class, tempered by masculine identities, normative expectations, and status hierarchies.

In our study of vulnerable families, fathers embraced the new normative expectations of the engaged father. When we asked Lorenzo, a 21-year-old unemployed African American father of two, how he thought his children would remember him, he replied:

> I think they will say he was a father that always, always had a sense of compassion towards us. He showed love. He nurtures us. He changes our diaper. He cooked for us. He did everything. Wash clothes. Took us for little walks. Helped us with our homework. Every aspect.

Kane, an African American father, a decade older than Lorenzo, described his involvement as a parent and his determination to do it differently from his own father:

> I am always here. I feed him. I can change his diapers—it's not too many fathers that can say they do that. I think I am doing pretty good. I try to go to a lot of his appointments. . . . I just want to be a good father, you know what I am saying. I want to be remembered as a good father. . . . Definitely, I don't want him saying, "Oh, my father was an asshole, man. He never was there for me." That's what makes me want to do right with him so that will never

happen. . . . Like me, man, I say my father was an asshole because he didn't give a crap about me. I don't want them saying that about me.

Vulnerable fathers are working hard to sustain this narrative. There is social worth in fatherhood, hope for creating meaningful lives or new beginnings, the fantasy of leaving something of value behind in the world, a stake in resisting stigmatizing labels like the deadbeat dad, and the prospects of feeling connection in alienating social worlds tightly wound around individualism. Sitting in living rooms and kitchens, in prison visiting rooms, in halfway homes, in small restaurants or soup kitchens, standing on street corners and in local bodegas, we heard similar messages: children were their worlds, their hearts, their priorities, and their reasons for changing their lives.

Their desires to be engaged fathers did not materialize out of nowhere. In addition to the images projected through popular culture and the media, the cultural narrative of the involved father is institutionally organized, and the men were exposed to these expectations in myriad programs, both inside and outside of prisons: fatherhood, substance abuse, cognitive-behavioral, and anger management programs. They were also exposed to these messages in state welfare, child protection, and probation offices, as well as in child support and family courts. They received similar encouragement from community nonprofit organizations, funded through federal and state grants—to be there for their children and to be engaged, nurturing fathers.

The men had adopted this language. Moreover, they had learned from institutional authorities and program leaders that only they could change their lives—it was up to them to make better choices, to get themselves together, and to be involved fathers. The men had internalized these messages, and they sounded determined.

The only problem is that they cannot do it on their own.

Perhaps a few "superdads" would—they would work two poor-paying jobs, navigate depressed neighborhoods, nurture their children, get some help from family members, pay child support, manage debt, walk their children to school, and show up for parent–teacher conferences. And they would be held up as the models of success—if they could do it, anyone could. This is an old story in America.

Most, however, would fall short for several reasons. First, while the cultural expectations for father involvement were increasing, the state and economic support for low-income families and for fatherhood was rapidly decreasing. Neoliberal economic restructuring increased inequality and decreased wages and reliable full-time employment. Likewise, the reorganization of the state tore holes in the safety net, redirected services to behaviorally manage the poor, and increased debt and punishment for those who failed or were unwilling to conform to the market. The political and economic foundation for families, marriage, and fatherhood was systematically deteriorating at the same time that normative expectations were increasing.

Second, vulnerable fathers were often left to become engaged fathers without any models to guide them. In fact, for many, their wishes to be involved fathers were driven by their desires to be there for their children, unlike their own fathers, who had abandoned, neglected, or abused them. Third, living in dangerous neighborhoods also compromised fatherhood and left them at odds with dominant institutional narratives about being nurturing fathers. And fourth, the dark side of poverty, inscribed on bodies and minds, had left some struggling with childhood traumas and unhealthy routines to mitigate or numb these painful developmental disruptions.

For these reasons, vulnerable fathers are not likely to do it on their own by making better decisions in their lives. The fathers' internalization of the cultural scripts about engaged fatherhood can be seen as an important achievement, but without economic, political, and social conditions to facilitate it, these fathers are being "set up."

The Gender Bind

Critical narratives of father disengagement and absence largely derive from a gendered lens. Many feminists have rightly argued that true gender equality is not possible until men fully share in the physical, mental, and emotional labor of childrearing, carework, and household labor.[2] The sociology literature suggests that the progress made toward more equitable co-parenting is encouraging, but remains inadequate across all social classes.[3] This should not be surprising. Second-wave feminists, particularly, understand that men and women's equal participation in the social reproduction needs of a society will not occur without social-economic transformation.[4] Unlike their first-wave counterparts, these changes are not about reforming current institutions so that men and women can co-participate on equal terms, a measure unlikely to be met under current power arrangements. Instead, current institutions will need to be transformed so that the material foundations of family and social reproduction, and the constructions of gender, parenthood, masculinity, and femininity, are changed to provide for true shared participation within and across different types of families.[5]

Radical transformation is not the direction that current concerns with father absence have taken. One direction underscores the irresponsibility of fathers who abandon mothers and children for their own self-indulgence. This has long been a social concern, referred to in the earlier part of the 20th century as husband desertion or "home slackers."[6] These dynamics are tied to the reorganization and idealization of the family in the late 19th and early 20th century, in which men became primary breadwinners and women the caretakers of homes and children to support the needs of an industrial labor force. The "cult of domesticity" and "separate spheres" normalized and institutionalized this organization of the family. It also fostered male economic power and privilege, by which father desertion or absence threatened family economic stability.

Toward the end of the century, with the advancement of no-fault divorce, the increase in cohabitation, the easing of sexual mores, and rise in out-of-wedlock childbearing, the manifestation of structured male privilege deepened family instability. Typically, divorce benefited men economically and disadvantaged mothers and children.[7] Too many men refused to pay child support after divorce or when children were born out of wedlock, and the issue was not taken seriously enough in male-dominated courts. The authors of this book were not spared these dynamics—both of us grew up in homes where fathers left and refused to support their children. More broadly, mothers and children suffered the effects of the imbalance of power, as men exercised their economic leverage and consumer indulgences.

Stricter child support enforcement was a potential mechanism to address this imbalance; unfortunately, it became wrapped up in neoliberal policies and discourses, which point to the second direction public concerns with father absence have taken. Father absence became racialized and viewed as a cultural pathology in black and brown communities. Conservative and liberal policymakers may have differed in their solutions to this problem, but they shared the perspective that the problem in inner-city communities was related to the scarcity of fathers in households.[8] Social science research supported this view, associating a range of social problems to father absence.[9] These views were consistent with the preoccupation with the black underclass beginning in the 1970s.[10]

Neoliberal policies promised smaller government and reduced social spending on the poor. Blaming the problems of poverty on cultural pathologies and on undiscerning war-on-poverty liberals, public assistance became more closely tied to managing the behavior of the poor and in enforcing market conformity.[11] The shift from a war on poverty to a war on welfare, as Michael Katz put it,[12] included child support enforcement policies that required fathers whose children had utilized public assistance to pay back the state for these costs and threatened incarceration for fathers who failed to do so. The retrenchment of public assistance in the 1980s and 1990s occurred along with the ascension of punishment and debt. These aggressive practices were symbolized by the "deadbeat dad," as paternalistic policymakers attempted to confront the presumed cultural pathologies of the inner city. The intention was to coerce father responsibility: to pay their debts to the state, financially support mothers and children, find employment, and to reclaim their place as heads of the household. At a time in which capitalism was being transformed from a social-democratic to a neoliberal model, provoking fear and uncertainty throughout the labor force, racial and class hierarchies were being reinvigorated and publicly exploited. This, too, is an old American story.

Even though the discourse racialized the problem of father absence, the policy focus remained on gender and the family—on male privilege and father irresponsibility. There was truth in this construction—fathers had leveraged male power and deepened burdens on mothers and children—but it was a fragile truth because it largely ignored racial and class marginalization. In other words, with only a few exceptions, the focus on gender failed to see how gender was embedded in racial and class hierarchies. Lacking was an intersectional lens, emphasized by third-wave feminists, that links gender, race, class, and sexualities to the organization of power, to the processes of inclusion-exclusion, and to the distribution of resources.[13] Father identities, conceptions, and practices are situated within these interlinking hierarchies. In this sense, these discourses failed to embrace the theories of both second- and third-generation feminists, who understood that true father engagement and gender equality would require the transformation of the social-economic system.

To understand how the system would need to be transformed, we examine how it is integral to the lives of low-income fathers. In this book, we examine class and racial marginalization, as well as gender dynamics as they are related to the lives of vulnerable fathers. At its elemental level, fatherhood is a relationship—a relationship embedded within a pattern of other relationships. But these relationships are not created anew upon the birth of a child; rather, they are structured within larger salient forces. We locate low-income fathers in relationships, families, and biographies but also take a broader view by situating these more interpersonal characterizations of fathers within the economy and labor force, the state and its relationship to families, national and local status hierarchies, and the changing boundaries of marginality that delineate patterns of inclusion and exclusion. In this regard, we adopt C. Wright Mills's analytical approach by examining fathers at the intersection of biography, social structure, and history.[14] We weave a narrative that is informed by macro-sociological forces but that preserves the voices of fathers whose fatherhood is expressed within and through these structural conditions.

Three Studies in Connecticut in the New Millennium

Understanding how political and economic structures affect the lives of families is essential to any discussion of low-income fatherhood. The decade 2000–2010 provides a useful examination of this. It is the decade that follows the optimism of the 1990s expansion, when the chickens came home to roost, so to speak. It is the decade in which the excesses of market-regulated capitalism imploded and the shocks to the labor market profoundly affected the lives of working-class families. It is the decade of two economic recessions— the first, a minor economic adjustment that was nonetheless followed by what was referred to as the "jobless recovery," and then the big one that devastated communities, families, homeowners, and workers. It is the decade that Nobel Prize–winning economist Paul Krugman called the "big zero" in which optimism of the 1990s turned up empty for everyone, except perhaps bankers who were again paying out bonuses before the dust had settled.[15] It is "the decade from hell" according to the 2009 cover of *Time* magazine, which pointed to the devastating bookends of the decade, beginning with 9/11 and ending in the Great Recession.[16] And it is the decade in which the warnings issued by many scholars concerning the 1996 welfare reductions in state assistance were painfully realized. We focus our attention on this decade that shaped the lives of fathers in our study as a pivotal decade that explains the trajectory of low-income families then and now.

In many respects, Connecticut provides a microcosm of neoliberal restructuring and its impact on the most fragile families in the state. In a small state like Connecticut, we can see how the remaking of capitalism and the state in the post-1970s affected the racial and class organization of social spaces across urban, suburban, small town, and rural areas. The geographical layering of communities segregated by race and class is stark in Connecticut because of the extreme wealth and poverty that gets spread across the state. Consider, for instance, that Connecticut has led the country in per-capita income for the past 20 years.[17] At the turn of the 21st century, it housed the third largest proportion of millionaires in the United States, while Hartford was ranked the second poorest city in the country.[18] A decade later, following the Great Recession, the state child poverty rate was 15 percent, while the rate in Hartford was almost one-half (48 percent), with New Haven (41 percent), Bridgeport (40 percent), New Britain (36 percent), and Waterbury (35 percent) following close behind.[19]

Further, Connecticut is a showcase for increasing inequality in the nation over the past 30 years, accentuating national trends in both the decades of the 1990s and 2000s. In the 1990s, the economic expansion was particularly good for the wealthy in the state—the top 20 percent of families saw their incomes in real dollars increase by an average of 21 percent ($31,635), while the poorest 20 percent of families lost 19.4 percent ($4,674) of their income. This increased the income gap between the top and bottom quintiles from 6 to 9 times within the decade, *the highest increase in the country*.[20] This trend did not end with the 20th century. From 2001 to 2006, low wage earners continued to lose wages in Connecticut, with the 10th percentile losing 6.9 percent and 20th percentile losing 9.2 percent in average wages, *the largest decrease of any state in the country*. Wage gains for highest earners were minimal, less than 1 percent, but they nevertheless did not lose ground.[21]

The social-spatial distribution of race and class in the state is also representative of the geographical organization of capitalism in the nation. At the turn of the century, almost one-half of blacks (49 percent) and Latinos (45 percent) lived in the four largest (and poorest) cities in Connecticut that housed only 14 percent of the state's population. Conversely, in 78 percent of towns in the state, the population was more than 90 percent white.[22] Median family income in Hartford at this time was 38 percent of its 17-town regional average, and while Hartford housed 24 percent of the region's children younger than six years, nearly 60 percent of all poor children in the region younger than six lived in Hartford.[23]

As striking as income and poverty differences are by race in Connecticut, wealth disparities are much greater. The average net assets for whites in Connecticut in 2002 was $153,900, securing college educations, home ownership, inheritance, and general future security to white children throughout the state. In comparison, the average net assets for blacks and Latinos in the state was $5,446, less than 5 percent of white wealth.[24] As we might imagine, racial disparities on a range of indicators lined up accordingly—in education, health care, infant mortality, labor force participation, and the like. One of the most striking disparities was in incarceration rates, where, in 2005, Connecticut had the greatest white-Hispanic disparity (6.6:1) in incarceration rates in the nation, and the fourth highest white-black disparity (12:1).[25]

Certainly, there is a lot of variation across states in terms of labor force opportunities, state welfare policies and programs, incarceration rates, inequality and poverty rates, educational achievement rates, and health indicators. Nonetheless, Connecticut tells one story about neoliberalism and its effects on low-income families and fatherhood. It is a story that will be both similar to and different from other states, general and particular in the lessons learned. Still, given the severity of inequality and the conditions of racial apartheid in Connecticut, it is a compelling story.

***

Three studies were conducted at the University of Hartford's Center for Social Research (CSR) during the first decade of the new millennium that provide the data for our book. We had been working with the Children's Trust Fund (CTF), then an independent state agency, to provide home visiting services to vulnerable first-time mothers in Connecticut. The program began at two state locations in 1995. With targeted research, legislative advocacy, and a carefully crafted staff training model that focused on supervision and home visiting practices, the program had expanded to every birthing hospital and to 40 communities in the state by 2010. Karen Foley Schain, the executive director of CTF, skillfully guided this process. Karen, Tim, and Dr. John Leventhal, a pediatrician and medical director of child abuse programs at Yale–New Haven Hospital, worked for more than a decade to design research that would inform program practices, assess their efficacy, and better organize a statewide network. John brought a wealth of research knowledge and a deep concern for child safety. Karen was a bold leader who was willing to go where few state agency directors would typically go. And Tim was committed to learning as much about the populations being served to better inform program services. Together, we combined our commitments and worked to provide support to the state's most vulnerable families.

The program defined vulnerability very loosely, using a parental risk assessment instrument that was typically administered at the birthing hospital to determine eligibility. Mothers were eligible if they met a combination of factors, which might include being single, poor, young, socially isolated, having less than a high school education, mental health problems, family problems, substance abuse issues, a cognitive deficit, late or limited prenatal care, or repeated abortions. These risk profiles told us one story about the mothers who volunteered to receive these services, but we wanted to go deeper. In 2002–2003, Mary Patrice Erdmans and Tim designed a life story study with program participants to learn more about vulnerable families across the state. They would later publish *On Becoming a Teen Mom: Life Before Pregnancy* based on these life stories.[26] At around the time of the study, Karen, John, and Tim had begun a conversation about fathers in these families. Fathers were not the target of home visitation services and had more or less been left out of the program orbit. We had an interest in learning more about them and in exploring the prospects of bringing them more into program processes. In our lifestory study, we were able to acquire consent from 48 fathers to participate. We trained male interviewers who sat with these men for a period of two to four hours across two interviews to record their life histories. Interviewers traveled to 15 different communities throughout the state to carry out the interviews. We would later match 41 of these fathers with mothers whom we had also interviewed and include them in our analysis for this book.[27] We will refer to this study as our *Couples Study*.

Around the same time of the life story study, the CSR also was working with the Department of Social Services in Connecticut to study their Fatherhood Initiative program. The program was located at three very different sites in the state. One program site, located in Norwich, served mostly white men and was managed by a man who deeply believed that fathers were victims of a female-friendly court system. For him, the program was a fathers' rights program. A second program was located in Bridgeport, one of Connecticut's poor cities, and served mostly black and brown fathers, heavily recruited from an Alternative-to-Incarceration program. A young charismatic Puerto Rican man, who many of the fathers admired, ran the program. The third program was located in Hartford, but targeted young, incarcerated fathers, almost exclusively African American and Puerto Rican. They provided services inside a prison and then followed up with fathers when they returned to their communities.

Our fieldworker on this study was Ronald Albert, a middle-aged African American man, who recorded ethnographic notes for six months at each program site and then interviews for the study between 2002 and 2003.[28] Ron had an unassuming, relaxed presence and easy laugh that contributed to an uncanny ability to engage these men without judgment and without imposing himself much into the conversation. We include the 62 interviews that Ron conducted with these fathers in our book, and we identify him as the interviewer where appropriate in the text. Fourteen fathers were from the Norwich site, 19 from the Bridgeport site, and 29 from the Hartford program, with 21 still incarcerated at the time of the interviews.[29] Interviews lasted between 60 and 90 minutes and were conducted at program sites, homes, and at the prison. We refer to this study as our *Father Initiative Study*.

The third study took place at the other end of the decade. Again, we coordinated with the home visitation program described earlier to identify 35 fathers to participate in a multiple-interview study. We began recruiting and interviewing fathers in the winter of 2008. Working directly with selected program sites, we received contact information and secured agreements with the fathers to participate in the study.[30]

Interviewers went to extraordinary lengths to maintain contact and conduct subsequent interviews. Phone contacts were made regularly during the intervals between interviews; however, many of the fathers ran out of minutes on their cell phones during the month and had to wait until further payments could be made, or else had phones permanently shut off. Several borrowed phones from family members to make calls, which contributed to our challenge of maintaining contact, while others moved households and, in a few cases, moved out of the state to take new jobs. In several cases, when cell phones were shut off, when fathers separated from the mothers, or when families moved without notice, fathers were successfully tracked through the assistance of program staff. At the end of our study in 2010, we had completed at least three interviews with one-half of the fathers (49 percent), which reflected the instability in their lives.

This sample represented a diverse group of men who had children participating in the home visiting program. Our respondents were from 13 program sites throughout the state and lived in 16 different cities and towns in Connecticut. Experiences varied considerably in terms of their family backgrounds as well as their educational achievements, arrest and incarceration histories, employment histories, and prior experiences as fathers. Sky was one of the interviewers who tenaciously conducted interviews wherever and whenever they could across the state. This study provides a range of voices and experiences during the worst economic crisis to hit the United States since the Great Depression. We refer to this as our *Nurturing Families Network (NFN) Study.*

Combined, we have interview data from 138 fathers during the 2000–2010 decade, and 41 interviews with mothers. As shown in Table 1.1, ages of fathers ranged from 17 to 49 at the time of the interview, although most were younger, with an average age of 25 and a median age of 23. Fathers were racially and ethnically diverse, with 29 percent identified as Puerto Rican, 26 percent white, and 24 percent African American. Nine percent identified as multiracial or multiethnic, and all but two of them included African American parentage. About one-half of fathers identified their relationships with the mother of their most recent child as a girlfriend, one-sixth were formally married, and one-third were no longer romantically involved.

Fathers were poorly educated. Only 35 percent had completed high school, while another 14 percent had earned a GED. Only 39 percent of fathers were working full-time at the time of the interview,[31] while another 12 percent were working part-time. Seventy-three percent of fathers reported that they had been arrested, 41 percent had spent time in prison, while 15 percent were incarcerated at the time of the interview. Thirty-eight percent of fathers reported that they had child support orders. Among this group of fathers who had current child support orders, a little more than one-half were paying the court-ordered amount, and two-thirds were in arrears for past child support.

The fathers represented vulnerable families in Connecticut. Only a few appeared to be economically stable, while the rest were either just-getting-by working class or were economically marginalized. The different data sets provide different snapshots that together tell a broader story about the lives of fragile families in Connecticut. For instance, the Couples Study profiles mostly young, white, and Puerto Rican parents, from communities throughout the state, with a little more than one-half employed full-time and about one-fifth formally married. On the other hand, two of the program sites from the Father Initiative Study represent the most socially and economically marginalized men in the state, residing in urban areas where structural unemployment is most apparent. All of the fathers from these sites had been street involved, 79 percent had been or were incarcerated, and only 12 percent were working full-time. Finally, the NFN Study includes a racially and ethnically mixed group of fathers scattered throughout the state, with about one-half employed full-time during at least one of the interviews. We

Table 1.1 Characteristics of the Sample (N = 138)

Age

Mean	25
Median	23
Range	17–49

Race/Ethnicity

White	26%
African American	24%
Puerto Rican	29%
Other Latino	8%
Multiracial/multiethnic	9%
Jamaican	2%
Other	2%

Relationship with Recent Mother

Married	16%
Nonmarried partner/girlfriend	51%
No intimate relationship	33%

Education

No high school degree	50%
GED	14%
High school degree	29%
Some college	4%
College degree	2%
Unknown	1%

Employment

Full-time	39%
Part-time	12%
Unemployed	34%
Incarcerated	15%

Criminal Justice

Ever arrested	73%
Ever incarcerated	41%*
Currently incarcerated	15%

Continued

Table 1.1 *Continued*

Child Support	
Current order	38%
Making payments	53%
Incarcerated with current order	13%
Not making payment/not incarcerated	34%
Owes arrears	66%

*In jail or prison for more than 90 days.

will provide more detailed statistical profiles from the different studies as we discuss issues throughout the book.

Organization of the Book

The book is divided into three parts. In Part 1, we examine the political-economic forces that have shaped the lives of vulnerable working-class families from the standpoint of fathers. A key objective in our book is to delineate these structural forces so that we can see what has happened to low-income fathers, how fathers make sense of these forces, and how they respond. Chapter 2 hones in on the economy and labor force. While four in ten men in our study were employed full-time, most of them were in jobs paying between $9 and $11 an hour. The majority of men were employed in part-time jobs or were unemployed, often deriving income from the informal sector, state assistance, family members, or from their intimate partners. We examine the political and economic dynamics that have leveled wages, increased inequality, and decreased family stability, and assess how families coped during the recessionary periods of the decade. Further, in this chapter, we highlight two industries that have become key employment options for men at the bottom of the labor force: fast food and the temporary employment industries.

Chapter 3 turns our attention to state welfare retrenchment. Drawing mostly from our Couples Study, we consider the strategies couples developed to survive the forbidding convergence of declining living wage job opportunities and decreasing governmental assistance, and we raise concerns about the effects this has had on relationships and parenting. In the latter part of the chapter, we turn our attention to fathers at the end of the decade and consider how they made sense of welfare reform amid the great economic collapse of 2007. In this context, we see how few state benefits are available to noncustodial or single fathers, and how benefits have become tied to market conformity. Moreover, we show how transferring more responsibility for public assistance to the states resulted in cuts to state welfare during painful economic recessions when state revenues declined.

Child support enforcement is the topic of Chapter 4. While child support courts can provide an important mechanism for distributing family resources across separate households, Child Support Enforcement (CSE) evolved from the 1974–1975 amendments to the Social Security Act, which were a response to a dramatic national increase in public assistance. In this chapter, we identify some of the key provisions added to CSE after 1975 that culminated in the Welfare Reform Act in 1996. These provisions reflected the neoliberal shift in poverty governance that redefined welfare from a system that provided basic support to families *for whom the market was unable to provide* to a system in which temporary support is provided to families *who fail to provide for themselves* within the market—and then only as a type of loan that the families are expected to pay back, even if it takes a lifetime. Child support enforcement was a central tenet of these reforms, and we examine their material and symbolic importance in this chapter.

In Part 2 of the book, we focus on the most socially and economically marginalized fathers in our study. We draw largely from our Fatherhood Initiative Study and examine the processes by which many of these men were channeled into the streets, drug trade, crime, and violence in and around public housing developments. A little less than one-fourth of fathers in our study grew up in a public housing development. Among these 32 fathers, 53 percent were African American and 40 percent Latino. We hear from the fathers who grew up in and around these developments in the 1980s and 1990s, and we consider the conditions in which many of them were becoming fathers at young ages.

Chapter 6 continues this discussion by focusing on policing and incarceration. A little less than one-half of fathers (41 percent) in our study had been incarcerated, while about one-sixth (15 percent) still were incarcerated at the time of the interviews. We discuss their experiences with the police in their communities, the streets, and prison. Here we raise concerns about the criminalization of this population and the effects this has had on their families and children, both in terms of what we call "fathering through the looking glass" while incarcerated but also in terms of the parenting strategies they adopt to prepare their children for negotiating social and economically marginalized neighborhoods. Together, Chapters 5 and 6 deepen our understanding of the "lived experience" of social and economic marginalization, as well as the neoliberal strategies for disciplining and governing the lives of this population.

In Part 3 of the book we turn to a deeper exploration of intimate relationships and fathers' perspectives about fatherhood and their futures—what we entitle "Relationships and Standpoints." We believe that we are only ready to talk about relationships—relationships with children and with mothers—after we have thoroughly examined the social and historical contexts in which these relationships are embedded. In Chapter 7, we discuss how fathers parent in these circumstances. We elaborate on their expectations of themselves as fathers; the stresses and strains that inadequate resources and dependence on extended families have on their relationships; how they manage fatherhood across multiple households or parent outside of the household; the problem of toxic masculinity and intimate partner violence, and the men's exposure to violence as children in their own households and neighborhoods; and how families and fatherhood are organized in social contexts in which intimate relationships have become casual. Finally, we also examine second-generation fatherhood, where fathers embrace parental responsibilities in families they establish when they are older.

In Chapter 8, we examine the cultural frames and narratives fathers articulated to make sense of fatherhood within their social and economic circumstances. We note that they rarely conveyed a systemic understanding of their lives. Instead, they constructed identities along three symbolic boundaries from which they attempted to derive moral self-value: by comparing themselves to their own fathers, to welfare-reliant fathers, and to deadbeat dads. These three constructions are defensive reactions to denigrating public discourses that have been directed at them. With the exception of some insight into social class and racial discrimination, systemic views tended to blame women and a system they believed favored women. They also conveyed individualistic and resilience narratives to project visions of the future and to orient themselves as fathers. In the latter they were focused on addressing violent, abusive pasts, or alcohol and drug dependencies, and they adopted therapeutic language to convey their personal travails. In the former, narratives consisted of "manning up," making better decisions, resisting the temptations of the streets, and succeeding through determination.

Throughout these narratives, fatherhood was almost always at the center—it was their motivation, their identity, their life purpose, their imagined future. Many of the institutional authorities in their lives supported and encouraged this identity, but emphasized that to become engaged fathers, they would have to change themselves and reorient their lives—it was up to them. These institutional messages fit well within a culture of individualism and an era of neoliberal reason, but without transforming the material and symbolic conditions through which fatherhood is lived, it is our contention that these men are being set up.

PART 1
NEOLIBERAL CAPITALISM

2

"It's the Economy, Stupid"

I don't need much. Pretty much I am a simple man. But without
a job . . . everybody goes through tough times and I know a lot of
unemployed fathers that was working at Sikorsky or whatever. So
people go through changes all the time. That's why they call it life.

—Robbie

Social structures are lived, usually in ways that are imperceptible to those
who live them. Seventy percent of the men in our study were born between
1975 and 1985, on the cusp of neoliberalism. Their families were located
within a class structure at the time of their births, and the changing economy
is reflected in their intergenerational experiences of work and family. Race
intersects with this class structure or, we might say, is produced within the
social relations of economic capitalism. The intersecting hierarchies of race
and class are apparent in the life stories of our study participants. Examining
their lives within a structural framework enables us to see how larger social
forces mediate their lives as fathers.

In this chapter, we examine how the economy has changed and the effects
this has had on families generally and fathers particularly at the bottom of
the labor force. We will listen to the struggles articulated by fathers in our
study in both parts of the 2000 decade—the early part when they were coping
with the so-called jobless recovery that followed the 2001 recession and then
the latter part after the Great Recession. Last, we will take a closer look at two
of the industries that men on the margins of the economy often turn to for
formal employment when job opportunities are particularly bleak—fast food
and the temporary employment industries—and consider the exploitative
nature of these industries as illustrative of the ways in which the economy
has undermined family stability. For much of Part 1 of our book, we suspend
our focus on fathers and instead examine how political and economic forces

It's a Setup. Timothy Black and Sky Keyes, Oxford University Press (2021). © Timothy Black and Sky Keyes.
DOI: 10.1093/oso/9780190062217.003.0002

have shaped fatherhood in low-income black, brown, and white families and communities.

For several of the white fathers in our study, their parents' work trajectories reflected permanent layoffs, plant closings and relocations, and downward mobility. Scott, 28 years of age, recalls: "As a matter of fact, when [my mother] moved to Winsted she started at SKF . . . she was the first batch of people when they opened that factory and she was the last batch of people let go when they closed that factory." Scott is referring to his mother's refusal to transfer to the plant in Alabama, where a large part of the production work was moved. Garrett, 24, told us that his father was a pipefitter for many years but was laid off. Unable to find work in his trade, he worked in the new booming industry in Connecticut—the casino—while Garrett worked as an assistant manager at McDonald's. Shane, 28, remembered when layoffs began to happen at two of Connecticut's' largest manufacturing employers: "What happened was EB [Electric Boat] started laying off thousands of people. Pratt & Whitney, that's when we had our big layoffs . . . thing is, when I was graduating, all the machinist places all closed down around here. . . . It really stunk." Shane was a restaurant manager, reflecting the shifting terrain of jobs toward the lower paying service industry. These white, mostly working-class fathers were getting by; however, they were cognizant of big changes that represented diminished opportunities for them and their peers.

We have similar stories from African American and Latino fathers. For instance, Roberto was a 22-year-old Puerto Rican father from Hartford. His father completed two years of college and worked as a butcher, in construction (asphalt paving), and was a security guard for an electric company (all in Puerto Rico). Roberto explained that his father usually worked multiple jobs, but he still fell short of meeting family needs: "It wasn't bad because there was always food on the table, there was always clothing to wear for all of us and everything, but my father always complained about the money, because it wasn't enough to cover all of the expenses." Roberto himself worked in maintenance in an apartment building and, like his father, had worked in a slew of jobs, from fast food to automobile detailing and construction.

Romeo, a 25-year-old Colombian from Hartford, was the most successful father that we interviewed. After working at Pizza Hut since 16 years of age, he graduated from college and acquired a good paying job with United Technologies. His father was an aviation mechanic for 18 years, after working as a truck driver for many years before that. And his mother, who had an associate's degree, had "always worked" to supplement the family wage.

George, an 18-year-old mixed African American and Puerto Rican father from New Britain, told us that his father always worked "two or three jobs," including at Friendly's and Applebee's, and other restaurants, and now worked as an in-home health care worker. Similarly, George, himself, worked multiple jobs from an early age, including employment at a lotion factory, a clothing store, and several other similar service jobs that enabled him to piece together a minimally adequate weekly paycheck to provide for his child.

Samuel, a 34-year-old African American father, grew up in a two-parent home in a New Orleans housing project. His father worked construction his whole life. Samuel had worked as a bellman at a casino for six years and had been previously in the Navy for ten years. Embracing working-class respectability and distinguishing himself from those he grew up with whose lives took the all-too-familiar route to incarceration, Samuel told us emphatically, "I was raised better than that."

These fathers' jobs reflected the changing times and provided a window onto the types of jobs that working-class fathers were acquiring in Connecticut. Working sometimes more than one job, these fathers were nonetheless providing for their children. Further, they demonstrated the racial make-up of the working class in Connecticut, reminding us of how black, brown, and white fathers were positioning themselves relative to the changing opportunity structure for working-class men in the state. Embedded within the class structure, however, is an intractable racial caste system, which is more evident in the geographical organization of race and ethnicity in the state and in the varying histories of working-class stability that race and ethnicity convey. Many more of our white fathers had family resources they could rely on that included family assets and job networks. These networks opened up job opportunities that reflected their racial characteristics, or what might be called their "complexion connection." White fathers were likely to work in more stable employment, even though their jobs often were characterized by the insecurity of impermanence as well as declining wages.

Black and Latino fathers operated within a similar class stratum, but they often lacked access to job networks and were located in racially segregated communities in Connecticut's larger cities. Some, as we saw earlier, gained access to working-class jobs and struggled in similar ways that white fathers did to provide for their children. However, we were more likely to hear stories that come from the belly of American ghettoes among our black and brown fathers. References to the illicit drug economy, hustling, violence, and incarceration permeate many of these stories. Speaking from a different, but distinct location within the working class, their intergenerational stories complete the spectrum of jobs and life experiences that range in this book from just-getting-by working class to economically and socially marginalized.

The men in our study are represented by the bottom quintile of income earners who lost 45 percent of their share of the national income between 1979 and 2009, dropping to just 3.4 percent. The quintile of income earners just above it did not do much better, losing 20 percent of their share of national income, dropping to 9.2 percent. In other words, the bottom 40 percent of income earners in the United States accounted for merely 13.6 percent of total national income at the end of the first decade of the new millennium, an all-time low. This is compared to the top quintile of income earners whose share of the national income grew 42.5 percent during the same time period to nearly one-half (49.4 percent) of total income.[1]

Layered in the bottom quintile are also those who have become largely economically superfluous and whose lives are largely managed by the criminal justice system. Given the consolidation and expanse of the international drug trade in the 1980s, leading to the locally profitable crack-years of the 1980s and 1990s, some of the fathers in our study span this period intergenerationally. Perhaps no story better illustrates the intergenerational footprint of the Reagan era as that of Brian, a 19-year-old African American from New Haven, who was locked up at the time of our interview. Brian, whose income history was limited to installing drywall under the table and selling crack cocaine, told us a story in which father absence, drug dealing, drug addiction, and emotional resentment all collided.

RON: Where was your dad?
BRIAN: My father I can't even say in and out. He wasn't even there. He would come through and drop off a little bit of money here and there, thinking it was all right. But it wasn't even about that. All I had to do was literally chase him down just to get him to come by.
RON: So what was happening with him?
BRIAN: As I got older, I didn't really know what it was all about. But now . . . I know he was using [drugs] strong and stuff like that. It came to the point where I was serving him myself.
RON: Oh really?

BRIAN: Yeah, so I really seen what it was all about, why he wasn't there when I was younger. All he wanted to do was get high, but he hold a job down.

RON: Okay. So how did you feel selling to your dad, man?

BRIAN: I mean I looked at it like this: I was out there like the first time I really found out, it was like he came by around where I be at and . . . running up to the car, I am like "Who is this right here?"

RON: You ran up to his car?

BRIAN: Yeah . . . I am like "I know that car." So I go over there and it's him. He looking at me all shocked like.

RON: Oh, man.

BRIAN: I got tired of him beating around the bush, so I laid it down. I was like "Yo, if you are going to do it, if you going to [be] coming out here getting, you know, what I am out here doing, come see me."

RON: Might as well.

BRIAN: It's only right. You ain't giving me no other money so let me get mine. You respect it. Started dealing with each other like that. Come through, buy a little something, give me a little money on the side. So really stopped dealing with him when he came through one day and he wanted some credit and I was "I can't do it." So he turned around the next week and I asked him, "Let me get some money." And he was like "You couldn't give me no credit." I was like "Oh, is it that serious?" I said "All right, you can't come back out here." Got into it with him. Last time I talked to him for a while. He got real sick, had a heart attack or something because he was using. I was like, "Man, I don't really care. You chose that life. Deal with it." That was basically it. I got locked up. That was my first bid in 2000. Maxed out 2001. I seen him a couple of times. He was doing the same old thing. It's like "Hey . . ."

RON: So, at that time the father–son relationship is . . .

BRIAN: It was never there.

INTERVIEWER: It was never there?

BRIAN: It was never there. My mother was the father and the mother.

Brian's mother, however, died when he was 13 years old, and he lived with his aunt until he was 15. Brian learned the drug trade at 15, when he began leaving school for two- and three-day stretches to hustle on the block.

Brian's story reflects the reorganization of family relations that occur in drug-infested communities where an illicit drug trade that creates and profits from drug addiction flourishes in the absence of other sustainable income opportunities. Both furious and embarrassed by his father, Brian told us his story behind bars at age 19, expecting his first child one month after the interview.

Stories of street involvement were more characteristic of fathers who lived in Connecticut's cities, often residing in public housing projects and surrounding communities where black and brown poverty was concentrated. However, white fathers were not immune to drug abuse, drug dealing, and other forms of street hustles, whether living in urban areas or more remote areas in Connecticut. Tyler was a 24-year-old white father and former member of the Hartford street organization, 20-Luv. Tyler's father, whom he lived with, was a negligent and abusive parent, a "pimp," while Tyler's mother was serving a 13- to 30-year sentence on two counts of manslaughter. Tyler was a high school dropout, former heroin addict, and currently had three children by three mothers. Tyler reminded us that the reorganization of capitalism in the 1980s and 1990s reproduced cleavages within the working class that were represented by race and space, but that by only focusing on racial inequality, we miss the broader dynamics of social class that were increasing distress in white communities as well.

The life stories in this book will underscore how changing opportunity structures for the working class, familial adaptations, the social-spatial organization of race and class, and a post-1970s restructuring of the state have generated a mix of lived experiences that have consequences for fathering in the new millennium.

The Standard of Living of the Average American Has to Decline

These were the words spoken by Federal Reserve Board Chairman Paul Volcker to the Joint Economic Committee on October 17, 1979. Soon after, Volcker took initiative to cut inflation by steeply raising interest rates—a policy that became known as "Volcker Shock"—that indeed started the economy down the road of lowering the standard of living for the working class. Placed in context, Volcker's quote was more about increasing oil prices and declining US productivity than a prediction about the future,[2] but his policies to wring inflation out of the economy became a turning point for economic policy and had severe immediate consequences: a deep recession in 1981, a dramatic increase in unemployment, the weakening of industrial labor unions, rolling back gains made by African Americans in urban areas, and ending any pretensions toward achieving full employment. Volcker's initiatives successfully decreased inflation and strengthened the dollar, but it imposed excessive competition on the economy and forced a proliferation of bankruptcies, setting the stage for an era of leveraged buyouts, hostile takeovers, and corporate mergers.[3]

While Volcker Shock may have been an historical turning point for economic policy, the Federal Reserve Board did not alone reshape the distribution of income and wealth that occurred in the ensuing 40 years. These monetarist policies were coupled with the restructuring of the tax code, reductions in public assistance, the evisceration of labor unions, the deregulation of finance and the economy, and the privatization of governmental land and services. In other words, monetary and public policies beginning in the late 1970s ushered in the era of neoliberalism that was intended to rectify the 1970s crisis in economic capitalism, restore corporate profit rates, and strengthen the position of US corporate firms in the rapidly changing global economy.

These changes reorganized the social structure of accumulation.[4] Further, they changed corporate boardrooms, business practices, and workplaces themselves. In the beginning of Louis Uchitelle's book, *The Disposable American*, he describes some of these changes by providing a historical profile of a manufacturing company located in the center of the state of Connecticut.[5] A brief summary will help to visualize this period of economic transition and provide a tangible context for understanding the shifting labor force.

Stanley Works

In Uchitelle's case study of Stanley Works, a tool-making company located in New Britain, Connecticut, we are immediately introduced to the CEO, Donald Davis, who led the company for 20 years. A graduate of Harvard Business School, whose education was paid for under the GI Bill, Davis began working for the company in 1948 as a junior executive. He represented the community-minded CEO who lived in the city and sent his kids to public schools, and who sat on local boards and knew many of his employees by their first names. Davis embodied an era of corporate leadership that recognized employee job security as important to their own interests, as a means to preserve a skilled and dependable workforce who would suffer only temporary layoffs during periods of economic downturn. Faced with foreign competition that eroded sales of Stanley Works tools in the late 1970s, Davis was forced to begin finding ways to reduce his workforce. He held meetings with employees to discuss the issue and began employee reductions among his white-collar workforce, mostly through attrition. When this proved insufficient, he turned his attention to his blue-collar workforce and began to move some operations to lower-cost cities.

Davis retired in 1988 and was replaced by CEO Richard Ayers, who moved the large distribution center in New Britain to Charlotte, North Carolina. Ayers moved other production operations to the anti-union south as well and forced wage reductions on New Britain workers. In 1997, however, the mantle of the company was passed on to John Trani, whose leadership completed the neoliberal transformation at Stanley Works. At General Electrics, Trani had been trained by Jack Welch and had excelled as CEO of the company that Uchitelle describes as having "invented the modern American layoff."[6] Trani signed for a six-figure salary at Stanley Works that was two to three times larger than Davis's or Ayers's salaries and included a signing bonus of $1 million in Stanley stock options. Trani moved several product lines to Thailand and China, closed over one-half of Stanley's factories, and reduced the workforce in New Britain to 900 employees, a company that had employed 7,000 in the city when Davis began working there in 1948.

Trani did away with annual dinners celebrating worker tenure at the company and had no personal relationships with his employees, which had been a hallmark of the Davis leadership. Trani did what he was expected to do—he finished what Davis and Ayers had started and retired at the end of 2003 with revenues, income, and stock prices rising. Trani retired after the 442 machinists remaining in New Britain walked off their jobs over job security and severance pay issues in 2003. They returned disappointed by Trani's unwillingness to compromise, while Trani retired later that year with a $1.3 million annual pension and an $8 million bonus for his resolute corporate restructuring of Stanley Works.

John Trani represented the new CEO, handsomely rewarded for his ability to respond to the new rules governing the economy and to subvert workplace labor unions. This pattern occurred across the corporate landscape as the ratio between CEO direct compensation and average pay for hourly, non-supervisory workers increased from 27:1 in 1973 to 275:1 in 2009. Of course, shareholders also benefit from cost-cutting measures that increase profits, and the post-1970s economy put more power in the hands of institutional investors who, in turn, placed more pressure on managers to increase shareholder value.[7] These pressures forced corporate management to sacrifice long-term development objectives for persistent, short-term returns.[8]

The restructuring profiled in Uchitelle's book is representative of corporate strategies to survive in an era of intensive competition, deregulation, and declining trade barriers. Corporations took on extraordinary amounts of debt, often to merge with or buy out competitors, in order to capture market share, which placed excessive pressure on cutting costs and wages. Debt in the financial sector alone increased six-fold between 1979 and 2007, to more than 100 percent of GDP.[9] In 2010, Stanley Works merged with Black and Decker through a $4.5 billion stock swap to form Stanley Black and Decker.[10]

Leaner and Meaner

Volcker's proclamation came true as average earnings for nonsupervisory workers in 2007 were below the rate in 1979. In fact, wage stagnation was the primary explanation for restoring profits and keeping inflation low. From 1948 to 1966, profit rates and labor income increased at similar rates; but, during the crisis period (1966–1979), the increase in wages slowed while profits barely grew at all. By the turn of the century, however, neoliberalism had changed this: from 2000 to 2007, profits grew at a rate 13 times income growth.[11]

More women entered the workforce, boosting family income, but the median income among all families grew only 18 percent between 1979 and 2007. For the poorest quintile, the group of concern in this book, income stagnated during these three decades, growing less than 1 percent.[12] The suppression of US wages occurred mostly through the use of old-fashioned workplace exploitation, including a disregard for legal worker protections, outsourcing, two-tiered wage structuring, a decreased social wage, investment in production technology and automation, mandatory overtime, increased production quotas, and the increased use of contingent labor. Workplace management strategies were organized to squeeze as much productivity from workers as possible, while changing workplace cultures normalized these practices. As Kim Moody put it, "your job had been stressed, reengineered, measured, monitored, standardized, intensified, and connected just in time to another stressed, reengineered, etc. job while you and your fellow worker had been informed that you were the organization's most valuable asset."[13] As illustrated in Figure 2.1, productivity and profits in the manufacturing sector increased dramatically compared to wages. Moreover, Arne Kalleberg asserted that the United States was the only advanced country in which large increases in production in the last two decades of the 20th century did not result in increases in income for the majority of workers.[14]

The only defense that workers could mount against these strategies was through labor unions, which were under assault during this period. In 1980, union membership increased to an all-time high of 20 million members, even though as a percentage of all workers, it declined from a peak of 32.5 percent in 1952 to 23 percent in 1980. In the following three years, membership dropped by about 3 million members to 20 percent in 1983.[15] More than two and a half million manufacturing jobs alone were lost in the 1981 recession as a result of Volcker's measures, deeply undermining labor union membership.[16] The increasing vulnerability of labor fostered a multi-million-dollar union-busting legal industry that assisted companies in neutralizing or

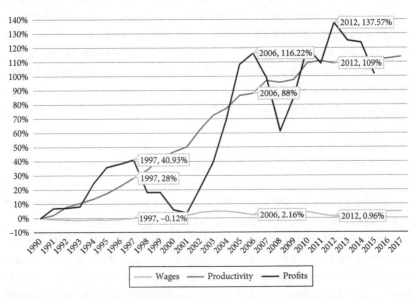

Figure 2.1 US Manufacturing: Wages, Productivity, and Profit Growth, 1990–2017 (% change over 1990 base year)

Wages equal average hourly earnings of production and nonsupervisory employees in manufacturing sector, seasonally adjusted (1982–1984 US dollars). Productivity measure is output per labor hour. Corporate profit rate is corporate profits after tax as a ratio of gross domestic product.

Sources: U.S. Bureau of Labor Statistics; U.S. Bureau of Economic Analysis.

eliminating unions in the workplace, while the politically appointed National Labor Relations Board, charged with overseeing labor laws and contractual processes, became staffed by many who were hostile to labor.[17] By 2010, the unionized workforce had plummeted to 12 percent (only 6.9 percent of private sector workers), while the spread of right-to-work laws across states was attempting to deliver the final blow.[18]

These macroeconomic changes had profound effects on everyone, but especially low-income families. Structural changes are hard to see, however, even though they create the changing material conditions, social relations, resource distributions, and opportunity structures through which we live our lives. In this book, we want to elucidate the material and symbolic conditions within which fatherhood occurs among low-income populations. In other words, we want to make the political, economic, and cultural story more visible and central to understanding the lives of low-income fathers. As Joseph Stiglitz reminds us, "American inequality didn't just happen. It was created."[19]

The Economic Decline of Men at the Bottom of the Labor Force

For men at the bottom of the labor force, their circumstances have been largely defined by declining wages, economic recessions, and incarceration. The wages for men, overall, decreased from 1973 through the first decade of the new millennium, but these losses were not equally distributed. Between 1973 and 2009, wages for men in the top 95th percentile increased dramatically from $39 to $55 per hour. Wages for men in the middle of the labor force remained stagnant at around $18 per hour, while men in the lower ranks of the labor force—at the 20th percentile—experienced a decline in wages from $12 to $10 per hour.[20] The failure to keep minimum wage increases current with the cost of living is key to declining wages at the bottom. In the 1960s, the minimum wage was equal to about one-half of an average worker's hourly wage; whereas in 2007, it had fallen to about one-third.[21]

Narrowing this group to young men more characteristic of our study, Andrew Sum and his colleagues show that hourly earnings dropped precipitously between 1979 and 2007 for 20- to 29-year-old men without a post-secondary degree—26 percent for high school dropouts and 27 percent for high school graduates. Wages also fell 10 percent for men with some college education and 3 percent for college graduates during this period. In their cleverly titled article, "No Country for Young Men," they conclude that falling wages have had a significant impact on falling marital rates, marital and family instability, and out-of-wedlock births among the lower-income population.[22]

Recessions over the past 40 years have also hit men particularly hard. The labor force participation rate for men in their prime working years has declined after every recession since the 1970s.[23] The 2008 recession was particularly brutal, resulting in historic long-term unemployment. By the end of the decade, it was taking laid-off workers, on average, 33 weeks to find another job, and most either took pay cuts or else jobs that provided fewer hours. Around one-fourth of displaced full-time workers returned to part-time jobs.[24] The recession was also distinctive in the large percentage of rehired workers who were subsequently laid off. A Pew study reported that one in three displaced workers experienced at least two layoffs. These trends fell hardest on low-income, less-educated men—more were laid off, more left the labor force, and more remained unemployed for longer periods of time.[25]

The decline in male labor force participation over the past 40 years would have been even greater if we were to count the vast numbers of men removed from the labor force through incarceration. Moreover, employment prospects for the formerly incarcerated population are bleak. In 2007, 1 in 31 adults in the United States, and one in three black men, were either in prison or jail, or on probation or parole. These concentrations of incarcerated and supervised adults are drawn largely from low-income populations, disconnected or weakly attached to the labor force. Bruce Western has shown that black men without a high school education are more likely to be in prison than they are to be working, and his research with Becky Pettit estimates that formerly incarcerated men lose, on average, nine weeks of employment and 11 percent in wages annually after they return, and 40 percent in lifetime wages.[26]

The loss of wages and the decline in the male labor force has reshaped families. The number of dual-earner families, as well as the number of single-parent families, has increased. Labor force participation for women between 1950 and 2000 jumped from 34 to 60 percent, and while women are three times more likely to work part-time jobs than men, both are working full-time in three-quarters of dual-earner families.[27] By 1990, white women had caught up to labor force rates of black women, mostly because the employment rate for less-educated women between the ages of 25 and 44 nearly doubled between 1960 and 1990, from 38 to 72 percent.[28] Another way to describe these changes is that the decline in wages and labor force participation among men has resulted in an increase in working hours in the family, and the increasing number of hours at work has placed additional stress on families attempting to meet home and childcare needs, a central issue in the lives of couples we profile in this book.

These trends have also increased the number of single-parent families as marriage has become increasingly unlikely among low-income couples. Among less educated women in the labor force, the percentage unmarried has increased from 15 percent in 1960 to 41 percent in 2010.[29] The economic incentive to marriage has evaporated even when men are working full-time. Ron Mincy and his colleagues point out that for noncustodial fathers who are employed full-time, around three-quarters of them make no more than $40,000 a year.[30] For men less attached to the labor force, marriage has become little more than a pipe dream. Recessions, low wages, and family instability have increased poverty, and have expanded extreme poverty, in America. Individuals living on less than $2 per day—a measure typically reserved for developing countries—doubled in the United States between 1996 and 2011 to 1.5 million.[31]

These are the larger forces confronting low-income families throughout the nation, who suffered the consequences of two recessions during the decade of our study. But what did this look like specifically in Connecticut and for the fathers in our study?

Surviving in the New Millennium

Jobs and Wages

As Table 2.1 describes, 39 percent of the fathers we interviewed were employed full-time at the time of the interview, while 34 percent were not working in the formal economy and another 15 percent were incarcerated. However, as we indicated in Chapter 1, there was considerable variation across studies. Among fathers we interviewed in the first half of the decade, a little more than one-half of fathers in the Couples Study were employed full-time, compared to only one-fourth of fathers in the Father Initiative Study. Moreover, because the latter study included an incarcerated population, two-thirds of these study participants were not in the labor force. In the second

Table 2.1 Employment Rates Across Three Studies

	Employment Status		Employment Status	
	Full-time	Part-time	Unemployed	Incarcerated
Couples Study	23 (56%)	5 (12%)	13 (32%)	0
Father Initiative Study	16 (26%)	5 (8%)	20 (32%)	21 (34%)
NFN Study	15 (49%)	6 (14%)	14 (37%)	0
Total	54 (39%)	16 (12%)	47 (34%)	21 (15%)

half of the decade, one-half of fathers we interviewed were employed full-time, while a little more than one-third were unemployed.

Wages among full-time workers were low. Even in the Couples Study where formal employment was the highest, the median wage was $10 an hour. Combining all studies, there was some range in the quality of jobs, but most were low-wage jobs with limited advancement opportunities. Of the 54 full-time jobs, two were semiprofessional jobs and two were decent-paying machinist jobs. Most of the jobs, however, paid wages that hovered around $9 to $11 an hour. Six were working in fast food joints. Casino jobs, low-paid construction work, and car service work (tires, oil change) made up a quarter of full-time jobs. Eight worked in warehouses and seven had jobs driving vehicles such as limousines, tow trucks, moving trucks, tractor-trailers, and pizza delivery cars, in which wages likewise varied. Despite working full-time, low wages located most of them at the bottom of the labor force. More importantly, these wages need to be understood in relation to the cost of living in Connecticut.

The cost of living in Connecticut ranks the third highest in the country. Connecticut has the highest cost for groceries in the United States and among the highest costs for utilities, housing, and health care.[32] In fact, the poverty rate in Connecticut is a poor measure of deprivation when it is compared to the self-sufficiency standard (see Table 2.2). Issued by the Connecticut Office of Workforce Competitiveness in 2005, the self-sufficiency standard showed that a single adult with two children would need to earn $44,141 a year to "get by" in a lower cost city like Hartford, and $61,181 in a more expensive city like Stanford.[33] A full-time, minimum wage income in 2005, at $14,768 for 52 weeks of employment, was beneath the federal poverty line ($16,090) for a family of three, but far beneath the self-sufficiency standard.

Table 2.2 Comparing Poverty Line and Self-Sufficiency Standard, 2005

Annual full-time minimum wage	$14,768
Poverty line for family of three	$16,090
Self-sufficiency standard in Hartford	$44,141

The self-sufficiency standard was updated in 2015. The equivalent figures for 2015 would be $19,032 annual income at minimum wage ($9.15/hour), the federal poverty line for a family of three at $20,090, and the self-sufficiency standard in Hartford at $59,553 for a single parent and two children. See Pierce (2015).

In other words, nearly one-half of children in Hartford in 2005 lived in families with incomes close to *one-third* of the self-sufficiency standard.[34] By these calculations, low-wage employment in Connecticut, even among full-time workers, is inadequate to making ends meet in a state in which affording the basics—housing, food, transportation, childcare, medical care, and clothing—reaches considerably beyond their wages.

Connecticut compares favorably with other states on the minimum wage. At the end of the first decade of the new millennium, its minimum wage was increased from $8.00 to $8.25, one dollar over the federal minimum and the third highest in the United States at the time.[35] However, while Connecticut's minimum wage may compare well to other states, the state's high cost of living greatly compromises the consumer reach of these wages. For instance, in 2009, wages for workers at the bottom of the labor force in Connecticut was the second highest compared to all other states, but when the cost of living was factored in, Connecticut dropped to 43rd in the nation in comparative wages among the lowest paid workers.[36]

One of the better paid, older fathers in our study, Ted, worked as a machinist, but he reminded us of the limited reach of his income: "Financially, anything could change; most people like us are only a couple paychecks away from having to eat at the shelter, you know." And many fathers could relate to 26-year-old Harry's description of bill shuffling.

My rent comes first. My bills come second . . . no . . . scratch that. My daughter's diapers and my daughter's needs come first. My rent comes second. My bills come last . . . but not the light bill. I have to have lights. . . . In the wintertime . . . the gas companies can't shut you off . . . so I don't pay my gas bill in the wintertime . . . I don't. I just don't. But also I get help paying for it, too. I get a program where I pay half and the state pays for the other half because there is only one income in this house.

Harry worked full-time at a factory and was therefore among the better-off in our study. When we remove the incarcerated population from our calculations, one-third of the fathers in our study were not employed in the formal economy. When resources are limited or unavailable, families face considerable emotional stress and risk losing their housing, separating, or relying on the kindness of family, friends, and even sometimes strangers to survive.

Before the "Big One"

Geraldo, a 23-year-old Puerto Rican father, told us in 2003 he had been laid off from his moving job, where he made $300 per week. He remarked, "Right now I'm waiting for anything. . . . I've been applying everywhere!" Geraldo said he started working illegally at the age of nine for Kentucky Fried Chicken, and that desperate for income, he had even returned to Kentucky Fried Chicken and begged for work: "I told them that I even know how to do the popcorn chicken." Speaking like others during this period of time, Geraldo expressed determination to find something, "I'm still looking for it [job], you know. It's not like I'm gonna stop."

Individual determination, however, was not enough for Geraldo and others who were searching for work in Connecticut in the aftermath of the 2001 recession. The labor force declined during this time and the slow recovery increased financial burdens on low-income workers, especially those who were black and brown. Not only did wages drop for those in the bottom quintile of the national labor force, but the decrease in Connecticut was, by far, the largest in the nation.[37] Those earning less than a "poverty wage" during this time grew to nearly 1 in 5 workers. Unemployment and underemployment rates were also increasing, especially for racial minorities, youth, and the less educated. Unemployment nearly doubled from 2000 to 2007, and for those without high school educations, unemployment reached 11.8 percent in 2006, while underemployment increased to 19.6 percent. For Latinos, the largest group in our study, unemployment was recorded at 8.2 percent and underemployment at 15 percent in 2006.[38]

This dramatic decline in employment conditions for those concentrated at the bottom of the labor force was occurring while the prosperity of the state was growing. From 2002 to 2006, the Gross State Product grew 10 percent, and from 1997 to 2006, 18 percent. And taking an even longer view, profits (the Gross Operating Surplus) increased from 28 percent in 1963 to 35 percent in 2006, more than a third of total GDP in the state.[39] This longer view tells a more complete story of growing inequality in Connecticut. Wages for those at the bottom of the wage force have stagnated since the late 1980s, while increasing for higher income groups. In fact, the increase in the wage ratio between the top quintile and the bottom quintile in Connecticut grew faster (3.8 times) between the late 1980s and the mid-2000s than any state in the nation.[40]

Much of the decline in wages for workers was tied to the loss of manufacturing jobs. Between 1990 and 2007, Connecticut lost 37 percent of its manufacturing jobs, almost twice the national rate. In one generation, Connecticut's economy was dramatically transformed from a state that after World War II employed nearly two-thirds of its workforce in manufacturing jobs to employing less than one-eighth in 2007.[41]

During the first part of the decade, living wage jobs were out of reach for many of the men in our study. Men's lives appeared to be in perpetual motion—searching, shifting, reorganizing, negotiating, but never settling. Jobs came and went, sometimes on a daily basis, while they shuffled to find on- and off-the-books jobs. As Jack, a 23-year-old Puerto Rican father, put it, "to make an all right living you have to work at least three jobs or one hell of a job." Jack had a lengthy work history for a young man and a job-training certificate from Job Corps, and was "looking into getting two other part-time jobs" in addition to the two he already had, "so I can just do what I have to do and take care of my daughter."

Dante, a 20-year-old African American father, captured the struggle for low-income men in the earlier part of the decade, when he said:

The economy is messed up. . . . I've been looking and it's like ain't nobody hiring. Jobs are laying off people. Like in school they cutting back on teachers and they don't got no money to pay them and stuff like that. It's hard. The temp agencies don't even have jobs. I've been looking. It's hard, man. It's a struggle . . . I do side jobs here and there like painting, moving. It brings a little bit of money to the table. Whatever it brings it helps out a whole lot. I might have a painting job with me and my friend split 50-50. Get $250. Jobs like that. But it's under the table. It's like really nothing.

Fathers on the margins, like Geraldo, Jack, and Dante, utilized whatever resources they could to manage their precarity and meet their financial responsibilities. Red, a 26-year-old African American father from Bridgeport, described his income strategy, which did not end so well.

RON: What kind of work were you doing?

RED: I was doing a lot of warehouse work. As a matter of fact, I was working at Stop & Shop at the time at the deli. I was doing that and warehouse work at night.

RON: How long would you say you were there?

RED: I was there on and off for about a year or two years.

RON: Is that the only jobs you have had?

RED: No, that ain't the only jobs. I had a little job at this [catering] company. I had a lot of odd jobs. I was doing temp agencies then, too.

RON: You ever work under the table?

RED: Recently, I was working for this dude moving pianos. That was pretty good. Just no benefits in it. Moving them pianos and that's dangerous.

RON: Yeah, man.

RED: You need benefits for that. I don't care. My cousin think it's sweet. He doing it right now. I said it's going to catch up with you in the long run.

RON: Hurt your back or your knees.

RED: He ain't giving enough for that straight up. $100 ain't enough. No, it ain't. It's not enough. What about some benefits?

RON: Hurt that back!

RED: Hurt that back, you got to come up with that money to pay for that on your own.

RON: Yeah. So, why did you leave the warehouse work?

RED: I started with the temp agency. I was on and off then. Just working for them and then I found Stop & Shop. And then I was doing Stop & Shop for a minute [long time]. And I got arrested.

RON: Oh, that will do it. [laughs]

RED: Yeah, that will do it. That did it.

Red was arrested for dealing drugs, a source of income he had relied on intermittently since his childhood to supplement low wages or pay for unexpected expenses that arose.

These were the labor force conditions for young low-income fathers in Connecticut and throughout the nation *before* the 2007 economic collapse. Things were not about to get better.

After the "Big One"

By the end of the decade—amid the aftermath of the Great Recession—more desperation had crept into our interviews. In our first interview with James, in February 2009, he observed, "Things are not easy. They are not going to be easier. Life is hard. There ain't many jobs out there. So what you can get, you keep." In September 2009 in his second interview, he commented, "I know a lot of people [looking for a job]. Every day I meet people that's looking for work. Even where I do work there are people looking for other jobs . . . I am one also that's looking for another part-time job . . . there are a lot of people that just say, fuck it. It's so hard. It's not easy. It seems like it gets harder every day."

Hard times had created tensions in his household and more arguments with his wife. "Well, yeah, [she will say] 'Get out and get another job. Get your shit together. Get another job. Help pay some of the bills.'" At the time, James, a 40-year-old white father, was delivering newspapers and working part-time at a supermarket. By the fourth interview, in 2010, James, who had worked as many as three part-time jobs at the same time, was down to one job at a supermarket, cleaning 24 to 36 hours per week. He never reached a combined 40 hours at any time in the study. He and his wife were still together, but arguments about money had not subsided. "I think that's a normal thing," James commented. "Everybody argues about money. Money is the all-evil thing in the world [laughs]."

At least James had work, even if only part-time. Many fathers in our study were not so fortunate, nor were many in the state. The state lost 119,000 jobs during the recession and another 22,400 manufacturing jobs.[42] By January 2010, the state had recovered only 19 percent of those jobs.[43] Unemployment more than doubled between 2006 and 2010, and for whites, like James, had increased to 7.5 percent. For blacks and Latinos, though, it had jumped to 17.7 percent for each group, and in 2010, one-third of Latinos without a high school education were out of work.[44] Workers at the bottom of the labor force earned less than they had in 1989 and experienced the greatest wage deterioration in the country. Likewise, from 2007 to 2008, Connecticut had the largest increase in the poverty rate in the country, and by 2010, nearly one-fourth of blacks and Latinos lived below the poverty line, about four times the rate of whites.[45] Moreover, blacks earned only 62 cents for every dollar earned by whites, and Latinos 60 cents, both considerably less than national disparities in 2010 (78 and 70 cents, respectively).[46] In the cities, poverty rates reached well beyond the state average. The child poverty rate in the state was 12.8 percent in 2010, but 44.5 percent in Hartford and 43.7 percent in New Haven.[47] This was perhaps best illustrated by *Hartford Courant* columnist Susan Campbell, who noted in 2010 that one Hartford homeless shelter had turned away needy individuals seeking its services 535 times in October alone.[48]

James's part-time employment during this period reflected the increases in underemployment in the state. This measure includes not only the unemployed (those still looking for work and those who were discouraged and no longer looking for work) but also those working in part-time jobs looking for full-time employment, referred to as involuntary part-time workers. The underemployment rate in Connecticut reached a historic high in 2009 at 14.4 percent, before jumping to 15.7 percent in 2010.[49]

Some fathers, like James, were working in part-time jobs, with the hope that as the economy improved they would be hired full-time. But in the era of cutting costs and maintaining production levels through lean management strategies, these hopes rarely materialized. James described:

> Where I work, [my co-worker] has been there since the place opened. I was told, "You are in a go-nowhere position. Once this guy retires you are just going to continue being a part-timer." There is no full-time [after him]. They ended it. . . . One less they got to pay.

As one of the older men in our study, James provided a longer perspective on the job market. His observations were sobering. "I remember in the state [of CT] many years ago in the 80s you could hop from job to job to job. And they would never stop. . . . Today, I work with college grads [and even] they ain't doing shit but bagging groceries . . . they can't get nothing."

James observation about college graduates turned out to be insightful. What he is referring to is what Andrew Cherlin calls the "downward cascade of workers" in which economic downturns result in workers being forced down the striated full-time, part-time labor force hierarchy. Wages for college-educated workers rose faster in the 1980s and 1990s than wages for less educated workers, but they quit rising for men after 2000 and slowed for women. Cherlin attributes this to some college-educated workers moving into "middle-skilled" jobs, where they replaced high school–educated workers and pushed them further down the labor force ladder.[50] In Connecticut, though, college-educated workers were not only being pushed down the latter, as James and Cherlin noted; they were being pushed out of the job market as well. The unemployment rate for graduates from Connecticut state universities doubled between 2005 and 2010 to 10 percent, a rate that was about one-half the rate for those without a high school education.[51]

Long-term unemployment was a distinguishing feature of the 2007 recession that severely disrupted the lives of low-income families. In 2009, Connecticut had the fourth highest long-term unemployment rate in the nation (the percent unemployed longer than 26 weeks) at 37 percent. In 2010, the rate jumped to 50 percent.[52]

Our efforts to complete four interviews with the fathers after the advent of the Great Recession were challenged by the men's harried schedules. They would often call us at the last minute to reschedule an interview because a temporary agency had called, or an under-the-table job opportunity had emerged, or they had a chance to work overtime. A few of the fathers followed job leads that took them out of the state, away from not only us but also their families. The larger challenge here is to understand and appreciate the daily grind of poverty where everything hangs by only a thread, and where the attention of accumulating and exchanging resources exhausts the day, even when there are no major eruptions. Life consists of balancing, juggling, stretching, borrowing, pleading, cussing, praying, running, and hiding in the daily struggle to navigate hard-living working-class lives. And we found that the small victories or failures, like maintaining a cell phone, making rent on time, keeping a vehicle on the road, or finding an informal income opportunity, could be the difference between getting up the next day prepared for the grind or giving into despondency and its more destructive outcomes.

All fathers in our 2008 study considered working to be an integral part of being a responsible father, yet less than one-half were working full-time jobs. The rest were either unemployed or working one or several part-time jobs. Many shared stories about feeling alienated, socially disconnected, and embarrassed that they were unable to pay their bills in a timely fashion. Even the more successful fathers working full-time were often living one paycheck away from family disaster, or in some cases one or two paychecks behind their wishes for stability. Those with criminal records or who were less attached to the labor market were much worse off.

Steven, a 20-year-old father of mixed Native American and white ancestry, left the state to seek better job opportunities after a lengthy spell of underemployment. We were only able to secure two interviews with him as a result of his departure. At the time of these interviews, Steven was working as a "super"—or maintenance man—in the apartment building where he lived. He was compensated with free rent, but no additional income. Although his job arrangement gave Steven plenty of time to spend with his newborn daughter, he desperately desired a job, but a criminal record and a bleak job market sealed his fate. Finding a job around here, he commented, "is harder than digging up gold, man.... I been looking around.... I went everywhere. Nowhere is hiring. And the few places that are, I mean I got a couple [criminal] charges and they are preventing me from getting those very few jobs." Before leaving the state, Steven insisted that "nobody should ever give up" on finding work, because he said with a sigh, "once you give up [on that] you give up on life."

Eric, a 21-year-old white father with whom we secured four interviews, was one of the rare success stories in our study. Recovering from drug addiction and possessing a felony criminal record, Eric told us he had been vigorously searching for a job for five months before we met him. He claimed that this was the longest he had gone without work since he was 16.

> I've been applying like crazy . . . going like every day just like from 7 a.m.
> until like 5 p.m. just straight up, just every single place I see, just stop in
> and going in [wearing] like a suit with a tie just telling them like my whole
> story. "I got a kid coming" and all this. But I guess they just weren't hiring
> around here.

He had been told by a few prospective employers that his felony record had prevented them from hiring him, and he told us that when "applying online [for a job], once you hit the felony [box] they just stop it right then and there." Eric's struggle to find employment with a criminal record was similar to the stories told to us by several fathers in the study. We did not secure another interview with him for almost a year after the first one, during which time he remained unemployed until just before we reestablished contact with him. He described finding his new job.

SKY: Last interview you were searching for work and having a tough time of it. . . . Can you talk about how you ended up finding a job?

ERIC: I just got real lucky. Just one day . . . I was going to go to the temp agency but on the way to the temp agency I saw a little restaurant with the doors open. So I was like "All right, I'll check it out." And I just got hired like the next day . . . as a busser. . . . I get $9 [an hour] plus tips.

SKY: Overall, how many applications do you think you probably put in?"

ERIC: Well over 100.

Walking into a restaurant because "the door was open" illustrated Eric's determination, if not desperation. Whether due to perseverance or a stroke of good luck—and being white most likely did not hurt—Eric was clocking slightly more than 40 hours a week at his new job. This provided him with a modicum of economic stability, enough to contribute toward some of his daughter's needs and to start a savings account for her, but not enough to move out of his parents' home or to pay off his debts. However, the benefits of Eric's job cannot be measured only in economic terms; it also provided him with a sense of self-respect and peace of mind. At the time of the last interview, Eric was meeting the expectations of fatherhood held by those around him, and Sky noted that although his relationship with the mother of his child had deteriorated, he seemed less anxious toward the end of the study, which Sky attributed to his job and his partial fulfillment of the provider role.

Jermaine, however, was not so fortunate. Jermaine, a 20-year-old father of African American and Jamaican descent, was another respondent who struggled with unemployment. He began the study unemployed and living in his partner's parents' home, and reported feeling the stress of his daughter's upcoming birthday. "Her birthday party is coming up, so it going to be a struggle to scrape up money. . . . I don't have a job right now [so] it's going to be hard to scrape up money and get her stuff for her birthday—clothes and all that because she getting bigger." Describing his circumstances, Jermaine said, "It's rocky, I'll put it like that."

By the time we secured a second interview with Jermaine, he was selling scrap metal to make money. A successful week might result in more income than some of his peers who were employed in formal part-time jobs, but the money was inconsistent. Jermaine wanted regular work but had been repeatedly rebuffed by the job market; he told us how even his efforts to get employed by a "temp agency" were unsuccessful and a waste of time.

JERMAINE: I had signed up for this temp agency. And they sent me to orientation for one job three times. They sent me to orientation before the winter hit and the job wasn't going to start until after the winter. After the winter hit, the summer started coming up, like right about now, they sent me to orientation two more times.

INTERVIEWER: I think I remember that because I was trying to call you around February, I think, and you had the orientation in the mornings, the real early mornings.

JERMAINE: Yeah. And I still ain't got a job.

INTERVIEWER: Oh, man.

JERMAINE: So I just recently took myself off they list. They want me to call them every day and everything just so I can hear "Oh, no, we don't have nothing yet! Call tomorrow!" [laughter] I am not calling you all tomorrow. Stop playing. I just had to take myself off. . . . I can pick up scrap metal.

Through the third and fourth interviews, Jermaine was still collecting and selling scrap metal but had augmented his income with an under-the-table roofing job as well as other odd jobs. His demeanor and comfort level seemed to change between the third and fourth interviews. At the third interview, he appeared particularly anxious about his unemployment and lack of income; by the fourth interview, it seemed that Jermaine had embraced his off-the-books jobs. He felt more competent in knowing how to get and where to sell scrap metal, which provided him with personal security that can only be understood in relation to his social and economic marginalization. Jermaine was searching for not only a form of subsistence but also a self-narrative that provided some semblance of dignity. He stated:

I tell anybody as long as there is metal around I ain't never going to be broke . . . I am always [gonna] have a job as long as there is scrap metal because I will always get out here and get my hustle on picking up scrap metal to make my daily quota to get my money to just survive, you feel me? . . . Cats be like "Yo, I hate life, man. Ain't no job trying to call me back." There are so many hustles out here, go pick up cans, man. You see bums— like I watched this dude, he picked up cans for three years, man. I just seen dudes, they go in [the junkyard] . . . with pure copper and come off with like $50. I know if I do two or three trips, man, that's a $150 right there. Buddy, I done already mapped this out. This is not a game. This is life.

Like many others, Jermaine longed for full-time employment, but he had worked out a contingency strategy for surviving a marginalized existence, especially in tough economic times.

In the remainder of the chapter, we examine two employment industries that are most available to workers at the bottom of the labor force: the fast food and temporary job industries. We do so because of the stories the men shared with us and to underscore the exploitative nature of these jobs. That is to say, we want to see the decision-making processes of fathers, but without losing sight of the decisions being made by economic and political elites who structure the labor force.

Fast Food: Marking the Bottom

Nearly one-half of the fathers in our study had worked at a fast food restaurant at some point in their working lives. The Labor Center at the University of California in Berkeley issued two reports, in 2013 and 2015, which documented the public costs of low-wage employment in the United States, with the first focusing exclusively on the fast food industry.[53] Further, the nomination of Andrew Puzder to be President Donald Trump's Secretary of Labor in 2017 brought media scrutiny to the industry, which exposed several additional issues, including wage theft, and demonstrated how the franchise model made it difficult for unlawful practices to be detected and for workers to defend themselves.[54]

The Labor Center reported that the median wage paid to front-line fast food workers in 2012 was $8.69, making many employees eligible for public assistance. Combining the costs for health care (Medicaid and the Children's Health Insurance Program), tax benefits to low-income workers (Earned Income Tax Credit), food (Supplemental Nutrition Assistance Program), and basic necessities (Temporary Assistance for Needy Families), the report conservatively estimated that taxpayers are subsidizing fast food companies about $7 billion a year in order for employees' families to have basic necessities. The largest public cost is for health care needs, since an estimated 87 percent of fast food employees do not receive benefits from the company.[55] This needs to be understood in relation to the prosperity of these companies. The ten most lucrative fast food corporations made $7.44 billion in profits in 2012 and paid their CEOs a total of $52.7 million in salary. They provided employment for an estimated 2.25 million workers at US restaurants.[56]

In 2015, the Labor Center broadened their study to examine the public costs of low-wage employment more generally. They found that taxpayer support for low-wage workers in 2013 cost $152.8 billion, what they refer to as the "hidden costs" of low-wage work. These costs have increased, the authors argue, because of stagnating wages and decreases in employer provided health care. They point out that nearly three-quarters (73 percent) of families receiving public assistance are working families and that a little more than one-half (56 percent) of total public funds go to these families. Fast food workers were the most likely to receive public subsidies, followed by child-care workers, homecare workers, and part-time college faculty. Connecticut followed this pattern, with working families receiving 54 percent of federal aid from public assistance programs.[57]

Most of the public is not likely to be too concerned, let alone disturbed, about the low wages or the working conditions of fast food restaurants, because they assume that these jobs are filled by young high school students who are first entering the job market and still going to school. While this may have been true at one time, it is less the case today. The percentage of workers in the fast food industry who are teens living with a parent is actually less (19 percent) than the percentage who have children of their own (26 percent), half of whom are married. In 2012, the median number of hours worked in fast food franchises was 30 hours per week, while a little more than a quarter (28 percent) of front-line fast food workers were employed full-time (at least 40 hours per week).[58]

Despite low wages, the fast food industry is nevertheless a last-resort job opportunity for many, like the men in our study. However, these jobs carry stigma. In contexts in which individuals are confronting regularly practices of exclusion, fast-food jobs become important symbolic markers. In other locations throughout the country, these jobs remain entry-level positions for high school students, who are learning to perform in a job environment and putting some spending money in their pockets. In fact, in wealthy suburban communities, fast-food restaurants pay more to recruit workers because there is less demand for these jobs. In poorer communities, and especially in poor urban communities, the lack of job opportunities creates more demand and, hence, more competition for these jobs that include adults in their prime-age working years. Studying the fast-food industry in Harlem in the 1990s, Katherine Newman found that for every job filled, there were 14 applicants—and because of higher demand for fast-food jobs in poorer communities, the pay was less than in the suburbs.[59]

In addition, when unemployment rates are high, or when there is a surplus of available workers, there is no pressure to raise wages or expand benefits, and worker discipline is enhanced. Workers must be on time, work hard, accept low pay and lack of raises, be deferent to supervisors, and be willing to work additional hours if needed—or even as the Puzder inquiries found, tolerate sexual harassment and other illegal behavior. Failure to meet these expectations can result in dismissal and replacement with one of the many applicants waiting to secure full-time employment.

Garrett, who we mentioned at the beginning of the chapter, told us a chilling story about working at McDonald's. Garrett had a history of suffering kidney stones. As an assistant manager at the restaurant, he had been offered health insurance through McDonald's, but he found the premium to be prohibitive, so he chose instead to enroll in the state's Medicaid program.[60] Having lost a job previously due to absences related to his son's medical condition, and aware of the lack of jobs at the time and the surplus of workers positioned to join the managerial ranks, Garrett had gone to extraordinary lengths to keep his current job at McDonald's. He told us that he had passed eight kidney stones in his life, two while he was working at McDonald's. He described the pain as the "closest thing for a man to ever having a child," which meant that for Garrett, screaming through the process in the bathroom at McDonald's was preferable to calling in sick, losing income, and risking the loss of his job.

The symbolism of fast-food jobs in poorer communities is shaped by these social and economic dynamics. Because these jobs are seen as entry-level employment for youth, adults working in these jobs as a primary source of income are stigmatized as "losers." This is especially true among street hustlers who view their peers as "suckers" succumbing to "slave wages." Fast food workers are viewed as the bottom feeders of the labor force, working in jobs that signify their lack of worth in the labor market. Newman found that this stigma affected even high school youth who went to great lengths to conceal their employment from their peers. We suspect that fast food jobs are less stigmatizing for suburban youth, because these jobs are seen as temporary, seasonal, and as a way to responsibly require youth to earn their own spending money. In communities where these jobs may become permanent, and where there is much more at stake in finding one's place in the economy, these jobs carry a heavier burden and are symbolically loaded with meaning.

Kevin and Nathan's reactions to fast food jobs in poorer communities illustrated the symbolic meaning of these jobs. Both were young African

American men with prison records for dealing drugs. When Nathan was released, he spent months putting in job applications without success. He told us that he had applied for jobs at fast food restaurants right out of high school, and that he felt discriminated against because he wore his hair in braids. Years later, Nathan approached these same employers, only this time older, with three felony convictions.

> I couldn't get a job at McDonald's. You know? That's crazy! Burger King . . . I had the manager sold at Burger King. They wouldn't hire me because of my record. The manager was feeling me, like vouching for me, like "He's a good dude" . . . I killed [impressed] them. [Nathan gets very emotional here and is trying to hold back tears.] The McDonald's thing was like "This is my last resort." The Burger King thing, I had just came home [from prison]. I was in a halfway house. I was amped up. "Yeah, yeah, I need this. I am going to go right by this." This was before my son was born . . . I was amped. Shot me down. Just went backwards. . . . I was hurt. Devastated. It's all right, though. But it's just like when a petty place . . . I can't even say "petty" . . . when a place like that won't hire you . . .

Nathan's emotions overwhelmed him, and he began to cry before he finished his sentence. For Nathan, being rejected by a fast food restaurant—"a place like that"—suggested that he had no value in the labor market, that he was useless, with his future hopes coming out of prison aborted.

Kevin, however, adopted an oppositional attitude toward fast food work. He was willing to work in other service jobs, but not fast food, which carried intolerable stigma for a young black man struggling to find a job that signified respectability. Kevin was 19 years old and locked up at the time of the interview for dealing drugs. He explained that he had turned to the street economy after his attempts to get hired by Home Depot and UPS failed. Working a fast food job was not a consideration. "The main issue really is," Kevin declared, "how can I get a respectful job. I mean I know everybody got to start from somewhere. But I really ain't trying to go to no fast food restaurant. I would work in a grocery store before I work in a fast food restaurant." Reflecting for a moment, he continued, "It's just the point of it. I won't do that." Kevin was trying to eke out working-class respectability in a context of constrained opportunities. To him, fast food work was a marker of failure.

Many in the public, including—as Newman demonstrates in her book— many of Kevin's peers, view Kevin's decisions as immature and indicative of a poorly developed work ethic, especially given that he is a father. Right or wrong, however, we need to consider Kevin's decision in terms of the symbolic boundary that fast food jobs represent in poor communities and the inner drama that plagues this young black man. Further, we need to realize that networks of youth participating in the drug trade are making similar decisions, despite the risks, in an effort to establish success and respectability.

Conceptions of masculinity, of course, mediate these decisions. In other words, this is a form of opposition, in which young men draw a line concerning what they are willing to accept in the legitimate job world and instead pursue alternative means to achieve widely shared masculine desires for status, respect, and conspicuous consumption. Of course, given the drug laws, and often the lifestyle that accompanies the drug trade, these decisions result in further economic and social marginalization and have long-term detrimental consequences for both employability and fatherhood. Nonetheless, these decisions are occurring in an economic and social context that is inextricably intertwined with the struggle to create lives of dignity and respect.

Temp Jobs

The Temporary Help Industry (THI) is a vital part of the flexible, contingent workforce. For men on the margins of the labor force, who lack viable job networks to help secure employment, the temp agency is a convenient, easily accessible vehicle for finding work. Many of the men in our study utilized these agencies at different times in their lives. However, THI benefits employers much more than it benefits marginalized workers. For workers, the hope is that they will get a foot in the door at a workplace that will eventually put them on the payroll as a full-time worker, eligible for the employee benefits. This is not an unreasonable expectation—it follows the "try before you buy" model. This strategy makes sense in an environment in which employers are looking for employees to invest in and develop as long-term productive workers. However, the post-1970s reorganization of the labor force and the role that temp agencies play, particularly in recruiting a low-wage workforce, have fostered a triangular relationship that is central to shaping a new regime of labor exploitation.

Private employment agencies have existed throughout the 20th century. Their changing role within the economy reflected the (re)organization of capitalism and the labor force in each period of the century.[61] In the 1970s, THI did not just find a niche in the reorganization of capitalism, but it played an active role in facilitating contingency work and restratifying the working class. The industry lobbied to avoid being classified as an employment agency to escape statutes that regulated, among other practices, fees, and instead pushed hard to be considered as an employer that could offload legal and administrative responsibilities from business firms and organizations.[62] The success of these lobbying efforts was astonishing. By 1971, only two states continued to regulate THIs as employment agencies, while 1973 marked the point at which explosive growth in the industry began. Citing the classic study by Barry Bluestone and Bennett Harrison, George Gonos explained that "the great spurt in THI growth" that began in 1973 also "marked the beginning of the 'Great U-Turn' in incomes of American workers."[63] Gonos clarifies the significance of this:

> The THI deregulation by the early 1970s had securely positioned the industry to play a key role in the tremendous growth of contingent work and in the restructuring of employment relations; it has now become widespread and accepted practice for corporations to use the THI's "services" to relocate work from their core to the "outer rings."[64]

The ring-and-core approach represented a shift from the asset to the liability model, as Erin Hatton describes it, in which workers were no longer seen as assets to invest in, but rather as liabilities that cut into profits. The cultivation of a long-term workforce became seen as an inefficient form of "overstaffing."[65]

The centrality of the temp industry in the new economy taking shape in and after the 1980s was unmistakable. For the first time, the temp industry began to provide temp workers as strikebreakers;[66] state unemployment agencies began referring unemployed workers to temp agencies;[67] and the federal government itself began to rely more on temp workers as a cost-cutting strategy.[68] The THI expanded into skilled white-collar work as well as into low-wage industrial work. It developed new "products" for its business customers that included vendor on premises, in-house outsourcing, day labor, and master vendor contracts.[69]

In the first year of the recovery of the early 1980s recession, the temp industry became the fastest growing industry in America.[70] Lesser known, however, is that even in the 1990s period of sustained economic growth that pushed unemployment rates down, one-half of the decrease in unemploy-ment was attributable to employment in the temp industry,[71] which grew 123 percent during the 1990s expansion compared to 22 percent in non-agricultural employment.[72] A *Time* magazine cover story in 1993 entitled "The Temping of America" announced that the temp firm, Manpower, Inc., had replaced General Motors as the largest private employer in America.[73] And in 1996, President Clinton invited the CEO of Manpower, Inc., Mitchell Fromstein, to the White House to discuss ways that the temp industry could help put welfare recipients to work.[74] Ringing it up on the cash register, at the turn of the millennium, the THI recorded more than $64 billion in business.[75]

In the first decade of the new century, when we were conducting interviews, the temp industry continued to thrive, with a few notable features. First, the length of time that temp workers were employed increased. In 2006, temp workers were assigned to jobs an average of 12.5 weeks, an increase of 600 percent since 1990, and one-third of temp assignments lasted more than a year. Second, the use of temporary staffing firms (TSFs) continued to be a central employment mechanism during periods of economic recovery. In the early 1990s recovery, temp jobs accounted for 11 percent of new jobs. In the slow recovery from 2002 to 2005, it accounted for 20 percent, and, in 2010, 27 percent of new jobs created were temp positions.[76] Currently, at any given time, around 3 million workers are employed in the THI; around 10 percent of workers are employed by temp agencies each year; and 9 out of every 10 American businesses utilize temp workers as a workforce strategy.[77]

Several of the fathers we interviewed talked about temp agencies as a common part of life in their neighborhoods.[78] These agencies provide needed services to residents in low-income communities, but much like other businesses—check cashing, furniture rental, secondary lending markets—they do so by extracting profits from already cash-strapped families and communities. Gonos estimates that temp workers are paid 25–40 percent less than regular employees.[79] He asserts that even though these agencies thrive in poor areas, "Labor markets mediated by for-profit agencies is not an effective anti-poverty strategy."[80] In our study, 29-year-old Todd was a reg-ular user of TSFs. At the time of our interview, Todd had two jobs assigned by a temp agency. He described his day at one of the jobs.

> I had to be at the temp agency at 5:00. So I had to get up at 4:00, take my shower, brush my teeth, make my lunch, and then head up to the temp

agency. Like drivers start leaving out around 6:30, 7:00 so you got to be there at least around 6:00 . . . and be gone like all day. Like leave at 7:00 and don't get back to the warehouse until around 7:00 at night. So that's like 12 hours a day working minimum wage. But it's better than nothing.

Todd was being paid minimum wage for a job that the TSF was making money from as an intermediary, and typically these markups for blue-collar or industrial jobs are at least twice the wage paid to the employee.[81] Todd was working a second job through the TSF at a laundromat.

Temp agencies move workers around with a phone call or text, and they keep a steady supply of workers in the wings waiting for that call. Jack, the 23-year-old Puerto Rican man we referred to earlier who said he needed three part-time jobs to make it, emphasized the unreliability of the work. At our interview in August 2010, he worked "at the temp agency for 10 bucks an hour," but described the stress that the unreliability of the work was creating for him. "Everybody is getting laid off. No jobs anywhere. And if you are working at an agency, they are only going to give you work for like two weeks, that's it. If I am going to work for a job, I don't want to work for two weeks . . . I want to stay there and work there." Jack was placed at a tool and dye company for $10 an hour, but the machine he was working on broke in the first two weeks of his employment. They told him, "We'll call you back when the machine is fixed. And they never did." Placed next at a warehousing job, Jack explained, "They call me in to go to work and then when I go to work, 'Oh, we don't need you.' Then why you going to call me to go to work when you don't need me? . . . That's why it sucks to work from a temp agency." Jack was describing the moment-to-moment decisions being made to place workers and the lack of accountability for when they are placed and released. Workers are simply ready labor at the whims of just-in-production needs. As we pointed out earlier, it was this dynamic that led Jermaine to give up on his temp agency and pursue collecting scrap metal full-time.

While some of the fathers sat at home waiting to hear from their TSF, a few others were placed at a workplace with long-term contracts. Because business clients no longer pay a one-time fee for an employee, the TSF has an interest in keeping the worker employed as a temp for as long as possible, since they are making money for every hour that the employee logs for their client. This has resulted in what is referred to as "permatemps," employees whose work is controlled by the client employer, but who legally are employees of the TSF. Permatemps have become an integral part of the labor force. From

1995 to 2005 alone, the proportion of temp workers employed for more than a year increased from 24 to 34 percent.[82] Deshaun was a 23-year-old Jamaican who grew up in a Kingston shantytown, but resided in Bridgeport. Like Jack, his employment circumstances at the time of the interview reflected the increasing use of temp workers in the manufacturing industries in Connecticut, as well as in the nation.[83] Once the backbone of good-paying unionized jobs that fortified middle-income families in the postwar era, manufacturing industries today have integrated temp jobs into their hiring strategies to reduce costs and liability, and to maintain a flexible workforce. Deshaun described his temp job.

RON: What kind of work are you doing? Full-time? Part-time?
DESHAUN: Full-time and part-time.
RON: Tell me about the full-time job.
DESHAUN: I work at [a manufacturing company]. We make plastic film. Like we make for all these big companies like cigarette companies . . . candy bar wrappers . . . so you got an idea of what I'm saying.
RON: How long you been there?
DESHAUN: I only been there for about four months.
RON: Is it a job that's going to give you benefits and health care?
DESHAUN: Well, I am a temp right now. I am a temp-to-hire. I have a two-year contract. I just try to show them that I know what I am doing and I got the skills for this and put me on their . . .
RON: Put you on their payroll. What about your part-time job?
DESHAUN: I work at [a] supermarket.

Deshaun referred to his job as "a temp-to-hire," but his two-year contract belies the point and instead represents the increasing reliance on permatemps as a labor force strategy. During these two years, Deshaun does not receive health care or retirement benefits, and the temp agency continues to extract their "fee" from the markup on his salary, without any guarantee that the job will become permanent after the two-year period. Low-wage temp workers rarely receive health or retirement benefits, and because of low wages, like fast-food workers, they must rely on public benefits to meet basic needs.

The THI is emblematic of the era of neoliberalism. It reflects the loss of power among workers to contest workplace issues, particularly abuses, and it represents the exploitative efforts of the industry to extract profits from the livelihoods of the most vulnerable class of workers through manipulation of statutory definitions and the normative reorganization of low-wage work. Listening to the fathers talk about temp work, it became clear that this type of work was part of a rotating matrix of income sources that men utilized. Forty-four-year old Marcus explained, "I have to call [the temp agency]. And they look for jobs for me. Sometimes they tell me they have a job; sometimes they don't have a job. So when they don't have no jobs, I have to run to someplace else and try to get a job from a friend of mine, under the table." The fathers rarely talked about temp jobs in isolation of other part-time jobs or revenue sources; in fact, temp jobs were often mentioned interchangeably with under-the-table jobs. In other words, to isolate a particular type of contingent labor does not capture the full experience of men who work in this labor sector. It is the day-to-day uncertainty that emerges in their descriptions of work that details the precariousness of their lives. As Richard Sennett put it, "What's peculiar about uncertainty today is that it exists without any looming historical disaster; instead, it is woven into the everyday practices of a vigorous capitalism."[84]

Conclusion

Neoliberal economic restructuring has greatly affected the earning potential of men at the bottom of the labor force. Pushed into low-wage, full-time employment that falls far short of meeting family needs or into part-time employment, or even out of the labor force, these men struggle to contribute as providers, and as fathers more generally. Financial stress in family relationships has become less episodic and more permanent, while marriage has ceased to be a viable institution in economically unstable social circumstances.

It is far too convenient to see economic restructuring as a natural development of the global economy. These constructions obscure the political agency of political and economic elites. The decline in the profit rate beginning in the 1960s and capitalism's crisis in the 1970s set into motion a set of practices that reorganized the economy. The only organization that represents workers' interests, the labor union, has been aggressively disempowered. Volcker's famous dictum that the standard of living of workers had to decrease became a reality, as the crisis in capitalism was rectified on the backs of wage earners. Precarious work, just-in-time production, the ring-and-core workforce, the franchise model, the steady supply of desperate workers, and downward pressures on the minimum wage created bleak opportunity structures for families at the bottom of the labor force. The unleashing of un-regulated market forces not only affected manufacturing plants, like Stanley Works, but it strengthened the franchise model that keeps wages low in fast food jobs, and it institutionalized the temporary help industry that manages a large portion of the contingency workforce. Without political representa-tion of their interests, these families and individuals had to battle alone to do the best they could within a set of circumstances that denied them.

Poverty and economic family instability do not cause poor parenting, but they certainly create and exacerbate stresses and constraints on families. The jobless recovery of the early part of the decade and the Great Recession that defined the end of it help us to see family vulnerability in a neoliberal con-text. But to fully understand the nature of this vulnerability, we need to ex-amine the effects that welfare retrenchment has also had on this population and on fatherhood.

3

Welfare Reform and Market Conformity

> It's funny I think I don't make enough, yet everybody else thinks
> I make too much.
>
> —Raymond

Since its inception, the US welfare system has always pegged its assistance to the poor beneath minimum wages in order to incentivize work, a standard adopted from the English Poor Laws called the principle of less eligibility.[1] However, the neoliberal transition after the 1970s affected both sides of the equation—it undermined the stability of jobs, allowed the minimum wage to decline in value, and reduced workplace benefits, while at the same time it retrenched governmental assistance, shredded the safety net for the poor, and increased the supply of low-income workers by pushing recipients into the labor force. Families at the bottom of the labor force found themselves caught in a vise—a destabilized low-wage workforce and dwindling social protections.

The welfare system, like all state institutions, is constitutive of gender.[2] That is, it both reflects and shapes the dominant conceptions and practices of gender (as it does race, sexuality, and disability). Throughout most of the 20th century, it had been organized around the breadwinner role for men and the caretaker role for women, and tied to the market swings of a manufacturing economy. Men have benefited from the privileges of the labor market, while the welfare system has provided aid that reflected their market status—mostly, unemployment insurance, social security retirement, and disability insurance. Further, it extended basic protections to families during cyclical periods when fathers were unable to provide for them in the labor market. However, because of the minimal role played by the US state, compared to the primacy of the market (income) and family (care), the government has rarely provided employment for men through either public or full employment policies.[3] Therefore, men unable to provide for families in the

It's a Setup. Timothy Black and Sky Keyes, Oxford University Press (2021). © Timothy Black and Sky Keyes.
DOI: 10.1093/oso/9780190062217.003.0003

market, disproportionately men of color, but also poor white men, are often left unsupported by the state and at a disadvantage in participating in the marital institution, in valued forms of masculinity, and as fathers.[4]

Neoliberal welfare reform modified the idealized model of the patriarchal nuclear family by promoting a model of the dual-earner family, woven together through marriage, in which fathers and mothers shared work and childrearing responsibilities.[5] In many ways, these changes reflected the reality of the declining quality of jobs and wages in the labor force, increasing numbers of women entering the workforce, and the changing norms and expectations of fatherhood. In essence, if fathers and mothers both worked in low-wage precarious employment and shared childcare responsibilities, they could eke out a living and presumably meet social reproductive needs by preparing their children for the 21st century. However, in keeping with the tenets of neoliberalism, there was little support provided by the state for these families—even less than had been provided in the past—but instead the state was reorganized to enforce compliance with labor market conditions and parenting responsibilities.[6]

While the federal government created the framework for neoliberal welfare reform, it left much of the work to the states to implement. Part of the devolution of authority for welfare provision from the federal to state governments was achieved by consolidating a broad range of categorical programs into block grants distributed to the states with reduced funding.[7] This created, in principle, 50 different welfare systems, with the states given more discretion in determining program eligibility requirements and benefit levels, but with less federal funds. Moreover, during recessionary periods, it left the states with the burden of addressing increased need with declining fiscal revenues, while meeting the imperative of balancing budgets.

In this chapter, we briefly summarize the post-1970s neoliberal restructuring of US state welfare that culminated in the 1996 welfare reform act. We examine how mothers and fathers from our Couples Study discussed the consequences of these reforms in Connecticut six and seven years after. While most of these couples were not married, they represented cohabiting families that were left to eke out their livings in a precarious labor market and to care for children with limited, and declining, support provided by the state of Connecticut.

We then focus our attention on the aftermath of the worst economic crisis to occur in US history since the Great Depression to see how this affected state support for low-income families within the new structure of the welfare system. Here we consider the effects not only on cohabiting families but also on noncustodial fathers. This chapter demonstrates how neoliberal welfare reform, combined with changes in the labor force, has destabilized families and left both low-income mothers and fathers with fewer options for subsistence, particularly during economic downturns. Further, by viewing the perspectives of couples in the first part of the decade and among fathers after the Great Recession, we see how neoliberal state changes are viewed through a gendered lens.

Neoliberal Welfare Retrenchment

Post-1970s US welfare reflected the changing role of the state. Under the prior New Deal framework, trade, finance, investment, labor, and consumption were regulated, while the welfare system, as John O'Connor put it, "smoothed out economic disruptions over an individual's life course (and working life)."[8] The role of the state was central to maintaining a largely domestic-based economy and mediating business competition as well as capital–labor conflicts.[9] US welfare provided basic protections during recessionary periods that preserved a workforce that would typically be rehired during recoveries with an eye toward full employment. Nonetheless, despite the key role played by the state in a New Deal structured economy, the welfare system was designed to minimally provide income and care toward the reproductive needs of a society, relative to the market and family.[10] Organized around a manufacturing economy and the patriarchal family, US welfare state intervention was mostly episodic, and its policies reinforced the nuclear family and gendered family roles.[11] Households unrepresentative of the nuclear family were stigmatized, received less assistance, and were often excluded by state authorities prior to the mid-1960s, particularly racial, ethnic, and sexual minority households.[12]

The state in the neoliberal era was itself transformed as it unraveled New Deal institutional provisions and accelerated market dynamics. Financial and industrial regulations, trade barriers, capital–labor accords, tax structures, and social protections were all reduced or eliminated as market forces were unleashed globally and domestically, and as market rationality was injected into all institutional and civic forms of social life, even the family.[13] Within this context, welfare was viewed as a market inefficiency and a waste of capital resources—perhaps best symbolized by Ronald

Reagan's famous quote that not only was government not the solution, it was the problem.[14]

The Reagan era was pivotal to the neoliberal reorganization of the welfare state. In addition to making deep cuts in unemployment insurance, employment and training programs, and housing assistance, his administration altered the eligibility rules governing many welfare programs, which fell disproportionately on the working poor.[15] Further, Reagan advanced the devolution of federal authority to the states along with the changing funding mechanisms described earlier. Military spending was increased while taxes were cut and restructured upward to benefit higher-earning groups, creating a spiraling federal deficit that placed more pressure on social spending cuts. Further, Reagan changed the welfare discourse from a war on poverty to a war on the poor, blaming the poor for moral degeneracy and big-government liberals for enabling a dishonorable poverty culture. His policies and rhetoric turned up the heat on parental responsibility and work.

Most importantly, neoliberal restructuring of welfare and its moral discourse advanced by Reagan would be deepened in subsequent administrations, Republicans and Democrats alike. The devolution of authority to the states would result in more disparate welfare systems. Deficit spending to reduce welfare spending, or "starve the beast," would reappear under George W. Bush.[16] The outlines of Reagan's Family Support Act (FSA) of 1988 that underscored father responsibility and workfare would become a centerpiece of Clinton's welfare reform.[17] Public assistance for the poor would be tied more closely to behavior, increasing the paternalistic role of welfare staff.[18] Further, the rhetoric of welfare dependency and the evils of big government would result in ending welfare as an entitlement.

Lived Effects of Welfare Retrenchment

In 2002 and 2003, six years after welfare reform had taken effect, we conducted life story interviews with each of 41 couples from vulnerable families. In Tables 3.1 and 3.2, we present demographic information for our sample of mothers and fathers, as well as their residential status and their use of public assistance. If neoliberal welfare reform was intended to discipline a low-income workforce, how did these family members experience these reforms? What role did the state play within the reconfiguration of the market, family, and state in providing needed support? In what ways did the

Table 3.1 Social and Demographic Characteristics of Couples Study (N = 82)

Demographics	Fathers	Mothers
Average age	25	21
Average number of children	1.6	1.3
Multiple family fertility	12 (29%)	3 (7%)
Race		
White	14 (34%)	15 (37%)
African American	2 (5%)	4 (10%)
Puerto Rican	18 (44%)	13 (32%)
Other Latino	3 (7%)	5 (12%)
Multiracial	2 (5%)	4 (10%)
Other	2 (5%)	0
Employment		
Full-time	23 (56%)	1 (2%)
Part-time	5 (12%)	14 (34%)
Unemployed	10 (24%)	23 (56%)
Disabled, unemployed	3 (7%)	3 (7%)

coercive role of a neoliberal paternalist state affect these couples? What were their struggles within this new context, and how did they make sense out of this?

As Tables 3.1 and 3.2 show, 85 percent of couples were cohabiting, most of whom were unmarried, with 4 in 10 couples living with a family member or another adult. A little more than one-half of fathers were employed full-time, while one-fourth were unemployed. All of the couples had a child under two years of age, so mothers tended to stay at home to care for the children, even though a little more than a third were working part-time, while a fifth were looking for work. Most of the couples were Puerto Rican and white and were in their 20s.[19] About one-third of fathers had children with other mothers outside of their household, while six (18 percent) cohabitating families included children from other relationships.

The use of public assistance varied depending upon need and eligibility. A little less than one-third of couples in cohabitating relationships were receiving cash assistance and food stamps, while about one-fifth of

Table 3.2 Couples' Residential Status and Public Assistance Use

Residential status (N = 41)	
Cohabitating	35 (85%)
Married	9 (22%)
Engaged	5 (12%)
Living w/ family member or other adult	16 (39%)
Living w/ nonbiological children*	8 (20%)
Living apart	6 (15%)
Public assistance among cohabitators (N = 35)	
TANF	12 (29%)
Food stamps	13 (32%)
SSI Disability	9 (22%)
Housing**	3 (7%)

* Households with children who were not biological children of the couple.

** Nine couples were on the waiting list for Section 8 housing.

these households received disability benefits. Less than 10 percent received housing benefits, even though nine couples were on the waiting list for Section 8 housing.

Merely six to seven years after welfare reform had taken effect, couples struggled with the reality and the symbolism of welfare reform. As the state withdrew resources and enhanced its enforcement role, reactions tended to cut along two different paths. For low-income couples who were working at above-poverty wages—that is, those who were better off in our study—they struggled with the income thresholds that defined whether they qualified for benefits to supplement their wages. In a high-cost state like Connecticut, state assistance with food, housing, health care, childcare, and utilities is vitally important to low-income families, even when there are one, and sometimes two, wage earners in the family. Families who make too much money to qualify for benefits but are still below the self-sufficiency standard experience what we call the welfare cliff problem.

Couples, who were worse off, struggling with unemployment and underemployment, were more cognizant of the new timeline imposed on receiving cash assistance and on the limited purchasing value of food stamps. Mothers and fathers confronted the institutional realities of welfare to work but also wrestled with the symbolic nature of welfare reform that advanced an ideology of work and responsibility.

Welfare Cliff

Welfare reform intended to move recipients into jobs and increase father responsibility did not resolve poverty or income inadequacies; it simply expanded the scope of need from the unemployed poor to the working poor or near poor.[20] In this respect, working families still relied on the state for assistance. Strong anti-poverty organizing and lobbying in Connecticut had resulted in more generous eligibility guidelines for benefits and services and higher levels of support than in many states. However, as discussed in Chapter 2, higher income thresholds in a state like Connecticut are needed because of the high cost of living in the state. The welfare cliff problem in a high-cost state refers to financial difficulties that working families experience when they make just enough money to exceed the eligibility cutoff for varying assistance programs.

Antonio and Polly illustrate. Not long after they were married and had their first child, they applied for public assistance. "Money was real tight," Antonio explained. "We were on food stamps for a couple months. We got money assistance for like two months and that certainly helped. We were both in and out of work with a brand-new baby." The more they worked, though, the less they were eligible for. Antonio continues:

> It got to the point where we weren't eligible anymore. . . . With money assistance for a family of three, the state says if you make more than $700 a month for three people, then you can't get money assistance. I'm like, okay, my rent is like four hundred a month. I was kind of pissed cuz we were struggling and at the time we needed help and it was like the state's telling us, "Well, you can live off of that much." I looked at the woman straight in the face and I said, "You tell me where I can live for $700 a month and I'll gladly move." And we weren't on Section 8 housing at the time, so I mean maybe that had something to do with it.

Antonio told us that they were "a hundred dollars over what they say you (can) make. Half of our income was just going right to rent. Then I have a car payment, car insurance; it's like I have almost no money left for food, plus utilities and everything. It was hard for a while." He and Polly made enough income to go over the cliff, but not enough to meet their basic needs.

Neoliberal welfare reform that placed more fiscal responsibility on the states increased the likelihood that benefits would decrease during recessionary periods whenever state revenues ran short. Two examples of this in the first half of the decade in Connecticut involved funding for childcare and health care. In 2003, the state's childcare program, Care for Kids, was available to families transitioning off of welfare if their income was below 50 percent of the state's median income,[21] but funding for state subsidized childcare was cut by more than half between 2002 and 2005.[22] As a consequence, waiting lists were long.

Similarly, in 2003, the state cut its Medicaid benefit to parents who qualified for the state's health care program referred to as HUSKY.[23] Bethany and her son received health care under the HUSKY program, but Bethany became one of 19,000 adults to lose her health care in 2003 when the state reduced its eligibility guidelines for parents from 150 percent of the Federal Poverty Line (FPL) to 100 percent.[24] Neither did they qualify for childcare, because their income exceeded the cutoff, even though they were both working at Taco Bell—Pablo, full-time for $8.37 an hour, and Bethany, part-time at minimum wage.

The welfare cliff problem applied to other forms of assistance as well, including food stamps, or the Supplemental Nutrition Assistance Program (SNAP). Program costs dropped significantly after 1996 welfare reform went into effect, mostly because as recipients moved into the workforce, their income exceeded the eligibility threshold. In Connecticut the SNAP eligibility cutoff occurred when gross income increased beyond 130 percent of the FPL—the national standard—which in 2003 would have been a full-time wage of $9.50 an hour for a family of three.[25] In Connecticut this meant that a single parent with two children acquiring a $10 an hour job would leave them far short of meeting basic needs but would nonetheless disqualify them from receiving food assistance. Studies showed that food insecurity increased across the nation as mothers left the welfare rolls after 1996.[26]

Energy assistance was another cliff issue for this group of families, as Melanie and Raymond indicate. Raymond was a 32-year-old father who worked full-time at a warehouse for $9.50 an hour. His partner Melanie was a part-time package handler at FedEx, and they lived alone with their

2-year-old. The only governmental assistance they qualified for was the nu-
tritional assistance program for mothers, infants, and children referred to
as WIC.[27] When we asked Melanie if she thought they needed more state
assistance, she said that they had looked into the Energy Assistance Program
but were told that they made too much money. At this time, Connecticut
households were eligible for energy assistance if their income was less than
150 percent of the FPL. Melanie told us that she earned $1,000 per month
and Raymond $1,200, for a total of $26,400 a year, more than 150 percent,
but less than 200 percent of the 2003 national poverty line, and well below
Connecticut's self-sufficiency standard. They had also applied for the Section
8 housing assistance program but found that they exceeded those income
guidelines as well.

Raymond articulated what seemed to be the angst among many of the
better-off families in our study whose family earnings were above the poverty
line but well below the self-sufficiency standard. "It's funny," he said, "I think
I don't make enough, yet, everybody else thinks I make too much." Raymond
described the couple's daily financial challenges as "getting by just by our
fingernails." For Raymond and Melanie, a white couple with two incomes,
every dollar counted, and they juggled bills to get by, especially in the wintertime. They were not alone. Nationally, around one-fourth of recipients who
left the welfare rolls in the late 1990s had their electricity shut off and nearly
one-half who left the rolls after acquiring jobs were unable to make their
utility payments.[28]

The welfare cliff problem was an issue for young working families in
Connecticut—not poor enough to qualify for benefits, but unable to meet
self-sufficiency standards in a high-cost state. Moreover, eligibility standards
also proved to be moving targets, depending on the shifting fiscal conditions
of the state. The retrenchment of the state in a neoliberal era is evident in
the struggles of working families in the bottom quintile of the labor force.
Those couples who were worse off in our study, however, were more concerned about time limits.

Time Limits

Most notably, the 1996 welfare reform act, designed to "end welfare as we
know it," eliminated cash assistance as a citizenship entitlement. The Clinton
administration accomplished this by establishing a five-year lifetime limit on

cash assistance, while allowing states the option to set shorter time limits. States competed for the headlines for setting the shortest time limits, and Connecticut won the contest at 21 months.

This powerful slogan that helped President Clinton win the 1992 election did not translate easily into policy, even though efforts to move welfare recipients, mostly single mothers, into the workforce toward self-sufficiency was not new. The Reagan administration's efforts to do so in 1988 should have provided sobering lessons. At the end of his second term, the 1988 FSA was passed, which more forcefully turned Aid to Families with Dependent Children (AFDC) into a workfare program and beefed up child support enforcement efforts. The FSA was a predecessor to the 1996 welfare reform act, and it garnered much support from liberals and conservatives as the legislation provided funding and assistance to welfare recipients—even long-term recipients—to transition them into the workforce.[29] However, with spiraling US debt, budget deficits, and an economic recession taking root, many states were unable to provide matching funds and the program failed to reach many of its intended population. By 1995, only about one-tenth of recipients were participating as expected.[30]

As suggested by its title, the Personal Responsibility and Work Opportunity Reconciliation Act (PRWORA) of 1996, acquiring work was given priority in newly coordinated one-stop welfare services, which were fortified by a set of rules, norms, and expectations intended to discipline the poor and to change the culture of service provision. The reorganization of poverty governance, as Joe Soss, Richard Fording, and Sanford Schram explained, combined neoliberalism and a new paternalism.[31] While implementation varied across states and localities, jobs were given priority over education, time limits for receiving cash welfare were implemented, paternity establishment and child support orders were strictly administered, statutory rape laws were vigilantly applied, marriage promotion was funded, drug felons were denied cash assistance and food stamp benefits, and teens mothers were refused benefits unless they lived with a parent or guardian and attended school. Further, states were given incentive bonuses for removing families from the rolls and granted flexibility in reducing benefits for not submitting reports, finding work, attending appointments, complying with child support enforcement, repaying a federal loan on time, or meeting state maintenance of effort requirements. An estimated 540,000 families lost their cash assistance, or Temporary Aid for Needy Families (TANF), due to these family sanctions alone between 1997 and 1999.[32] Likewise, TANF rolls plummeted across the

nation after the law took effect. In Connecticut, the rolls decreased 62 percent between 1996 and 2005.[33]

Because yearly cash assistance increases had not been pegged to inflation,
the value of cash assistance already had fallen considerably—nationwide by
42 percent after 1970 and before the 1996 law took effect.[34] Consequently,
cash assistance had been only one source of income that poor families relied
on, often turning to family members, off-the-books employment, the drug
economy, or income from unreported sources in the home.[35] In 2005, the
average wage for adults in Connecticut still on the TANF rolls was $8.77 an
hour, so most families in our study continued receiving cash assistance to
supplement these wages. They did so recognizing that when they exhausted
their time limit, they would have to find another source of income to replace
it, if the state did not grant them a six-month extension.[36]

At the time of our study, families reported between $300 and $545 per
month in cash assistance. When cash assistance was combined with other
benefits, like food stamps, Medicaid, energy assistance, or WIC, it still often
fell short of meeting basic family needs, especially for families unable to obtain housing assistance. If families could not get a housing subsidy, their entire monthly check might go toward paying rent—or, worse, they would find
themselves in situations in which the rent was more than their cash assistance. In this respect, TANF time limits threatened the housing security of
many recipients and, nationally, resulted in an increased demand on homeless shelters.[37]

While the amount of cash assistance that families received was inadequate,
it was still an important revenue source. As intended, time limits created fear
in families with limited wage income, who relied on governmental support.
When we asked these couples what they thought about the welfare-to-work
program that was intended to facilitate their transition off of cash assistance
within the 21-month window, mothers' and fathers' responses reflected their
gendered locations within the family and welfare system.

Twenty-one-year-old Madelyne and her 25-year-old partner Mateo,
both Puerto Rican and unemployed, were seeking work at the time of their
interviews. Mateo had completed Job Corps, received SNAP and Medicaid,
had previously worked at McDonalds, and did odd jobs when opportunities arose. Madelyne, who was pregnant, had previously worked as a telemar-
keter, in a grocery store, and at a nursery. Because of income and housing
limitations, Mateo stayed with his sister and Madelyne with her mother.
Madelyne was approaching the end of her 21-month period and was applying

for an extension. She expressed frustration at the unrealistic expectations of finding work.

> They expect everybody to get up and overnight find a job . . . and it's not that easy. Because God knows I've filled out applications everywhere. No calls back. And I've called. No response and stuff. You know? It's not easy. You're not just gonna get a job overnight like that. And then they sit there and say, well, maybe you're not trying hard enough.

Madelyne was responding to the central provision of welfare reform intended to force welfare recipients into the labor market. Working was not new for Madelyne, but the state's withdrawal of support removed a form of security that could be utilized when jobs were not available or did not pay enough. It forced Madelyne to compete in the labor market, and it placed blame on her for "not trying hard enough" if she was unable to support herself in the market. At the time, the unemployment rate was 10 percent and the underemployment rate 17 percent for Latinos in Connecticut, so Madelyne had a lot of competition for low-wage jobs.[38]

Her partner Mateo's perspective was different. He told our interviewer that finding a steady job was the most pressing need he had. He was unemployed and felt fortunate that his sister provided him with housing, even if it meant not living with Madelyne. However, he was conflicted about relying on state support; it undermined his manhood. He asserted, "I don't ask them people for nothing; I don't ask them for handouts or nothing like that. You know, I'm a man; my father taught me how to be a man." Relying on welfare was a sign of weakness for Mateo, and yet, he acknowledged that if the market failed to provide for him and his family, he had to swallow his pride. "At one point I did you know [receive aid]." He hastened to add, "I didn't want my friends to see me." Describing this to an interviewer with the tape recorder running sounded painful and difficult for Mateo. "I see it now like this," he reasoned, "that they're helping me to put food in my mouth and in my kid's mouth, you know? So why should I be ashamed with that?"

We heard a similar narrative from 26-year-old Hiram, who began his interview singing the praises of the welfare-to-work program.

> The 21-month thing is wonderful, you know . . . [people] were just becoming dependent on the state and they didn't want to work, you know. So it's like right now they got that, what is it, like, uh, Welfare-to-Work . . . It's

straight cuz that's how it should be. You know what I'm saying? Like, like we're not gonna be on the state forever.

Hiram was expressing the prevailing view about welfare and state dependency; however, as the conversation continued and he talked more about his own situation, his position softened. A former street hustler, he was currently working 30 hours a week as a chef at a chain restaurant. With a prior felony, he did not qualify for federal aid to go to college, as he preferred. Moreover, despite Hiram's support for the 21-month time limit, he recognized the significance of public assistance in his own family's life.

> I'll put it to you like this. I do my thing and I got my job now, but it's like without the state and without this [Healthy Families] program, we would barely be making it. You know what I'm saying? It's like it's hard. It's hard. It's hard when you don't got nobody to help you. You know what I'm saying? And it's hard when you just barely make it. The eight hundred that you make a month is going to everything else. You feel what I'm saying? [cough] So it doesn't hurt to get help cuz everybody needs it, I guess.

The realities of Hiram's own life could not support the political narrative he had internalized. He did not want to be "dependent" and yet he needed material aid (food, cash, medical care) and social support (parent support program). He tried to preserve a masculine identity that conveyed his responsibility of taking care of his family—his sacrifice, dedication, and hard work. Even though the market had not supported this image of him, he nonetheless embraced it. We would hear similar perspectives at the end of the decade when circumstances were much worse.

Mothers' and fathers' perspectives converged when discussing how welfare-to-work was being implemented in Connecticut. The notion that the state was not properly facilitating the transition to work was a more socially acceptable criticism, than, say, arguing that state assistance was a right, the position advanced by the National Welfare Rights Organization thirty years earlier. Several of our respondents, men and women alike, argued that the problem with welfare-to-work was the *jobs first orientation*—Jobs First was, in fact, the name of the welfare-to-work program in Connecticut. Nicki, a single white mother, transitioned off welfare as a Certified Nurse Assistant (CNA). Due to her low wages, she still qualified for WIC and Medicaid. Nicki argued that the program funneled mothers into low-wage jobs instead of helping them build a career with a living wage.

> They were real reluctant to give me money to go to school so I could get off of state assistance. I think that's one of the biggest problems of the state system. They want to just cut you off of state, but they don't want to help you. They want you to get a job at like seven or eight dollars an hour. If you're a single mother and you're living in your own apartment, that's not enough. They do help you get a job, but they don't pay for schooling or anything, or they won't pay for daycare if you're going to school, just if you're working.

Antonio, the 24-year-old white father referred to earlier in the chapter, may not have been a single mom, but he was a living example of Nicki's point.

> I'm going to school full-time and taking care of her [pointing to his daughter] whenever I'm not working and at one point they denied us help, saying that the only way we could get help was if I was working because I was the man and the man had to work if you wanted help. I'm like I can understand if neither person is working you don't want to help us, we gotta help ourselves before you'll help us. I understand that, but I mean she was working full-time, I'm going to school full-time so I can get a better job, and they're like, oh well, he has to work. At that point I was just fed up with 'em. I'm like, if you're gonna give me a hard time about asking for help, I don't need your help, you know.

Antonio did concede, however, and left school where he was learning computer technology and took a job as an assistant manager at Domino's Pizza. Nicki and Antonio were articulating a common criticism made of the welfare-to-work initiative, that it did not resolve poverty, but instead had expanded the ranks of the working poor.

Finally, we also heard objections from fathers about the way they were treated by staff in welfare offices. Condescending treatment was not new for women who had been more likely to interface with welfare professionals in the past.[39] But the new culture of provision not only encouraged a process of removing recipients from the rolls through sanctions; states were rewarded with federal bonuses for reducing the rolls. As more men came into these one-stop-welfare facilities, these attitudes were more apparent to them. One of the fathers, Shane, seemed to be searching for a rationale for why welfare staff treated him and others with such condescension:

> State workers should be more willing to work with them instead of constantly looking for reasons not to help them. That's the biggest thing nowadays. They look for so many reasons not to help. I can understand there are a lot of people out there taking advantage of it and I think they should take it right away from them people. But when there are people that really need it and are sincere about getting ahead in life, then I think they should help them 100 percent. I think their whole attitude stinks, the way they look at things. But they have their reasons, I guess. I don't know what they are.

The process of roll-purging exposed fathers to moral condescension among state authorities, but, as will see, not nearly as much as they would experience in the child support courts.

The 21-month time limit for cash assistance injected fear into the lives of recipients, as it was intended to do. It disciplined recipients by pushing them into low-wage work that fell short of providing a self-sufficiency wage—so short that they usually kept their cash assistance, even though their time clocks were ticking. The purge of recipients from the rolls was extraordinary—nothing like it had ever occurred in US history.

Mothers struggled with the realities of balancing work and caretaking with less support from the state, while fathers wrestled more with the symbolism of welfare, eschewing welfare dependency, while living in households that relied on these benefits. These perspectives among fathers would remain fairly consistent even as things got much worse at the end of decade.

Decade from Hell

There is really no way to compare the decade before and after December 2007. Certainly, conditions had deteriorated after a minor recession in 2001, and workers suffered from the vastly growing discrepancy between productivity and wages that was being fueled by new technologies and aggressive management strategies. And certainly, the slow recovery, which became known as the "jobless recovery," was contributing to the suffering of workers as inequality deepened. It is perhaps worth restating that the decline in wages for workers in the bottom two deciles of the labor force was greater in Connecticut than any other state in the first half of the decade. And, as discussed earlier, the state of Connecticut decreased state spending on the poor during this period. All that said, nothing can compare to what became the longest recession in US history, what Carl Van Horn called the Hurricane Katrina of US recessions. During the Great Recession, unemployment rates exceeded 10 percent, the long-term unemployment rate was unlike anything seen since the Great Depression, more than 20 million workers were either unemployed or involuntarily employed part-time, and private-sector job loss was greater than the four prior recessions combined.[40] Suffering was broad and deep.

Our interviews from 2008 to 2010 reflected the stresses and strains on relationships that were weaved through tales about joblessness, inadequate state aid, lights being turned off, deadbeat roundups, childcare costs, rent-consuming paychecks, acrobatic bill juggling, and couples living in parents' homes.

Food stamp usage was a good barometer of economic distress in the New Millennium. Despite the "success" of the 1996 reform act in removing recipients from the rolls in epic proportions, and the immediate decline in food stamp usage, the demand for food stamps increased considerably after 2000. Even prior to the 2007 recession, SNAP usage had increased 36 percent in the state. But in response to increased need after the advent of the recession, in 2008, Connecticut increased the SNAP eligibility standard from 130 to 185 percent of the FPL, which pushed the number of recipients receiving food benefits up 172 percent across the decade.[41] What is perhaps most striking about this increase is that it highlighted the policy constraints that had been placed on cash assistance by the 1996 legislation. At the same time that food stamp usage was increasing, the number of needy families with children receiving TANF in Connecticut was decreasing—by 21 percent during the years most impacted by the Great Recession, 2007–2010.[42]

The increase in the SNAP eligibility criteria was important to reaching more families, but SNAP policies restrict spending discretion that cash assistance permits. Nonfood items cannot be purchased with SNAP. For example, one of the fathers in our study, Charles, argued that he could acquire food from church food pantries, while other needs of his went unmet. Charles had been laid off for one month and described, "There are lots of resources for food. There is food banks. There is churches . . . which provide a lot of your basics—your breads, your cereals, your canned goods." Charles said that funds needed to be "directed to housing needs, whether it was rent, the gas, the electric, whatever financially." He argued for a system:

> where the stipulation was that you would tell them specifically what needed to be paid and they would say, "Okay, you have X number of dollars in assistance available" and you can say, "I want this much of it to go towards my electric bill and this much to my rent." And the check was cut directly to whoever the payment needed to be made to. That way your assistance went to where it belonged.

Personally, Charles needed money to be directed toward his rent. But he connected these needs to fatherhood and being a provider. "I mean financially speaking there are things that would put less burden on me as a father to be able to provide for my home. Obviously, being able to provide better makes for being able to parent better because you have less stress at that point." Reductions in cash assistance and increased oversight of recipients, however, had created just the opposite—it had narrowed family discretion.

Despite increases in SNAP coverage, the overall trend during the decade continued to be less state spending on low-income households. Confronting steep declines in tax revenue during and after the Great Recession, the state made spending cuts to balance the budget, but it continued tax expenditures (or credits) to businesses. Across the decade, from 2002 to 2010, low-income family assistance was reduced by $68 million, or 19 percent.[43] But in 2009, the trend of extending corporate tax credits continued as the state issued a record $305 million in credits to businesses, a more than 60-fold increase over 1987.[44] These state strategies were not unique to Connecticut. Fearful that businesses would find a more advantageous tax environment in another state, combined with strong business lobbying, states shifted their resources toward corporate businesses at the expense of needy residents.[45]

Most of the fathers in our study at the end of the decade were either working involuntary part-time jobs, temporary jobs, or off-the-books jobs, or they were unemployed. They struggled on the margins of the labor force, where they attempted to find some semblance of stability that would provide for a longer view of fatherhood. That is, caught in an unstable world structured by shifting income sources, job opportunities, housing conditions, and familial and social networks, the time frames in their lives were restricted. Adjustments or coping strategies were made daily, or seemingly in the moment.

The Great Recession was a disruptive force to our study as well. We lost funding and had to scale back the study. In addition, the difficulty of unsteady lives became evident to us as we attempted to track these fathers across as many as four interviews. Because of the precarious nature of many of their jobs, fathers would call us at the last minute to reschedule an interview because a temporary work agency had called, or an off-the-books job opportunity had emerged, or they had a chance to work over time. One father called us to say he had relocated to Maine for work and had not just severed ties with us, but had left his family behind as well until he could acquire more stability.

Maintaining continuous phone service with fathers was challenging as one temporary cell phone was exchanged for another when prepaid minutes ran out. At one point during our tenure with Harry, his cell phone was disconnected, then his wife's phone was disconnected, then their cousin's phone was disconnected. And Harry was one of the fortunate men to hold on to his job during the recession. Sky was given permission to stop by Harry's home unannounced; he was shown the appropriate place on the apartment building to knock so that Harry would know someone was outside, and he was eventually shown (in the third interview) how to use a makeshift card to pry open the outside door to the building so that Sky could knock on the actual apartment door. The process was difficult and resulted in a lapse of 18 months to secure the last of four interviews with Harry.

Housing for fathers was fluid. They moved into households where they could make it work given the contingencies of that particular moment. Movement created instability, and these were not conditions for making long-term commitments. The stresses and uncertainties of daily life wore down relationships and some breakups occurred as men and women moved across households. Usually, if marriage was a consideration, it was off in the future, when finances would hopefully stabilize, parents would mature, or when they could finally move out of their parents' homes.

Welfare support provided little for these men and their households. For those who lost jobs, they might draw unemployment insurance (UI), but even this benefit was limited. The most an individual could draw was 50 percent of his former income, and this was in the most favorable conditions, which for the men in our study was rare. For those who were working sporadically and part-time, it was difficult to meet eligibility qualifications for UI, and when they did, benefits were very low. One father told us he received $11 a week. Very few laid-off fathers received UI benefits; Jairo received the most at $133 a week. This was true throughout the country. A Government Accountability Office report in 2007 found that low-wage workers were one-third as likely to receive UI benefits as higher wage workers, and that part-time workers, whether low- or high-wage, were significantly less likely to receive benefits than full-time workers.[46] And, of course, those who were working under-the-table jobs or as independent contractors were ineligible. To a large extent, these restrictions reflected the failure of policies to adjust to a workforce that was becoming more casual and less permanent, what Jacob Hacker refers to as "policy drift."[47] But it also reflected key policy changes made during the Reagan administration that had narrowed eligibility for UI.[48]

State assistance was especially limited for noncustodial fathers. So far in this chapter we have focused mostly on fathers living in households with children. However, in the latter part of the decade, we captured the experiences of some fathers not living with their children. Very few benefits remained for this group. In addition to UI, unemployed noncustodial fathers might draw SNAP benefits, but only if they were meeting work requirements. PRWORA limited able-bodied adults who were unemployed or not enrolled in an employment training or workfare program to only three months of SNAP in a 36-month period. This included noncustodial fathers who were paying child support.[49] Further, the 1996 legislation disqualified anyone from SNAP who had been sentenced to a drug felony but allowed states to modify the legislation. Connecticut is one of 24 states to modify the ban (another 20 states eliminated it entirely).[50] For convicted drug felons to receive SNAP in Connecticut, they need to have finished their sentence or be reporting to a parole officer, and to have completed or be participating in court-ordered drug treatment and testing.

The Earned Income Tax Credit (EITC) was another potential source of revenue for fathers. Originally intended as a temporary program to bring relief to families suffering the effects of increased social security taxes and inflation in the 1970s, it was expanded in nearly every subsequent administration, with Presidents Clinton and Obama significantly increasing benefits.[51] Today, it has become the largest cash transfer program for low-income workers with dependent children. However, for some in our study, EITC was not a viable option. Not only does it not benefit unemployed fathers or fathers working under-the-table jobs; it has only minimal benefits for fathers not living in the homes with their children since *EITC is not available to live-away fathers as parents, even when they are paying child support.*[52]

Cash assistance through the TANF program follows children, so this was not a possibility for noncustodial parents either, and besides, as we have seen, program rolls have been cut precipitously. Five men received disability benefits through the Supplemental Security Income (SSI) program.[53] With neoliberal reform, this is one of the few places poor, single adults can still turn for relief. And given histories of neighborhood and family violence, trauma, incarceration, or stress-related illnesses, many living in poor communities might qualify. In this respect, neoliberal reform has essentially medicalized poverty.[54] This creates a murky area for determining eligibility, since in order to receive benefits through SSI, poor adults need to demonstrate that they are too "damaged" to sustain continuous full-time work, and that they are poor.[55]

Finally, the only other form of assistance that these men might qualify for was General Assistance (GA).[56] In Connecticut, the program is used mostly by poor adults who have a documented mental or physical condition that prevents them from working and who are not receiving SSI, or else are waiting to receive a decision concerning their SSI application.[57] Only one man in our entire study reported ever receiving GA.

In short, in the aftermath of neoliberal welfare reform, noncustodial fathers who are unemployed have few places to turn for state support. Quite the contrary, as we will see in the next chapter, this group was more likely to be brought before court authorities for child support arrears, underscoring another key provision of 1996 welfare reform. US welfare, historically, has been intricately related to men's employment status. Neoliberal reform, however, withdrew state support further from low-income working families, noncustodial fathers, and the unemployed, while enforcing stricter compliance with the low-wage labor market. Given these dynamics, how did fathers located at the bottom of the labor market make sense of and react to these circumstances?

Men's Views of State Welfare and Fatherhood

Fathers' perspectives of welfare reform complemented what we learned from fathers earlier in the decade. Generally, they conveyed disparaging views about welfare dependency, distinguished themselves from welfare cheaters and deadbeat dads, constructed their identities as heads of the household and as fathers making sacrifices for their children, minimized the importance of public assistance, and directed anger toward state authorities.

Several men struggled with their feelings of failure as their opportunities to provide for their families narrowed, particularly those like James, who remained committed to conventional gender role expectations.

SKY: In your experience growing up, what does it mean to be a man?
JAMES: Get out there and earn that money.
SKY: And what type of things do you think a man should or should not do?
JAMES: For one, I don't think he should put his hands on his wife. I don't
    think he should walk away from his family. I think they should be the
    number-one priority on anything in his life, besides holding down a job
    and doing what he has to do. That I do. And making sure his child is well
    taken care of.

These men, mostly white, were ashamed of telling the interviewers that they were relying on the state, and they worked hard at impression management.

When we asked Ray, a 30-year-old white father who had been out of work for 13 months, if he had received any state assistance, he replied that he had received unemployment insurance for 10 weeks before it got cut off, and then "I went on state aid for three months and got back on my feet." We followed by asking if state aid had been important to getting back on his feet. He replied, "It was. I mean it helped me out. It kind of like, oh, somebody does care. Somebody does want to help me out." He then quickly added, "But I never like stopped looking [for a job]. I was always on Craig's List. I was always on Monster.com. I was always on the unemployment office computer. I was doing interviews." Later, Ray made sure to distinguish his need for welfare from the "leeches."

> I am very big on the man is the breadwinner . . . you've got to do whatever
> you can to make sure your family is well taken care of. And part of that is,
> well nowadays, working a full-time job. If you keep bringing children into
> this world just for welfare or other people to support, then what kind of a
> person does that make you? It's more like a leech. If you go swimming, they
> are going to suck off of you, instead of going out and doing what they have
> to do to make sure they can survive.

Other men made similar statements that validated their sacrifices as heads of the household. When we asked Harry (who gave Sky the makeshift key to get into his apartment building), if his daughter ever lacked anything she needed, he exclaimed, "Never! Never goes without nothing. She comes first. I put her first and my girl goes second and I go last."

These statements communicated fathers' masculine identities as willing to make sacrifices for their families. But it also made asking for and relying on state aid difficult. As has historically been the case, Harry associated the use of public assistance with women. Referring to his own wife and one-year-old living in the same residence as himself, Harry said, "She gets food stamps and everything. And WIC for the baby," as if he was not also receiving these benefits as part of the household. Moreover, we would later find out that the apartment that Sky got special permission to enter was a government-subsidized (Section 8) apartment that was in Harry's mother's name. In Harry's mind, his wife received food stamps, the baby WIC, his mother housing, while he assumed his place as head of the household by working a full-time low-wage job and eschewing state assistance.

Steven took it further. As we described in the last chapter, Steven and his fiancé were living in an apartment complex along with their 10-month-old baby, before he eventually relocated to another state for employment. Steven worked informally as the building superintendent for reduced rent but no cash income. He and his fiancé relied on their families for help, and Steven said they that they received "a little bit of assistance in cash, a little bit of assistance in food stamps" from the state. Steven articulated disdain for the state and for welfare. He claimed that his wife had discontinued her appointments at the WIC office because they decided that with SNAP benefits, they did not need it, and besides, if they came up short they could rely on his fiancé's mother to "throw some groceries" their way. To make the point clear, he asserted, "And I was always raised on the fact of don't take what you don't need to." When we asked if his daughter ever went without anything he thought she needed, Steven snapped, "My child does not go without a damn thing." Softening a little, he continued, "Me and my fiancé would go without food for a year before she went out without socks." Distinguishing between dependency (feminine) and rebellious initiative (masculine), Steven asserted that he would "hustle again [deal drugs] if it was 100 percent necessary," even though he knew that for "all the legislators and people of law, it's never necessary." But he quickly added with a defiant smile, "There is always an alternate route" and said that he would "rather take from the streets than take from the state, if need be." In the end, Steven chose employment in another state instead of the streets.

It was easier for these men to acknowledge help from their families than from the state. As Steven indicated, both his and his fiancé's mothers helped out. Similarly, in almost every reference to help from family members, fathers referred to women—mothers, grandmothers, aunts, or sisters. It was rare that they might identify a man in their lives helping out, let alone caretaking. We also noted that men rarely understood the details of public assistance. In our Couples Study we were able to record more clearly families' use of state assistance because of our interviews with mothers. Mothers interfaced with the system. Men were removed. Public assistance was an integral part of care-taking, and it had been designed to reflect and constitute the gendered roles in the family.

Steven, Ray, Charles, and Harry were all hard-living, white, working-class fathers trying to hold onto their identities as heads of the household. Their status derived from the narrative of making sacrifices for their fam-ilies and providing for their families. Their need for state assistance cre-ated ambivalence—it symbolized weakness—and they navigated these contradictions by distinguishing themselves from the "others" who were abusing the system—the "leeches," as Ray said. This was made particu-larly clear by Robert's tirade about the highly publicized octuplets born to a woman in 2009 whom the media named "Octomom."

Robert was a 31-year-old white father who worked at a local factory, was the sole provider in his household, and lived with his wife and five-month-old daughter. He considered himself "an average American" who was "just getting by," unlike "people out there who are popping out kids" to live off the state. During the interview, he asked Sky if he had "heard about that lady with the octuplets?" The media exposed that the mother, who had become preg-nant through in-vitro fertility, already had six children, was unemployed, and was receiving state aid before the delivery. Robert exploded:

> That's fucking horseshit. She can't even afford the six she got and she wants eight more? Get the fuck out of here. Now you are taking my tax money, you know? The state is already fucking hurting and now they got to give you fucking $800 more a month because you got eight more fucking kids. Get the fuck out of here. That's why our state is hurting. So, what happens when the state is hurting? They raise the taxes. What happens when they raise the taxes? Now they are fucking with my kid because this bitch wants eight more that she can't afford.

Robert was adopting a racialized discourse made popular by Ronald Reagan's reference to welfare queens in the 1980s, who were draining the state coffers and living off the backs of hard-working white families, like Robert's. A little later, though, Robert boasted that he was able to get a tax return for $5,000. His hours had been cut back at work due to the recession. He proclaimed, "Thank God I was married and had a kid because I got $5,000 back. So that $5,000 was able to keep me alive until the business where I work picks up."

Robert was referring to income he was able to acquire through EITC. The program is particularly useful to families like Robert's. Fathers not living in the homes with their children are only eligible to receive EITC as a single wage earner without dependent children, and for this category of wage earners, the benefits are quite low.[58] For instance, in 2012, unmarried wage earners without children only qualified if their income was below $13,980, and the maximum credit was $475. This is compared to a father living in the home with one child, who qualifies with an income up to $36,920 and can receive a maximum credit of $3,169.[59] EITC is an important anti-poverty program for low-wage earners, and it allows fathers like Robert to benefit from state distribution policies without the same stigma of receiving public assistance.

Reliance on public assistance did sensitize some men to state aid differently, and it enabled them to be critical of cuts to state welfare programs, especially given the increased need for assistance. This included a few white men in our study, such as Patrick, a 23-year-old father, who had experienced homelessness. He described living in his car for six months with his pregnant girlfriend.

> Dude, I am talking about I am a grown-ass man, but I would cry. I mean hungry. I hated it and it sucked. It was nothing like I know. Man, you don't know if people are looking in your car, looking at you while you are sleeping. I mean you got your clothes and shit all in the back.

Patrick was the father of two daughters in addition to the son he had on the way. He did not live with his daughters but indicated he was involved with them. He received SNAP and his daughters relied on Care for Kids, but he was under the impression that these programs were going to be cut—that he was going to lose a quarter of his SNAP and that Care for Kids was being taken away. He remarked, "I don't agree with that. Man, I got kids I need to feed. Are you kidding me?" It is not clear if Patrick had the details right about these program spending reductions and their consequences, but certainly he had the general principle correct, that the state was reducing state assistance.

More marginalized fathers in our study also wrestled with the stigma of public assistance, but, like Patrick, their experiences enabled them to see the value in it, even when they insisted on making a distinction between those who need it and those who abuse it (we will return to this topic in Chapter 8). In segregated poor communities, public assistance was a vital resource, especially as economic conditions worsened. Jermaine, a black father from Hartford, whom we introduced in the last chapter as a scrap metal collector, observed, "I don't know what some of the black females or males [would] do out here without, like, food stamps and WIC and all that, without the state help. Man, I thank God that the state help us. You feel me?" Jermaine went on to talk about the high costs of baby formula and diapers.

The burdens of the recessionary period at the end of the decade particularly fell heavy on racial minorities in the state, as shown in Table 3.3. As Douglas Massey and Nancy Denton demonstrated in their classic *American Apartheid*, economic downturns cut deep into areas of concentrated black poverty.[60] In Connecticut, black and brown residents were disproportionately concentrated in poor cities—cities with child poverty rates three to four times the state rate (see Table 3.4). In the 2007–2008 school year, about one-third of all children in Connecticut qualified for free or reduced-price school lunches, but in Hartford and Bridgeport, nearly every student did (8 in 10 in Hartford; 9 in 10 in Bridgeport).[61] During the recession, black and brown poverty rates in Connecticut were nearly four times the rate of whites, unemployment and underemployment rates more than double the rate of whites,

Table 3.3 Racial Minority and Poverty Rates by City and State, 2010

	% Minority	% Poor*	% Children Free/ Reduced Lunch
Bridgeport	60	23	89
Hartford	70	31	80
New Haven	56	29	63
Connecticut	22	10	34

*Income less than the 2010 federal poverty level for an individual.

Sources: United States Census Bureau; Connecticut Department of Education, Bureau of Health, Nutrition, Family Services and Adult Education.

Table 3.4 Connecticut Poverty and Employment Rates by Race, 2010

	% Poor	% Unemployed	% Underemployed
White	6	7.5	13
Black	22	16	25
Hispanic	24	18	30.5

Sources: Santacroce, Matt, and Orlando Rodriguez (2011) State of Working Connecticut, 2011: Jobs, Unemployment, and the Great Recession. New Haven, CT: Connecticut Voices for Children. http://www.ctvoices.org/sites/default/files/econ11sowctfull.pdf

wage income relative to whites lower than the national average, the median value of assets (or wealth) for black- and brown-headed households less than 2 percent of white-headed households, and racial and ethnic disparities in incarceration rates among the highest in the country.[62]

Unemployed fathers from our study residing in urban areas had few places to turn for income and material support in the waning years of the decade. This was particularly true for those who had felony records. They relied on under-the-table jobs, can and metal scrap collection, family members, churches, food pantries, homeless shelters, the drug trade, or whatever state assistance was available to them, which we have seen, was not much.

Nathan, who in the last chapter expressed the despair he felt from being rejected by fast food restaurants for a job, was living with the mother of his second child. Unemployed, he worked intermittently in off-the-books jobs in construction and as a bouncer. His girlfriend received public assistance, so he benefited from this in the household. However, Nathan contacted Sagacity, our interviewer, about a month after he had completed the study to ask for advice. The police had been to his apartment with a warrant for his arrest for violating a child support order. Nathan was not at home and was now on the run. He called to ask Sagacity whether he should turn himself in.

Because of the magnitude of child support enforcement policies in the lives of fathers in our study, and because of its significance in the 1996 welfare reform act, we will devote the entire next chapter to it. For now, it is worth pointing out that so-called deadbeat dad roundups were happening regularly during the 2000 decade in Connecticut and because of the thickness of law enforcement in black and brown areas, these aggressive efforts resulted in targeting many black and brown fathers.[63] One strategy for men was to try to avoid having any association with state authorities for these reasons, which included applying for state assistance. We turn to Jermaine again to illustrate.

Jermaine, the scrap metal collector, and his girlfriend lived with her mother. He was also very close to his own mother and his older siblings. Childrearing was an extended family practice. In addition to support from family, he said that "the state helps and I pick up the rest of the slack, man." He then emphasized, "It's not that we really *depend* on the state." Later in the interview, we found out that the only state assistance he received was WIC. He asserted that his partner "want to go and get some food stamps but I tell her not to get food stamps because if she gets food stamps and I find a job it will cut my pay back." This comment is remarkable in a few different ways. First, what Jermaine is referring to is that if his partner goes on the SNAP rolls—a form of public assistance—then he will be required to provide child support. This money would be deducted from his check when he secures an on-the-books job (we will more fully explain this policy in the next chapter). Jermaine was thus advising his partner not to apply for benefits that she was entitled to so that there would be no negative repercussions in the future. He seemed adequately informed about this process.

Second, however, we find out later in the interview that Jermaine was not the biological father of his 15-month-old "step-daughter." He was the social father, which in many households has more meaning to the residents and those parenting the child than it does to policymakers.[64] What Jermaine did not realize was that because he was not the biological father, he could not be held legally liable for child support. In his mind, though, he was the father of the child. He was there when she was born and was raising her; therefore, the laws would apply to him, as he saw it. This illustrates the different conceptions of fatherhood that many family members and policymakers have concerning childrearing in socially and economically marginalized communities, especially when families do not resemble the traditional nuclear family.

The recession produced suffering in low-income families across Connecticut. For fathers like Jermaine and Nathan—unemployed and black—they were cognizant that receiving public assistance might trigger attention from child support authorities. For fathers, mostly white, trying to maintain their status as head of the household, they wrestled with the implications of receiving public assistance. Benefits that reflected their status as breadwinners were not considered public assistance—unemployment compensation and EITC—but when they received cash assistance or SNAP, they largely disassociated themselves from these benefits by attributing them to their partners. She and the baby receive food stamps, cash assistance, WIC, and Husky. Moreover, they worked the symbolic boundaries to distinguish their household's use of public assistance from those who did not need it: the welfare cheats, the slackers, the welfare queens, the Octomoms.

In the Couples Study, in the earlier part of the decade, mothers and fathers worried about the welfare cliff and the 21-month time limit. At the end of the decade, when we just talked to fathers, we did not hear as many criticisms about reductions in benefits. Some, like Patrick, were aware that cuts were being made or that benefits were being reduced, and that there was something not right about this. But for the most part, caretaking and public assistance was the province of women. Men may have lived in households that benefited from this aid, but they seemed more preoccupied with trying to maintain their identities as providers, or else in avoiding the punitive arm of the welfare state, especially child support enforcement.

Nonetheless, state support was being retrenched and was adding to the suffering of low-wage families and the precariously employed. It was especially adding to the hardships of noncustodial fathers. Men wrestled with their masculinities—their own conceptions, expectations, and practices of manhood and fatherhood. Most had been prepared for hardship, but their embodied routines for dealing with it varied, and some were healthier than others. And as sociologist Richard Sennett observed, "Only a certain kind of human being can prosper in unstable, fragmentary social conditions."[65]

Conclusion

Rounding out the decade for low-income families, we see a dramatic increase in inequality (particularly in Connecticut); a decrease in wages for those in the bottom quintile of the labor market; and increased unemployment, underemployment, and long-term unemployment. In addition, we see the retrenchment of government assistance used to soften the harsh blows of the market. The gradual decade-long decreases in state assistance to low-income families increased hardships for families in Connecticut and elsewhere, especially as the economy went into a tailspin, while the "hidden welfare state" was channeling generous tax benefits to assuage businesses and higher income groups in the state. As the safety net was being shredded, forced compliance to a competitive labor market was advanced to replace it.

In the United States, the state has always played a minimal role in providing for households, compared to the roles of the market and family. In the neoliberal era, its support was even further withdrawn, while families were left with more of the burden of making a living in a low-wage labor market and providing care to prepare children for 21st-century labor and citizenry needs. As more families became part of the working poor, or near poor, they struggled with meeting a range of basic needs that market wages might not cover, including food, housing, utilities, clothing, health care, and childcare. There was considerable variation across states in supporting these needs, and many low-income families exceeded program eligibility guidelines set by the states. Moreover, when state revenues decreased during economic downturns, austerity measures resulted in lowering these eligibility standards further and excluding more needy families. For single-parent families and the unemployed poor, welfare reform sent the message that they, too, would have to find their way in the labor market and that the time for doing so would be limited.

The fathers we interviewed during this pivotal decade grappled with the material and symbolic dimensions of welfare reform. Their sense of manhood valued individual initiative, sacrifice, and familial responsibility. While they often lived in households that benefited from public assistance, these forms of state support were largely an extension of caretaking duties and household management which fell within the purview of women. They may or may not have acknowledged benefiting from state aid, but they were more likely to disassociate themselves from the specifics of public assistance and instead focus on the symbolic dimension of welfare reform—its stigmatizing discourse. In this regard, many of them saw state assistance, or more colloquially, state dependency as weakness, and they embraced the public discourse that was advanced by welfare reform architects.

Fathers navigated symbolic boundaries to distinguish themselves from those being disparaged by stigmatizing public discourses. White fathers were not having droves of children that were draining state coffers, as popular images of welfare queens or the Octomom would suggest. Black and brown fathers were not like those other black and brown fathers caricatured in the media—they were different, resilient, determined. Some fathers whom had experienced extreme poverty seemed to better understand how vital public assistance was, and some could develop a more critical perspective concerning program cuts. But even these fathers wrestled with disparaging moral discourses. They preferred to rely on state aid only temporarily or to disassociate themselves from public assistance as something only their part-ners and children received. Before turning to the state, these men preferred to rely on support from extended families, various hustles, such as can or scrap metal collecting, or the illicit drug economy.

Single-parent families, usually mothers, and noncustodial parents, usu-ally fathers, were particularly targeted by 1996 welfare reform. While neo-liberal economists viewed welfare expenditures as a market inefficiency and waste of capital that disrupted the social and economic virtues of a deregulated, competitive marketplace, the conversations that were occurring in Washington, DC, and states throughout the nation advanced the goal of cost-cutting through paternalistic endeavors to root out cultural pathologies associated mostly with black, urban poverty. The imperatives of the global market may have left us with a less stable, more precarious labor market, but compliance to the competitive demands of the market through value reso-cialization would presumably pave the way for family sustenance. The pa-ternalistic arm of the state appeared confident that dual-earner, low-wage families could meet market demands, and that through marriage, discipline, sacrifice, and individual initiative the state would coercively demonstrate how households could sustain themselves in a precarious labor market and overcome presumably cultural and social pathologies that prevented many of them from finding this path themselves. In this respect, fathers' repugnance toward state assistance was not the only challenge to masculine identities; the new paternalism also brought men closer to the faces and voices of state welfare authority.

This was particularly true for the part of the 1996 welfare reform story we have yet to tell. Child support enforcement was a key part of state welfare re-trenchment in which families were expected to shoulder more of the burden for raising and providing for children. The 1996 welfare reform act signified the transition from a welfare system intended to provide basic support for families *for whom the market is unable to provide* to a system in which tempo-rary support is provided for families *who fail to provide for themselves* within the market—and then only as a type of loan that the families are expected to pay back, even if it takes a lifetime. Child support was a central tenet of wel-fare reform and its material and symbolic importance is where we now turn.

4

"I Ain't No Fucking Check, I'm a Father"

These were the words spoken by Lawrence, a 24-year-old African American father of a 19-month-old daughter. "That's cool, pay the money," Lawrence told us. "But, okay, what about the other factors of being a father?" Lawrence felt misunderstood and humiliated by the courts. He was not alone. Others also felt that their efforts to be fathers were reduced to being only a provider and they had plenty to say about it.

> *"And when you are in front of the magistrate, 'Get another job [or] don't see your children.' That's the attitude they have. . . . They are getting paid really good money to treat us like this."*

> *"I was in court one day. I was about to cuss out the judge because . . . he tried to put me down like. The judge made me real mad. I been depressed since I been going to court. . . . I don't be going to sleep half the time."*

> *"If I miss two or three payments, why should I have to go to jail when I've been paying for like 15 years?"*

> *"That's how I felt the whole time. You are a deadbeat dad so you are worth nothing to us. You are just worth money. This is how much you need to be paying us and if you don't this is where you are going."*

> *"Yeah, I know how to be a father. But just the court stuff and all that other child support crap, I don't understand that."*

> *"They don't know your background. You can't throw all kinds of things at me and you don't know my background. You don't know how I am towards my kids. You don't know the relationship of me and my kids or my ex-lady."*

It's a Setup. Timothy Black and Sky Keyes, Oxford University Press (2021). © Timothy Black and Sky Keyes.
DOI: 10.1093/oso/9780190062217.003.0004

"They don't care about you being with the kids. They don't care about baby-sitting. They don't care about day care, being with them at school. They don't care about none of that. Just the money."

These fathers were angry and scared, and felt disrespected by the courts. They were responding to the interlinked child support enforcement and criminal justice institutions that were designed to collect child support debt and were advancing a public narrative of father irresponsibility and neglect conveyed by the popular trope the "deadbeat dad."

In this chapter we extend our analysis of the changing social and political landscape that was contextualizing fatherhood among low-income families in Connecticut and across the United States. We turn our attention to child support policies that were central to 1996 welfare reform, to the organization of Child Support Enforcement (CSE) in Connecticut, and to Fatherhood Initiative programs that proliferated across the nation after 1998. Again, we explore how low-income fathers made sense of and responded to this changing landscape, paying particular attention to their gendered locations in the family but also to their different racial experiences. Further, we examine how the reorganization of state welfare and child support enforcement was about "getting the money" in an era of state austerity but also about the institutionalization of symbolic power, through which the courts defined, stigmatized, and managed the lives of a marginalized population, reaffirming racial and class hierarchies.

In addition, we expand the voices of fathers in this chapter by drawing more extensively from our Fatherhood Initiative Study, which recruited noncustodial fathers from three locations in Connecticut.

Family Support Magistrate Court

In Connecticut, court magistrates were the arbitrators of the child support system. The men were quite aware that jail time hung over their heads, while three had been already incarcerated because of child support debt. They also knew that they were at the mercy of the magistrate. There were five magistrates and no one wanted to draw the magistrate they referred to as the "hanging judge." As we did our interviews, the stories about Magistrate Aronowitz accumulated.[1] Rayshawn, a 22-year-old African American father from Bridgeport, with one child, described his experience in the court.

During my time of incarceration, the court sent me a letter for child support saying for me to be there. Unfortunately, I was locked up. I was not
aware of it. So, when I was released from jail I received a letter in the mail,
maybe about a week or two after I came home, saying I owe $142 a week
and that my arrearage . . . was something like $5,000. I was told the best
thing I could do was go for modification and try to get the weekly amount
lowered. When I went to court, I was kind of unprepared because, you
know, this is my first time ever in child support court. I wasn't aware of
what I needed to show them at that time. When I got there, it seemed like a
setup [laughs] because I went in and I had to meet with a guy and he says,
"You are in deep trouble . . . you are not working. You haven't been working.
You didn't come to the first date. They give you the amount to pay and you
haven't paid anything." I didn't know I had to pay anything.

Rayshawn said that his case was continued for two weeks by a female magistrate, and he was charged with contempt of court. He was ordered to return
in two weeks with proof that he was looking for work. Upon his return, he
went before Magistrate Aronowitz with the good news that he had found a
job and had $200 cash in his pocket.

I went back to court with a letter from my boss saying I was working and
how much I was getting paid and so forth. And I had $200 to give them as
well. The magistrate acted like he didn't want to take the money. He still
wanted to lock me up. So I informed him that I was working. I was trying to
do the best I could do. He says to me, "If I send you to jail today, you could
possibly go to jail for six years." And I said, "Yes. I could."

Rayshawn had been arrested for dealing cocaine, and his sentence included
a six-year suspended sentence. According to Rayshawn, this was Magistrate
Aronowitz's leverage in the case—being held in contempt of court for failing
to pay his child support apparently could trigger his six-year suspended
sentence.

Magistrate Aronowitz underscored the seriousness of the situation by
appointing Rayshawn a public defender before determining whether to
incarcerate him. Rayshawn was then given time to meet with the public
defender in another room. When they returned, the public defender communicated the efforts Rayshawn had made in a short period of time. The magistrate continued the case for two more weeks and structured the payments

that Rayshawn was to make: a $142 payment the following day to meet his weekly support requirement, the same amount, $142, the following week, and then a $500 payment when he returned to court, bringing the total to $784 in a two-week period. Meanwhile, they took the $200 Rayshawn had in his pocket.

The next day, Rayshawn was able to pay $100. He got paid every two weeks, so he did not submit any payment the following week. At his next court date, he paid $400. He said this was the entire amount of his check. In the two-week period he had paid $500. Rayshawn said that when he returned to court, the magistrate asked, "So where's the other $284?" Rayshawn explained: "I am working. I am paying you all the money that I am making right now. I am not even paying my bills right now. I am not even paying rent. I am paying you every dollar that I make." Rayshawn owed the state $5,000 and the mother of his child $1,200. He was not sent to prison that day, most likely because the director of the Fatherhood Initiative Program (FIP) was standing at his side and vouched for him.

We heard many other stories like Rayshawn's, which were variations on related themes: the accumulation of debt during incarceration, unawareness that a warrant had been issued, and feelings of vulnerability and disrespect in the courtroom. Listening to them, it would seem that they were victims of a punitive system and at the mercy of a heartless magistrate. To learn more about the magistrate court and the enforcement system, we interviewed two of the magistrates, including Magistrate Aronowitz. As part of his interview, he invited our fieldworker, Ron, to court to observe the proceedings. Magistrate Aronowitz was dedicated to his work and to the mission of the court, and he was eager to share his perspective. Since he was the magistrate whom the men mentioned most and, for our purposes, represents the spirit of the legislation to track down these men and hold them accountable, we will focus on our interview with him.

Judge Peter

Ron travelled to the state courthouse to observe and interview Magistrate Aronowitz. The magistrate had agreed to participate in our research, and he was friendly and forthcoming. When the field worker arrived, the court was in session and Magistrate Aronowitz was presiding. The following field notes were recorded prior to the interview.

1:00 p.m.—I proceed to the courtroom, where Magistrate Aronowitz is in session and it becomes clear the interview will not begin on schedule. . . There were nine people [defendants] in the courtroom, one of whom was a woman. Four of these were men being held in custody. They were flanked by six sheriffs. All were handcuffed and wore leg shackles. The handcuffs are connected to a waist belt, which does not allow arm/hand movement above the waist. . . . In one instance a man came from home to court, but was ordered held in lieu of $1,000 bail, which was the total of what he owed for child support. He stated that he had the money and could go to work and pick it up. The magistrate told him he would have an opportunity to make calls and get someone to pick up the money and get it to court. The prosecutor stated the money would have to be in cash, money order, or certified check. Another dad was there on a support warrant, he stated he had paid some money, was working at a nursing home, but was laid off after a strike was over. He had a letter from the court stating he was to pay $120 per week, but his original letter had stated $120 per month. . . . The magistrate ordered the child support worker to investigate and come back with a finding, the judge then told the dad "since you are in contempt of the support order, the $120 per week would remain in effect until such time the original order could be located." The matter was continued for two weeks, and the dad was remanded into custody until such time. The judge stated "should you make bail before that date it is your obligation to be here and to continue support payments. The matter will be reviewed at that time."

Another dad . . . was a Latino male and had petitioned the court for a child support modification. The hearing began with the magistrate asking the dad, why had he stopped payments to begin with? The dad stated he had gotten back into drugs and was unable to work, he had gone into treatment, but relapsed. The magistrate then asked, "Did somebody put a gun to your head and make you use drugs?" The dad said, "No." He was unemployed at the time, could not find a job, and it just happened. The magistrate said, "Well, this is a consequence of you making that decision, on your own, to get involved with drugs. Your motion for modification of the child support order is denied." The dad then asked, "Does that mean the money is building" [meaning does the weekly rate continue to accrue although he is incarcerated and has no job]? The magistrate told him "yes" the support continues at the court-ordered rate. The dad then shrugged his shoulders and gave a look of exasperation, which echoed his thoughts of unfairness. "When will you be released?" the magistrate asked. The prosecutor said he believed the dad would be incarcerated for another year, at least, depending on the decisions of the parole board. The magistrate said, "I suggest when you are released, you make every attempt to find a job and begin making payments. I also think it would be wise if you got yourself involved in a drug treatment program."

2:00 p.m.—Recess: I approach the sheriff and explain I am here to meet with the magistrate. He goes to chambers, comes back, and I am escorted to the magistrate's office. He is removing his robe, apologizes for the delay, and states "that happens a lot around here."... I prepare to take a seat and he says, why don't we get out of here and have lunch. The atmosphere will be better for talking.

Outside of the courthouse, the magistrate was referred to warmly as Judge Peter. Seated by a hostess who appeared to serve Judge Peter regularly, the field researcher started the recorder. The magistrate explained that the child support court was set up to only address child support issues—all other family issues, including visitation and custody issues, were "upstairs" in family court. His job was solely to adjudicate child support cases. He said that he and his fellow magistrates each heard around 250 cases per week.

Judge Peter began the interview by identifying "the potential" for his job "to do a lot of positive things for some people that could use the help. You know, you get some kid or some children some child support that they weren't getting otherwise." He went on to tell a story about a man whom he sentenced to jail twice and would later see him on the street, who would thank him. This father had found work at a casino and was making sufficient money to pay his support orders. The magistrate recalled that the father said to him, "I'm even paying the one you didn't know about," as they shared a laugh. Judge Peter reiterated that sometimes "you get to do something positive for custodial parents" who "have been in the system so long that they really have given up."

The magistrate gave a number of reasons for why fathers don't pay: (1) they aren't making much money; (2) they are angry at the mother; (3) they are irresponsible or "they think they have other priorities that are more important"; (4) they have a new girlfriend and are more interested in supporting her children; and (5) they are not good at managing money. His job was simply "to make sure that the child support gets paid." What was most challenging, he said, was determining a "number that somehow he may be able to actually reach so that we get the money." Each case is unique, he claimed, and discerning the truth was no easy task when "you're dealing with people in the most emotional issue in their entire life. You know, it's like expecting President Clinton to tell the truth about his sex life," the judge quipped. "Why would he? Nobody else does!"

The burden of proof, Judge Peter explained, falls on the nonpaying parties. By this he meant that the father must prove that the child support arrears could not be paid in a lump sum, or that the weekly order was too much. "The bottom-line point," the judge explained, "is to get some money for the family, or if it's a welfare case, for the state."

For Judge Peter, this meant that the men needed to get their priorities straight. He explained:

> Support Enforcement will bring them in and they like haven't paid any-thing in six months of their child support . . . "Well, how far behind are you on your rent?" "Oh, god, I'm a month behind on my rent." You know, six months on child support and a month behind on rent. "How far behind are you on your telephone bill?" "Oh, well, I'm really bad, I'm two months on that." You know, like, almost invariably none of them are as far behind as their child support. I don't take that too well, but I mean it clearly tells me where their priorities are and part of what I have to do is say you have to ad-just your priorities.

The magistrate understood that, in many cases, there was not enough money to go around. "I mean guys will complain about half their paychecks disap-pearing," and ask, "How am I going to live on half my paycheck? And they don't think about, well, how is my ex-wife or ex-girlfriend and a child or maybe two or three or four children going to live on the other half of that paycheck?" He continued:

> But it gets even worse because you're dealing with younger and younger relationships breaking [up]. . . . It's also especially the sign of the times that both sides are getting into new relationships. And particularly from the guy's standpoint, they're the ones that want to be macho or whatever and "I want to support my new girlfriend, too." It's like, "Wait a minute, support your kids first." But they don't see the fact that the money isn't gonna go around to pay for all these things that they want to do.

According to Judge Peter, the magistrate's challenge is "to get the money" when there is not much to go around. Incarceration is used as a punitive mechanism to do this. However, incarceration places a burden on family members to cobble together money so that the father can be released from jail, and this money, as we have seen, is coming from already dwindling employment and welfare resources.

Judge Peter described a case in which a father was $40,000 in arrears. His job, as he explained, was to find a reasonable figure to ask the man to meet—to do "a reality check"—and to use incarceration as leverage to get the money, but not to "put this guy in jail until the next millennium." He continued:

> If the guy pulls in all of his chips and calls in all of his resources and gets all of his, you know, new girlfriends and parents and aunties and uncles and everything to chip in . . . and goes to, you know, some loan company and gets a loan and everything, what's the maximum amount he can show up with? It's probably not gonna be $40,000, so I actually ended up on $4,500 with that guy and so far he hasn't raised that either [so] yeah, he's in jail. . . . What I'm trying to keep in mind [is] that I still want a number that somehow he may be able to actually reach so that we get the money. We track our incarcerations and about 80 percent of the guys that we send in [to jail] end up coming up with the money and getting out.

Judge Peter admitted that he was hard-nosed when it came to getting the money and negotiating.

> I'll set a number, you know, hope that I got it right, but if I didn't, I kind of want to put the burden on them to come to me. And sometimes the ones that are represented by a lawyer, you know, will get in touch with me and say, "Well, look you wanted two thousand, he's got a thousand. Will you let him out for a thousand?" And I'll say, "Bring him in, I want to see the money on the table and we'll talk about it." I've had too many times where you bring him in and say, "Okay, we'll lower it to a thousand" and then he doesn't come up with a thousand. And they'll say, "Well, we've got five hundred." Well, you know, maybe its $480. Bye. I want to see the money!

At the end of the lunch interview, which lasted an hour and a half, Judge Peter graciously paid and returned to the court along with Ron. Judge Peter was one magistrate among five who was located within a system designed to *get the money*. He is not necessarily representative of all the magistrates, who were given considerable discretion in deciding cases. His aggressive demeanor, however, lays bare the institutional mission and inspiration of federal and state policies that were being passed in the era of neoliberal welfare reform.

Judge Peter's interview raised important issues. First, he identified a key problem—what he called the half-paycheck problem—when fathers have children with more than one mother and their income is not enough to support one household, let alone two. Relatedly, he noted that young relationships were unstable and likely to result in repartnering, what he saw as a generational problem. Second, the determined mission to "get the money" not only targeted fathers, but entire families. Judge Peter acknowledged that when he determined an amount of money to be paid to avoid incarceration, he included in his calculations money that the extended family might be able to scrape together. Further, he noted that even when he sent fathers to jail, that most of the time, the family came up with the money. Thus, these financial penalties extended to family networks. Third, the magistrate lived up to his reputation—he was hard-nosed and seemed to use incarceration quite liberally to discipline fathers, even when he was aware that arrears were accumulating while men were locked up. Fourth, Judge Peter indicated that he derived satisfaction from his job when he was able to get money for mothers and children, and for the state. This raises the question: where was this money going? Who was benefiting from these payments, and why? To better understand these issues, the Connecticut Family Support Magistrate Court, and Magistrate Aronowitz, we need first to consider some of the historical context.

Neoliberal Welfare Reform and the New Paternalism

Divorce, Nonmarital Births, and Male Privilege

The need for an institutional mechanism that would enforce child support collection and distribution was urgently needed in the latter half of the 20th century. With the near universal adoption of no-fault divorce by the states in the 1970s and 1980s, divorce rates increased precipitously. The courts and the legal profession were dominated by men, and men's privileges in the labor market meant that while their financial circumstances often improved after divorce, for mothers and children it became a significant cause of poverty.[2]

The poverty rate for single mother–headed households was 37 percent in 1990.[3]

Fathers were getting away with a lot. One estimate in the late 1980s indicated that one-half of mothers with child support orders were not receiving full payment, while one-fourth received nothing.[4] As mentioned in the Preface, both authors of this book lived in families that were victimized by this dynamic—fathers left, did not pay child support, blamed mothers, and found little to no repudiation from the male-dominated courts. Our fathers were not unique. With the increase in postwar incomes, divorce unleashed masculine exuberance among men expressed through consumption and personal indulgence, leading ultimately, we would argue, to the damaged grandeur of 20th-century white masculinity.

As bad as it was for divorced mothers with children, never-married mothers received even less from fathers. In the mid-1980s, the rate of fathers who had legally established paternity in nonmarital births was less than a third and, according to one study, only 13 percent of never-married mothers reported receiving child support.[5] This was particularly a concern because of the increase in nonmarital births in the 1980s, which was occurring simultaneously to the decrease in births among married couples. By 1990, the percent of births to nonmarried women was more than a quarter and, by 1995, was three times higher than it was in 1970. Interestingly, the rate of births to unmarried white women continued to increase through the 1990s and after, but decreased precipitously for black mothers and moderately for Latinas. Still compared to their married counterparts, by the start of the new millennium, around one-fifth of white births, two-thirds of black births, and more than one-half of Puerto Rican births were to unmarried mothers.[6]

Increasing divorce, nonmarital births, and poor single-mother-headed households, coupled with father self-indulgence, spelled trouble and underscored the need for state intervention—for a system that produced a fairer distribution of resources across a changing family landscape.

Child Support Enforcement

Federal child support policies can be traced back to the 1950s, but the current system was shaped by the 1974 and 1975 amendments that created part D of title IV of the Social Security Act and established the Federal Office of Child Support Enforcement. Key to this legislation was the 1975 amendment that required welfare recipients (those receiving Aid to Families with Dependent Children [AFDC] or cash welfare) to assign their rights to child support over to state authorities and to assist in identifying and securing support from noncustodial parents.[7] In 1977, the same protocol was extended to families receiving Medicaid.[8] This legislation provided a mechanism for the state to recover costs by tracking fathers and requiring that they pay back the state for assistance that had been provided to their children. This is what Judge Peter was referring to when he said that his mission was to get the money for mothers *and the state.*

This was a different concern from creating a system that distributed resources more fairly across households. The notion that state aid should be paid back was a government response to the dramatic increase in public assistance that occurred in the 1960s and 1970s. From 1965 to 1979, the numbers of families receiving cash assistance more than tripled from one to three-and-a-half million.[9] The increase reflected a shift from black family exclusion to inclusion, as the percentage of black recipients increased to 45 percent, a much better representation of the black poverty rate at the time. When Latinos were added, racial minority families made up the majority of families on the rolls, a major accomplishment that would change public discourse about the poor.[10]

Social movements, along with the enforcement of the 1965 Voting Rights Act, compelled states to lift barriers to enrollment.[11] The most politically organized group to broaden access to governmental assistance was the National Welfare Rights Organization (NWRO).[12] The NWRO targeted welfare offices across the nation to demand public entitlements for millions of black women who had been denied access.[13] They also turned to the courts, where a series of rulings struck down barriers to access, including "midnight raids" in 1967, "man in the house" and "substitute father" provisions in 1968, and "length of residency" rules in 1969.[14] In 1966, the year that NWRO was established, 15 percent of the poor received AFDC; by 1973, the rate had increased to 48 percent.[15] Without the mechanisms of "man in the house" and "suitable home" rules to exclude black families from the rolls, and with the rising costs of state welfare, child support became a new frontier for reducing costs and scrutinizing nontraditional families.

Child support policies ironically reversed the strategies that states had adopted to monitor AFDC families. Up until the 1968 Supreme Court ruling, state welfare agencies had routinely sent staff to inspect homes to see if an unreported man was living in the home, instituting the infamous "midnight raids." These policies discouraged cohabitation and forced men out of homes, even if they were unemployed or underemployed.[16] Beginning in the 1970s, however, fathers were penalized for not living in the homes, and by 1977, a partnership was developing between federal and state agencies to track non-compliant fathers through the use of burgeoning computer technology.[17] In short, before 1968, the state penalized poor families when fathers were in the homes, but after 1968, when they were not.

In the 1980s, while President Reagan was cutting social support for the working poor, he also was broadening CSE measures. Among other provisions, 1981 legislation authorized the IRS to withhold tax refunds to delinquent fathers and distribute the funds to the states, while 1984 legislation required the states to seize tax refunds as well.[18] Tax withholdings would become normative over the next two decades. Ironically, in the same way that the Earned Income Tax Credit would provide a once-a-year income boost used to pay down debt in poor families, noncustodial fathers with child support arrearages would learn to rely on the IRS to pay down their child support arrearage at tax time each year. Many of the men referred to this in our study. Garrett, for instance, paid off $5,000 in two years. He proudly exclaimed, "I just finished paying that off with my last tax return!" However, for noncustodial parents who owed child support to the state, any federal tax return intercepted went to the government, not the family.[19]

In 1984, child support legislation allowed states to garnish wages and impose liens on property of delinquent fathers. It also required states to pass through the first $50 of money collected as an incentive for mothers to be more complicit in identifying and providing information about absent fathers.[20] The tax reform act that same year required states to give information on arrearages to consumer reporting agencies. Soon after, in 1986, the Bradley Amendment prohibited the retroactive modification of child support orders, which meant that even if a noncustodial parent could prove that their income had been significantly reduced for a period in their lives, the arrearages accumulated during that time could not be modified.[21] This particularly affected fathers who had been incarcerated when support orders were active.[22]

This 22-year history culminated in PRWORA in 1996, which, as we have seen, unleashed a national wave of state action to move families off of the welfare rolls by transitioning mothers into jobs and by increasing fathers' financial responsibility for their children. The penalties for fathers' noncompliance were severe, including driver's license revocation, professional license bans, financial penalties (including interest and fees on arrears in many states), and incarceration.[23] The 1996 act also eliminated the federal pass-through $50 requirement and allowed states to decide how much, if any, money to pass along to families. More importantly, the act reinvigorated a national effort to establish paternity and child support orders, which broadened the net to include more economically vulnerable families. Consequently, while collections grew, arrears grew faster and larger.

In the early 2000s, in Connecticut, if a child was receiving public assistance, the state gave the custodial parent the first $50 of child support money collected each month and kept the rest.[24] The federal government paid bonuses to states that met collection benchmarks, and the states offset their own budgets with bonuses and collections.[25] The stage was set. Fathers who owed child support were labeled deadbeat and the state went hard to get their money. Fathers were swept up on the streets for warrants when they did not appear in court, were exposed to public humiliation rituals in court, and went to prison. Magistrate Aronowitz was an institutional actor who had been incentivized and encouraged to act aggressively.

What might have begun as a reasonable challenge to address gender inequities that were taking shape in the 1970s and 1980s due to changing attitudes and practices concerning marriage, childrearing, sexual relationships, and the distribution of family resources, instead, began to resemble a moral crusade.

Father Responsibility

Lynne Haney and Miranda March tracked federal legislation beginning in 1998 concerning "responsible fatherhood" and examined four years of discourse from invited public testimony related to different iterations of this legislation.[26] They identified two ideological camps. One conservative set of views saw fatherhood policies as a way of restoring men to their "rightful" place as heads of the patriarchal nuclear family—as financially responsible and morally driven fathers. This group focused more on marriage and the value resocialization of fathers. The liberal set of views promoted the idea that men would become more marriageable if they acquired human capital, which would improve self-worth and father involvement, while advancing the dual-earner family model in poor communities. These two groups converged, however, on the idea that father absence was central to the cultural pathologies that had taken root in poor urban communities and that family restoration through work and marriage was the needed antidote.

These culture of poverty theories, reinforced by the preoccupation with the black urban underclass at the time, were occurring simultaneously with neoliberal economic reform and discourse about reducing the size and reach of government.[27] The reorganization of market capitalism that pushed down wages by increasing the global and domestic supply of wage earners, that increased the number of precarious jobs, and that withdrew state support for low-income and indigent populations was transforming the labor force at the same time that a moralistic assessment of the black urban poor was being amplified in legislative hearing rooms. It was not a historical anomaly, by any means. In fact, it has become a well-established formula, by which racial and class hierarchies are reinvigorated in times of economic crisis and uncertainty—a formula that has left in its aftermath much of the moralistic legislation in the United States today, from drug laws and incarceration policies, to immigration laws and citizenship policies.

Like the era of mass incarceration, aggressive CSE discourses, policies, and strategies drew on several cultural and social threads that were woven together into a punitive, paternalistic, moralistic tapestry. In fact, the overlapping circuitous institutional processes between the criminal justice and CSE systems were striking.[28] In the era of neoliberal austerity, it was about getting the money, as Magistrate Aronowitz asserted, but it was about much more.

Getting the Money

While the scrutiny of welfare families that produced the 1974–1975 child support amendments was largely a backlash to increasing numbers of black and brown families on the welfare rolls, in order to get broad support to pass the bill, both welfare and nonwelfare families were included in the legislation.[29] Welfare families made up only a part of uncollected child support debt. Still, the CSE initiative specifically targeted welfare families, since there was less incentive to collect monies for nonwelfare families in which the full payment was passed through. For welfare families, the state could reimburse itself. In the 1980s, with state welfare retrenchment taking root and a deepening discourse that held the poor as morally culpable for their own poverty, the jurisdiction of CSE expanded across the states. Just as Reagan had invented the story of the welfare queen to lampoon black welfare mothers, the era of the deadbeat dad would soon follow, as the institutional foundation for it was expanding.

Was it then about getting the money? Certainly, given the large amount of unpaid child support that had accumulated, a bureaucratic, administrative response would seem reasonable. In these terms, the success of the 1996 legislation was championed by the U.S. Department of Health and Human Services, which documented an increase in child support collections from less than $10 billion in 1993 to $23 billion in 2005, providing for nearly 16 million cases.[30] The Urban Institute reported that the percentage of poor custodial mothers receiving formal child support increased from 20 percent in 1983 to 33 percent in 2005,[31] while Sarah McLanahan and Marcia Carlson documented steep increases in established paternity cases, support orders, and collections from both welfare and nonwelfare families alike.[32]

On the face of it, who could deny these achievements? However, the benefits of policies targeting welfare families went disproportionately to the states, rather than to the well-being of the families. According to an Urban Institute report, of the $635 million collected by the states on behalf of welfare families in 2004, only 27 percent was distributed to the families, which resulted in an average income increase of merely $337 a year or an estimated 2 percent of cash income among welfare families.[33] Moreover, the amount collected from poor families was declining over time, in part because declining caseloads after 1996 had decreased the amount of money that was available for collection from welfare-assisted families. The federal and state governments spent $23 billion on cash assistance in 1994, but only $9.6 billion in 2011, so there was simply less money to recover. Even with declining caseloads, aggressive efforts by the states had increased collections from welfare-assisted families from $2.5 billion in 1994 to $3 billion in 2003, after which it began to decline. As a percent of money recovered compared to money spent on cash assistance, states improved their recovery rate from 11 percent in 1994 to its peak of 31 percent in 2002. By the end of the decade, however, the recovery rate had declined to 18 percent.[34]

What is most striking is that during these decades of aggressive state efforts, child support arrears were growing astronomically. From 1987 to the end of the first decade of the new millennium, child support debt increased from $14 billion to $108 billion.[35] A study by Elaine Sorenson and her colleagues at the Urban Institute in 2007 estimated that 70 percent of this debt belonged to fathers who made $10,000 or less income per year, while a report from the Office of CSE in 2004 indicated that 60 percent of this debt was owed by 10 percent of debtors.[36] Arrears were spiraling upward on the backs of debtors who were unable to pay, while hyperaggressive enforcement efforts were not even dulling the edges of debt growth.

In short, the outcomes of the child support provisions of PRWORA are similar to outcomes of its welfare-to-work provisions in that the touted successes of these measures belie serious shortcomings. In the latter, welfare rolls have been cut drastically, leaving the most difficult to employ on cash assistance (in the best-case scenarios) through a process of waivers and extensions, while most others were moved from the status of welfare to working poor (or near poor). Regarding child support outcomes, collections increased and paternity was nearly universally established, but limited amounts of these monies reached poor families, while fathers without resources to meet state demands suffered the indignity of rising arrears.

Within the courts, however, the mission to "get the money" persisted, even while state reimbursements for welfare outlays were in decline. For instance, when we asked Magistrate Aronowitz if he thought that the state's effort to collect these monies was cost effective, he replied, "Actually, I think it is cost effective." He considered CSE to be "one of the few, if you want to call it that way, profit centers in the state. We actually bring in . . . something like three-and-a-half dollars for every dollar" spent on the process. He qualified that "not all of that's going into the state coffer," but he quickly pointed out that by collecting child support money from nonwelfare families he could be saving the state money by preventing families from applying for welfare later. The magistrate stated, "We collect I think a decent percentage of the child support that's charged. We don't collect all of it. The last time I saw the number I think we were around 50 percent. Which sounds horrible, but it's actually pretty darn good."

Magistrate Aronowitz was partly correct. When all monies collected from noncustodial fathers were included, state collections exceeded state costs. As illustrated in Figure 4.1, this was because, in Connecticut, collections from nonwelfare parents had increased 74 percent between 1999 and 2009. Meanwhile, collections from welfare-assisted families declined by 23 percent during this period.[37] State expenditures for the CSE system in Connecticut reached $73 million in 2009—an 88 percent increase since 1999—even though they were only collecting $42 million from welfare-assisted families.[38]

Across the nation, these patterns were similar. In 1999, between federal cost sharing and bonuses, and welfare recovery, states increased their coffers by $50 million; but ten years later, in 2009, they were running a

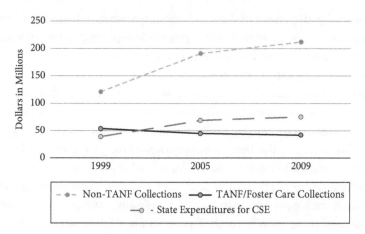

Figure 4.1   Child Support Collections and Expenditures in Connecticut, 1999–2009

Source: Data from Solomon-Fears (2012), Tables A-4, A-5, and A-8.

deficit in the amount of $718 million.[39] Between 1978 and 2010, annual expenditures on CSE activities increased from $312 million to $5.8 billion. And yet, in 2010, there was $143 billion in child support debt still on the books—$33 billion for current support and $110 billion in arrears. CSE collected $20 billion, or 62 percent, of current obligations in 2010. However, they collected only $7 billion, a mere 7 percent of total arrears. And frankly, this mammoth bureaucracy is unlikely to ever decrease arrearages beneath $100 billion.

It is hard to say that the mission of the court was not to "get the money" in an era of welfare retrenchment and neoliberal reform. After all, the use of fees, fines, and debt leveraged on indigent populations was increasing across a lot of different institutional spaces—the courts, the prisons, probation and parole services, bail bonds services, electronic monitoring surveillance, driver's license bureaus, lending institutions, hospitals, and proprietary schools, to name a few.[40] Neoliberal state austerity has increased the use of more nefarious funding mechanisms. But there was more at play—something more moralistic; something that galvanized institutional authorities and practices; something that reconfigured the constructions of marginality and race. These were symbolic practices that reflected the new developing forms of poverty governance that defined, stigmatized, and institutionally managed the lives of marginalized fathers—stamped as deadbeat dads. Magistrate Aronowitz did not appear to be a deceitful or merciless man; instead, he was eager to show us his work and how well he performed it. He was embedded within a system that was organized ostensibly to "get the money," but that was also an invigorated institutional organization of symbolic power.[41]

The Deadbeat Drumbeat

The decade of the 1990s recorded the longest period of unending economic growth in US history, and yet during this time, the racially charged vitriol directed toward teen moms, corner boys, and deadbeat dads crescendoed. The prison rate increased 44 percent between 1993 and 2000 alone, while the divide between the rich and poor mushroomed.[42] Concerns about inequality were minimal amid good reports about the economy, while state institutions were reorganized to deny women public assistance and lock up indigent men.[43] Pre-1960s welfare that systematically denied black families assistance and ran state worker raids on households gave way to a new form of welfare paternalism that scrutinized the behavior of those who received assistance and paraded men through the courts for their neglect. These state initiatives and moral discourses shaped the culture of state welfare offices and the courts. Well-intentioned public aid workers and court magistrates committed to doing their jobs effectively and boosting their federally rewarded numbers embraced these discourses and became the agents of symbolic power.

Clinton's 1996 welfare reform squarely targeted noncustodial fathers. It released a full-court press to establish paternity, boost child support payments, and collect "welfare debt," while it emboldened states to revoke drivers' and professional licenses, to deny passports, to enhance wage garnishment, and to seize assets of delinquent fathers.[44] Rounding up and shaking down deadbeat dads was part of a moral campaign and, after all, what could be more noble than making sure that absent fathers, shirking their responsibilities, would pay money to mothers who were bearing the costs of childrearing? This was ostensibly about fairness and responsibility, and as we have seen, with rising divorce rates, single-mother households, and nonmarital births, there was an argument to be made for it.

Public discourse fanned the flames. Some scholars see the Bill Moyers award-winning documentary, *The Vanishing Family: Crisis in Black America,* which aired as a CBS Special Report in 1986, as critical to shaping public discourse.[45] Indeed, responding to one of the men in the film, Timothy McSeed, a proud father of six children with four mothers, columnist George Will wrote, "The Timothies are more of a menace to black progress than the Bull Connors ever were."[46] As Kathryn Edin and Timothy Nelson pointed out, a series of "deadbeat dad" laws soon followed from Congress, beginning with the Bradley Amendment introduced by New Jersey liberal Democrat Bill Bradley, in 1986, which, as we have seen, forbade retroactive modification to arrears. Conservative scholars like Charles Murray and Lawrence Mead had already laid the groundwork for the deadbeat drumbeat with earlier excoriations of the black underclass that attributed moral degeneration and familial irresponsibility to liberal welfare legislation that had purportedly given license to the licentious. However, it was David Blankenhorn's 1995 book, *Fatherless America: Confronting Our Most Urgent Social Problem*, that gave father absence academic imprimatur.[47] For Blankenhorn, the breakdown of the traditional family and the failure of men to step up and assume their familial responsibilities were cause and consequence of America's waywardness, its amoral drift. During one of our presentations at the Legislative Office Building in Hartford in 2005, a prominent local political leader and black minister responded by raising a copy of *Fatherless America* for everyone in the room to see and announcing that this was the answer to our problems in the inner city.

These moralistic claims, directed mostly at the poor black family, were as publicly infectious as they were simplistic. Daytime television and nightly news programs provided incendiary reporting on deadbeat dads, from Jerry Springer, Judge Mathis, Steve Wilkos, Judge Judy, Judge Joe Brown, Maury Povich, and Dr. Phil to Bill O'Reilly ("Deadbeat Dad Confronted"), Wolf Blitzer ("Most Wanted Deadbeat Dad Captured"), and other headline news features (CNN: "Man with 30 Kids Asks for a Break"; Headline News: "Should Man with 22 Kids Have Reality TV Show?"; Fox News: "Judge Orders Deadbeat Dad To Stop Having Kids"; Fox 5: "Operation: Deadbeat Parents"; and NBC 41 in Missouri: "Cops Target Deadbeat Dads and Dopers").

The black bourgeoisie joined the fray. Bill Cosby, a then respected member of the black community, castigated black fathers in his 2006 speech at a black church in Baltimore for "having more children than you have jobs."[48] Retired District Court Judge Greg Mathis declared that deadbeats are responsible for the "downfall of black people in general" on his daytime Emmy

Award–winning television program.[49] Even President Barack Obama exercised the highest public office to reinforce the message.

Obama used his public platform to restore the black family, or put the "black house" in order. Obama's deep commitment to his 2014 initiative, My Brother's Keeper, targeted male youth of color in an effort to raise their hopes and opportunities and to keep them "on the right track." In his now famous 2008 Father's Day speech, given at a Southside Chicago church, Obama stated, "But if we are honest with ourselves, we'll admit that too many fathers also are missing—missing from too many lives and too many homes. They have abandoned their responsibilities, acting like boys instead of men. And the foundations of our families are weaker because of it." Obama went on to identify the need for more police officers, school funding, outstanding teachers, jobs and job training, and opportunities, before taking further aim at absent fathers: "But we also need families to raise our children. We need fathers to realize that responsibility does not end at conception. We need to realize that what makes you a man is not the ability to have a child—it's the courage to raise one."[50]

Conversations occurring across many public spaces—legislative hearing rooms, the White House, social media, and academia—converged on how to correct the cultural pathologies of the black inner city. Father absence was presumed to be the central problem, and the new paternalism of the welfare and child support enforcement systems would target black fathers—and by extension misdirected poor brown and white fathers as well—to teach them how to embody and enact responsible fatherhood. As we saw in earlier chapters, this was occurring as neoliberal reorganization of the economy was decreasing living wage jobs, increasing inequality and a precarious workforce, and imposing more spending austerity on the states. One response to this transformation of capitalism was then to enhance the institutional power of institutions that interacted with marginalized populations to enforce discipline and moral responsibility. Thus, the system was not out of whack—people were. And if only they learned to buck up, enact personal responsibility, and conform to the needs of the system, then they and everyone else would be just fine. Within these institutions, a professional and semiprofessional class were left to carry out the mission, and to secure funding for their missions by producing scientifically measured success and, thereby, advancing the heralded social science achievements of "best practices."[51]

"I Am Scared of Child Support More Than Life Itself"

Child support magistrate courts, working in partnership with DSS, CSE, and State Marshals, assumed a heavy hand in the neoliberal era, which included rounding up "deadbeat dads" who were held in contempt for failing to comply with a child support order. As Magistrate Aronowitz illustrated, magistrates were there to force men into jobs and into their responsibility of providing for their children. He and others used the bench to harass, shame, or cajole fathers—whatever it took to direct household revenue flow to the right places: to mothers and taxpayers.

Not being able to find work was not an option. Men chafed at this. Travis insisted, "I don't have a problem paying when I'm working. I really don't." Lorenzo agreed, "As long I'm working and I can pay my child support, I'm straight. I ain't be worrying about nothing else. My kids are set." The magistrates' allegations sometimes left these men feeling befuddled. Marcus, at 44 years of age, was one of the older men in our study. He had three children with three mothers. When we knew him, he was calling a temp agency daily to find out if they had any work for him. He owed nearly $10,000 in arrears. Marcus expressed shame for not being able to afford holiday presents for his kids and told us that he had to make choices in his own life, like deciding whether to attend an appointment with an eye doctor or pay child support. He felt misunderstood by the child support courts and wished they could order workplaces to give fathers jobs.

MARCUS: They don't understand me at all. I told them right out, "I don't have no job right now." He said to me, "Well, you are going to find one or we are going to have to put you in jail." They don't give me a chance. They think jobs are so easy. I wish they would find me a job or give me the opportunity to find a job and then they could see I go to work every day. . . . I told them I am going to the program right now in the morning time. He didn't want me to go to the program; he just wanted me to get a job. I said to him I have a job, but they are calling me a temporary. And he said to me, "This is not a job."

RON: He said that's not a job?

MARCUS: No, when I told him that I was working under the table for this guy, he said to me, "Oh, I thought you said you don't have a job." What I don't understand is how you see work under the table for somebody is a job but working for a temporary agency is not a job.

The determination to get the money or lock'em up added stress, especially for those men who had never been incarcerated before. Faheen, a 24-year-old African American, who had been laid off from his job, was one of them.

> The judge wants me to have a job before the 22nd and here it is, it's what, the 15th . . . If I don't have one, he probably sit up there and give me like 30- to 60-day lockup, doing my little time and I don't want that to happen because I never been locked up. I can barely rest. I lose a lot of sleep. After that judge said what he said to me last time, I was just restless. I am picking up cigarettes. I am trying to quit at the same time, but still I am stressing. Whatever, I got to find this job thing. It's just running me crazy. I feel snappy here [and] there, but I try to front and put on a happy face when I know I am feeling kind of down. I don't want to kill my own self and have worries and thoughts in the back of my mind and end up into a tumor or something like that. All I need is a job. That's it. That's where it starts and that's where it's gonna end. Just a job.

Alberto, on the other hand, had spent time in prison. A part-time grocery store worker and former street hustler, who lived with his child and the mother, Alberto also felt inordinate stress, because he wanted to stay out of jail and connected to his family.

ALBERTO: I am just barely surviving. Trying to find work so I can just be able to keep my rent.

RON: You need to hustle still?

ALBERTO: Not really because she's working. I am just trying to do the right thing. I just don't want her coming to welfare. And then child support hit me up my ass. I am scared of child support more than life itself. I don't want to go back to jail for some dumb shit over some child support for money. They don't give two shits about nothing.

RON: "They" meaning who?

ALBERTO: Court. The judge. They don't care. The prosecutor. They don't care.

What men like Marcus, Faheen, and Alberto were experiencing was intended. The courts were pressuring them to find work and make their child support payments—to force them against the wall, to feel anguish, and to resolve their distress by complying with court demands.

The charge of the deadbeat dad carried heavy symbolic significance, while the threat of prison was intended to scare them straight. But for fathers with connections to the street economy, these measures seemed to do just the opposite. Several of the men felt as if they needed to hustle on the streets to meet the court's demands. Richard explained: "The hustling money is easy to get and I could pay everything off with the hustling money, but I want to go positive. I really do. But it's hard. The judge will tell you, 'Bring $1,500 back.' 'So where am I going to get $1500?' 'Do what you got to do,' that's what he tells you." Aaron observed, "You see a lot of people go to the street and sell crack, marijuana, whatever, cocaine. Got to get money. And it's unfortunate because I see the court, that's all the court cares about. The court is like, 'I don't care how you get the money. Just get it.' Now what?"

Richard and Aaron's point seemed logical to us. If judges were pressuring street-connected, unemployed fathers to produce significant amounts of money in short periods of time, how else would they expect the men to meet these demands other than by working in the street economy? Chris expressed desperation: "I've been depressed since I been going to court. . . . I don't be sleeping half the time. When I'm asleep, that shit still be in my mind. I am going to court, Damn! I got to pay all this money and shit. Where am I going to get this money from? I'm going to go rob somebody, or something?"

In these instances, where fathers felt channeled back to the streets, it seemed that the enforcement arm of the state had reached a place of irrationality—where getting the money, shaming father absence and irresponsibility, and disciplining fathers as both workers and providers had come off the tracks. Or was it? Perhaps judges were taking fathers making unreported income to task, whether that income was from off-the-books jobs or drug dealing. Perhaps, they were letting fathers know that they were on to them, and that they needed to cough up some of this money for mothers and children. Either way, if men were being guided back to doing what they knew best—dealing drugs or sticking up drug dealers—then they were being pushed back into the deadly cycle of what Lynne Haney astutely calls the imprisonment of debt and the debt of imprisonment.[52] In this scenario, fathers are incarcerated for child support debt, and then accumulate more arrears while they are incarcerated. Or they are incarcerated for committing crimes to pay their child support, and then land in prison where child support arrears continue to accumulate.

We saw the beginning of this process among the 29 fathers we interviewed at the Hartford FIP site. All of the fathers in this program had been street involved; all but eight were incarcerated at the time of the interview; all were young, between 17 and 21 years of age; about one-third had a second child; and none of them were married. At these young ages, some of the men were expecting children, some were living in the homes with the mothers and children before incarceration, while others had worked out informal arrangements of support and had managed to avoid using public assistance. Still, seven of them were aware of child support arrearages that were accumulating while they were incarcerated. These debts were likely to be the beginning of a lifetime of child support debt for these 18- and 19-year-old fathers, which would then add to the $143 billion currently on the books.

Where in these processes, we might ask, was the concern for the new fatherhood—for the softer side of these practices that were supposed to encourage marriage and enhance father engagement?

New Fatherhood

The Fatherhood Initiative programs—sometimes referred to as Responsible Fatherhood programs—that spread throughout the nation in the late 1990s and early 2000s were predicated on the assumption that father absence was a preeminent cause of inner-city cultural pathologies. The programs emphasized both financial responsibility and father engagement, and they found considerable research to support these twin objectives. Financial contributions, the research showed, increased with father contact, while father contact increased along with financial responsibility.[53]

The DSS commissioner and her staff in Connecticut were deeply committed to this vision and organized programs to value the full expression of fatherhood—the dual investment of money and time. Inside the state bureaucracy and legislature, these twin goals generated bipartisan support— fiscal conservatives leaned on financial responsibility, while liberals embraced father engagement. The commissioner and her staff were liberals and were particularly concerned about creating programs that supported fathers' emotional involvement with their children. As such, the programs advanced the view of the "new fatherhood," in which the social value of nurturing and caregiving were elevated relative to contributing financially.[54]

The "new fatherhood" was highlighted in public campaigns across the country, as the historic image of the detached breadwinner of the family gave way to the nurturing, engaged father. For marginalized fathers, who had little else working for them, fatherhood was a form of status that could provide them with a respected identity, a direction forward, a fantasy, a glimmer of hope. Edin and Nelson went as far as to suggest that this set the stage for serial fatherhood, so when relationships failed men jumped into new relationships chasing, if you will, a new fatherhood moment.[55]

One of the key benefits of FIPs was the advocacy that staff provided to fathers in their efforts to combine both financial responsibility and father involvement. Fathers relied on FI staff to help them with custody, visitation, and child support issues, for encouragement, guidance, and support in their fathering practices, and for finding jobs and job training opportunities.[56] The magistrates we interviewed expressed their gratitude for these programs and their dedicated staff. They helped them make decisions about the cases before them and attempted to balance out their mandate to "get the money." Financial responsibility and father involvement became the mantra in the field, something that all parties could get behind that made the push toward "government recoverables" appear more humane. Moreover, these programs provided a space for the men to make sense of and respond to the aggressive actions of the courts.

The FIPs in Connecticut were diverse, providing services to different populations of noncustodial fathers that emphasized the varying needs of fathers. This allowed us to see how race operated within these institutional processes. In this chapter, we contrast two of these sites (most of the fathers at the third site were incarcerated and will be the focus of Chapter 6). One, located in Norwich, a small city in Connecticut, provided services mostly to white working-class men (see Table 4.1). The men in this program often reported strained relationships with the mothers of their children; they also tended to be more educated and more often employed, to have less street involvement and histories of incarceration, and to have more access to family resources. While most of the fathers were struggling with poor-paying, unsteady jobs, their problems were less a reflection of social and economic marginalization and more a result of troubled relationships with the mothers of their children. The program had a "father's rights" emphasis. At the time it was directed by a man who felt strongly that the courts were biased against fathers and that one of the central missions of the program was to assist men in obtaining child support modifications, visitation rights, and child custody from the courts.

One of the fathers in the program carried the mantle. Aaron was a biracial, 37-year-old father of a 15-year-old-daughter. He completed high school and

Table 4.1 Social Demographic Characteristics of Norwich and Bridgeport Fathers

	Norwich (N = 14)	Bridgeport (N = 19)
Race		
White	57%	5%
Black	14%	47%
Puerto Rican	14%	32%
Other Latino	7%	5%
Multiracial	7%	0%
Jamaican	0%	11%
Employment		
Full-time	71%	11%
Part-time	7%	21%
Unemployed	21%	68%
Age		
Mean	28	26
Median	26	24
Mean no. of children	1.8	1.9
Mean no. of mothers	1.5	1.6
Relationships		
Good/fair with recent mother	57%	84%
Good/fair with child(ren)	86%	95%
Child Support		
Does not have an order	29%	16%
Currently paying	57%	37%
Not currently paying	14%	47%
In arrears	36%	68%
Incarceration		
In past	21%	47%
Marital status		
Married	29%	5%
Separated/divorced	29%	16%
Single, never married	43%	79%

had served in the Navy. He was separated from his wife and worked as a self-employed contractor doing odd jobs for mostly unreported income. Aaron had a regular presence in programs at the agency, where he encouraged fathers to pursue their rights in the courts as parents. In Aaron's view, the child support courts were "like a system of apartheid, where they make one person superior, usually that's the custodial parent."

At around the time of Aaron's interview, the DSS Commissioner and her staff were conducting public hearings throughout the state to learn more about the needs and experiences of noncustodial fathers in the CSE system. Aaron said he attended one of the hearings, where he elaborated on his views.

> I said when you create a situation like that people will not invest in the system. So if you have no equity in your child eventually what happens, unless you are extremely strong-willed person, you give up because you are not making any impact on that child. You are not doing anything and you become demoralized and leave that child. And that's what they really see happening to fathers.

Aaron continued his critique by suggesting that the gendered make-up of the court reinforced this system of apartheid. He described the female magistrates as "rude" and Magistrate Aronowitz as the male enforcer, and saw the paternalism of the court as similar to the disciplinary role of the corrections officer (CO) in a prison.

> I have found them to be extremely rude. Their mentality is like a CO in a prison. Like when you get down to child support court, like especially Sandra Green . . . she's extremely rude and the other woman is rude, too. . . . I said, "Well I am self-employed and sometimes my income isn't steady and blah, blah, blah. . . ." "Well then you can't be self-employed." They are like the Gestapo. They are like, "We are just going tell you what to do. We are going to run you. You will do what we say and if you don't you'll go to jail." And then Judge Aronowitz gets behind them and starts trying to throw you in jail and unless you really get up there and do Johnny Cochran or a Larry Elovich or somebody [laughs], Alan Dershowitz, you are going to go to jail.

In a statement that summarized Aaron's perspective, and the views of many men in the CSE system, he asserted, "They call them deadbeat dads, but what they don't seem to understand is that they created the deadbeat dad thing because they don't create the stable platform that you require to see your child."

The 1996 legislation, the CSE system, and FIPs stressed the gendered role of fathers in the family. The aggressive paternalistic form of the CSE system made fathers feel as if mothers and the courts were out to get them. The FIPs created a space for men to react to these perceptions—it reconstituted their identities as men and as fathers. In hostile relationships, the courts provided an instrument of power that the different parties might use. Mothers might acquire leverage in these situations by threatening to take fathers to court to pursue more aggressively a child support order. In these cases, fathers felt ganged up on. Tyler, a 24-year-old white father from this program site, said:

> Well, I remember my ex for a while back she would take me to child support and nothing really to make a big scene about. Again, this was all out of spite, out of just vengeance. And they would really believe her wholeheartedly and not try to consider my situation or see what I go through as well to be a father. It's all about the money.

Fathers, on the other hand, could counter with the argument that if they were being pursued for child support, then they had the right to see their children and to require that mothers adjust their lives to make sure that fathers had regular access to their children. The paradigm of the "new fatherhood" advanced these rights, even in relationships that were contentious. Justin illustrates.

Justin was part of the same Norwich FIP as Aaron. He was a 33-year-old white father, with an 8-year-old daughter, and was also a self-employed contractor—a carpenter whose work was sporadic. He was married at the time of the interview but said that the child was a result of "a one-night stand" with a woman from Rhode Island before he was married. At the time, he questioned whether the child was his and apparently demanded a DNA test, which he said the mother refused. He explained that he retaliated by not paying child support, nor was he involved in the child's life. This worked out for him, until the mother applied for Medicaid when her daughter was five. The state then intervened and demanded a paternity test, which came out positive. They then pursued him for child support arrears calculated retroactively to the time of his daughter's birth.

Justin turned to the agency for help in navigating the courts. He said that staff assisted him, but that he obtained a lawyer to resolve the case. It was rare for fathers who went before the magistrates to be represented by an attorney, until they were threatened with jail, at which time, one was appointed. Justin was an exception and his story validates Aaron's point about doing "a Johnny Cochran" to challenge the culture of the courts. Justin said the state was pursuing him for $45,000 for almost six years. Justin continues: "I fought it. I was cooperating with the state the whole way. I didn't say that I didn't sleep with her. I didn't put up a fight about going for the paternity. I went along with everything. And they dropped most of it." Justin was still indignant because the lawyer had cost him $7,000. Feeling some momentum, Justin then asked when he could see his daughter. He described:

> The judge laughed and said, "You have to come back and you have to fight for that." I said, "Well, why don't you take care of that now?" "Well, that wasn't on the docket for the case today." Nobody explained any of that to me or anything until that day in court. And then I felt like I was taken advantage of and that's when I started getting angry. The whole system was working against me. They just wanted to take my money and hold me from my kid. The lawyers and then the judge and then the mother.

Justin was angry. He had spent money on the case, had accepted paternity, and felt like he was now entitled to see his child. Unlike some of the black and brown fathers living in cities, who never expected the system to work for them, Justin did. He felt more entitlement than his urban counterparts, who were more likely to express fear of the system—"more than life itself," as Alberto had said. Justin continued.

> So I was like very angry, very confused. . . . And the lawyers kept saying, "You are too angry. You are too angry." I said, "I am angry at you guys. I am not angry at my child . . . I am angry at the lawyers who are keeping me away from the child. If the mother is keeping me from my child, I am angry at her too. If the boyfriend of the mother is, I am too." The boyfriend I heard nothing good about. I heard he was a crack-head. Heard he was a coke dealer. Heard he was a drunk. Heard he was violent. Everybody that I asked said, "Oh he's probably beaten your kid already." So I am hearing all this and the lawyers aren't willing to help me because they think I'm angry.

Even though Justin was angry, legal representation had helped him considerably. The amount he owed retroactively was mostly eliminated, which was highly unusual. Justin lashed out by demanding that the courts enable him to see his daughter regularly, even though this had not been a concern of his before. This appeared to be a retaliatory measure—the use of the courts to strike back at the mother and to assert Justin's paternal rights within the paradigm of the new fatherhood.

Justin's case was unusual at the Norwich site. Very few of the men were brought before the court because their children had received public assistance. They were in the CSE system because mothers had filed for support—they were the so-called nonwelfare cases. A few of these men were struggling with the "half-paycheck" problem that Magistrate Aronowitz had identified—they were in second families and made poor wages that did not stretch far across the two households. One of the fathers said his whole paycheck went to child support, while his household lived off of his wife's check. Others complained about the expense of lawyers and some admitted to alcohol and drug problems. The quality of postseparation relationships varied, even though several expressed hostilities toward their former wives and partners. In estranged relationships, anger was directed at mothers and magistrates, while they relied on the program to assist them with court issues. Fatherhood was central to their narratives, and several of them reported that they appreciated the parent education program that the agency provided. Moreover, several of them talked about their devotion to their children and expressed their insistence that they see their children regularly. Jobs rarely provided satisfaction and the new fatherhood promoted by the program enabled them to deepen this part of their identities.

At the second FIP site, located in Bridgeport, fathers were more likely to be young racial minority men, living on the social and economic margins, struggling with limited education and marketable skills, little to no formal work history, unemployment or underemployment, probation and parole officers, anxiety and depression, the lack of transportation and driver's licenses, no medical insurance, no access to credit, and accumulating child support debt. They did not see the courts as an instrument of power that they might use to represent their interests—quite the contrary.

Most of the fathers in the Bridgeport FIP had accumulated child support arrearages due to incarceration. The program was directed by a young charismatic Puerto Rican man whom the fathers seemed to hold in high esteem. The director did what he could to assist the fathers in court, but his and their main interest was finding employment, which was a huge challenge for men with felony records. Despite the father's respect for the director, when the program failed to provide jobs, the men stopped showing up. The attrition rate in the program was very high. Only 10 percent of fathers entered the Bridgeport program with full-time jobs and 83 percent had arrest histories. After six months, only 17 percent were left in the program and, of those, 39 percent were employed full-time.[57]

The fathers who remained did rely on the director to help them with court issues. Many felt uncomfortable standing before a judge to represent themselves, and they rarely had the skills and experience to do so. We interviewed 19 fathers from this program. Nearly one-half had been incarcerated and were on probation or parole. Only two held full-time jobs, while four reported part-time employment. All of them had been involved in the street economy. For these men, their past experiences with the state had not been positive—in the schools, the welfare office, the police stations, or in the courts. Their failure to appear in court often reflected their feelings of vulnerability. Moreover, the practices of the court and the processes of modifying support orders and establishing visitation rights and custody were complex and culturally dislocating, and left the men feeling inadequate, scared, and misunderstood. Speaking for himself and others in his situation, 44-year-old Carlos said that a person:

> gets intimidated and gets fearful when you are in front of people who come down with a ruling or decision that devastate and change your life. And when it comes to your own personal family that's really devastating. They don't have no idea how much I have lived and done for many years. And then all of a sudden, they get into our lives within a couple of months, a month or whatever. They make this type of decision which is really traumatizing.

Fathers like Carlos had different perceptions of themselves from how they felt the magistrates saw them, especially when the magistrates' mission to get the money was expressed in threatening or contemptuous ways.

Arturo, a 25-year-old Puerto Rican father of two, felt the rebuke of the court even when he behaved proactively to inform them that he had lost his warehouse job and needed to modify his $50 a week child support payment. Already $3,900 in child support arrears and without a job, Arturo thought he would be praised by the magistrate for taking initiative. Instead, according to Arturo, the first words from the magistrate were: "Do you know I could hold you in contempt right now?" Startled, Arturo asked why and was told because he was not paying child support. Arturo said he responded, "That's why I came here to let you know that I can't pay because I am not working," conveying both confusion and exasperation. The magistrate spared Arturo jail, but only if he enrolled in the FIP and brought back evidence from the unemployment office that he was looking for work. Armed with the authority to incarcerate fathers for their support arrears, the magistrates' threats and chastisement left fathers feeling powerless and vulnerable, and at the mercy of the magistrates' discretion.

We have heard from several of the Bridgeport fathers already about their courtroom experiences—Rayshawn who opened the chapter about appearing before Magistrate Aronowitz just after his release from prison; Marcus who was confused by the magistrate's definition of what qualified as a job—a temp job versus an under-the-table job; Faheen who was losing sleep over the prospect of going to jail for the first time; and Chris and Richard who felt the courts were pushing them back to street life. These were fathers who feared the courts and were often unemployed with few job prospects. Their feelings of powerlessness and vulnerability also meant that they were more likely to have warrants for not appearing at court hearings. As in Rayshawn's case, this might be because they were in jail when the summons was sent. It might be because they were living at an address that the court was unaware of when they sent the summons. Or it could have been simply avoidance behavior to stay out of jail. Robbie was part of a round-up, and he did not remember receiving a summons. Robbie's case represented a generation of fathers attempting to navigate child support, unemployment, and the changing expectations concerning father involvement.

Robbie was a 32-year-old African American father from Bridgeport. His father was an absentee father, something that Robbie deeply resented. Robbie's father, however, paid child support. Robbie's father was not unlike a lot of fathers of his generation who paid child support but had little to nothing to do with their children. Robbie, on the other hand, was an involved father with two children from two mothers, but was unemployed, reportedly receiving $11 per week in unemployment compensation after losing a part-time job. Robbie owed $11,000 in child support arrears and was caught in one of Connecticut's "deadbeat dad sweeps." Robbie's story made the local newspapers—a deadbeat dad apprehended—while his father had been viewed years earlier as the model live-away parent because he paid his child support. And yet Robbie had relationships with his children, unlike his father. Robbie's mother paid $1,000 to get him out of jail after the sweep. Robbie described the incident.

> When we first went [to Child Support Enforcement] I guess they give you a paper or something and you got to come back in a year. I never received it, but even if I did receive it, I couldn't remember to come back in a year. So, I got rounded up. It was a deadbeat dad sweep. . . . I stopped by my mother's house to see if she wanted to see her granddaughter, spend some time with her. And the doorbell rings no sooner than I got there. I looked out and it was the sheriffs. I opened the door. So, I spent the weekend in there [jail] . . . Handcuffed me, dragged me out in front of the neighbors. Luckily it was early, but there were still people out there. Deadbeat dad roundup. It was just one of those things where I felt like my civil rights were violated because at the time I was paying child support. It was a misunderstanding that could have been avoided had they sent a letter out or something. I am pretty sure I know I would have went. [If] the only alternative you give me is to show up for court or get locked up, I am showing up for court.

Robbie and his father reflected a generational shift in norms and expectations, but Robbie's experience also enabled us to see that the story on the surface is not always the most accurate story. What's on paper—or in the papers—does not necessarily reflect a father's relationship with his children.[58]

Unlike the Norwich site, most of the Bridgeport fathers were summoned to the magistrate court because their children had been on the welfare rolls. This did not mean that the fathers felt any less ganged up on by mothers and magistrates, especially when relationships with mothers were estranged. Richard, a 33-year-old African American father, said:

> So on that day I went to court. I brung the fatherhood papers in and everything just went bad. They didn't even care about me. They didn't even care. And the judge looked at my baby's mother and asked her what she wanted to do and she said, "Lock him up." And the judge locked me up and I had $250 in my pocket.

Several of the fathers indicated that without the FIP they would have avoided the courts and remained at large. The program had enabled them to enter the courtroom and navigate complex contingencies, just as it supported and nurtured a father identity. However, when we consider that only 17 percent of

fathers remained in the Bridgeport program after six months, we might sur-
mise that many of them felt like there was no hope for their circumstances,
even with the director in their corner. They were unemployed with felony
records, felt that the courts, if not the mothers, were against them, and could
not see how anything could change their circumstances. They may have
appreciated the efforts made by program staff, but ultimately, they were
acting with their feet.

In summary, the two FIP sites provided a few similarities, but many more
differences. Men in both programs felt that the culture of the CSE system was
biased toward mothers and was out to get them. In some respects, of course,
they were right. These efforts were an attempt to address the inequities that
occurred after divorce, or when fathers refused to contribute toward children
born out of wedlock. Moreover, the courts provided a mechanism for dealing
with the "half paycheck" problem when fathers had children in more than
one household and made incomes that could, at best, contribute minimally
to each of them. The FIPs responded to this differently.

In Norwich, the program served mostly white fathers and the emphasis
was on fathers' rights. Many of these men were in estranged relationships with
the mothers of their children, and they were brought before the magistrates
when mothers filed suits against them. They were bitter and resentful, and
felt victimized by these processes. They advanced a sense of entitlement in
the courts and were supported by program staff. They attempted to invert
the court mechanism to their own advantage, under the assertion that if they
paid, then they had distinctive rights to their children and that mothers had
to adjust to their needs and desires to see their children. In this way, mothers
could not act as gatekeepers, and fathers could develop relationships with
their children more or less independently of mothers. In many instances,
however, this turned up the heat on contentious relationships that valorized
gendered struggles for power and control.

Most of the fathers in the Bridgeport programs, on the other hand, were
issued child support orders because their children had received public assistance. These men, mostly black and brown, were usually unemployed or underemployed and were involved in the criminal justice system. Several had
accumulated debt while they were incarcerated. Relationships with mothers
varied more for these men. Some were in contentious relationships in which
they, like the Norwich fathers, felt as if they were being dragged into a father-
bashing courtroom. Others were in cooperative relationships, which were
disrupted by the paternalism and aggression of the CSE system. Moreover,

these men were the faces of deadbeat dads, which reflected the inspiration of CSE legislation to remedy the problem of father absence and cultural pathology in the inner city. Most program participants left the program because it could not provide them with what they wanted most—jobs. For those who remained, the FIP helped fathers negotiate a hostile system and prevented some from resorting to their default disposition—to avoid or run from state authority. Moreover, the program provided these men with a sense of value as fathers—a discourse that for some of them centered their identities and offered purpose in otherwise bleak life circumstances. We will learn more about this in Chapters 7 and 8.

State Austerity and Child Support Enforcement

As we have seen, child support collections from welfare families fell continually across the decade, from a peak recovery rate of 31 percent in 2002, to 22 percent in 2005, to merely 18 percent at the end of the decade. Together, states rang up more than $700 million in deficit spending in 2010 to chase these monies, while total arrears soared to well over $100 billion. A large part of this decrease was attributable to declining welfare caseloads and the limited amounts of money that states could squeeze from fathers of low-income families remaining on the rolls.[59] For instance, an internal CSE report in Connecticut determined that in 2007, 40 percent of the noncustodial parents with open child support cases had been formerly incarcerated and that 11 percent were currently incarcerated. Looking at these data more closely, they found that noncustodial parents with criminal records were three times less likely to pay their child support in full, and that one-half of them paid nothing toward their child support orders.[60] In other words, socially and economically marginalized fathers were unlikely to pay much, if anything, toward current orders and accumulated arrears. These findings were not unique. A 2010 national study by Laura Wheaton and Elaine Sorensen of the Urban Institute found that only one-fourth of fathers living outside of the home making less than $34,000 paid the full amount of their child support orders, while less than 5 percent of fathers earning below the poverty line for a single household ($10,830) were able to make these payments.[61]

In 2005, Congress made some changes to the CSE system by passing the Deficit Reduction Act (DRA). The DRA changed the incentive formulas so that states would receive less federal dollars for collections. The decline in state child support revenues already had resulted in cutbacks in CSE appropriations and in fatherhood programs. The DRA budgeted a mere $50 million to promote fatherhood programs (and $150 million to promote marriage), which did not go very far across the country. Foremost, the DRA allowed states to pass-through $100 each month to TANF families and $200 if they had two or more children, without having to pay the federal government its share of those monies.[62] Some states (Connecticut one of them) experimented with passing through the entire payment collected.[63] These policies established the potential of turning a cost recovery and cost avoidance program into a governmental subsidy program that would increase, however modestly, the incomes of the poorest families. However, there were two key problems with the DRA.

First, the DRA did not require states to adopt the pass-through policy—it was voluntary. The states' willingness to turn child support enforcement into a subsidy program varied by state and required states to invest more of their own monies into fatherhood programs. Research had shown that when states use more of their own money to fund fatherhood programs, the outcomes were better compared to states that rely mostly on federal subsidies.[64] Still the problem remained that some states would make these investments while others would not—or at least not without significant political organizing around the issue to pressure state legislatures.

After the 2008 recession that sent shocks through the financial system and turned states into dens of austerity, the DRA incentives to provide more subsidies dissipated. Moreover, it appears that once states adopted their child support policies after the collapse, they were reluctant to change them. If we compare data on pass-through state policies between 2008 and 2016, we see that, for the most part, states refused to adopt generous pass-through strategies. In 2008, more than one-half of states (27) provided no pass-through monies, ten states provided $50, and only seven states passed through the entire payment to welfare families. In 2016, little had changed—one-half of states (25) did not pass through any of the payment to families, and now only five states passed through the entire amount. Ten states had changed their pass-through policies between 2008 and 2016, with one-half passing on more money and one-half passing on less.[65] Our analysis reinforced the 2011 GAO report that concluded:

Most states nationwide have not implemented "family first" policy options since DRA. Several state CSE officials GAO interviewed said they support "family first" policies in principle, but funding constraints prevented implementing these options, because giving more child support collections to families means states retain less as reimbursement for public assistance costs.[66]

With 50 different child support enforcement systems, it was apparent that implementation would be uneven across the country, but it was also apparent that state fiscal crises would result in most, if not all, state governments putting fiscal concerns above family concerns.

The second and more important problem was that the DRA, like most other policy initiatives on the table, was not going to address the needs of the most socially and economically marginalized fathers—the structurally unemployed and underemployed—despite the research that had been done on fatherhood programs intended to reach this population.[67] Welfare reform and child support enforcement had clearly exposed the limitations of the market in meeting the needs of low-income populations, and so had the ballooning amount of child support debt that remained on the books.

Conclusion

While neoliberalism was increasing insecurities among workers and families in a highly dynamic and competitive economy, the discussions among lawmakers, media pundits, academics, and nonprofit leaders doubled-down on the cultural pathologies of black and brown inner cities. How were these incendiary spaces to be managed and controlled became a predominant concern. In other words, as major transformations were occurring within the political economy, social policy focused on shoring up and reaffirming racial and class hierarchies.

As the economy provided less for those at the bottom of the labor force, the institutional strategies of poverty governance increased state authority in determining compliance to declining market conditions. Further, as the perspective that government spending on the poor was nonproductive and wasteful became dominant in the neoliberal context, state assistance was retrenched and tied more closely to behavioral requirements, while the needs of families were more firmly embedded in market contingencies and family caretaking.

CSE extended the arm of the state as part of its reformulation of poverty governance. The poster boy of the system remains the "deadbeat dad" and CSE wields extraordinary power over indigent fathers whose lives are being managed by debt and punishment, many of whom will never be able to pay off their debt in a lifetime. These are economically and socially marginalized fathers who have been most affected by the changing post-1970s labor force and by the reorganization of the neoliberal state. Moreover, these fathers— the deadbeat dads—join teen moms, welfare queens, gang bangers, and drug dealers as symbolically the scourge on a market economy that therefore require tough-love paternalism from the courts, police, welfare bureaucrats, social service providers, and teachers to get their lives in order. These institutional processes discipline the bottom of the labor force into the new normal of underemployment, without any pretensions of a living wage, pension, medical care, vacations, or sick leave. By keeping our eyes trained on the deadbeat dad, we need only to rehabilitate him, and given the debt leverage against him, we have a lifetime to do so.

These state systems are filled with professionals, like Magistrate Aronowitz, who are doing their jobs effectively, passionately, and with good intentions. In fact, Magistrate Aronowitz summed up well the problems he faced in trying to figure out how to make inadequate resources stretch across more than one household, and he recognized that mothers were often the main victims of these dynamics. What could have developed as an instrumental mechanism to address gender inequities stemming from increases in divorce, cohabitation, blended families, single parenthood, nonmarital births, and father self-indulgence instead became a punitive mechanism for controlling and symbolically denigrating the most marginalized populations. This was easily justified as an endeavor to make sure that mothers and children were getting the resources they deserved and needed to raise children— it was a socially honorable quest. However, most of the money collected from poor fathers was going to taxpayers, and, besides, had the state been serious about transferring resources to poor and working-class families, there were clearly better ways of doing so. Further, dynamics in the courtroom and among CSE professionals turned these distributional mechanisms into symbolic practices that impugned the poor and rearticulated racial and class hierarchies.[68]

In short, CSE advanced a gendered understanding of the problem, which indeed was warranted, but did so by neglecting racial and class inequalities. As Laura Curran and Laura Abrams explain, this "reasoning reduces male powerlessness to the axis of gender and ignores other structural impediments such as race and class marginalization."[69] Without a narrative that would recognize and affirm their racial and class vulnerabilities, it is no surprise that fathers directed blame at mothers and the courts, or that they felt ganged up on. To fully understand the depth of their racial and class vulnerabilities, and how these dynamics were affecting fatherhood, in Part 2 of our book, we focus exclusively on the most marginalized fathers in our study.

PART 2

SOCIAL AND ECONOMIC MARGINALIZATION

5

Public Housing and the Streets

I'm not saying that I carry my thing all the time, but when times get rough and I get nervous, I get scared. I am going to pop my heat, man. [laughs] By all means . . . I'm not going to call it do or die. I call it "If I got to beef with you, I'm going to get you before you get me." I not out there for beefs, not at all . . . but the way the streets is, man, listen here, I ain't going to be that one, hell no. I'm straight . . . can't be me, not at all.

—Jamal

Slovakian-born Roman Catholic priest Father Stephen Panik would not miss the groundbreaking ceremony for Yellow Mill Village in Bridgeport in 1939, Connecticut's first public housing project. Father Panik had lobbied hard for the project, which he called "the greatest Christmas present Bridgeport has ever received."[1] Mayor Jasper McLevy was also there. A socialist mayor, elected by a strong industrial unionized labor force in early 1930s, McLevy referred to the Village as "the biggest event in the history of Bridgeport."[2] Even Governor Wilbur Cross got into the act. He asserted that the development would "take boys and girls off the streets and into the playgrounds" and declared that "good housing open to sunlight and fresh air and ample play areas are the best preventatives against disease and crime." Yellow Mill Village included 40 acres, 36 buildings, a shopping center, a playground, and apartments adorned with lace curtains and copper awnings.[3]

In June 1940, six months after the ceremony in Bridgeport, ground-breaking occurred at the first housing development in the state capitol, which would be quickly followed by two more in 1941. Again, the rhetoric of hope and opportunity prevailed, only this time, it was State Senator Alfred N. Bingham who waxed patriotic at one of the Hartford ceremonies:

It's a Setup. Timothy Black and Sky Keyes, Oxford University Press (2021). © Timothy Black and Sky Keyes.
DOI: 10.1093/oso/9780190062217.003.0005

Here will be 500 families more with a stake in the democratic way of life, a stake that they lack so long as their country allows their children to grow up in unhealthy back alleys. We can no longer afford slums. We can no longer afford poverty in America. The contest between totalitarianism and democracy is a contest between two ways of life. It must be won on the home front as well as on foreign battlefields.[4]

Similar speeches were being made by public dignitaries at new public housing developments throughout the country over the next few decades.

By the 1990s—only 50 years later—these same housing projects had fallen into disrepair and had become places where residents struggled to create healthy, safe environments to raise children. Yellow Mill Village, renamed Father Panik Village in 1955, was already half demolished, with the remainder scheduled to be raised in 1994. Poverty, illicit drug markets, drug addiction, and violence invaded the lives of residents who had moved into these housing projects in more promising times. The New Deal strategy to build safe and inspiring public housing for the poor turned out to be an historical anomaly.

Slumlords had long extracted exploitative rents from poor immigrants and southern black migrants pouring into the cities looking for work in the early part of the century.[5] However, amid the greatest economic crisis to confront the modern world, the National Housing Act was launched in 1937 with the hope that it would stimulate the economy and expand opportunities for the poor. Nonetheless, capital interests had registered their opposition to public housing from the beginning and had a strong impact in limiting its capacity and its quality.[6] Awash in money during the postwar years, capital accumulation strategies would eventually turn to suburban development, leaving behind fiscally declining cities and redlined poor black neighborhoods. Highway construction, urban renewal, housing policies, budget cuts, and racial segregation led to the decline of these housing developments, as many became spaces of social and economic exclusion.[7]

By the new millennium, not only had the conditions of public housing become a social hazard in many cities, but the availability of housing for the poor had also become a crisis. As Matthew Desmond points out in his groundbreaking book, *Evicted*, by 2013, the percentage of the rental poor living in public housing had fallen to 15 percent, while those receiving some form of government subsidy—mostly housing vouchers—added another 17 percent. This means that two-thirds of the poor are receiving no housing support, pushing them into the shadow economy of overpriced, poorly maintained housing.[8] With neoliberal changes to the labor market, the reduction in state support, the increase in debt and punishment, and the geographical disinvestment in poor black and brown urban areas, the result has been what Desmond describes as incarceration for black men and evictions for black women.[9]

The response to the devastation created by the demise of public housing and the systematic neglect of black and brown urban neighborhoods was to police and incarcerate the problem—to increase surveillance, militarize the police, and build more prisons. In other words, it was to meet violence with violence. It is important to place this issue in its social historical context—to understand how public housing could be launched with such public exuberance and then fall into the cauldron of capital reorganization, racial segregation, discrimination, and systemic exclusion. It is in this context that opportunity structures were (re)created, dreams were engendered, decisions were made, and lives were funneled into interpersonal violence and deep enclaves of personal distress. We need to realize that this is the backstory to the lives of many marginalized fathers; and to fully understand fathering on the margins, we must first understand this backstory.

In this chapter and the next, we focus on the most marginalized fathers in our study. It is perhaps more apparent that prisons have become an institutional mechanism for warehousing the most socially and economically marginalized populations in the United States—those who have become largely redundant in the post-1970s neoliberal economy or who have refused to accept their place within a precarious labor force.[10] But public housing developments in the 1970s and after also provided a similar institutional mechanism—they became depositories for the poorest families in urban America.

A little less than one-fourth of the men in our study spent some of their childhood growing up in a public housing development, and nearly all of these men were racial minorities (93 percent). Further, among this group, nearly three-quarters of them were either locked up or unemployed at the time of the interview. This does not include fathers who grew up in surrounding neighborhoods, many of which had similar reputations as the "PJs" themselves. It is in these urban spaces where they became exposed to the drug trade, robberies, and structural and interpersonal violence, and it is here where they became fathers.

Its Origins and Its Demise in Connecticut

The 1937 National Housing Act gave birth to Housing Authorities in cities throughout the country with the charge of planning urban housing. The chief purpose of the legislation was to stimulate the economy during the Great Depression and to create temporary shelter for transitional populations and better housing for slum dwellers. Public housing developments shot up in Connecticut cities in the 1940s, especially in prosperous industrial centers along the rivers flowing southward through the state and emptying into Long Island Sound.

In the 1940s, with the advance of World War II, public housing in Connecticut was expanded to house industrial workers and to address housing shortages for migrants pouring into the cities to obtain industrial jobs. Connecticut had been an arms manufacturer long before the war. In 1914, a contract to produce 37,500 rifles for the Czar in Russia created the largest factory in America at the time, the Union Metallic Cartridge Company in Bridgeport, which became known as the "Russian Rifle" plant.[11] But it was Remington in Bridgeport, Colt in Hartford, and Winchester in New Haven that laid the foundation for Connecticut's early reputation as a military contractor. Yellow Mill Village rapidly became home to many workers in the defense industries in the 1940s, while public housing expanded rapidly in other Connecticut cities to house defense workers.

Hartford already included 52 defense-related industries at the time of the bombing at Pearl Harbor, and plans went into effect immediately to add 11,000 workers by the middle of 1942.[12] The fourth public housing development in the city, Charter Oak Terrace, would be built during this time in the southwest corner of the city on sprawling farmland along the Park River. Charter Oak was among 128 public housing developments planned across the country to house defense workers as the war-time economy advanced, and its 1,000 units would be the largest in New England. Applications overwhelmed the opening of Charter Oak Terrace in late 1941, where two-thirds of residents would work for the three largest defense manufacturers in the city.[13]

During the war and in its aftermath, public housing provided shelter for manufacturing workers and temporary housing for soldiers returning from the war, while they accumulated enough savings to take advantage of housing subsidy programs available to veterans.[14] But there were problems in sustaining public housing in the United States from the beginning. Despite its celebrations and its symbolism of hope, private developers had lobbied against using expensive materials or elaborate designs in the construction of public housing when the act was passed in 1937, and within a decade, many of these buildings were already in need of steady repair.[15] Efforts to undermine public housing continued through key housing acts in 1949 and 1954. As David Ratcliffe explained, "Claiming that such housing was the opening wedge of socialism, the industry convinced Congress in 1949 to limit public housing to the very poor," which required an exodus of residents in public housing who had incomes over the threshold.[16]

In 1954, the Housing Act shifted priorities from low-income housing to urban renewal, directing public monies toward private development. Federally guaranteed mortgages and redlining were providing an exclusive ticket for whites to move to the suburbs, while manufacturing plants were moving to industrial parks outside of the cities or to the anti-union south. Consequently, cities were becoming blacker and poorer.[17] Urban renewal was an attempt to slow, if not reverse, this trend, but it resulted in less commitment to housing provision for the poor. In New Haven, Connecticut, for instance, by 1966, less than 1 percent of new units were built for low-income families, while the waiting list for public housing reached above 1,500 families. Moreover, the rate of demolition of low-income housing in the city to provide spaces for urban renewal projects far exceeded the low-income housing being built, which became a national trend after 1954.[18]

In 1969, Congress passed the Brooke Amendment, which capped the amount that families receiving public housing would pay toward rent to 25 percent of their income. This was landmark legislation that provided important income relief to many families, but it placed more strain on operating budgets. In response, Hartford Housing Authority Chairman submitted a letter to Washington decrying that the legislation "cost the Hartford Housing Authority over $1 million, wiping out slender reserves. We've had to make drastic cutbacks in services to all our clients."[19]

Despite promises to plug these holes, the federal government would make deep cuts in the public housing budget in the ensuing decades. In the 1970s, the loss of manufacturing jobs and the exodus of middle-income families pushed cities toward fiscal collapse. Public housing developments not only suffered from these forces but also from high inflation in the 1970s that increased the costs of labor and materials, the loss of revenue tied to the 1969 Brooke Amendment, and Nixon's moratorium on "all federally subsidized housing programs" in 1973.

When Nixon took office in 1969, 29 percent of all housing production in the United States was federally subsidized; by 1972, this figure had dropped to 14 percent—before the housing freeze.[20] Fiscally deprived cities could do little to fill the void. Large-scale repairs were desperately needed, but unaffordable, while basic services were neglected, including road repair, public safety, garbage collection, and school transportation. Cities were broke, and poor neighborhoods and public housing were not at the top of their priority lists.[21]

One glaring illustration was in Hartford, where housing abandonment, declining city services, and public housing neglect resulted in a rat infestation in the south end of the city in the area of Charter Oak Terrace. In 1978, a pastor of a city church organized a rat day, in which he and others collected bushels of live rats that they intended to let loose in a downtown federal building. The day before the action was to take place, HUD appropriated $1 million for extermination practices and other improvements to the public housing stock. Forty units at Charter Oak Terrace were restored with this money, the first time that any improvements had been made on the premises since its opening in 1941.[22]

After the 1970s, public housing developments became blacker and poorer, and more socially and economically isolated.[23] In New Haven, Hartford, and Bridgeport, units remained vacant and in disrepair, and the targets of vandalism and youth rebellion. Many of the residents in public housing were deeply invested in their communities and some had lived in the developments for decades. Tenant councils organized and fought back against deteriorating conditions, while waiting lists for housing continued to grow. Father Panik Village housed a formidable tenant council.[24] However, drugs and violence had consumed the Village in the 1980s, where homicides averaged four to five a year. Council leaders stressed that most of the drug dealers did not live in the buildings, but that physical structures had made it easy for drug dealers to operate in boarded-up apartments, dark hallways, and doorless entryways.[25] Outsiders were invading their communities, while the public scapegoated them.[26]

By the 1980s, with the flourishing cocaine drug trade, public housing was awash in governmental neglect, flatlined budgets, crime, and violence. The Reagan administration responded with more budget cuts to housing and beefed up law enforcement. In fact, no president did more to decimate public housing than Ronald Reagan. Funds for subsidized housing were cut from $26 to $2 billion between 1981 and 1985, while housing starts fell from

185,000 in 1980 to 28,000 in 1985. Housing had become an incendiary issue in the 1970s, stoked by housing and school desegregation efforts, which made it a politically expedient issue for Reagan. Addressing the Urban League in 1985, HUD Deputy Assistant Secretary stated, "We're basically backing out of the business of housing, period."[27]

Outlaw capitalism took hold in many of these public housing complexes. As city resources plunged in the 1980s and 1990s, the international drug trade became more organized to meet the demand of soaring illicit drug consumption in the United States and Europe. Public housing developments became drug distribution centers in many urban neighborhoods—what residents in New Haven referred to as "insulated crime dens."[28] Further, the labyrinths of interstate highways that cut through cities near public housing complexes created ideal conditions for open-air drug markets. In the early 1990s, the Bridgeport police chief said that suburban drug users accounted for 70 percent of drug sales in the city and that Father Panik Village had become an ideal location for sales because of its location next to Interstate 95.[29]

The illicit drug trade became defended and enforced by paramilitary street organizations, while violent drug turf wars rolled through cities in Connecticut and elsewhere. In New Haven, housing developments that had been the neighborhood anchors in more prosperous times would become markers of rival gangs in illicit drug markets.[30] These groups would compete, negotiate, merge with, and sometimes evolve from larger street gangs— like the Latin Kings, and then later the Crips, Bloods, and Black Gangster Disciples—in carving up territorial spaces of the drug trade.[31]

Charter Oak Terrace in Hartford—the development that had been built to house defense workers in 1941—would illustrate these conditions far too well. Hartford is not a black-white city. In 1990, Puerto Ricans numbered 60,000 in Hartford and, by the turn of the century, the Puerto Rican diaspora extending from New Britain, Connecticut, to Holyoke, Massachusetts, was arguably the largest on the mainland. At the beginning of the new millennium, Hartford would elect the first Puerto Rican mayor to office in a US city. By the 1980s and 1990s, the city had become extremely racially and ethnically segregated with blacks concentrated in the north end and Puerto Ricans in the south end. The majority of the residents at Charter Oak Terrace were Puerto Rican and, in the 1980s, the development had become a warehouse for the poor, with 70 percent unemployed, 85 percent headed by single mothers, and an average family income of less than $10,000.[32]

One Latino street gang, Los Solidos, controlled one-half of the Charter Oak complex in the 1990s, while the other half was staked out by their rival gang, the Latin Kings. Gun violence escalated and, by 1994, Hartford's crime rate had jumped ahead of Detroit, Washington, DC, and New York City to be the fourth highest in the nation.[33] Public housing residents bore the brunt of these exploding circumstances, as did neighborhood residents. The tenant's association at Charter Oak Terrace and a neighborhood organization were spurred into action, but it was the shooting death of a seven-year-old cradled in the lap of her mother sitting in the passenger seat of a car in front of the housing development that horrified the city.[34] The car had been mistaken for belonging to a rival gang member and peppered with bullets.

The solutions in Connecticut cities followed the models that were being developed throughout the nation—to beef up militant anti-gang and incarceration strategies and raze and rebuild public housing. In the former, RICO statutes that had been devised in the 1970s to incarcerate organized crime members were employed to lock up street gang members.[35] Wiretap-generated gang sweeps resulted in sending many black and brown youth to prison, where they would remain for years and age into adulthood. Meanwhile, dilapidated public housing would be targeted for demolition and new construction that would reduce its size, would restrict its occupancy through rigorous selection criteria, and would attempt to economically stabilize the areas through homeownership, mixed-income strategies, and more attractive designs.[36]

Certainly, by the 1990s, varying forces had created the perfect storm: urban fiscal crisis, federal and state welfare retrenchment, massive unemployment, concentrated urban poverty and social exclusion, lucrative illicit drug markets, and a militant governmental war on drugs.[37] Cities had become poorer and public housing developments, once the beacon of neighborhood hope, had deteriorated into depositories for concentrating the poorest black and brown residents of the city. In the early decades of the 21st century, these buildings were being torn down and residents displaced and dispersed into already distressed communities. Some of the fathers in our study who grew up in these developments experienced these demolitions, displacements, and relocations, and some were from families who had resided there for several generations. Moreover, their experiences demonstrated the changing opportunity structure that drug markets provided, as poverty became more entrenched in their cities, neighborhoods, and schools. Their lives would un-fold within these historical circumstances, and it is here that they would be-come fathers.

Living the Dream

I'd be there every year for the reunion.

—Richard

Many of the fathers in our study were exposed to the drug trade as young boys—to its attractions, drama, and risks.[38] Richard, the 33-year-old father whom the magistrate had told in the prior chapter to return to his court with $1,500 in hand, grew up in Father Panik Village. He had fond memories of the Village and expressed his strong attachment to it, even after it had been razed in 1994: "I'd be there every year for the reunion." He also explained that his entrance into the drug trade at Father Panik was easy. "You lived next door to the biggest drug dealer. You see him every morning. You idolize them sometime, you know? They had everything, big cars, nice vans, brand new sneakers; I mean they didn't have to work. I just flow right into the system."

Colin, a 19-year-old African American father, who grew up in a different Bridgeport housing development—PT Barnum—explained that his older brother had exposed him to the trade. He started by holding drugs for a pros-perous dealer, "and I was getting paid," he added. Then Colin was asked to sell marijuana.

> I am like "Well, yeah, I could sell some weed." And when he got it, I am thinking I am going to make a couple hundred dollars and then here he comes and he has thousands of dollars worth of weed and I am like, "Man, I'm never going to be able to sell all this." And when I got started, I mean two weeks; I was like, "Whoa!" It was gone. I mean like $10,000 in like two weeks. And my cut was long and I am like "Man, I can do this." And then I just got smarter and smarter. You just evolve in it. Some don't. Some do. I am like, man, I want to be my own boss, and he telling me, "Man, get your money involved." So that was it. I knew math. I knew my weight. School smarts was street smarts and it got on from there. It was just something that you grow and you get more experienced at it. You learn more at it.

Established in the drug trade, Colin became a father at age 17. He had never been incarcerated on a drug charge, but he was in prison during our interview for a probation violation stemming from a domestic violence charge.

Most of the fathers talked about entering the drug trade at very early ages. Jacob was 12 when he began selling: "I just went and got my first pack [of heroin], like a half a stack, five bundles." Jacob, with mixed Puerto Rican and African American ancestry, was an 18-year-old Hartford father of two—a daughter and son, each just shy of four and three years of age. He grew up in Hartford and had been locked up for most of the prior three years and was not due for release for another year on a robbery charge. Turning over heroin and crack was easy, he claimed, and as he aged, his skills and connections increased to where he was making huge windfalls of money. He continues:

> Your eyes just glow green like, "Damn!" . . . dope [heroin] is the number-one drug. It goes fast. And then crack goes. . . . I lived in a million-dollar project. So everywhere you walked somebody wanted something. I started getting on. Started getting them on the cell phone, the pager. Started getting the money. Just not going to school. Waking up like I am going to real work; six in the morning, I was there hustling.

Elmore was so young that he could not remember his age when he started. "I was like 11, no, younger than that," he said. Unsure, he added, "All my life I was around it." A 19-year-old African American father of a 2-year-old daughter, Elmore had been displaced from the housing development he grew up in during its conversion. With his skills, he found similar opportunities in his new location. "When we moved out the projects, I moved to a neighborhood. It was the same way as the projects was. And then we moved from that neighborhood to another neighborhood. . . . It was just all the same." Elmore was serving a two-year sentence for drug possession.

The drug trade was lucrative and provided an opportunity structure that resembled the American dream—the rags to riches story—to these young fathers growing up in public housing.[39] As corner boys, they were a small part of the illicit global drug market, but their eyes glowed green, as Jacob said, especially when they looked around at how others were living in their respective communities.[40] Like Jacob and Elmore, all of the fathers in our study involved in the drug trade started at very early ages; they flowed right into the system, as Richard said. Going to work in the trade, leaving school for "real work," and earning money, they also became fathers at early ages. But risks came with the lawlessness of the trade, and they had to prepare themselves for violence.

Illicit drug dealers create organizations that compete with other organizations over market share, territorial dominance, supply chains, delivery methods, marketing strategies, and product development.[41] However, these business operations are not governed by law. Consequently, disputes are not mediated in courts or argued before arbitrators of the law. In lieu of this structure, organizations expand and protect their own business operations through gun violence. Moreover, the lawlessness of the trade encourages start-up operations—especially when law enforcement alters market dynamics after drug sweeps—that violently challenge established groups for market shares. Networks of predatory stick-up artists also target lucrative members of drug markets for cash, and sometimes large quantities of drugs, that in turn may provide venture capital to start their own drug operations.[42] This outlaw capitalism has resulted in the development of a violent street culture, in which youth socialized into these trades prepare their minds and bodies for violence.[43]

Gun Violence

Several of the fathers in our study who grew up in public housing developments witnessed gun violence. Chris is the 23-year-old African American father who told us in the last chapter that his encounters with the magistrate had left him unable to sleep at night and wondering if he would need to rob someone to pay his child support and, ironically, stay out of jail. Chris was raised in Father Panik Village, where he witnessed a shooting.

CHRIS: While I saw dudes sitting there and bleeding I used to sit there and watch. Everybody be like "Call the cops. Call the cops." I said, "Hey look, I ain't calling nothing."

RON: You saw him get shot?

CHRIS: Yeah.

RON: Did he die?

CHRIS: No, he sitting there bleeding, hurting. See the smoke coming out through there.

RON: Out of where?

CHRIS: Dude's leg.

RON: The smoke?

CHRIS: It was hot. The heat.

RON: Well, I don't know what's you talking about, man? [both laugh]

CHRIS: When people get shot, man, it burns on the inside, you see smoke . . .

RON: Coming out the body?

CHRIS: Yeah.

RON: So anybody you knew?

CHRIS: Yeah, I knew him. My mother used to talk to him that's why I knew him. I didn't like him.

Ron had a hard time imagining what Chris was describing—smoke coming out of the body. More disturbing, though, was that Chris's description of the event was dispassionate and his concern for the young man indifferent. Chris was a lot more stirred up after his meeting with the magistrate than he was about a shooting he had witnessed. He shrugged and said, "I seen a lot of things." Chris, whose involvement in the drug trade began at age 12, was the father of two boys, ages seven and five.

Nineteen-year-old Colin, whose brother paved his way to becoming a lucrative drug dealer, described the violence he saw at the PT Barnum projects.

There's a lot of drugs where I'm from, it's just all around . . . Waking up, I heard a lot of gun shots. I seen people get shot. I seen people just walk up and just shoot people, point blank in their head [long pause]. You see a guy walk up with a gun, point it at the guy's head, and I turned my head and, pow, you heard the pop. I look and the guy is laying there leaking. . . . A guy sliced my ear right here. I got stitches in my ear. Stitches in my forehead— getting hit with a big rock.

Red, a 26-year-old African American father of a two-year-old boy, was expecting his second child at the time of the interview. He also talked about growing up in the PT Barnum projects. "Back in the day it was real wild. If I could change anything, I would change that whole environment we was living in. . . . I've seen a lot of violence there," Red acknowledged. He said that he did not participate in the violence, but he had to learn to navigate it in public spaces where he lived. His memories of the violence he witnessed remained vivid.

Actually, I was going to my grandmother's house one day. They started shooting. Somebody was shooting him in the back while he was running. He just fell out, right there. And I saw another dude get shot like almost 16 or 17 times. Holding an ice cream. Fell and everything, still holding the ice cream. Laying on the ground, still holding it and then eventually he just let it go. He still lived through that though. He lived through that because it was all in his leg. They wasn't trying to kill him. They was just trying to hurt him up, from one leg to another leg. Bam. Bam. Bam. Back and forth. Until he fell. He was standing up for a while, that's what it was. If he had just fell, they would have stopped early. He was trying to take it.

Like Chris, Red's exposure to violence made him indifferent toward it or, as he said, "It's a way of life." Ron pushed him on this.

RON: Is it scary? Does it make you anxious?
RED: It ain't affect me . . .
RON: Do you think it could happen to you?
RED: Yeah. Hell, yeah. It could happen to me. It could. Everything is a possibility. It could happen to you, too. It could happen to anybody.
RON: Yeah, anybody?
RED: Anybody, anywhere, doing anything. You could be going to the ATM machine or something and you just catch somebody at that wrong time.

Certainly, anyone could be a victim of a robbery or an act of violence, but Red's exposure to violence and his needs to navigate it were clearly a consequence of growing up in his social circumstances. Neither he nor Chris was incarcerated at the time of their interviews, but both had been before—Chris for domestic violence and Red for a probation violation stemming from a drug transaction charge.

Donnie, a 19-year-old African American father who grew up in New Haven housing projects, was also familiar with violence. He had been involved in the drug trade and stabbed once. He was the father of two—a three-year-old and one-year-old—and was locked up on a domestic violence charge and for a probation violation, a failure to appear in court. He described an incident in which he transported a victim of gun violence to the hospital emergency room.

DONNIE: Yeah. I brung people to the hospital and stuff.
RON: Oh, you have?

DONNIE: Yeah.

RON: Could you tell me about one time? I don't need to know who it was. Just give me a situation.

DONNIE: We was outside, somebody just jumped out of the car and just started shooting. Shot him up. Shot him at least like nine times.

RON: Nine times?

DONNIE: I had to bring him to the hospital. I took my car and they kept it for a while.

RON: The police?

DONNIE: Yeah.

RON: Because you took him to the hospital?

DONNIE: Yeah. . . . And in the projects if somebody gets hurts, the ambulance take forever so I had to bring him to the hospital. I brung a couple people to the hospital a couple of times.

RON: The ambulance don't come quick?

DONNIE: They don't come quick.

RON: Because it's the projects?

DONNIE: Yeah. If it's somebody white, you know they going to go there quick. They ain't worried about no black people.

RON: You ever seen anybody die?

DONNIE: Yeah.

INTERVIEWER: What are you thinking when you see something like that happen?

DONNIE: Just you got to move on. You can't dwell on it. It will eat you up if you keep dwelling on it. But you just got to keep it moving.

Chris, Red, and Donnie witnessed life-threatening violence and had learned to "just keep moving," to accept it for what it was, as part of living in and around public housing in the 1990s. If you resided there, random events of violence had to be reckoned with, whether you were directly involved or not.[44] Gun violence was a form of aggression and protection. People armed themselves for many reasons, including to protect their income-generating practices, to expand their businesses into other areas, and to protect themselves.

Dante carried a gun to protect himself and his profits after his rise in the drug trade. Dante was a 20-year-old African American father from Bridgeport. His early exposure to the drug trade resulted in him dropping out of school after a two-week school suspension for skipping class, and devoting himself full-time to making money in the trade. He was the father of a daughter, nearly two years of age, and had just been released after serving 11 months in prison for possession of narcotics.

RON: You were in the streets before you were 16?

DANTE: Yeah.

RON: How did you happen to end up out there?

DANTE: I just followed the wrong path. I wanted to be like this person with a good name, like you wild. I just wanted to be in the crowd. So I did. I made a name for myself.

RON: Doing what?

DANTE: Just getting money. It's all material things, showing off for the girls, man. Looking good for the girls, going out with my fellas, having a good time.

RON: Okay.

DANTE: Being grown before I'm supposed to be.

RON: So how did you start selling drugs?

DANTE: I said, I was following the wrong crowd. I seen my people they getting money. I seen the money they was getting and I was like "I want to get money, too."

Dante described his "rags to riches" story.

DANTE: I went to the people, like they would put me on.

RON: Did you have to pay anything up front?

DANTE: Nah. Give you like say 15 bags, that's $150.

RON: Bags of what?

DANTE: Crack.

RON: Oh, okay. That's $150.

DANTE: So, sell that, give them back $100 and keep $50. So, saving my money . . . Got my own.

INTERVIEWER: Oh, okay. So now you are independent?

DANTE: Yeah, yeah. So now I am cool with everybody. So, it wasn't no problem for me to be out there with my own stuff. And then I had other people under me now . . . and then I got deep into it. I started, like, it was me and my man. I wasn't worried about nobody else. We had our little phone. Driving around, making mad sales all day.

RON: How much money would you say you ever made in one day?

DANTE: I was making like 3 Gs.
RON: 3 G's? In a day?
DANTE: [agrees]
RON: You were making mad money. So you get addicted to it after a while?
DANTE: The lifestyle, yeah.

As Dante developed his business and hired more people to work for him, he also had to protect himself from stick-up artists that targeted drug dealers on the rise.

RON: Was it dangerous?
DANTE: Yeah, because you got people that don't like you. People hating on you. See you shining and they want to take your shine.
RON: They want to take your shine?
DANTE: They see you doing your thing and people hate on you.
RON: Anybody ever try to hurt you?
DANTE: I got into a couple things. Nothing major though.
RON: Did you have to carry a gun?
DANTE: At one point in time that was the only thing I was trusting in.
RON: The only thing you trusted in? Is that right?
DANTE: Felt secure.

Dante's need for a gun was pragmatic; it was to protect his business and himself in the lawless world of the drug trade.

Guns are symbolically and aesthetically a form of power. Carrying a "burner" not only provides protection, it gives a person a sense of power or significance.[45] Moreover, a gun facilitates a form of masculinity, whether it is carried by trained militia, used to resolve disputes between "southern gentlemen," used by mass murderers, or carried by adolescent boys. Guns reinforce authority and domination. They provide the ultimate measure for resolving differences, settling competing resource claims, avenging physical or psychological injuries, or redressing disrespect. In areas of social and economic isolation, neighborhood identity is intensified, where social and economic exclusion creates contentious interpretive claims on geographical space, meaning, and experience. The drug trade and incarceration, along with structural unemployment and idleness, have deepened street identities and neighborhood boundaries, and the proliferation of guns far too easily turns emasculation, disrespect, resentment, jealousy, retaliation, and reputation into death. Guns as a part of business become guns as a part of everyday life, and the ultimate measure for resolving disputes.[46]

Much of the work, if you will, of youth who live in violent areas is learning to physically and psychologically master the fear, hypertension, and distress that accompany the uncertainty of neighborhood violence—with or without guns.[47] Returning to Richard, the 33-year-old father who grew up in Father Panik, we see how conflicts emerge, escalate, and ultimately get resolved through the use of guns. Richard said he walked through a part of "the Village" every day where a man resided who was romantically involved with a woman he used to date. The man would confront and fight him in an effort to dissuade him from walking through that area of the complex, which Richard attributed to jealousy. Rather than changing his course and showing "weakness," Richard continued walking and fighting with him on a regular basis until, as Richard put it, his rival "met .38. After .38 hit him one time and that was it. It was over." "You had to pop him?" Ron asked. "I had to do something, man. That's how bad it was."

Men who live in these areas often find themselves with the dilemma of whether to carry an unregistered gun and risk being arrested by the police, or whether to move around on the streets without self-protection. Nineteen-year-old Joshua articulated this dilemma well.

> I mean I had two choices: either walk around without a gun and have to look behind my back all the time and worry about I could get killed today or tomorrow, or walk around with a gun and worry about the cops [but] feel a little safer. Even though I got to still look over my shoulder, I still feel safer. Regardless of whether a gun or not, I could still get killed, but I got a better chance.

Joshua started in the drug trade at 12 and had his first child at 15. He was the father of two biological children and one "stepchild" and was serving a 20-month sentence for a second gun possession charge.

Others found ways to negotiate these conditions without assuming the risk of carrying an unlicensed gun. Robbie, the African American father, who in the last chapter had been mistakenly rounded up in a deadbeat dad sweep, grew up in Bridgeport housing projects. He had lost friends to violence and been shot at, but said he never carried a gun. Robbie explained, "When the shooting starts, I am out [both laugh]. I don't look back to see who's doing it. As long as I don't get hit, I am gone. It was one of those things where I felt like

I never had to carry a gun . . . and I think that's one of the reasons why I've never done a year or more in jail."

Similarly, Richard also pointed out that not everyone who lived in public housing carried guns, nor did they get involved in the drug trade. Richard observed, "I guess that's how most people fall into the drug game because once you living in that environment, man, it's hard to break out. I mean there are a lot of people that went to college because they had their mothers and fathers backing them up." Richard reminds us that in urban ghettos there is a significant presence of working families.[48] Still, children from working families living in areas where the drug trade is visible and accessible also venture into the "drug game," including Richard himself. He was raised in a two-parent family in which both parents worked or, as he said, were "backing him up." But Richard's parents were working multiple jobs due to low wages, and left Richard and his siblings unsupervised much of the day and evening. As Richard described, "My father was working two jobs. My mother was working three, so we hardly see each other."

These young men made decisions within the circumstances that defined their lives, including the negotiation of the drug trade and the opportunities it provided, as well as the violence that stemmed from the drug trade. In telling the backstory to the men's lives, it is important not to lose sight of the fact that these men are fathers. They entered the drug trade at early ages and had children at early ages. They grew up fast and as part of their entry into adulthood went to prison. Their street histories—or street habitus—shaped their fathering practices, which we will discuss in the next chapter. As they aged through the life course, many would remain in this social location—between the streets, precarious work, and incarceration—and some of them would develop drug addictions. At 36 years of age, Daniel's story illustrates this pathway.

Daniel is an African American father of two children—one grown and the other a teenager. He grew up in the Bellevue Square housing development in Hartford and, by age 13, was holding heroin for dealers, when he began sniffing the product. The ensuing course of his adult life had been a continual battle with heroin addiction and incarceration. Daniel had seen both sides of the gun barrel: "I been shot two times. . . . Dude that I grew up with my whole life came with the gun . . . He shot the shit out of me twice. . . . I've carried a gun. I have hurt people, I have. That's the way I grew up man. . . . That's the way it is out there." In many respects, Daniel is a true veteran of the streets. Injured twice in these combat conditions—earning two "purple hearts" in the drug wars, if you will—and also having "hurt people" himself, he experienced the traumas associated with living in an area where the local drug trade forms a powerful segment of the local economy—all a part of "the way it is out there." At the age of 36, he had been through street combat, survived it, battled addiction successfully, given up hustling, and entered the job market.

Daniel's only previous work experience, outside of street hustling, was doing under-the-table landscaping work, which he described as "chain gang" work. Working his first on-the-books job and getting paid $9.50 an hour in an entry-level warehouse position, with $95 being taken out of his check weekly for child support for two children, he was entering the legitimate labor market that a peer, not reared in Bellevue Square, was more likely to have begun 10–15 years earlier. In many ways, Daniel was a success, and this may be the most that other young fathers in our study can hope to achieve.

These stories bear telling in their own words—stories of warzone conditions often in or around housing projects associated with the drug trade. If a soldier or refugee finds it difficult to adjust to "normal life" after experiencing trauma, then perhaps some of these men might also be entitled, in a compassionate society, to some sort of assistance in handling the mental baggage of witnessing and experiencing extreme brutality. Besides, they are fathers, and many of them will play some role in their children's lives.

Psychological and Emotional Costs

There are many consequences to the violence that occurs in these socially and economically marginalized spaces. There are psychological and emotional consequences of loss. Robbie, who claimed earlier to never carrying a gun, but being the first to run when the shooting broke out, described falling into a three-year depression after losing a friend to gun violence.

ROBBIE: I lost my friend in '97.
RON: You lost your friend, how?
ROBBIE: He was killed. I lost a few friends.
RON: In the street?
ROBBIE: Yeah.
RON: How did he die?

ROBBIE: He was shot and killed. It was a big scene that day and I had just left him. . . . I kind of putting it with going to church and being watched over by a guardian angel. It's like while I was running and doing my thing . . . the guys that I was running with, most of them are dead.

RON: Wow.

ROBBIE: And I was either with them the night before or right before. Like in '97 we grew up together basically. . . . We were hanging in the Terrace and smoking weed and everything. And I went to make my mom something to eat. It was like a chore. I had to do it. Get it done. The street could wait. I get that done and all heck was breaking loose in the Terrace. It's like I don't even know what's going down. And I get back to the Terrace and I am looking for all my friends and everybody is looking at me like "You don't know what's going down? It just went down like 10 minutes ago." . . . Basically, a drug turf type of thing. He chased him around in the car. A couple of shoot-outs. I'd say a half an hour or 10 minutes between each shoot-out. He is driving the car. They are up in [Trumbull]. He gets shot in the head. The car flips over. He's dead. Something that you only see on TV. But had I just said the heck with the chores [pause].

RON: You probably would have been with him?

ROBBIE: Yeah. Most likely I would have. I was real depressed from like '97 until 2000. I was working but I was just going through the motions. My daughters kept me from being like completely a mess with myself.

Several of the fathers in our study experienced the loss of friends to violence. After doing five years in prison, Richard was sent to a halfway house as a transition to his release. A counselor at the facility emphasized that if he returned to the streets, he would likely die. Richard reflected during the interview, "And that was real because like four people that was in that halfway house with me [either] died or they are in jail for life right now"—which, for all intents and purposes, is another form of death.

Despite the glorification of violence in popular culture and its association with hypermasculinity, interpersonal violence is not easy to physically and psychologically master.[49] Participation in or the threat of violence can have lasting psychological or emotional consequences. Todd, a 29-year-old father with mixed Caribbean blood lines, lived in New Haven most of his life, before moving to the Dutch Point housing development in Hartford. He lived in Hartford for four years before returning to New Haven. He described his experiences and the "anger problem" that he developed during these moves. He began by talking about his move to Hartford.

It was crazy for me because I didn't know anybody. I was getting in fights every day just because I was from New Haven. Oh, my god, it was crazy. There were a couple of dudes just picking on me and my brother because we were from New Haven. . . . And then we just get in a fight just because I said I was from New Haven. And that was like an everyday thing. That's pretty much where I learned, because I never used to fight. Even now I still don't like violence. But in Hartford I had to fight. If I didn't fight, I would get my ass whooped every day. . . . I ended up taking boxing for a year up there, and then I ended up taking kick-boxing for 2 years, and I ended up learning how to fight. But my mother didn't like me fighting, but I would defend myself. And I would defend my little brothers. Like if somebody got into a fight with my little brother, I am going to jump in it and have my little brother back out and I take over the fight. . . . And me living in Hartford I ended up getting an anger problem.

Todd said he later returned to New Haven different from when he left.

I had a serious anger problem. And then when I moved back to New Haven the dudes were like "Yo, you different." I was like "I ain't different." "Yeah, you are." And I would just punch them. I had a serious anger problem. I had to take medication for it because I would black out. I would get migraines from my anger. . . . Me living in Hartford changed like my whole, whole attitude. Just because I went from being humble and quiet to being quiet but with an attitude. Like if anybody say anything to me, I would snap. But as long as nobody say nothing to me I won't say nothing. Where before if somebody say something to me I'd just be look at them like "Yo, whatever" and I walk away. But when I came back from Hartford, it was totally different.

Todd was physically and emotionally impacted for which he took medication to address migraines and "blackouts."

There is a popular tendency to believe that violent people enjoy violence, and while it may satisfy some, for many, it can create maladaptive psychological and physiological symptoms, like Todd's.[50] Enhancing public safety is not simply about protecting the victims of violence, but in many cases the perpetrators as well, who may be engaged in violence for a number of reasons, including their own past victimization, as well as their own fears about being victims of violence.[51]

What is perhaps most disturbing is when individuals come out of prison without a reason to live. Usually due to their prison experiences, their social disconnection and alienation, and a general malaise, they return to society with what some refer to as a death wish, and others on the streets call "wylin' out." They no longer fear death and are willing to tests the boundaries of life itself on the streets. They put themselves in life-threatening situations that violate even the norms and codes of the streets.

Jacob, who earlier described Stowe Village in Hartford as a "million-dollar project," was locked up before the age of 16 after a street shootout and subsequent car chase with the police that resulted in him hitting a young boy with his car. He turned himself in, but prison did little to rectify his reckless behavior. He continued:

> So during that time I came out of jail a menace to society. I just started doing everything. Robberies . . . like whoever would sell drugs I would run into their house or something and take their drugs. No face mask. Just didn't care if I got shot or nothing. I don't know what was wrong with me. I almost got killed like five times. . . . Once I was in a car with a dude that I buy from him and would front me. So, I just told him straight up "I ain't giving you nothing back." He just put the child locks on the door. Because it was like three niggers in the car, in a Jeep. All of them just put guns to my face. So, I just paid. He let me out. I went home and got my gun. I went and go look for him. I never find him. He got locked up.

Sitting in jail, Jacob continued by reflecting on his life and his prospects for change:

> I been in jail for so long—I was only 15. I didn't live life. I didn't really see nothing. When I smoked weed, I always wanted to fight somebody. When I am drunk, I always wanted to shoot somebody or go rob somebody. I just started smoking dust. And dust is a bad drug . . . Now knowing that, why should I do that again knowing what I am going through? Plus, my kids. They are just too precious for me.

While sitting in a prison cell, Jacob was trying to come to terms with his self-destructive past. Interestingly, in doing so, he pointed to the one, and perhaps only, motivation he had that might pull him through his imagined personal transformation—his kids, whom he described as "too precious."

The consequences of structural and interpersonal violence are profound. These conditions get negotiated in different ways, with varying outcomes. In the shadows of this violence is the anarchy of the drug trade that pervades the daily lives of those living in neglected, disinvested neighborhoods. Violence has its consequences, but so does the drug trade in these areas, where far too many residents will spend the rest of their lives wrestling with drug addictions. Several of the fathers reported ongoing struggles with drug addiction. For some, like Daniel, they entered the drug trade in their early teens, began using addictive drugs, like heroin, and have spent their lives in and out of treatment. The prevailing contradiction is that they work in a trade where they sell the product to which they are addicted. Making money in the drug trade requires extraordinary discipline for addicts, and the more successful they are in practicing self-discipline and making money, the more they are tempted to binge on the drug that gives them so much pain and pleasure.

Viewed from a community perspective, the drug trade creates its own contradictions. On one hand, it brings badly needed money into poor communities and pays for rental costs, transportation, school clothes, and utility bills. On the other hand, it does so at the expense of residents' addictions, often residents who have little income. Of course, the success of the drug trade requires that it reach beyond these communities to the suburbs and surrounding areas. Beginning with the death of the actor Seymour Phillip Hoffman, more attention has been directed to the so-called heroin epidemic that has reached the white suburbs.[52] In other words, drug addiction is not reserved for the urban poor, but, then, neither is drug dealing.

Illicit drug dealing is determined by law—by the definition of what is deemed a legal and illegal drug. In the largest drug-consuming country in the world, illicit drug dealing occurs across social class and racial groups in urban, suburban, and rural spaces throughout the nation. The legalization of marijuana has demonstrated how quickly the political and economic landscape can change when the definition of a drug changes. John Boehner, for instance, the former Speaker of the House, who was among the many legislators to advance careers on anti-drug crusades, has become the poster boy for the burgeoning marijuana industry, encouraging investment in the multi-million-dollar market.[53] The drug is now defined as legal in many states because members of Boehner's social class write the laws. Boehner's current motives, however, while hypocritical, are not any different from those whom he locked up—to take advantage of a market and make money.

Illicit drug markets and drug addiction among the urban poor, however, create its own set of issues, in part because of aggressive law enforcement in these areas but also because of the lack of resources to address addiction problems.[54] It also creates the absurd scene where successful dealers, fashionably dressed, seize on the opportunities provided by local addicts who swarm open-air drug markets to sustain their habits. The most painful illustration of this was provided in Colin's story.

Colin is the 19-year-old described earlier from the PT Barnum projects in Bridgeport whose brother introduced him to the lucrative drug market at an early age. Colin said that he never used illicit drugs himself, other than marijuana. He claimed he never even drank alcohol. When we asked why he did not use drugs, he laughed, "Because I seen people on it. Why would I want to do that? I see how people look when they on it. I see what it do to people, what it do to families, what it did to my mother." Colin tells the story of his mother becoming addicted to crack cocaine and the realization that he was part of a trade that was a destructive force in his family and community.

COLIN: I think it started out from prescription medication.
RON: For her?
COLIN: Yeah, I think that's where the addiction started through prescription medication. So, nobody really knew, but it started coming more and more to the light and it's embarrassing, man.
RON: What do you mean?
COLIN: Like the final straw, like right before she went to the rehab, like where I am from, I ain't kidding, but like in the morning certain times of the day, you would see like a rush with the dope fiends, and they would rush to come buy these drugs and everything. And I would see like my friends' moms and stuff and I know it's embarrassing, but one day, man, I seen my moms, man. My moms never walked around the hood, never, ever. And to see her, I had to double look and I am riding with my friend, man, and I started to stop and say, "What the hell are you doing?" But it was something that was so far gone, it was going to happen. So, I just turned my head and tried to avoid it, man. It was so embarrassing. It was like wow I know everybody know and one or two like real friends would be like

"Yo, man, you know, your moms, man, I think your moms is slipping." It's so embarrassing. I would just deal with it in my own way.

Psychological and emotional suffering come in different forms in these social and economically neglected areas. And while our study focuses mostly on the lives of men, Colin's mother reminds us of women who are suffering the psychological and emotional consequences of living in these spaces of political and economic neglect as well.

Migdalia from our Couples Study is another reminder. A mother who grew up in Hartford's Stowe Village projects and was interviewed along with her husband Miguel, Migdalia described what witnessing violence did to her: "And then there, in Stowe Village, I got sick from my nerves because I was seeing a lot of people shoot up and a lot of killings and stuff like that. That really affected me in my childhood. I was like, probably like 11, 12 years old." Our focus on the lives of fathers may provide a different lens through which to examine structural and interpersonal violence and its consequences, but mothers face these same circumstances, albeit through a different gendered location.[55] The number of men we have already alluded to going to prison because of domestic violence underscores this point. Intimate partner violence is an issue we will return to in Chapter 7.

Conclusion

At the turn of the 20th century, Connecticut's cities were thriving manufacturing centers. Even Hartford, known for its insurance legacy today, was central to the advancement of US industrialization through its precision craft ingenuity, where names like Samuel Colt, Amos Whitney, Francis Pratt, and Frederick Rentshler were etched into our history books.[56] By the turn of the 21st century, however, Hartford was the second poorest city in the country, while Bridgeport and New Haven were not far behind. At the end of the decade, after the Great Recession, close to one-half of the children residing in these three cities would live below the poverty line, which is a marker of extreme poverty in a state with such a high cost of living.[57] Inside these cities were some of the worst concentrations of poverty in the country, and these were anchored by public housing developments that a half-century before had been launched with hope, pride, and patriotic zeal.

In post–World War II America, metropolitan areas would expand to become race- and class-organized spaces and places that determined advantages and disadvantages. In the wealthiest per-capita state in the country, these socio-spatial representations of inequality would resemble a racial apartheid system, with black and brown populations occupying the most politically and economically neglected areas in the state. Several of the men in our study grew up in the housing developments that geographically marked these areas and in families that had intergenerationally experienced the demise of public housing and the decay of its surrounding neighborhoods. The global drug trade turned these areas into distributional nodes and the men talked about flowing into the drug trade, eyes glowing green, dropping out of school to do "real work," and developing lucrative entrepreneurial skills.

Participation in the lawless drug trade and its ancillary predatory activities would expose these fathers to gun violence at young ages. Moreover, in areas of deprivation and neglect, the proliferation of guns would affect the negotiation of respect, honor, and reputation. Men in our study were perpetrators, victims, and witnesses to extraordinary violence, to the extent that they expressed indifference toward it and minimized it as simply a way of life. Still the psychological and emotional consequences of violence and street life were also apparent. Men lost friends to gun violence, lived with the physical and emotional scars of violence, suffered episodes of palpable self-destruction, and struggled with their own and loved ones' drug addictions.

The state response to socio-spatial poverty was to intensify law enforcement in these areas, militarize the police, and incarcerate the problem. Rather than addressing the political and economic roots that caused the demise of public housing, the discussion turned to how to address the cultural pathologies that drugs and violence symbolized. As we have seen, these strategies included disciplining men to conform to the low-wage labor market, demanding financial responsibility for children, and encouraging marriage and father involvement. Men were making "bad choices," and the paternalistic arm of the state was strengthened to force compliance with their presumed places in the labor market and the family. Ultimately, though, both debt and punishment would lead to incarceration and criminal justice supervision.

The state's response tightened the institutional linkages between state welfare, the police, and the prison, or as Loïc Wacquant described, between the ghetto and the prison. The ghetto became more like the prison and the prison more like the ghetto as the punitive arm of the state was extended to discipline labor, neutralize resistance, and symbolically stigmatize, racialize, and

marginalize a population of mostly black and brown men who cycled between these two spaces of institutional confinement.[58]

As we have seen, these fathers grew up fast; they became involved in the
drug trade and had children at early ages. They also went to prison and
started accumulating debt at early ages. Moving between the ghetto and
the prison, they were also enacting fatherhood. Moreover, they were being
exposed to the discourses of the new fatherhood both inside and outside of
prison. In the next chapter, we delve further into the institutional contexts
of fatherhood by examining the fathers' experiences in the criminal justice
system, and we begin to shift our attention to how these structural dynamics
were shaping fathers' relationships with children and mothers and their own
perspectives on fatherhood.

6

Fathering Through the Looking Glass

Not finding work drove me back to the streets because I needed to support my son. At the time he was small so I needed to support him.

—Arturo

It's hard to see your son through a glass and see him reach for the glass and put his hand and his face near it and stare at you and making you feel like he wants to grab you or something. And there is no physical contact at all. It's tough. It's really hard.

—Javier

The end of the 20th century will be historically remembered as the era of mass incarceration in the United States. The numbers are extraordinary and tell a chilling story of neoliberalism and the reorganization of poverty governance. The Connecticut prison population followed the national pattern. At the beginning of 1980, there were 3,845 state residents behind bars. The prison population would peak in 2008 at 19,894 inmates, a fivefold increase.[1] This increase fell disproportionately on black and brown communities, where law enforcement was concentrated. In fact, in 2005, Connecticut distinguished itself for having the largest white-Latino disparity in incarceration rates and the fourth highest black-white disparity in the nation.[2]

Fathers in our study, located at the bottom of the labor force, experienced the colliding social forces that have rendered their lives precarious and risky. This chapter rests at the apex of the prior four chapters, where we see how declining living wage opportunities, welfare retrenchment, accumulating child support debt, and public housing neglect have culminated to create social spaces that detach many from the labor force, push people into the informal economy, concentrate poverty, increase interpersonal violence, and situate masculine identities. The political response has been to create new forms of poverty governance that have utilized more fully the state repressive

It's a Setup. Timothy Black and Sky Keyes, Oxford University Press (2021). © Timothy Black and Sky Keyes.
DOI: 10.1093/oso/9780190062217.003.0006

apparatus. Not only did the US prison and jail populations reach their peaks during the 2000 decade, but the rate of US adults under the supervision of the state penal system (in prison, jail, probation, or parole) reached 1 in 31 adults in 2008, and 1 in 3 black men.[3]

Similarly, the number of mothers and fathers incarcerated has also increased dramatically. More than one-half of prisoners are parents, and nearly one-half of those parents were residing with their children at the time of their incarceration. In 2008, 2.6 million children had a parent in prison and, of those, 1.7 million were locked up for a nonviolent offense. While the number of mothers incarcerated has more than doubled since 1991, still, in 2007, 92 percent of incarcerated parents were fathers. More shocking, among children of high school dropouts, 15 percent of white children and 62 percent of black children can expect to have a parent in prison before they turn 17 years of age.[4] Sara Wakefield and Christopher Wildeman assert that prison has become not only an institutional mechanism that produces inequality in the United States, but it has become a form of tracking much like the system that channels students in the schools.[5]

In our study, 57 of the fathers, or 41 percent, had been incarcerated at some point in their lives, while 21 (or 15 percent) were incarcerated at the time of the interviews. In this chapter, we look more closely at fathers' lives on the streets, the ways in which the criminal justice system has intersected with and shaped their lives, their experiences of relating with children and mothers while incarcerated, and their perspectives on fatherhood within the institutional interstices of the streets, police, prisons, and community reentry. We examine key contradictions that challenge marginalized fathers, including reconciling masculinity on the streets with being available and present to children, as well as reconciling norms and expectations of being nurturing fathers with preparing children for living in violent social spaces.

Getting Paid

As we saw in the last chapter, many of the men in our study engaged in criminal behavior in heavily policed areas. They grew up with ready access to the illicit drug trade and started at young ages. Many would be locked up in juvenile facilities and then later adult prisons, before returning to their communities under thick probationary and parole supervision. There were different reasons they provided for their involvement in the drug trade. One common narrative was that, as youth, they were pursuing money, girls, status, masculine identities, and name-brand clothes. The dreary lives of many around them, the regimented, meaningless routines of school, and the "shine" of sharply dressed "players" with big wads of bills in their pockets made this an easy decision. Nathan, whom we have heard from regularly, a 27-year-old African American from Hartford, put it this way:

> Mother fuckin' drug dealer is like a mother fuckin' rap star or basketball player. . . . He even ain't got to be the biggest drug dealer. As long as he making some type of money, bitches is going to throw herself at him. Ain't no damn nigger if he in that position, basically you are in the position of power. . . . That's just how dudes live.

Nathan is describing the masculine rush where pleasure and power mesh on the streets, something usually reserved for elite white men, as the 2017 exposure of sexual assault and harassment by powerful men from the White House to Congress, and from Hollywood to Fox and NBC News illustrated.

For other fathers, though, it was less about the lifestyle and more about paying bills. They paid rent for their mothers, bought food for the family, and school clothes for themselves and their siblings, albeit name-brand clothes that gave them some schoolyard recognition. Nineteen-year-old Bernard described:

> One thing, too, I wasn't selling drugs because I wanted to. It's because I had to. See? I needed clothes. My mother would buy us stuff but, hey, I was trying to help myself. I wanted the finest things, too. I wanted Timberlands, name brand things. You feel me? If I don't got to sell drugs, what am I going to do it for? Fun? No, man. That was the white kids. White kids wanted to be down like that. I am not like that, man. I had to sell drugs because I had to. I had to buy new things. I had to feed myself. I had to buy me clothes. I had to do it. Help my mother out, too.

Of course, these two explanations were not always mutually exclusive. Family poverty might push youth into illicit money-making opportunities, which then might lead to a desired pursuit of status and masculine indulgence.

For a few, however, these opportunities were less about the individual spectacle or paying bills, and more about learning business skills, entrepreneurial discipline, and saving money. As we have seen, Colin studied the trade under his brother's tutelage:

> I just soaked it up like a sponge. He was no dummy at it. . . . He wasn't the type to just go get a pack or do this and that. He did his smart. He analyzed it more. These guys, they sit out here and they sell $1,000 worth of drugs and they only keep $200. He was the type, he get his money. He taught me, "Get your money involved."

Similarly, 19-year-old Marshall added: "When you are doing it, it got to be for a reason. Like some people do it just to buy new clothes. You got to stack your money up." For these young men, they rarely, if ever, used drugs, and they refused consumer temptations and status symbols. They remained focused on profits, investment, and expansion, and on drawing minimal attention to themselves—in other words, they focused on learning the ins and outs of outlaw capitalism.

For some of the men, drug dealing had become normative. It is what they did because wage-earning alternatives were poor. In this sense, they were rejecting the low-wage labor market. To explore this, Ron asked Alford how he responded to adults when they said things like, "Man, you got to stop that," or "Go to school or do this or that." Alford, 20 years old and incarcerated at the time of the interview, responded:

> Because, to tell you the truth, I done tried to sign up for jobs, I done tried all that. And these people ain't never put no money in my pocket, so I feel how they going to tell me what to do and what to not do. And I ain't got it as easy as them [and] I don't got the good stuff they got. . . . It wasn't like I was trying to diss them or nothing. It was just I got to do what I got to do.

For most of the men who agreed with Alford, coming to this conclusion was not always easy. Drug dealing was not necessarily a first option. As 21-year-old Antwan put it, "First I won't stop looking for a job. Probably get under the table, but if that don't work, the streets." This was especially the case for men coming out of prison, who faced barriers to employment. While some moved right back into the drug trade, typically, the process began with looking for formal employment, turned to under-the-table employment, and then to the streets as the final solution.

Motivations varied. Young men entered the trade for different reasons, but they did so where networks and opportunities existed. They pursued money and status, and chased the prospects for personal achievement.

Hitting Licks

As we saw in the last chapter, making money in the illicit drug trade sowed competition and conflict into neighborhoods, where robbing drug dealers also became commonplace. Money was rarely put in banks. Some put it in locked safes; others paid people to hold their drugs and money. However, most hid it in their apartments or carried it in their pockets. This made them vulnerable to robberies. In an unlawful and unregulated marketplace, robberies—or "hitting licks"—became a type of hustle. Several of the men talked about being robbed, and some about being shot, while a few talked about doing the robbing.

Calvin, an African American father of a newborn, was just shy of 18 years when we interviewed him. He was serving a two-and-a-half-year sentence for marijuana possession. He described a scenario where he was trying to help out his mother, but was being robbed by a presumed friend. His story illustrated the complexity of poverty, family, drug dealing, and predatory consequences.

> I was trying to make my mom happy, but [if] she would have knew it was coming from drug money, she probably wouldn't have took it. People were stealing from me. I was like "Mom, you seen some money hid this place?" She be like "No, you shouldn't be selling drugs." . . . So, I always thought she was taking it and be holding it. It was this boy I was chilling with. He was robbing me and stuff. . . . I had $5,000 for her. This boy stole it from me. I found out when he got locked up, so I couldn't do nothing. So I had to start all over again. When I started all over again, I kept getting locked up, so I had to bond out and pay for a lawyer, bond out, pay for a lawyer. I could never see my goal. I wanted to buy a little house like.

Having money in the house made Calvin vulnerable to robbery, and robbery disrupted his vision of buying a small home for his family.

Robberies increased risk on the street. Drug dealers found themselves always looking over their shoulders, carefully answering doors, looking behind the corners of houses and behind the bushes. Or as Dante put it, people "see you shining and they want to take your shine." Sociologist Randol Contreras argues that robberies increased after the heyday of the 1990s crack trade. As money dried up and the trade become more competitive, redundant dealers turned to robbing lucrative dealers.[6]

Alberto, a 21-year old Puerto Rican father of two children, described the intense competition that exists on the corners among young dealers and how this led him down the path of robberies. "It's not something I wanted to do," he said. But "somebody fight over a corner. Somebody fight over who gonna work next. If it comes down to a last resort, give me your goddam money. You getting stuck up." A stick-up artist, Alberto explained his rationale.

ALBERTO: My M.O. was sticking people up and then doing it for my family. Cuz I was the only man in the house at the present time.
RON: Okay. So you would take that money.
ALBERTO: Yeah, I'd take the money and buy food with it and give my mother the rest of it. . . .
RON: Take it?
ALBERTO: Straight taking your money. And I have done that before to my friends. That's why I can say I ain't got no friends. . . . my father always told me. He says, "Never keep friends close to you."
RON: It's all part of the game?
ALBERTO: All part of the game. . . . it's like you being a wolf, like you being the sheep. Something like that. Kill or be killed.

The competition on the streets in a lawless world can be vicious—getting money by any means necessary. Alberto described the predatory nature of the street economy and underscored the rationale for why people living in these spaces carry guns, whether they are street-engaged or not. He rationalized his behavior as necessary to providing for his family.

As Alberto suggested, part of the code of the street is to not trust anyone—to maintain a self-reserve that recognizes that greed or desperation can turn a friend into an enemy when a compelling opportunity arises. To negotiate these spaces, a person must learn the cues, codes, and conduct through which money is made and relationships are managed.

The Streets and the Prison

Elijah Anderson argues that the concentration of poverty in black urban neighborhoods has entrenched street life and violence in these spaces. In turn, it has generated a code of the streets that provides a set of norms or rules that govern behavior—particularly violence—that both "street" and, what he terms, "decent" residents have to learn in order to negotiate interpersonal situations. For Anderson, street codes regulate a "desperate search for respect" that precipitates violence and is a "cultural adaptation to a profound lack of faith in the police and judicial system."[7] Douglas Massey adds to Anderson's argument by illustrating how black poverty and black residential segregation create an "ecological niche for black Americans" in the inner city, "within which violent behavior becomes a logical, rational adaptation." Massey reasons that if crime and violence are strongly associated with income deprivation, then concentrating poverty "also concentrates crime and violence." In these circumstances, violence is not only a survival strategy but "constitutes a valuable form of human capital."[8]

Alford's story provides an example of how street codes presuppose violence, and while knowledge of these codes might reduce personal violence, they also define situations in which violence is requisite. Alford was serving an 18-month prison term at the time of our interview for first-degree assault for shooting someone in a dice game. He explained the sequence of events that led to the shooting.

> Somebody tried to rob me . . . I was playing C-Low, playing dice with somebody. I had tripped up—when you trip up, you get paid double. Whatever, the guy didn't want to pay me. So I pulled out a gun and shot him, an older person. And they wrote statements on me and stuff. But I almost beat the case because they stopped coming to court and stuff. But the judge didn't want me to just walk, so he said, "Do this little bit of time," and he gave me a bunch of probation, too.

Alford continues by explaining his dilemma:

> It's the way it goes. If I had pulled out a gun and didn't shoot him, I'd have been "he a bluffer." I am pulling out for nothing. Then he could have caught me slipping and hit me up or whatever. So really, if I pulled out a gun, I had no choice but to shoot him. If I didn't pull it out, what's even the sense of me

having it on me? It's like I am just fronting with a gun on. Plus, if I wouldn't have did nothing about it, there was other people gambling and "Oh yeah, the next time I'm gambling with Alford, I'm doing the same thing he did." Just take my shit, and I can't have that. So I am like, whatever.

Sitting inside prison, Alford lamented, "I wasn't thinking. I was stupid. I didn't care if I killed him or nothing." On the street, though, he was responding to the situation in a prescribed manner; carrying a gun, he used it accordingly. When we asked Alford why he had the gun in the first place, he insisted, "Just had to. Had beef out there, dudes trying to stick dudes up. I had to survive out there, man. Part of the deal. Comes with the package."

Alford carried a gun to protect himself and to navigate a violent social world. Not everyone would have pulled a gun and shot the man in this situation, but the rationale that Alford provided for doing so was a street rationale—it followed a logic that if he pulled the gun, he needed to use it, and if he did not pull the gun, he was pretending to be someone he was not. Either way, his actions, he thought, would have bearing on how others would respond to him in the future—as someone with or without "heart," or in other words, as someone who would or would not use his gun in that situation. Alford's willingness to use gun violence and his knowledge of how and when to use it earned him a degree of respect on the street which decreased the chances that someone would try to take advantage of him on the streets "to take my shit."

Alford landed in prison, and like many street-engaged men, he will move back and forth between the prison and the street, where his understanding and participation in street culture will deepen and where his life will be managed by criminal justice institutions and authorities. Since the 1980s, drug dealers and gang members have been swept off the streets in extraordinary numbers—disappearing and reappearing in neighborhoods—and creating social and cultural ties between the prisons and the streets. Loïc Wacquant made this important connection in a couple of seminal essays in the 2000s, demonstrating the institutional and cultural linkages between prisons and the streets.[9]

Wacquant's thesis focused on the institutional enclosure of the ghetto and the changing role of the state in poor, black urban spaces in the wake of structural unemployment and welfare retrenchment. Further, Wacquant noted that the infusion of large numbers of street youth into the prisons in the 1980s and 1990s transformed an inmate culture from one organized around a code of conduct that generated solidarity in defiance of prison guards—the "convict code"—to a code of the street, much like Anderson had described, that coveted hypermasculinity and predatory violence.[10] In this respect, the code of the streets did not simply originate in the socially and economically isolated ghetto, but *between these spaces*, as the prison and the streets became institutionally bridged and socially symbiotic. Street gangs and oppositional culture were incubated within prisons, which were bursting at the seams with exploding numbers of urban youth swept from the streets and dumped into facilities lacking the capacity to house, feed, and service them through prison programming. Certainly, the code of the streets overwhelmed the vestiges of convict culture, but the social and cultural ties between the prison and streets affected street culture on the outside as well. Gang members and neighborhood affiliates crisscrossed the institutional spaces of the prison and the ghetto, as efforts to create fluidity and continuity extended networks between each. Street codes germinated and crystallized across both of these spaces, as men cycled between the prison and ghetto.

The uncertainties and the violence of the ghetto were no less apparent in the prison, especially where boredom and tedium stemming from segregated idleness festered inside these overcrowded facilities. Using physical violence as a primary means for resolving conflict was regularly employed in prisons, where a little less than one-half of our respondents had spent some part of their lives.[11] Most of the fathers agreed that staying away from violence was their goal, but just as neighborhood violence was difficult to avoid, so was prison violence. James described:

> You get caught up in the drama every day. You could be keeping your cool and sitting there like conversations like we are having; like say if I knew you from the world and we were in jail right now and we were bullshitting. "Yeah, remember them good times going to the beach" and all that. And then you got another dude that will come over, "Yeah, fuck them beaches. I never liked swimming anyways." And you are like "Oh, mind your business, bro." And they'd be like, "What did you say?!" And then the conversation would escalate throughout. It would just start a free-for-all. . . . I've seen people get in a fight over a cup of coffee and get his dome split open. I've seen people get stabbed in the face, stabbed in the head, get locked [hit by a padlock enclosed in a pillowcase] . . . I've seen people get hot water and baby oil thrown in their face—skin come right off them. Broken arms. Broken legs. Yeah, I've seen some serious, serious ass whoopings in jail that

you don't forget. . . . They always tested people. I been in jails where there's been riots in the jail. You see 200 people on this side, 200 people on that side, people coming out with homemade shanks. First thing that comes to your mind? "I am going to get mine. I am hitting the first fucker that hits me."

At 40 years of age, James was one of the older fathers in our study. He was a white former member of the street gang Los Solidos and had done 12 years in prison for felony assault and gang involvement. His street experience had prepared him for violence in prison, where he could read the signs and codes in potentially violent situations and respond accordingly. Conversely, prison would also prepare him for his return to the streets.

George, an 18-year-old father, with both Puerto Rican and African American lineage, invoked the code of the streets, as he prepared himself for prison. George had violated probation during the course of our study and was expecting to begin a prison sentence. He reasoned:

I know (deep sigh) off rip [right away] somebody going to try pressing me. Somebody going to try to come up to you and say something, or try to take something from me. It's not going to happen. You only got one chance to make an impression, you feel me. And as soon as somebody touching my shit, if I let that shit slide everybody going to think that's all right. As soon as somebody touches my shit, I am going to punch them in the face. I don't give a fuck if he's six foot seven or whatever. It's the whole principle. You are going to know that I am going to fight for mines at the end of the day. It's like whatever. I am not a little kid.

Whether in prison or on the street, the same cultural framework and personal dispositions operated. Interestingly though, George's father had prepared him long ago for this rough-and-tumble male world, where respect is violently exercised and protected. George recalled an incident in which he reported a playground fight to his father. "After that time my Pops told me, 'You come here and I find out you got your ass whooped, somebody did something and you didn't do nothing, I am going to fuck you up.'" George could feel his father's presence as he prepared for his prison term. "I feel like my Pops, if I go back to my [prison] cell, my Pops is going to pop out of nowhere and fuck me up. You know what I am saying?"

George's comment is important for our purposes, because it brings fatherhood into the loop with prison and the streets. Parenting strategies need to be considered in this context as well. The role of the state in institutionally reorganizing the governance of poverty through its repressive and symbolic measures must be understood as a key force that created the conditions for reconstituting street culture, just as parenting needs to be understood as well from within these grooves. Fatherhood is reflective of these processes in a few ways. Fathers living in areas of concentrated poverty must consider how to prepare their children for these social conditions—one, how to parent within the confines of repressive surveillance and predatory violence, and two, how to parent through the cycles of recidivism. The social context is riddled with contradictions.

Sitting in a prison cell, Alford, who shot the man in the dice game, cannot imagine how the situation could have been avoided—he was caught in the dictates of the street, the fear of looking soft and surviving on the street. And yet he felt anguish and regret for missing out on the birth of his daughter. "I got a lot of regrets, like being in jail when my daughter was born. That's my biggest regret is not being there for her right now.... She know who I am and stuff, but it ain't the same thing." His "not being there for her" is a direct result of his street-influenced life.

Fathering does not occur in a social vacuum; it occurs within the interstices of institutional processes through which lives are lived. How did the institutional reorganization of poverty governance shape fatherhood among this group of fathers? How were they intending to raise children within social contexts dominated by prison and the streets? To answer these questions, we need to examine one more part of the institutional framework through which the lives of the most marginalized fathers were being managed and controlled: the police.

Policing and Incarceration

In the context of the streets and, especially the drug trade, policing and incarceration have been embraced as a key strategy of poverty governance, and have become a nearly seamless part of a broader system that includes the courts, probation and parole offices, state and nonprofit social service agencies, halfway houses, and homeless shelters. Policies that bridge urban communities and the criminal justice system create varying forms of surveillance and empower agents of the criminal justice system to enforce strategies intended to control the "refuse" of the structurally unemployed and defiant who reject precarious work.[12]

Brutally policing the black ghetto is not new. Cell phone recordings have made lethal policing more visible to the public, but certainly policing with impunity has a longer reach than 21st-century technology might suggest. Policing the neighborhood borders of the ghetto in the north as blacks migrated to escape Jim Crow terrorism in the south was first enacted by white mobs with police complicity, and then more systematically by local and state government.[13] The black ghetto was the institutional mechanism of the 20th century through which a racial caste system would be reconstituted in the north, while the role of the police would become entrenched in a new organization of state repression.[14]

In the 1960s, many of the ghetto uprisings were instigated and fueled by police brutality. The Kerner Commission, convened by President Lyndon Johnson to study race relations in 1968, affirmed the assertions long made by ghetto residents that many police officers acted on the premises of white power, racism, and repression.[15] In the post-1970s, with the decline in the city tax base and the reduction in federal funding, the old models of city management gave way to entrepreneurial cities as urban government sought ways to entice capital and homeowners back to the city.[16] As investment moved downtown, the suffering in poor, neglected neighborhoods deepened. The dual city took shape and the success of these entrepreneurial strategies meant controlling the areas of the city where crime and disorder were likely to flourish amid neighborhood disinvestment. Attracting capital investment and professionals was, in effect, dependent on the success of controlling crime and disorder. The "blue line" would get reconstituted to protect the dual city, manage urban disorder, preserve spaces for capital accumulation, and make the human sacrifices of neoliberal reorganization invisible. The desperation by which city governments pursued these entrepreneurial measures would create lethal conditions where police were given license to act with impunity.[17]

Similar dynamics were occurring in Puerto Rican communities after the mass migrations from the island in the 1950s and the 1980s. Puerto Ricans were concentrated in poor urban areas as mobile capital was hollowing out the manufacturing labor force. These communities were also stigmatized, stereotyped, and scapegoated as neighborhood poverty deepened, the drug trade flourished, and policing intensified. Piri Thomas's classic, *Down These*

Mean Streets, graphically conveyed some of these dynamics, as have several ethnographic studies.[18]

Whether in the 1920s, the 1960s, or 2000s, policing in urban minority neighborhoods was driven by the mission to manage and control the spatial borders marking race and ethnicity in metropolitan areas. Still, today, despite GPS technologies that allow for electronic tracking of state-supervised individuals, policies still tend to be spatially targeted, including hot spot and community policing, school and public housing zone surveillance, targeted anti-loitering and no panhandling areas, and the like. These policies are justified by so-called broken-windows policing, where police focus their attention in areas showing signs of disorder. In other words, broken-windows strategies target policing in areas where neglect and disinvestment have had their most apparent effects.

Throughout large and small cities in Connecticut, anti-loitering laws were passed that, by the 2000 decade, restricted citizens' movement in areas that were considered "hot" for drug activity and violence, areas described by the fathers in the last chapter. These areas were in predominantly black and brown neighborhoods, which placed residents in these areas at risk of police surveillance and, according to many of the men, police harassment. Geographically targeted anti-loitering policies cast a broad net and grant the police excessive authority in enacting those policies. In most instances, the police not only did not reside in these areas, but were white and had little familiarity with neighborhood cultures. The fathers had much to say about anti-loitering laws and the police.

Loitering policies were enacted in Hartford, in the area where the Charter Oak housing development was located. Joaquin, a 21-year-old Puerto Rican, described:

> Flatbush is mostly hot [so] you can't be outside too much. Cuz there's usually the cops harassing you. Like if you're out there on the sidewalk, they'll come and harass you. [This happens] anywhere, but mostly on Flatbush. Cuz Flatbush, since there's a lot of youngsters that sell drugs, they try to pick 'em up.... But they do it differently—they'll give you a ticket no matter what. Yeah, even if you don't got nothin' on you, you just right there getting air or looking, they give you a ticket—it supposed to be loitering.

Jack, a 23-year-old Puerto Rican, described the enactment of anti-loitering policies in the small city of Meriden:

Like right here in Meriden you can't walk around by yourself. You just walking around and they'll stop you. "Where you going? What's you doing?" . . . They do that shit. And you can't stand on the sidewalk. They'll give you a $95 ticket just by standing on the sidewalk.

Jack added that the enforcement strategies were abusive, that he had been "slammed against the car" and cursed at on several occasions. He believed the police were "prejudiced" and said unequivocally, "They're assholes!" Jack asserted that the police were so out of line that when he went to court for loitering, the judge "dropped the charges."

There were several fathers who agreed with Jack's perspective of the police and provided stories of police brutality and racism. Juan, a 25-year-old Puerto Rican from Bridgeport, described an incident.

The cop pulled me over, whatever. . . . And I put the car in park and when I put the car in park he opened the door and he dragged me out and he threw me on the [ground] and this guy was big. And at the time I wasn't as big as I am now. I was all anorexic looking. And the cop just dug his knee in the middle of my back with my shoulder blades just like collapsed in the middle. And then he pulled my hair and he just looked at me and called me a piece of shit. And I was like "What are you talking about?" I was like "I didn't even know the car was stolen, this and that." They handcuffed me and everything. And then the state trooper swung by and he was like "You caught them pieces of shit, them Spics?" And I was like "What?" And I spit on his windshield and I got mad. I was like "What you going to be saying something like that?"

Pito, a 38-year-old Puerto Rican from Waterbury, described an encounter he had with the police:

PITO: They have dragged me across the floor. They are abusive, these white guys. They are! [laughs] I have seen them kicking people around here.

RON: What did you do?

PITO: Nothing, stay quiet, because they are blue and they are the law—one has to swallow the words, one cannot do anything. They are brutes and they beat you.

Red, a 26-year-old African American, elaborated on the problem of un-checked authority in Bridgeport.

> They is the same way as the judges—got a little bit of authority and they just don't know how to act with it. Trying to be super cops. It's all it is. It's crazy. You can give the wrong people authority. That's what it is. They be buggin' now, too. Connecticut is a wrap. I am ready to get out of Connecticut.

Bernard, a 19-year-old Nicaraguan from Meriden, asserted that anyone living in these conditions understands that these policies and practices are unjust.

> We deal with reality. Even if a dude do something good, man, he's going to get jammed up for something. You could be successful, walking in the street, and then anything can happen to you. Police could come in and ha-rass you or arrest you for anything . . . just to earn his badge or his stripe or something. That's reality. Ain't no justice, man. Everybody know that. Ain't no justice.

These men are referring to what sociologist Victor Rios describes as the crim-inalization of the poor, in which institutional authorities in poor urban areas manage the lives of black and brown youth through surveillance and pun-ishment. This results in what Rios calls the "youth control complex" where harassment, scrutiny, provocation, and emasculation push these youth into defiant criminal activities.[19]

When white fathers talked about the police, their narratives tended to be less belligerent and violent. Certainly, their relationships were conflic-tual and they did not like the police, whose job had been to apprehend them. Still, their responses reflected the difference between the ways in which the police were likely to respond to a white and black man on the streets, where the constructions of blackness and criminality evoke danger and fear.[20] When we asked Shay, a 23-year-old white father from Willimantic, whether he would characterize his contact with the police as good or bad, he replied:

> Sometimes they treated me good because they knew I grew up with fucked-up [parents] . . . they knew my family. They used to come to the house all the time when I was little. But then there were some that were bad.

In Shay's case, the police appeared to attribute his criminality to his family, not his race. Johnny, a 23-year-old white father from Manchester, described the police:

> They like to harass you sometimes when you're just sitting out there hanging out. They just come up and harass you and ask what you're doing and everything and shine their bright light in your face. I never had 'em like in a helpful situation. Never had 'em really help me in anyway. I mean, I know they're just doing their job but sometimes they take it too far, I think.

Ray, a white father in his late 30s who has lived his whole life in Willimantic, told us his experience:

> RAY: State police, they kind of look at the age [of someone from Willimantic] and make assumptions. Like one time I got pulled over on Route 2 for going five miles over the speed limit. And they insisted I had drugs in the car. . . . I mean they brought the canine unit and everything.
> SKY: What about when they didn't find any drugs? Did they apologize or anything like that?
> RAY: No. They gave me a stern warning, gave me a ticket, and sent me on my way.

These stories from white fathers betray irritation and perhaps even resentment toward police treatment of them, but their stories are quite tepid compared to descriptions of being pulled from cars, dragged across floors, kicked, and beset with racial slurs. Reading across the transcripts, it was clear that the descriptions of and interactions with the police were qualitatively different between black and brown men and their white counterparts.

Policing is only one part of the criminal justice system. It works in conjunction with the courts, prisons, jails, and probation and parole offices, which together manage the lives of the chronically marginalized across the spaces of the prison and the neighborhood. Many of the men in our study were suspended in this cycle and were attempting to father within it. Consequently, their perspectives on fathering were also developing within the contexts of the streets, prison, and criminal justice system. As we will see, many of them would see their street experiences and knowledge as important to what they had to offer their children. They were street smart and could teach their children the dos and don'ts of the streets. They could better protect daughters, often from men like themselves, and teach their sons how to become men in these social circumstances. This is what many of them valued most about their capacities to be fathers.

Street Smarts

Culture is not something that is easy to describe or even to see. It is something we perform that is semiconsciously encoded in our bodies and minds, but rarely something we reflect upon. So, when we explored the culture of the streets—the codes, symbols, dispositions, practices, routines—with the men in our study, we found that it was not easy for them to articulate it. Fathers said to be on the streets, you had to be street smart, and that it was something they valued about themselves and that they imagined would benefit their children. So we asked, what is "streets smarts"? What does it mean to be street smart? They generally responded, "Well, it means that you experienced the streets—you been out there." In other words, it is something you possess because you possess it; not something you explain.

Experience was key—living and learning. Lawrence said, "You got to read the angles. When you can't see the angles no more, you in trouble. That's the truth." Deshaun remarked, "I mean can't nobody tell me nothing on the street or try to fool me out there, try to trick me into anything. You always got to be on your Ps and Qs, on your toes." We heard the alphabet again from Red, "Street smarts to me is just basically you are able to think quick, Ps and Qs at any moment." Red continued, "It's just about the street codes, what you doing and what's not to be done." Travis said, "You can drop me anywhere and I'll survive."

Being street smart was described as having awareness on the streets, being able to read situations and people's intentions. It usually involved making money and negotiating interpersonal situations and social networks. Nineteen-year-old Jamal explained:

> You got to live the life. . . . Basically, you can't teach nobody, you got to be there. . . . I got to go out there and get what I got to get, by myself. . . . It's like if I take a person somewhere and he don't know where the hell he at; if he's street smart, he going to know how to get to that place. . . . He'll know how to jump on his feet, go to the streets to get what he want. . . . How can I put it? It's knowing what you got on the top of your head.

Nineteen-year-old Jose emphasized that you need to be able to identify who people are on the streets.

> When you can look at a dude and you can tell if he's a gang member or not. When you look at a dude and you can tell he's selling or not. . . . Basically, when you look at somebody and by just looking at him, [you] describing who he is, the way he looks, the way he acts, all that.

Nineteen-year-old Brian described street smarts as a form of both engagement and self-preservation. He suggested that when you are in the midst of the action, the reality of the streets engages your intellectual faculties.

> Me personally to be street smart you just got to be aware of everything, man. I mean anything is possible when you on the streets, man. Seriously. Especially when you running wild. Once your name and stuff start getting around and stuff people want to push your buttons to see what you really about. It's real. When you are getting that money, it comes with a lot of strings attached, man. A lot of strings. Believe me. It's real.

Bruce, a 20-year-old white father who had served four years in lock-up facilities, sounded much like an ethnographer who claims to understand a culture when he or she can participate in it.

BRUCE: If you go out on the street and people talk the way they do or they act the way they do and, if you can't understand that or if you can't be around it without looking out of place, then you are not street smart. Because if you are, you are going to be able to communicate with them people and deal with them and work with them in a way that nobody else can. So that's what street smarts is to me.

RON: So what happens if I am out there and I don't blend in?

BRUCE: Either you are going to get picked on, you going to get robbed, you are going . . .

RON: Oh really?

BRUCE: Something is going to happen to you.

Kevin proves his street smarts by his survival, "Nobody didn't shoot me dead or nothing like that." Robbie agreed, "If you've been out there doing your thing for a year or more, you'd be dead if you hadn't gotten street smart by then."

Others talked about the interpersonal skills that are required to operate competently on the street—the ability to develop social networks, manage, and use people. Nathan explained:

> I go places and I will interact with anybody. . . . You got to keep a snake in the grass at times. I mean I'd rather have a snaky person around me than somebody else because you ain't going to snake me. He may be cool but he got some grimy issues. I'll keep you around but certain things I am not going to deal with it. . . . You always got to have some fighters around you because you don't want to be around a bunch of people that can't fight. You got to have all types of friends. There are friends you can talk to about certain things, friends you just joke with, friends you may smoke with, some you may drink with.[21]

Keen perceptions and interpersonal skills allow men to see types and differences, and to engage people adroitly.

Other discussions about being street competent expanded the narrow constructions of the street to include the surrounding community. Being street smart was about being community-minded, or interacting effectively with families and community leaders. Marcus elaborated on this.

> To be street smart, you have to know how to deal with the people that you around. . . . Because me, I call me street smart because when I was selling drugs and the kids that were coming out of school, I giving those kids the most respect that I can give to them. I don't let them see nobody selling drugs. Nobody have no time for them. So when they were going to the store, I will pay for those kids. . . . I make the people that's around me like me. Because I know I am doing wrong. I might as well instead of doing wrong trying to do something right around the community. . . . I remember one time the police came, approach me, and somebody came to me and said to the police, "Excuse me, this is my husband. No, no, no, no, he just walk the street to get something with me. Excuse me." And the lady held my arm and she gave me a kiss and brought me to her house and saved me. But they were one of the ladies that always take the money for the kids when they go to school. And I make sure that people stop selling drugs when the kids that were

coming through. This is street smart. When the person was telling me, "Excuse me, this guy is selling down here," whatever, whatever. I say, "Okay, man. I will make sure this never happen again." And I went and tell them, "Hey, I don't want you to sell no more. You go over there or over there." . . . This is how you ought to be street smart. You have to work up the neighbors.

Marcus was not alone in this orientation to the streets. When we asked, "What makes a bad drug dealer?" 18-year-old Martin replied:

> I feel like a bad drug dealer is somebody that if you are out on the corner of the street hanging around selling drugs that if he don't have respect for the community and the people around him and don't show them respect, then, in my eyes, that make a bad drug dealer. Because when you don't show people respect that's around you and they watching you do that, they end up not showing you no respect and calling the police on you. But if you show them respect, nine times out of ten they go ahead and mind their business.[22]

Working with and in the community was stressed by several fathers; however, most focused on their own skills, orientations, sensibilities, or discipline when discussing their street life.

Given the dangers of the streets, several of the fathers talked about the need to master fear. In this respect, men had to discipline their bodies. They had to control the physical signals that move through the body to protect it against danger—beating hearts, sweaty palms, trembling hands and jaws. These are the bodily sensations that sociologist Randall Collins says lead most people to perform acts of violence poorly, despite masculine bluster and posturing.[23] In his book *Toxic Schools*, Bowen Paulle demonstrates how school-based fights are often won before a single punch is thrown. Squaring up in a fighting posture itself requires the mastery of fear and in training bodies to perform in highly stressful situations.[24] Like any embodied performance, the discipline of bodies can only occur through repeated practice, until the act is seemingly natural, conducted with relative ease.[25] For the men on the streets, disciplined fighting bodies are crafted on street corners, in bars and after hour clubs, in schools and prisons, and sometimes in families. They become what Travis referred to as street soldiers engaged in street war. He explained:

Like I had guns to my head and I'm still telling the kid, "Fuck you. You don't scare me. What? Shoot me bitch. Your kids will die." You know what I mean? It's fear. Everything is control. Everything in this world is controlled by fear. If you can control your fear and know how to use your fear to release fear in other people, you'll survive . . . not fearing death. I welcome it. In my own eyes I know when I die I am going to die as a soldier. You heard before, a coward dies a thousand deaths, a soldier dies but once. And I believe that. I believe when I die I'll be considered a vet. You know? Even though I never fought. I fought many a war, but none for our government.

Travis's quote describes his brutal living conditions by comparing it to war and himself to a veteran of war. It also underscores the preparation and discipline of his body and mind that are necessary for performing effectively.

Articulating street culture in their own lives was not easy. It came out in fragments, spurts, and sometimes insights. It included interpreting motives and actions of others, networking effectively, mastering fear, negotiating violence, accommodating community needs and concerns, and making money.

When we turned to issues of fathering and the streets, more clarity emerged. For when fathers had to consider how they were going to raise children in these environments, they reflected on the challenges posed by the streets and the skills their children would need to navigate them.

Hyperviolent Bully, Nonviolent Punk, and Nasty Little Girls

When talking about fatherhood, fathers often compared themselves to their own fathers. They wanted to "be there," which meant doing more than dropping by once in a while with a few dollars. Like their own fathers, they may have been parenting outside of the household, but, still, they wanted to be engaged fathers. In fact, new normative expectations of fatherhood gave them the opportunity to compare themselves favorably to their own fathers; further, it provided them with a legitimate channel to express their anger at their fathers for neglecting them, an issue we take up in Chapter 8. Most importantly, it provided an opportunity to find value in their lives, where few avenues existed.

But how did they intend to do this from their social locations? Moreover, how did they intend to reconcile the normative expectations of being nurturing fathers with the violent worlds in which they lived? Contradictions abounded. While they dreamed that their children would attain jobs that paid a decent wage and provided a stable working-class lifestyle, they mostly hoped that, at minimum, their children would achieve more than they had. At the same time, they also had to prepare their children for the violent worlds that awaited them.

Many of the fathers in our study not only witnessed or participated in violence of all kinds; most articulated the importance of developing one's own violent capabilities as an invaluable survival skill. As parents, they felt the need to teach their children how to defend themselves and how to prepare their bodies for violence. George, for instance, whom we described preparing for a prison term earlier and imagining his father appearing to scold and toughen him up, insisted on teaching his children fighting skills. Not unlike the lessons passed along by his own father, he wanted to instill these values and skills in his children at young ages, and he compared these skills to learning a trade.

> Especially while they are young, you know what I mean? At a playground you always going to get into confrontation about something. As you get older you probably won't have to use it as much, but it's just good to have, you know what I am saying, because you don't know what's going to happen. It's just like going to school or taking a trade or taking up something in school. Like you might not need it when you are older, but it's always something good to have. That's just the way I see it.

Other fathers made similar arguments when discussing the schools their children would attend. They needed to learn to take care of themselves rather than rely on institutional authorities. "See, here's the problem," Rayshawn explained:

> If you are like fifteen or sixteen and you are in high school and someone pushes you and you go and tell the teacher, you are going to get your ass whooped [by the students]. So, if you are a teenager, the only thing I can really pretty much say is posse up your boys because there is gonna be some action.

Another father, Ray, asserted:

> I am not going to tell my kid, "Hey if somebody hits you, then just take it." If somebody hits you, you have a right to defend yourself. [If you don't] they are going to keep at it. The adult in me says talk it out. I would hope that physical repercussion would be the last resort.... Do I condone [violence]? No. Would I do it? Yeah.

Will Ray uphold the normative expectations of the nurturing father and advise his child to respond to a physical confrontation by talking it out or walking away? Will he help his child develop the verbal negotiation skills to deal with conflict that can deftly mediate one's physical reactions to fear or confrontation? Or will he advise his child to do what he would do and respond to violence in kind? Tre articulated what appeared to us to be the general consensus among the fathers about how to navigate these competing expectations.

> I'll teach him to defend himself, but I ain't going to teach him to just be like a bully.... I am not saying I want him to run away and be a punk about everything, but I don't want him to throw his life away because he's out there looking for fights.

These fathers hoped their children would act in a manner somewhere between the two caricatured poles of the "hyperviolent bully" and the "nonviolent punk," and in this way stake out a satisfactory position in their local social hierarchies. For these men, violence can be seen as social currency in its own right; however, they also know firsthand that violence can also be a legal liability and result in arrest, and perhaps even incarceration. It seemed that only a nuanced navigation of this contradiction would help their children avoid the pitfalls of violence—physical injury or prison—and avoid the stigma of the emasculated "punk."

These men generally believed that although everyone will face violence from time to time, the frequency and magnitude of it will be drastically affected by one's initial response to it. In other words, they aimed to not only deal with the situation they were confronted with at any given moment, but to respond to it in a way that addressed the pervasive atmosphere of violence in which they lived. Whether in prison or their own neighborhood, these men made it clear that without a strong initial showing one would likely become a permanent victim of abuse. These fathers were keenly aware of the miserable quality of life endured by the people at the bottom of their local social hierarchy. The specter of "losing all respect" haunted them and not only guided their own behavior but their parenting strategies as well.

These parenting values and expectations, of course, had to be negotiated with their partners, who did not always agree with the emphasis on self-preservation and violence. We interviewed Jack four times during a 16-month period. Jack, who spoke about his experiences with police brutality earlier, had two-year and three-month-old sons. He lived in a cluttered apartment in Meriden with his in-laws. Jack described his father as physically and verbally abusive throughout his childhood until he left home at age 16. He was expelled from school for violence. He was adamant that his son would learn how to fight or, more importantly, learn how to stand up for himself. "Not every kid is perfect," Jack explained, "you are going to lose a fight regardless. If you lose a fight with the guy, just come back to them. You might beat them the next time. [laughs] . . . It's not only about losing or winning, you showed that you do fight."

On a warm night, our interviewer, Sagacity, sat on the porch to do the first interview with Jack, when his partner, Raquel, and a cousin wandered out and joined the conversation about parenting. Very quickly, their parenting expectations and strategies began to differ.

RAQUEL: Okay, but he wants to know what would [our son] learn from you? . . . I can give you a great example, something I can't do—teach him how to use the bathroom standing up.

JACK: That's a good one. . . . I fight with him—play fight with him so he won't be a punk [laughter] and defend himself when he has some problems.

RAQUEL: Are you calling my son a punk?

JACK: I said so he won't be a punk. So when he gets into a fight and someone hits you, hit him back. Just don't go around crying to mommy, "Mommy, I just got hit."

RAQUEL: As long as it doesn't get him suspended out of school or expelled, I am fine with it.

JACK: Hey, if that's the reason he gets suspended; if he get in a fight in school and he got a reason to defend himself; if he needs to fight, he needs to fight. He's not going to come home and started crying because he got hit.

COUSIN: But in my point of view, I am not a father or nothing, but in my point of view when I think of that, I would wait until after school. Because you don't have to worry about anything in the school, teachers calling.

JACK: That's true. That's true.

Their oldest son is only two, but Jack and Raquel are attempting to determine the lines of when and where violence is appropriate, and how to make sure their sons do not become "punks."

It appeared that the fear that their children might fall to the bottom of their local social hierarchies in violent neighborhoods was a powerful determinant in these fathers' views on parenting and masculinity. Moreover, it seemed to us that, for the more marginalized fathers in our study, *their primary concern was not to what heights their child might achieve but rather to what extreme lows they might successfully avoid.* This was also true for raising daughters; however, gender altered the description of extreme lows.

For sons, fathers feared violence and drugs; for daughters, they were concerned about early sexual activity, predatory men, and the stigma of teen pregnancy. Here the fathers' role as family protector or in "patrolling the borders" of their families was apparent, whether they were in the home or not.[26] In a few instances, they expressed different, and even contradictory, attitudes about the dating behaviors of sons and daughters. Tre, a young father of a two-year-old boy, explained, "I think it depends on what you have, a son or a daughter. . . . When it's a daughter, the father is going to be more protective of the daughter with like her boyfriends when she gets older. But then like when it's a son, it's like 'Yeah, you got a girlfriend! Yeah!'" For many fathers, adolescent pregnancy was their greatest fear for their daughters, suggesting that the stigma of the "teen mom" was viewed as a failure of parenting, even though many of them had been teen fathers themselves. Rex, a father of two daughters, stated very candidly how many of our fathers felt about adolescent pregnancy.

> I am going to do my best to not let them be a young mama. I think that's important. That's going to be like almost like number one, because I don't want my damn daughters, any one of them, pregnant at 15 or 17 or 18. I want them to be like in their mid-20s or late 20s if they can help it. I am going to imbed it in their head because it's crazy the way these young girls today are all pregnant. I ain't saying that's bad, but that's bad.

When talking about their daughters and early pregnancies, several fathers expressed fears that their daughters would acquire a reputation for being sexually promiscuous at an early age and become a target for predatory men—what George referred to as becoming "nasty little girls." For George, a young father of two girls, very young mothers symbolized the worst outcome for his daughters, or as he said, "that she'll end up like all these nasty little girls, you know what I am saying? All these girls who are young having like babies. Having babies at 14, 13. That's wild—you really are a child. That's my worst fear."

George placed the greatest onus for managing this situation on himself as a father.

> I got to be the first man she ever loves, you know what I mean? Her father, I got to treat her like every man should treat her. She is a princess. She is a queen. She got to be treated right, you know what I mean, so she knows what to expect from a man when she is old enough to date. It all starts with me.

In George's narrative, male predation is less the concern; it is young, female vulnerability that, as a father, he must protect against. His role is to show his daughter that she is special and deserves to be treated with respect, so that she does not succumb to the advances of predatory men at a tender age.

Parenting was influenced by local social hierarchies, which reflected the intersection of gender and sexuality within poor, racially segregated communities. The fathers' expressions of heterosexual masculinity define a location of power within socially and economically marginalized spaces. To be emotionally controlled and physically capable of violence allows men to embrace a version of manhood that gives them moral status when (1) they choose not to exercise violence—to avoid being the bully; (2) they exercise violence to stand up for themselves—avoid being the punk; and (3) they exercise violence to protect daughters—to patrol the borders of the family—from other hypermasculine, hypersexualized men.

Like fathers across all social groups, the fathers in our study were struggling with questions about how to relate to their children and to develop open and honest communication with them, while also establishing parental boundaries and a structure for them to develop into healthy adults—but were doing so within their own social locations and social hierarchies. Further, there seemed to be an expressed sense of urgency, if not desperation, in getting it right that stemmed from different sources: in some cases, from their own past mistakes; in other cases, from their efforts to be the father that their fathers were not; and still in other cases, from the fear that there was only a small margin for error when parenting in the neighborhoods and schools where they lived. They wanted to teach values that reflected the conditions in which children were growing up, and they wrestled with whether their primary responsibility—whether living inside or outside of the house—was to be a disciplinarian or a confidant, an issue we will return to in the next chapter.

Raising children in socially and economically marginalized spaces, where violence, trouble with the police, and teen motherhood are disproportionately manifested, shaped how fathers imagined their roles in raising their sons and daughters. But for many of these young men, they were preoccupied less with what they thought they should do as fathers and more with how to establish fathering relationships as they moved across the spaces of the prison and the streets.

Fathering and Incarceration

The Agony of Fathering Through the Looking Glass

Many of the men in our study described the experience of fathering through the "looking glass"—the Plexiglas that separates prison visitors from inmates when visits are designated noncontact visits. Communication occurs by using phones secured by steel wires tethered to visiting stalls, and through intimate gestures, like placing lips and hands against the glass to "kiss" and "hold hands." The prison where we conducted interviews rarely permitted contact visits; thus, with only a few exceptions, visits were conducted through the looking glass.[27]

In *Dangerous Masculinities*, an ethnographic study of fathers in two prisons in Connecticut, Anna Curtis described prison visits with children as an opportunity for fathers "to drop their 'game faces' and instead emphasize their value as something more than prisoners." She explained: "In particular, men were able to express deep emotions about their children even as they acknowledged that there was little space for emotions within the context of prison."[28] Curtis is identifying two parts of the men's identities that are in conflict with one another inside prison: the tender, loving father and the distant, emotionally controlled inmate.

The fathers in our study described their agony of interacting with children through the looking glass. Javier, a 19-year-old Puerto Rican father of a seven-month-old son, was incarcerated for three years with a five-year suspended sentence for armed robbery. He claimed that he robbed the store with a butter knife to satisfy his cocaine and alcohol addiction. He described:

> You can't hold your son. Knowing that you never met your father, it's hard to see your son through a glass and see him reach for the glass and put his hand and his face near it and stare at you and making you feel like he wants to grab you or something. And there is no physical contact at all. It's tough. It's really hard.

Gerard, a 19-year-old white father of a five-month-old son, was sentenced for 18 months for conspiracy to commit robbery for leaving the back door of a McDonald's restaurant open during a robbery. Gerard lamented the looking glass.

> I just hate myself for being in here [crying] when he was born. It's horrible. I let me down; I let my family down. What kind of role model is this for my brothers and sisters, you know? Now that I am a father, this is no good. I realize how I have been wrong. It's time to change everything. . . . I see him in front of me, and there's like this much glass in between us and I cannot touch him. I mean it's the worst pain knowing you have your child right in front of you and you can't even touch them or nothing. I hate it.

Benito agrees. At 18 years of age, Benito served 18 months for robbery and was on probation when we interviewed him. Reflecting on fathering through the looking glass, he commented:

> It's not the same as holding them and giving them what they want, loving them or showing them that you love them. It's tough. I mean you could let the kid know that you love them and you are their father and that when and if you are getting out you will be there for them and everything, but there's nothing else you could do but say stuff to them.

Sitting behind the bars, the loss of their children was painful for Javier, Gerard, and Benito, and seeing their children through the looking glass, unable to touch them, augmented their desires to be fathers.

Elmore's desire to be an involved father was not only generated by the pain of seeing his two-year-old daughter through the looking glass but also through the experience of his cellmate. At 19 years of age, Elmore was serving a two-year sentence for cocaine possession. He described:

I had a cellie in Walker; he had 25 years and he was on the phone talking to his daughter. His daughter was 12 years old. And she was like "You been in jail, in and out of my life twice. It's been so long. You don't even know what I'm out here doing." She was explaining to her father and like telling him like, "I could be out here doing what I choose to do. You ain't care about me. Now you got 25 years." She 12 years old. . . . He was telling [me] like "Youngblood, you got a chance to go out there and see your daughter, have kids. Me? I ain't going to see none of that. The only thing I can see is a picture if she send it to me—if my baby's mother send it to me." I was sitting there thinking like, man, my daughter say some of that to me that would hurt me. That would break me the most. That would break me! Like my daughter saying, "You ain't care about me. You wasn't there for me." I was sitting there like "You took all that? You got balls. I couldn't take that."

With lots of time to think, it was common for the fathers also to worry that their partners, usually the mothers of their children, would start a new relationship. The loss of the relationship and the prospects of not seeing their children left them feeling vulnerable, while thoughts that someone else might replace them as dad was often unbearable.[29] Elwin, a 20-year-old Puerto Rican father, had applied for parole after serving 18 months and was waiting to hear the decision at the time of the interview. He described himself as a devoted father and said that he wanted to marry the mother. He had heard things though while he was incarcerated which suggested that she might be seeing someone else. Elwin lamented:

My son, I don't know now. He got like people around him. I don't know if my baby's mother is doing stuff that I don't know and she bringing him [new boyfriend] around, he is going to see him around more than me. And he's going to start calling him "Daddy" and I ain't going to like it.

That's why I am trying to get visits and stuff like so he can at least see me and stuff like that.

It is difficult to know from the interview if there was another man involved or if this was just something that Elwin feared and, sitting inside prison, was unable to control. Certainly, prison takes its toll on relationships. We will expand on this in the next chapter.

For the most part, the agony of fathering through the looking glass, the attenuation of romantic relationships, and the organization of the prison around "dangerous masculinity" bear down heavily on men in prison. In this context, men often accept that they made bad decisions and need to change their lives, if for no other reason than for their children. Sitting in prison and upon release, fathers embraced fatherhood as their motivation to change.

Fatherhood as Motivation to Change

The fathers are caught in a web of contradictions. As Alford's story illustrated, the codes of the streets and its expression of unforgiving masculinity may lead to consequences that remove them from the people they love and need, including children. Similarly, the emotions that get invoked while they sit in a prison cell may need to be suppressed as the men adopt masculine postures to negotiate the prospects for violence and domination in spaces too small, too restricted, and too self-denying. Moreover, from the perspectives of many prison guards and administrators, men are rarely seen as fathers at all; in fact, as Curtis writes, "incarcerated fathers' connections with children and family are most often ignored or dismissed within the prison system."[30] Our interviews, therefore, provided men with the opportunity to express a part of themselves that is often suppressed in their performances of masculinity inside the prison, or denied altogether by prison authorities.

Sitting across from us in a private room inside the prison with the tape recorder running, fathers said over and over again that children were their primary motivation to change. The men embraced fatherhood as their hope for a different future, as their ticket off the streets. For instance, Todd, a 29-year-old African American father of a newborn, described how his daughter might disrupt the embodied routines of the street that he had acquired through his adolescence and early adulthood. This is the same father who described to us earlier how his involvement in neighborhood violence in Hartford and New Haven had left him short tempered and violent. Todd believed his two-week-old daughter could give him pause and could help him to change his "total way of thinking" represented by the code of the streets.

> If somebody do something to me, I figure is it worth me doing something back to him, and we get in a fight, and one of three things is going to happen—either I am going to end up in jail or he's going to end up in jail; one of us going to end up dead and then the other one is going to

eventually end up dead; or we just going to keep fighting [and] every time we see each other we beef and shooting at each other or stabbing each other. And I got to ask myself, is that worth it? And when I was younger, it would have been like "Man, I am going to fuck the nigger up." But now it's like "You know what? You got this one. We good. I don't want no problems with you." . . . I be talking to a lot of young dudes and they be like "Man, fuck that nigger. He disrespected me I am going to fuck him up." And I am like "Yo, you all got a daughter. Stop right there." The first thing that pop in your mind when somebody disrespect you, say, "Is he worth me going to jail and losing my daughter over? Is he worth me dying and my daughter not having a father?" Because if you go to jail or you die, your daughter ain't going to have a father. Even though she can see you in jail, it's just you are dead, because you can't hold her like you want to. You can't see her go to sleep. You can't put her to bed. You can't tuck her in. You can't kiss her goodnight. You are not there to see her first steps or like I know this dude when I was locked up, this dude was in jail for 35 years. He had his daughter and he got locked up when his daughter was like three or four weeks after she was born. He missed everything. His daughter got married, got divorced, got married again. His daughter got five kids and two of her kids got kids. So he got grandchildren. It's just like mad crazy. I can't see myself doing that. That's why I got to stop and think before I act. That's why I am glad I am just changing my total way of thinking.

Todd was giving himself a chance to remake himself, to adopt new routines. And his daughter was the catalyst.

Brian, a 19-year-old African American man, was about to be a first-time father. He described his ambition to change.

The street ain't even worth it no more, man. I did a little bid. I did a year. Maxed it out. Came home. Was home for eight months. I was doing my thing or whatever. But it didn't even last for eight months. After doing a year I come back with two. It ain't even worth it. Then I got her right there. She pregnant. I am like, I got to come home and get my mind right. I got to take a new route. It's over with. It ain't even worth it. I am going to give my child everything I never had. A full environment. A mother, a father, and everything dead right. I am going to be there from the start, for real. When she say "daddy," he either in the room laying down or he on his way home from work. That's how I want it to be, personally.

Unable to avoid the streets after his first release, Brian imagined that his new-born would be the incentive he needed the next time around.

Manolito, a 20-year-old father with Cuban and Puerto Rican parentage, had started selling drugs as a teenager to provide for his mother. His first arrest was at the age of 16 for selling crack in a public housing development, where he and his mother lived. Manolito had been locked up three times and was serving a two-year sentence when we interviewed him. He was the father of a two-year-old and had conceived a child two months prior to his incarceration, whom he said was "on the way." Like Todd and Brian, he insisted that this would be his last time. "In July, I'll be 21," he said. "So, it's like time to grow up. I am about to have two kids. I grew up without a father. I know how that shit is."

These stories are representative of how the men talked about their children and their desires to change their street lifestyles for their children. Away from the streets and the prison blocks, they could express this part of themselves—this part of their masculinities that was rarely heard or acknowledged by institutional authorities. It represented their own fragmented understandings of themselves.[31]

Fatherhood is complex within this scenario for two key reasons. First, for many of the men, caught between the dangerous and stressful world of the streets and the inadequacies of structural unemployment and underemployment, fatherhood is one form of redemption; it is one way to stake out a moral identity—to be a father and, in many cases, to be the father that their fathers were not. Fatherhood comprises one of the few remaining opportunities for deriving social value that can be affirming of a masculine identity and self-worth.[32]

Second, and perhaps less apparent, fatherhood is also an escape route from the streets. It is a legitimate way to leave the streets without compromising one's masculinity. For men caught in the streets versus precarious work dilemma, who grow tired of the intractable perils of the streets, fatherhood provides a face-saving avenue off the streets. Jamie, a 19-year-old African American father of a one-year-old, expressed a deep sorrow of loss when he failed in this quest and was headed back to prison.

I went up the street, got on my cell phone. Called my baby's mother and told her I am on the way to her house. I was at her house the whole day, inside her house, holding my daughter, looking at her. I started crying like I don't want to be away from my daughter. I don't want to be a deadbeat father. I am not going back to jail. I was like I already been, I am not going back.

But Jamie was going back. He had been an accessory to a robbery, and he was also wanted for failing to appear in court.

Christopher, a 17-year-old African American father, had also failed to stay out of prison. He had been locked up repeatedly, but in between these episodes, he decided to intentionally have a child as an incentive to remain free of crime and prison. He said that after being released, just before Christmas, he told his girlfriend that "If I get locked back up, you are going to be pregnant." He and his girlfriend successfully conceived and Christopher was incarcerated when his girlfriend took a pregnancy test on Valentine's day and found that Christopher's revelation had come true. Christopher said that the emotions he hoped he would experience inside prison did indeed follow: "I felt embarrassed, ashamed of myself, everything," he confessed. "I don't know. I felt all types of stuff. I left her out in the world. I wasn't supposed to do that." Christopher said that he conceived his child "because I wanted a kid. It probably would slow me down. That's how I was feeling. I was stressing on the streets." If we can accept Christopher's construction of the pregnancy, his story illustrates the point well, that children provide a credible exit off the streets. Whether his strategy would be successful or not, Christopher, beleaguered by the stress of the streets, had a child to augment his chances of ceasing his street involvement upon release.

With only a few exceptions, the men insisted that fatherhood and the streets do not mix. They needed to choose. Nineteen-year-old Elwin put it this way:

ELWIN: It ain't no good being in the streets and being a father. You want to be a father or you want to be in the streets. You got to make the choice.
RON: You got to make the choice?
ELWIN: Because if you don't in a way it's going to be hard for you and be hard for your kids because one day you could be with your kids in your house and, boom, your kid is going to see that and that ain't good for the kid.
RON: No, that's not good at all.
ELWIN: Seeing your father getting arrested. That ain't good. Or your kid seeing you on parole or seeing you in a casket or something like that. That ain't good for the kid. So you got to choose.
RON: Can a guy live and have a street life and still be a good father?

ELWIN: I don't think so.

RON: You don't think so?

ELWIN: No. Because it's chance . . . there's a 50 percent chance you could live and a 50 percent chance you could die.

RON: Not good odds, huh?

ELWIN: That's not good odds. You could be the best criminal in the whole world and there is going to be a day when you are going to get caught, some kind of way.

RON: So it's not going to work out very well.

ELWIN: Nope. You could have everything, cars, money, house. It's going to go. Nowadays, it's FBI—they know everything.

Dante, a 20-year-old African American father of one child, agrees with Elwin.

In the streets there's a lot of things that go on. And like I was saying earlier, I want to be there for my baby. I don't want to be caught up in the street. Like I said, I'm shining and somebody hating on me and try to come get me one day. I don't want to give them that and they put a bullet in my head.

Elwin and Dante were not alone. Many of the men talked about the toxic mix of the streets and fatherhood. Not only did the streets put them at risk of prison, violence, or even death, but the streets-fatherhood duality enacted different parts of their masculinities and identities that apparently were not easy to reconcile—certainly not for Jamie and Christopher.

Most of their desires to be better fathers and leave the streets were expressed while men were inside the prison looking out. Fatherhood was a catalyst for change, but what would happen after they were released? What would happen when their own determination to change was not enough? We will pick up this thread in Chapter 8.

Conclusion

In Part 2 of our book we have focused on the lives of the most marginalized fathers in our study. These men started in the drug trade early, left school early, were locked up early, and had children early. In their 20s, they sounded tired and were looking for a new direction in their lives. Fatherhood provided one possible route that could advance a socially valued identity and a socially respectable expression of masculinity. But how would these fathers parent within the social spaces that contextualized their lives, particularly the streets and prison? How would they teach their children to navigate the neighborhoods and the streetlife that existed just outside their doors? This scenario allowed for the men to extrapolate from their street experiences and thereby squeeze some value from these experiences by becoming an authority on the streets with their children. They intended to protect their daughters and counsel their sons—they were experts in consequences and derived authority and purpose from telling their children what to and not to do.[33]

Further, the programs that were engaging these men about being fathers were reinforcing messages of father involvement. Most of the marginalized fathers in our study were enrolled in the state's fatherhood initiative program and many had been exposed to fatherhood programs in prisons. But the norms and expectations of the engaged, nurturing father had to be rearticulated by what the fathers saw as the need to prepare their children for violent worlds. They wanted their children to find jobs and stay away from crime—to make better choices than they had—but they also wanted to be sure that they had the skills and awareness to negotiate the violence that they would encounter in their neighborhoods, schools, and with the police.

The prisons created complicated and contradictory spaces for imagining and engaging in fatherhood. On the one hand, prison authorities, not unlike the general population as a whole, saw these men as dangerous criminals. Many of the men had contributed to these perceptions through their participation in robberies, assaults, and drug abuse. While strategies varied, they lived as outlaws within the social grooves provided for them. On the other hand, fatherhood programs encouraged and rewarded their perceptions, identities, and feelings as fathers. It gave expression to this part of themselves in an institution in which it is difficult to betray any sign of tenderness and compassion—to guards or fellow residents. This is a part of these men that is less publicly visible.

We provided a setting to discuss these issues. We saw the agony that they experienced when they could not touch their children, saw tears when they talked about how they had failed their children, heard determination when they discussed changing their lives for their children, and were able to see the fragmented and often contradictory parts of their selves that these fathers were struggling to reconcile. How, though, would these desires get institutionally supported when the fathers were released back into their communities? How would these fathers develop and maintain connections with their children when relationships with mothers broke down as they moved across the household, streets, and prison? If fathers were being encouraged to embrace responsible fatherhood, but the labor force and state institutions were failing to support the "new father," what then? Here is where we see the outlines of the setup. Responsible fatherhood is not simply an individual choice; it is also a socially and institutionally constituted process.

In Part 3 of our book, we turn our attention more fully to fatherhood and return to our larger sample of fathers to include the voices of just-getting-by, working-class fathers as well as marginalized fathers. While fatherhood cannot be separated from the policies and institutions through which it occurs, fatherhood is ultimately a relationship, or perhaps a set of relationships between fathers, mothers, and children. Structural forces shape these relationships, but they do not determine them. How did men relate to their children and the mothers of their children and how did the institutions governing their lives affect these relationships? And what were these men's perceptions of themselves and intentions as fathers, and how were these culturally and institutionally shaped?

PART 3

RELATIONSHIPS AND STANDPOINTS

7

Intimacy, Masculinity, and Relating

Earlier when I was doing time [I was thinking] like maybe I need a child to take me away from this negativity. But once I found out I was having a child is when everything around me stopped. I began to get stuck.

—Lorenzo

Maybe like, after I am dead and gone, my son will grow up and know that like, "Hey, he had a rough life, but look how I turned out. He did a good job. . . . He was a good person, even though [he trails off into thought, before saying] I still think he was a good dad."

—James

In this chapter we pivot our analysis from the forces of family destabilization to how fathers talk about relating within these circumstances. The previous chapters have delineated the forces that make up a matrix within which the fathers in our study are located, the place where they make sense of their lives as fathers, develop and perform identities, make decisions, create strategies, and engage those around them. In what follows, we focus on relationships between mothers and fathers and between fathers and children, but we do so in the shadows that the last five chapters cast upon low-income families in the 21st century.

The era of neoliberalism has made it more difficult for low-income men to be fathers, at the same time that the expectations for them to be involved fathers has increased. The norms and expectations of "father involvement" have changed rapidly within one to two generations, and yet the labor force and state institutions have not supported low-income families in a way to achieve this. In this chapter, we examine how fathers have adapted to these

It's a Setup. Timothy Black and Sky Keyes, Oxford University Press (2021). © Timothy Black and Sky Keyes.
DOI: 10.1093/oso/9780190062217.003.0007

changing circumstances. We consider how the casualization of the labor force has structured the casualization of family life; the essential and yet complicated role that kin play; the neotraditional formation of the family and the "new father" role; the efforts to father through generational family violence and to address toxic masculinity; and the contours of fatherhood as men age into second-generation fathers.

Financial Distress and the New Fathering

Arguments were often about money—too little money, too many bills, too many needs. In a context of low wages, reduced government entitlements, excessive rents, and the need for food and diapers, many of the fathers expounded on their financial distress.

Men who worked full-time talked about bill juggling, the costs of childcare, heating costs during cold winters, the car breaking down, or having the deepest pockets that extended family members depended on. Eddie described his stress:

> What has caused me a lot of stress has been the problem of money. Because sometimes we run out of oil, we don't have money to put oil in [for] the heat because now the children, one of them has asthma and he gets sick with the cold. Then there is where you start to worry and sometimes the money isn't sufficient because you have to pay the rent, you have to pay the other bills, food for the children, diapers for the children. Sometimes you get desperate and this causes you stress thinking about the money.

Rex was employed in the heating, ventilating, and air conditioning (HVAC) trade and was among the more economically successful wage earners in our study. Rex's wages were enough to provide for him, the mother of his child, and his stepchild, but he was from a poor family and others looked to him as a financial resource. Rex described making bail for an uncle, paying family members' rents, and buying furniture for his mother. He was trying to set limits and boundaries. "Shit, I got responsibilities, too," he said. "I can't just give you my money like that. When you can't do it, you just can't do it. I don't want to stretch myself out that far where I am going to be hurting and I don't have nobody to fall back on . . . it's not rational." But could he really say no to his family?

Then there were the fathers who were precariously employed—working temp jobs and part-time jobs, and collecting meager paychecks that for some amounted to $3 to $4 an hour after taxes and child support were deducted. These were the men living Jack's prophecy that you either work three part-time jobs or one hell of a job. There were the fathers who were unemployed, searching for daily under-the-table employment, or collecting scrap metal, like Jermaine. And there were fathers making money in the drug trade, dodging the police, street predators, and the courts.

Money was the Achilles heel. Marcus said it was unbearable to hear his daughter's voice when she called to say, "Daddy, I need a coat." Illegal activities filled their imaginations around Christmas time. Some avoided their children because they could not afford an ice cream cone when they took them to the park. And they fought with the mothers of their children. As James said earlier: "Everybody argues about money. Money is the all-evil thing in the world." And Tre said, "Sometimes we'll expect to have money that we end up not having and we just blame each other and end up bumping heads and fighting about it."

Unemployment added to the distress, not only because there was not enough money, but because there was too much time in the home together to take frustrations out on one another. Rachel commented, "We both fight all the time. [laugh] It's really, it's just being stuck in a house together for so long." Distress and uncertainty led to physical fights. Emily and Johnny had repeated fights, which led to police intervention on at least one occasion. Emily said things were better because "Now he has a job, I'm like, yes!" (laugh). She explained, "I mean me and Johnny fight when we're together all day long and I think that's with every relationship. If you're stuck with one single person, you're just gonna get on each other's nerves." Emily noted that their lights had nearly been turned off during Johnny's spell of unemployment and that the stress and frustration had mounted, but then, voila, Johnny got a job and suddenly they have "gotten closer, a lot closer," she proclaimed.

Similarly, Greg and Jenna described arguments that also led to police intervention and separation. Greg explained:

> Me and Jenna got into an argument a while back because I was in-between jobs and I was home a lot. With me and her being around each other a lot like that for two months, ehhh, it started a bunch [of fights] and she went to her mother's. Well, the same time the cops ended up coming because she

packed up all her formula and started packing up all her clothes, and I got a little perturbed about it and I said if she leaves with my daughter, come on. The cops ended up being here.

Of course, domestic violence is not simply about money and unemployment—as we will discuss later—but economic hardship in couples' lives triggers distress that can invoke vulnerability, shame, and deeply felt injuries that get expressed as violence toward those they care most about.

Casualization of Family Life

One of the key insights in Andrew Cherlin's book *Labor's Love Lost* is that the casualization of the labor force is being manifest in the casualization of relationships. He states, "It is likely that the changes in the labor market that underlie the casualization of work and the changes in values that have contributed to the casualization of family life have influenced and reinforced each other."[1] If the institutions that stabilize adulthood transitions through resource distribution and security, normative routines and expectations, continuity and predictability, no longer hold for a broader swath of the labor force, the grooves through which life is guided become less certain. Work, education, marriage, and family have been key to adult transitions, but, as we have seen, they have become less stable in the past 30 years.[2] For fathers, this can lead to transitory father involvement in the household and with children, or what Kevin Roy describes as liminality in which the father is neither "here nor there," searching for place amid ambiguous roles.[3]

Fantasies and longings emerge from the unanchored moorings of life, leading those most victimized by disinvestment and institutional abandonment to imagine their way out of the chaos and uncertainty into pathways that still designate lives with some modicum of dignity and respect—parenthood among them. Teen motherhood in poor communities is located within this mix when young teens search for a new direction and trajectory that holds out the possibility of starting over and living meaningful lives within narrowing opportunities.[4] Fatherhood, too, projects new possibilities: for being the fathers that their fathers were not; for leaving the empty promises and risky exigencies of the streets; and for attaining the fading prospects of working-class respectability. These hopes, however, are battered by the realities of unemployment, precarious employment, dwindling state support and their consequences: living with extended kin, too much unstructured time, too many people in too little space, tensions across relationships, self-blame, mutual blame, irritation, frustration, rage, and varying forms of escape—drugs and alcohol, infidelities, one last robbery or run on the streets, and starting over, yet again.

In our Couples Study, nearly a third (31 percent) of cohabiting couples lived with extended family, two lived in homes owned by parents, and three took in renters to pay the rent. Nearly one-half of the children lived with three or more adults in the home. This was almost exclusively for financial reasons. Living with extended family has been historically more common in African American and Puerto Rican households, where limited income and resources have created intergenerational strategies for meeting basic needs and taking care of children.[5] The care and perseverance of black grandmothers has been well documented.[6] However, white families in our couples' study were also relying on extended family for childcare, paying debts, and housing. While these forms of support have been necessary for survival and are considered a strength of working-class and poor families, too many people living in close quarters creates tensions and arguments. Rachel, one of the young white mothers living with the father and his parents, told us that she and Jaime fought all the time. "It's just, you know, everybody gets sick of it and everybody starts bothering each other. I mean I think that's mainly a problem, cuz when I lived by myself with him, we got along very well and there weren't any problems."

Because of limited household space and the emphasis on childcare needs, it is not unusual for fathers to be forced to live apart when the mother and child move in with extended kin.[7] Young parents living apart work out arrangements to be together and for the father to see the child, and they often work toward saving money to eventually get their own place. Eldis said that his child and partner "stays with her mother, but that's what I am working towards, like saving. First, I had to save to get the car. And now I am working to save to get the apartment." But when the young couple moves into maternal or paternal homes together, they may live in basements or pull mattresses stacked against the living room wall to the floor at night, sleep on couches, crowd into spaces traversed by other adults and children throughout the day and night, and have to negotiate resonances of old emotional family dynamics, all the while taking care of an infant. As tensions roil and tempers boil, blame moves in different directions and members of the household get pulled into the drama.

Lorenzo, a 21-year-old African American father of two children, both younger than two years, had been together with the mother of his children since he was 18. Lorenzo grew up in Bridgeport in his grandmother and mother's home. He did not finish high school, but completed his GED through a local program. He had struggled with employment, had relied on street connections for income, was arrested for drug trafficking and on probation at the time of the interview, and owed child support, which he was not paying. While Lorenzo was in jail awaiting his hearing, he said he had time to reflect on his life and "felt something was missing," that he was "stuck" and was "crying out" for a different path. He said at one time he felt that "I need a child to take me away from this negativity," but when "I found out I was having a child is when everything around me stopped. I began to get stuck." He asked himself, "What I'm gonna do? I love this girl. She is about to have my baby. I ain't really working. What I'ma do?"

After his release, Lorenzo, Shemariah, their two children, and a third child that Shemariah had from a prior relationship moved in with Lorenzo's mother. "Mom's held us down," Lorenzo said. And when Shemariah was able to get state assistance for the children, Lorenzo "didn't really even sell any drugs or anything. I left it alone," even though he was "tempted always. When them Pampers and stuff got low, I was tempted, man. But I was like 'Naw, I can't do it man.' I just came home not too long ago. . . . It ain't worth it right now." But Lorenzo stressed, "We struggled for a year, man. All we did was struggle. All we did was get money on the first of the month, use it, and struggle every month."

Lorenzo found a job at a fast food restaurant through a friend to ease the pressure, but living with his mother was key. With the extra income, Lorenzo said, "We didn't have to pay no rent. All we had to do was buy the kids what we needed, buy food to last us for the month, and we had our little money to play with. Beautiful. It get no better . . . you in heaven, man." It wasn't heaven. Tensions simmered and tempers flared in the household. Lorenzo and his mother felt like Shemariah favored the older child and Lorenzo said his mother started telling him she was a "loser. She don't want to do nothing. You are struggling for her. C'mon man, leave her alone. And I am like trying to explain I really care about her. But at the same time, 'I understand what you are saying, moms, because

I am starting to feel the same way.'" According to Lorenzo, the breaking point came when Shemariah wanted to go to an amusement park with her family and friends to celebrate her birthday. She left the children home with Lorenzo to take care of and left despite his protest. They got into an argument and, adhering to gendered norms and expectations, Lorenzo's mother drew the line:

> So now moms is like, "Hold up. Yo, you got to go. You ain't going to be acting like this. I am tired of your mouth, bad enough. I am keeping it real with you, keeping a roof over your head for my son. You all don't got to pay rent really. I am getting tired of this. What you going to do? You don't got time to go to no Great Adventures. You got three kids." She just keeping it real. And she getting smart with my mother, so, you know what? Leave. Take your daughter and leave. And that's that.

Lorenzo did not bother to call in after the blowup and missed work the next few days; he stayed home with the children and then helped Shemariah find an apartment. His job was terminated.

Shemariah moved out with her oldest child, while Lorenzo and his two biological children continued living with his mother. Caught between his mother and his partner, Lorenzo eventually moved in with his partner, reuniting the three children. At the time of the interview, Shemariah was receiving public assistance, they were on a waiting list for public housing, Lorenzo owed $6,000 in child support, he was in a training program making no income, and said he was resisting the call of the streets.

Extended family are essential to young parents who cannot sustain themselves financially, and grandmothers are often heroic in their efforts to help out—to raise grandchildren and provide housing and food. Moreover, given the tenuous circumstances in Lorenzo and Shemariah's lives, it is very likely that his mother, and maybe Shemaria's as well, will be called on again for housing and other forms of support. But crowded housing conditions, poverty, division of loyalties, and old family dynamics place much stress on residents living in these conditions, and on young couples trying to establish their families. The casualization of family life extends where the institutional structures that facilitate the life course recede. It is here where informal networks of support become normalized, but not without the persistent churning of impermanence.

The "New Father"

In a very short period of time, family roles and norms have changed. And so has the economy and labor force. And the state welfare system. And prisons. In other words, we live in an era of flux, in which uncertainty has become the norm. Moreover, the burdens of uncertainty have fallen heavily on individuals and families, as the privatization of risk and the triumph of entrepreneurial reason have taken hold.[8] Kathleen Gerson, who has studied these trends closely across all social classes, describes, "Families are situations in flux, not fixed arrangements. Labels such as 'dual earner,' 'single-parent,' and 'traditional' are only snapshots, while family life is a moving picture."[9]

At the bottom of the labor force, this uncertainty has its own unique configuration. The increasing number of temporary jobs and jobs that don't pay sustainable wages, the withdrawal of government support for those precariously employed or no longer looking for work in a dismal labor force, and the concentration of poverty, social isolation, and idleness policed in urban ghettoes and prisons create dismal conditions that manifest in interpersonal family relationships. Within this mix, fathers are hearing different messages about fathering than was characteristic of their own fathers. The controlled, emotionally distant, breadwinner image of fatherhood and its attendant forms of masculinity have been rapidly replaced with the expectation that the father will be involved in his children's lives as a nurturing, caring father who will contribute to their emotional development.

Fathers receive these messages from a variety of sources—from the media, institutional authorities, social service programs, court personnel, intimate partners, and from peers. The proliferation of fatherhood programs at the turn of the new century, like the ones that we studied in Connecticut, emphasized the dual role of the father—to provide financially and to be emotionally involved.[10] The duality of financial responsibility and emotional involvement was enacted in different ways, often depending upon family resources.

Neotraditional Families

In our study, some fathers talked about playing with their children, giving baths, and changing diapers. However, in many instances, the children were very young and fathers often remained on the perimeter of childcare; instead, they talked about how they intended to parent as their sons and daughters aged. Negotiating these new roles was not easy, and mothers were often suspicious and reluctant to turn over too much care to the fathers. They adopted more traditional attitudes and gendered boundaries.

Lina and Riza were a young couple living apart with their respective parents. They did not live together for two reasons—because Lina's father, who was Peruvian, did not like Riza, who was Filipino, which Lina attributed to racism, but also because Lina desired her mother's help in taking care of the infant, who was only seven weeks old at the time of the interview. In instances like this, the mother and grandmother bond around the care of the child, pushing the father out of these emotional ties—and in some cases like Lina and Riza's, out of the household altogether.

Maggie and Slim lived in the same household, but Maggie did not trust Slim to be alone with their two-year-old. "I wouldn't leave him [the child] alone with Slim for up to four or five hours, only because Slim is a guy." Of course, there may be good reasons for both of these scenarios. Young mothers rely on their own mothers to take care of their infants and toddlers because they have experience and are a resource. Rarely have fathers been prepared to take care of children, let alone infants, and given the rapidly changing norms and expectations concerning fatherhood, it is unlikely they have had male role models to learn from. Harmony left their two-month-old son with his father one time and reported, "I came back and he had throw-up stains all over [the bassinet]. Now I keep all his stuff clean and I know I didn't leave him like that. That's the last time he was with him alone." And as John Leventhal, the medical director of Yale's child abuse clinic and a leading scholar in the area of child maltreatment knows all too well, an unprepared and impatient father can unintentionally do serious damage to an infant.[11]

Some mothers tried to involve the fathers more in childcare, but traditional gender roles and expectations usually defined divisions of care.[12] Janelle described Elijah's involvement with their two-month-old daughter, "He looks after her and picks her up when she cries or something, but the one that changes her and bathes her and gives her milk is me, you know. If he notices that the girl dirtied herself, he calls for me and tells me about it [laughs]. I don't like [to leave the baby with Elijah] as you can imagine. It's just . . . I don't trust anybody."

Perhaps it is understandable that mothers did not trust their fragile infants to the care of fathers, but several of them projected other traditional gender expectations as well. Returning to Liza, she not only excluded Riza from childcare duties, she was annoyed that he was not stepping up and being "the man" in the relationship. Lina explains, "But as a person, he's, he's very sensitive. I guess in a way I did like that but now I really don't cuz I want him to be the man in our relationship and not me taking control of it and telling him what to do. I keep on telling him, if you want advice, don't ask me. I'm younger than you. I'm a girl (laugh). You have to do it." Similarly, when asked the question if a child needs a man in the home, most mothers wanted them there to teach gender norms, especially to their sons. Several like Jenna, a 25-year-old white mother, explained that she wanted the children to know "this is what a mommy does like basically clean house and cook supper and this is what the father does is basically work around the house and fixing things."

With the changing norms and expectations of fatherhood, mothers created more openings for and made more demands on fathers to share childcare and household responsibilities, but typically they remained the primary caretakers and homemakers. Similarly, fathers talked about their involvement in these activities with a sense of achievement and pride, but their primary responsibility remained as the provider, even when they were not working. In other words, in households where couples cohabitated, they were bending toward the "new fatherhood" while maintaining traditional values and roles. Gerson refers to these families as neotraditional.[13] Fathers nurtured when and where they could, and their involvement was negotiated with the mothers, and sometimes maternal grandmothers. The mothers' "neotraditional" orientations usually included the intention to go (or return) to work when their infant was old enough, and in several cases, they did not stop working after the child was born. Their primary responsibility, however, remained the home and childcare, often shared with maternal and, in some instances, paternal grandmothers. Work was not their primary sphere of concern or influence, and yet they knew they needed to contribute income to the household. Similarly, they did not expect fathers to be primary caretakers, but they did expect them to be there and participate in childcare.

There were several examples of father involvement in nurturing activities with their babies. In our interviews we listened for how they were engaged. Jairo, 19 years old, described the best part of his day was before leaving for work:

Just waking up in the day and just seeing him there and know that he's there and I am going to have a good day with him.... That's the best part about it. You always got to thank God for that.... I would wake up, give him a kiss.

But I wanted to say "Good morning," be there for breakfast, have fun with him and feed him in the morning. That's like beautiful.

Twenty-year-old Eldis described his 10-month-old daughter as "wild. She wants to be everywhere, touching everything. She crawls. But she can like grab something and pull herself up and move along on something. But she can't walk, she'll fall." Eldis talked about her putting things in her mouth. "Even the littlest things you can't see. [laughter] Like how in the heck did you see that?" When talking about what he does with her, he said, "I take her out somewhere—the park, Chuck E. Cheese—things like that. I play with her on the floor. I mean at Chuck E. Cheese she can't really do much. I'll sit her on the machine and like it moves up and down or something. I'll sit her on my lap or something, or I will shake her toys for her. Just play with her." Eldis was not living with his daughter at the time of the interview, but he saw her every day. He was living with his mother, working at a fast food restaurant, and saving money for an apartment for the three of them to move into. Because he did not live with his daughter, he stressed, "I feel like I just always have to be around her every spare time I get, because if not she is not going to really know who I am."

Nineteen-year-old Rosa said about Tommy: "We don't go out much. He works from three at night until sometimes one or two in the afternoon. And then he comes home and I go to the store or just little things. He baby-sits. He changes diapers. He cooks. He cleans" [laughs]. The "neo" part of neotraditional, however, suggested that these couples were negotiating new gender territory, which invoked tensions, differences, and power struggles. Gloria and Ted, an older white couple, were trying to define the lines of work and home responsibilities. Ted was the main provider—he worked full-time in a machine shop, while Gloria worked part-time for a dry cleaner and did most of the childcare. Their son was 14 months of age. Gloria expressed her frustration with Ted.

The house is a mess and he's so stressed that, what the hell does he think I do when he leaves at five-thirty in the morning and doesn't come home till five at night. . . . I mean he does more than a lot of people. He does do bath time which is nice; it's kind of like their little thing. Um, and he does kind of keep him like at night because Ted doesn't go to bed till like midnight. I go to bed pretty much when the baby goes to bed unless I'm doing laundry or I've dishes. I, um, go to bed fairly early. So, like if the baby wakes up before midnight, he gets him. But, everything, it's like a little kid. Like, well, how come you get to do this and I didn't, well you got this and you know, what's the point? I hate that.

Couples were trying to work out their gendered routines with increasing expectations that fathers would share in child caretaking and mothers would contribute toward the family wage, but they were negotiating the traditional boundaries of the patriarchal nuclear family. There was considerable variation in terms of what fathers would and could do, what mothers expected of fathers, and how childcare and homecare were negotiated. And these negotiations often included larger kin networks, in which generational norms sometimes came into conflict. Gendered norms, household circumstances and dynamics, income opportunities and sources, and kin network involvement generated ambiguity, uncertainty, and conflict.

While fathers were figuring out how to change diapers, to take care of crying babies in the middle of the night, to give baths when they returned from work, and to feed the baby a bottle before they left for work in the morning, they were also articulating their more traditional role as the disciplinarian in the family, often by trying to figure out how to do it differently from their own fathers. Several had grown up with fathers who used extreme forms of corporal punishment, and they were trying not to emulate their fathers, if for no other reason than this type of punishment, today, is defined as child abuse by the state. Instead, they were wrestling with issues about whether to spank their children, or how to punish children that would not draw the attention from state authorities, but would teach their children right from wrong. As such, this was also an expression of neotraditional fathering. Jose, a 19-year-old Puerto Rican father, told us,

I don't like hitting him. . . . Sometimes I have to if it's necessary. She let him do whatever he wants. And I don't want to be with that. I don't want to spoil him; if I let him do whatever he wants, he is going to be disrespectful to people. I don't want to do that. So, I guess, I mean I discipline him in a regular way. I ain't going to do it my father's way because I already know the errors my father did. So I am going to try not to be in that area right there. . . . I am trying my best.

Luis, a 27-year-old Puerto Rican father, put it this way:

If you don't spank them, you end up yelling at him anyway or getting so mad and frustrated, but you don't want to take out your frustration on beating him either. Being a parent is hard; to each their own. I mean I don't say abuse your kid, but parents should be allowed to discipline their kid to a certain extent without it acting like they are killing their kid. Because maybe they spank them on their butt with their hand a couple of times to give him a little wake up. I don't see nothing wrong with that. But if you are beating him with an extension cord or a stick, well that's different.

A few of the white fathers were particularly angry at the state for infringing on their liberties to parent. Robert, 33, said, "I am going to raise my son the same way my dad rose me. You fuck up, yeah, you need to get a spanking. The fucking cops want to send me to jail, you can go fuck yourself, because guess what, cop? I am sure when you were little you got your fuckin' ass whooped, too. Don't even play fuckin' games with me." Scott, 26, attributed the crime rate to:

the fact that parents have been forced to become more lax on discipline by society, by governing agencies like DCF. Everyone is afraid of getting accused of child abuse. So I think parents are so gun-shy on discipline that our kids younger and younger and younger are being allowed to get away with more and more and more.

Some fathers, like Huey, a 37-year-old white father, was less concerned about the state and more focused on whether corporal punishment was effective.

A little smack on the hand or somethin' like that is fine, but I mean I've seen parents get a little ridiculous, in grocery stores parents literally sockin' their kids. To me, that's wrong. They ain't gotta beat 'em up just to get 'em to listen to ya. You beat 'em up then, I wouldn't listen, either. They figure if they scare 'em that way, they're gonna listen better. It don't work that way.

Elwin, a 20-year-old Puerto Rican father, took Huey's logic further:

When you hit them, it's going to make it worse. Your kid is going to think dad is a bad person. He hit me. You might as well not hit them than hit them and be hated. My baby's mother spanks my daughter and she be telling "Mommy, I don't like you. You hit me. I don't like you." Her grandmother hit her too, she spanks her too. And she told her, "Grandma, I can't wait. When I grow big, I am going to hit you."

Many fathers were articulating neotraditional forms of disciplining children in response to state child protection standards, their familial traditions of discipline, and their own personal experiences with corporal punishment. The most marginalized fathers—those incarcerated, unemployed, and street involved—were also wrestling with the norms and expectations of the "new father" and with their roles as disciplinarian and nurturer, but given the social-spatial conditions in which they were parenting, their narratives were somewhat different.

Turning Vices into Virtues

In our study, 1 in 4 fathers were teens, while 4 in 10 were younger than 21. Among the young fathers who were incarcerated at the time of the interview, more than one-half were considered to have good relationships and a little less than one-fifth poor relationships with the mothers of their most recent children.[14] Only one father indicated that he had no relationship with his child, and three-fourths indicated a fair to good relationship with their recent children. These were fathers, who despite being young and incarcerated, were already learning to father from the margins—literally, as their relationships were developing through the looking glass.

We discussed with the more marginalized fathers how they expected to parent children growing up in poor neighborhoods, or more specifically how they intended to engage their sons and daughters as fathers. As we saw in Chapter 6, they were trying to figure out how to prepare their sons and daughters for violent neighborhoods and schools. These fathers were also being exposed to the expectations of father involvement from fatherhood programs inside and outside of the prison, and from institutional authorities as well. These expectations were then being negotiated in relationships with the mothers and filtered through the fathers' conceptions of their own masculinity. Just as the working fathers living in the households were learning new expressions of fatherhood and masculinity within a neotraditional milieu, more marginalized men were searching for new expressions of masculinity and parenting situated in a different set of family and neighborhood dynamics.

Living in a twilight period of changing fatherhood norms, fathers were often left without parenting models or skills for how to meet the role of the engaged father. Most of the more marginalized fathers wanted to do it differently from their own fathers—they wanted to be there and be emotionally close to their children. Growing up in lives saturated with violence—in homes, schools, neighborhoods, juvenile facilities, prisons—they were trying to figure out how to convert violent street histories into parenting capital. Many described a desire to have a strong relationship with their children, one where their children could speak to them about any subject, no matter how personal or difficult it might be. In fact, many of the more marginalized fathers believed that their street experiences and "bad boy" lifestyles provided them with insights and wisdom about how to navigate the difficult worlds that awaited their children. In some ways, many of these fathers imagined turning their vices into virtues. To avoid prison, the streets, drugs, predatory men, and so on, their children would only need to talk to them about it, because they had been there.[15] Nathan avowed:

> I am not going to hide anything from them. I can easily show them, point them out certain people, "This is what happens when you do this. Look at this person. Look at that person." . . . "Look at the choices I made. You don't want to end up like that."

This narrative valorized Nathan's life experiences: "Nine times out of ten, they going to understand that," he insisted.

Many fathers wanted to talk about how to be a nurturing, caring, and sensitive parent who listened and maintained open communication with their children and, at the same time, a disciplinarian—what many believed was their primary role in the family. This was sometimes expressed as the difficulty of being a "comforting ear" and, at the same time, an "iron fist," or as being what many described as a "friend" to their children, while also making sure that their children learned to respect their parents and elders, learned that they were not equals, and learned their place in the family—values that typically mediate working-class households.[16] Jermaine imagined how he would walk this line with his daughter.

> I just basically want her to talk to me and have an open relationship. . . . I know this lady right, she got kids and her kids just walk all over her because they look at her as a friend. . . . Like me, I'll play that parent role.

Like she [my daughter] knows right now I am a parent. But as she get older, I want to play the friend role so she can always come sit and talk to me and discuss anything.

Eduardo reflected:

Being a father is nothing that is easy because it is a constant battle. You have to love [and] be very patient in a clever way be able to manipulate him and guide him. . . . Because you know that sometimes children are rebellious and all of that. [So you need to] completely turn into their friend—not contradict him but tell him yes and later on deviate from him, but cleverly so he can understand. When a father is a bit strong with their kids, that's when they do the opposite, and here they show you a personality and out there, away from their parents, they are a totally different person. . . . I feel that it's a lot of work, but it can be done.

Many of these fathers were figuring this out alone, without their own fathers in their lives and without many places to turn for direction. Often, their own mothers served as their models and advisors. Understanding the full context of this struggle for marginalized street men can be seen in Rio's story, where past street life, unemployment, estrangement with his father, and his orientation to fatherhood come together.

Rio's Story

We did four interviews with Rio across an 18-month period from the spring of 2009 to the winter of 2010. Rio turned 22 years of age and his daughter 21 months by our last interview. Rio referred to the mother of his child as his wife, even though they were not legally married. Rio met his "wife" in high school and they had been together for five years. They lived with Rio's mother in New Britain in 2009, but had moved in with his "wife's" parents in 2010. The move located them in a poorer neighborhood, with a lot of street activity, and in a crowded apartment shared also with his wife's sister and her boyfriend.

Rio grew up in Willimantic, a smaller town, but one with a publicly recognized drug problem.[17] His mother moved them to New Britain because of problems Rio and his brother were having in Willimantic, but Rio explained that with the move to New Britain, "I was exposed to more shit than Willimantic—more drugs, more drama." Rio was very street involved in his adolescence and had been incarcerated for possession of drugs with the intent to sell and released on probation one month before our first interview. He had also been arrested before on a larceny charge. He claimed that he had taken the fall for these crimes, which involved others, and had left the streets and drug dealing behind. He spent seven months in prison and was there when his daughter was born. His "wife" brought his daughter to the prison the first time Rio saw her.

Rio had an estranged relationship with his father. He described his father as a "con artist," a "big hustler type" who had been in and out of prison much of his life, including one five-year bid. His parents had migrated from Puerto Rico, where Rio was born, but then split up. He said after trying to have a relationship with his father, he gave up, disappointed by his father's inability to live up to promises and to make time for him. Meanwhile, Rio's mother brought Rio and his brother to Willimantic, while a godmother and grandmother raised his sisters.

Rio described his wife as the opposite of him in high school. She was quiet and studious, or as he said:

> My girl is smart—real educated. Unlike me, I am a dumb-ass. . . . Like she is more like book smart, like school-wise and stuff like that. I am more the street smarts. So she can whoop my ass in like some fucking Physics and shit, but I can whoop her ass in teaching her what up with drugs and guns and just shit on the street.

He appeared to have a close relationship with his "wife" and was very angry at himself for not being there when his daughter was born.

Rio and our interviewer developed a good rapport during the 18-month period, especially bonding around their shared love for hip-hop. Sagacity was an artist himself and encouraged Rio to "spit a few verses" at the end of their third interview. Sagacity described Rio as street oriented, and Rio seemed comfortable talking to Sagacity about his street past. At the end of third interview, Sagacity recorded in his field notes:

> You are starting to see the whole stresses of working under-the-table jobs and stuff like that getting to him. He told me he was like "I don't want to get back to the streets but that street money is calling me." He seems a lot more

shaky on that. Whereas before, like the first interview definitely, he was sitting there saying like "I can't do that. I won't do that. I won't go back to the
streets." Now he's like "I don't know." That's a viable option for him right
now. So he's really hurting hard. I mean he still has a couple under-the-table
jobs. One is picking up checks for the police department, like for donations.
Then the other one he delivers pizzas.

Rio had a job working part-time at a grocery store, but he lost the job for
insubordination. When the manager told him that he needed to greet the
customers when they entered the store, Rio recalled saying, "Nah, you know,
don't talk to me like that. You feel me? I will try my best" and he was like
'Well, you better.' " The manager fired Rio, but Rio said he won his case when
the unemployment office investigated his claim. He felt triumphant since, in
his view, his supervisor "thought I was like some little street hoodlum that
don't know what insubordination means." He was receiving $50 a week in
unemployment compensation.

His job working for the police department was an odd one, especially
given his criminal history. Rio would drive to the home of people who had
answered telephone solicitation from the police department and agreed to
donate money. Rio was picking up the checks. He did this three times a week,
until he made a trip into a white community.

A couple of weeks ago we was in Cromwell and we almost caught like a
home invasion 'cause people thought we were trying to break in the house.
All we was doing was getting them checks for the police. They pulled out the
burner [gun] and everything on us. They felt like shit because they called
and then they had to let us go. We don't got nothing. Everything matches
up. They let us go.

By the fourth interview, Rio was still receiving his $50 per week and was
delivering pizzas for cash under the table. His hours at work, while irreg-
ular, were increasing. His "wife" had been let go from her cashier's job at a
grocery store, so money was tight. When Sagacity asked what was causing
stress in his life, he answered without hesitation: "Money. [laughter] That's
the biggest stress. Money pays car insurance—you don't got money you
can't do that. Money is a lot. And that's my biggest stress—getting a job
and trying to do what I got to do to feed my family and to get money to
be okay."

At the last interview, Rio confided that he had been diagnosed with obsessive-compulsive disorder (OCD). In his fieldnotes, Sagacity related this to Rio's sense of powerlessness and described Rio's reflections on his condition.

> And he was like "Living here is hell." And what's also interesting is that he thinks that like a lot of his OCD is coming from being so stressed out of like taking care of his family and stuff. Now he's really meticulous on where things should be and how things should fit into their own place. Because he is feeling like he is more powerless and stuff. So he's trying to have control . . . he was like "Yeah, I think it's because I ain't got control over certain things so I just want to have control over what I have control over."

Rio's favorite time of the day was at night when he would go out on his second-floor porch and smoke a "bogey" and try to figure out his life. He did not drink or use drugs during this 18-month period, except he did enjoy smoking cigarettes. He described these moments:

> That's why I smoke bogeys like it calms me down. . . . I don't do it to be cool. It's just a stress reliever. Have my little alone time. It's straight to come out here at like night time and just look up at the sky and smoke and just think about shit. And at nighttime when the stars is out and you be like, wow, you just start thinking of like 100,000 things that come through your mind.

Given the circumstances of Rio's life and his family history, how did Rio describe himself as a father during the first two years of his daughter's life?

Rio said that he shared in the caretaking of his daughter as soon as he was reunited with the family. At the first interview, he described:

> I am learning how to wake up all the time she cries. Go make her bottle. You know what I am saying? Shake her so she fall asleep a little bit. Then change her diapers. It's pretty much easy. I can't wait until she gets older. . . . At first it was like "Wow, diapers." How the heck you put a diaper on? I don't know how to put no freakin' diaper on. But I just learned. My girl was like "Look it. This is how you got to do it."

As his daughter aged, Rio assumed the more gendered role as the disciplinarian.

I got to spank her a couple of times because she got to learn to listen to dad, you know? . . . And she'll test you. What she'll do is say you put a soda on the table. She'll grab it. The first time you say, "No, don't do that. Put it back." She'll smile and grab that shit again. "No!" Then the third time when she does it "I am going to spank you, you feel me? You are going to learn." So I have to spank her. Because she'll keep on doing it. If you don't discipline her, and it's not like I hit her hard. I just spank her in the butt real fast, you feel me? Boom, you feel me? And then she'll cry. She'll run to her mom, you feel me? . . . But she got to learn. She acts up big time with her mom. When she's with me, she's straight. But when her mom gets home from work, she acts up. That's that trigger, like "Ha, ha, mommy is here!" [laughter] She'll take her glasses off and throw them.

Like many of the fathers mentioned earlier, Rio was trying to discipline his child differently from how he was punished, and yet he wanted to maintain a modified form of corporal punishment to teach his daughter "respect" and "humility."

As his daughter ages, Rio imagined that his fathering role would be more as a protector of his daughter. Rio desired open communication with his daughter, but he did not see how this might contradict his need to be a strict disciplinarian that constrained an adolescent daughter's freedom. In a somewhat humorous flip of the switch, Rio began by saying, "I don't want her to be scared to tell me everything," before imagining a conversation with his daughter: " 'Oh, Daddy, I like a boy.' 'Yeah? Well, don't like him. Change your mind. You don't like the boy. Where is that boy going to get you? He ain't getting you nowhere. Give me five reasons that you should be with that boy. And five legitimate reasons!' "

Sagacity challenged Rio's deep desire to protect his daughter from boys who might mistreat her: "How are you going to handle situations like that with your daughter? Because you can't go around jacking up little kids." Rio responded:

I don't know. I'll probably even scare the little nigga. I am just going to be real with the dude, because like I don't want the nigga to be scared of me, but know how to respect me. You going to know how to respect me. You are going to learn what it is and you are going to respect my daughter, nigga. . . . Like I hear about niggas hitting them daughters and shit. That's not going to roll with me. Even if I got to pay a couple little niggas to whoop your ass [laughter] I am going to get it in, believe me. . . . Just because you a minor don't mean shit. I might not touch you but I'll get little niggas to touch you. Shit, don't get twisted. I got a lot of little mother-fuckers around here. . . . So I don't sweat it.

Rio did not see the conundrum between imagining open communication with his daughter and his overprotective disposition, mostly because he was preparing his daughter for the conditions in which she lived and because he saw this as part of his parenting expertise derived from his street experiences. He explained:

I want to show her what it is. Let her know I went to jail. Let her know that she can't trust everybody. Watch who you trust, you know what I am saying? And just look out for yourself because nobody else is going to look out for you. When you out there by yourself, you out there by yourself regardless, who going to [say they] have their back. . . . But when she is in the situation, it's only going to be her.

Rio was invested in parenting—it was his primary motivation for staying away from the streets. He imagined that his daughter would have a well-rounded upbringing because she would get "book smarts" from his "wife" and "street smarts" from him. "I'd rather [her] have both," Rio said. "I'd rather have her book smarts and the street smarts. Then, damn, she is on top of it. She sees both of the worlds; she can be more ahead of most kids."

Rio's story reflected similar dynamics that other street-involved fathers in our study were confronting, even though situations varied. Some lived outside the home, some used drugs or alcohol, some had more contentious relationships with their partners, some returned to the streets for income, and some relationships broke up under the stress of inadequate income, overcrowded apartments, intimate relating, mental health issues, infidelities, and addictions. What was similar though was that these fathers rarely had their own fathers in their lives, they were parenting in poor neighborhoods, and they were expected to figure out on their own how to adjust to changing fathering norms and expectations in a rapidly changing political and economic context that provided little support. Rio was making it up as he went, drawing on what experiences he could and whatever resources were available to make sense of the changing world within which he was structurally located.

***

Neotraditional parenting extended fatherhood into more nurturing, care-taking roles in the home, whether men lived in it or outside it. They measured their own involvements by how "engaged" they were. But the shadows of the provider and disciplinarian roles were still paramount, even as fathers leaned toward the "new father" identity. These values were usually shared by mothers, and sometimes grandmothers, who for their own reasons, maintained control of their households even as they expected fathers to step up and be more involved. In these spaces, fathers were trying to figure out how to be engaged, and how to integrate their masculine and fathering identities. Some borrowed from their own fathers, even as they attempted to do it differently, especially when it came to their disciplinary roles. Some rejected their fathers entirely and were determined to "be there" for their children in ways their fathers were not, an issue we take up in the next chapter. Finally, more marginalized fathers struggled with how to raise their children in the contexts of dangerous neighborhoods and untrustworthy institutions, suspended in a liminal space of how to nurture and yet prepare their children for potential violence, and of how to discipline and yet be their children's confidants in negotiating complicated social spaces.

Break-ups

Most of the fathers in our study were involved in the lives of their most recent children and most were still involved with the mothers of the children. These two sets of relationships—parenting and partnering—are not always linked. As the literature on fragile families has documented, the "package deal," in which fathers' relationships with children were largely defined by their relationships with the mothers, has given way to the "new package deal," in which fathers' relationships with their children define the parents' relationships.[18] Under the former, when divorce occurred—and the package deal had been violated—fathers involvement likewise declined. However, with the increase in divorce and nonmarital cohabitation, the new package deal provides a normative route for sustained father involvement, and for more marginalized fathers, a chance to derive social value even when they cannot contribute financially.[19] The new package deal, however, comes with added complications and challenges, which also results in a decline in father involvement over time, only for different reasons.

In our Couples Study, almost one-third of fathers had children with another mother, while one-fifth of couples had children in the household that were not born to them. In the Father Initiative Study, fathers rarely resided with the mothers of their children, but reported better relationships with their children than with the mothers. In both of these studies, the fathers were young, with a median age of 25 in the Couples Study and 21 in the Fatherhood Initiative Study. The median age for fathers at the two program sites that served the most marginalized fathers in the Father Initiative Study was 19, and a little less than one-half of these young fathers had more than one child, and about one-third, with more than one mother. Still, even among the most marginalized—with nearly one-half incarcerated—more than eight in ten were considered to have fair to good relationships with the most recent mother (83 percent) and children (85 percent).

Relationships in both of these studies, however, will not necessarily sustain the test of time. These were snapshots of young couples and young fathers describing their relationships. They were—and will be—confronted by many challenges despite the prospects of the new package deal which encourages family formations around relationships with children. As the literature indicates, some relationships will dissolve around incarceration, drug addictions, infidelities, partner violence, and street lifestyles.[20] Meanwhile, income problems will remain at the center of many of these relationship difficulties. Fathers, with limited formal employment opportunities and criminal records, combined with the need for mothers to acquire income from multiple sources to support themselves and their children, will create insurmountable problems.[21]

Contrary to the color-coded images of the deadbeat dad, however, research has shown that black father involvement with children is highest compared to other racial groups of nonresidential fathers.[22] Kin work helps to sustain this. Maternal and paternal kin provide for flexible family formation that allows for father involvement, familial dynamics of reciprocity, relationship suspensions and renewals, and second-chance relationships.[23] Given the inadequate structural support for families at the bottom of the labor force, these family formations become fluid and dynamic, and negotiated across time.[24] Women are at the center of these extended familial networks, through which responsible fatherhood is defined, demanded, enacted, and resisted.[25] The ambiguity and uncertainty that result from these variable processes place an emphasis on the now—on a family formation that rests at any given moment upon the turbulence of economic, state, housing, and neigh-borhood vagaries. As Aasha Abdill eloquently put it:

> You may not be committed forever, but you are together now and for the foreseeable future. Or you are not together now, but you live with the possi-bility that you may reconnect in the future. Or you are together now but not living together because of circumstances. Family becomes planned with *now* as the most important unit of time.[26]

Relating Through Episodes of Incarceration

There are few life events that disrupt family formations more than incarcera-tion, or that underscore Abdill's insight about changing configurations of the now. The 29 fathers who were incarcerated and receiving services from the Hartford program provide a good illustration. About one-half (52 percent) of fathers were not receiving visits from their children while incarcerated.[27] The main reason was that they were largely dependent upon the mothers to bring their children to the facility. Relationships were disrupted by the incar-ceration. Four had broken up before the prison term, eight broke up during, five were still together, but pulling apart, while eight remained solidly to-gether and four indicated that prison had made their relationships closer.

Benito, 18, provided a familiar script of break-up during incarceration.

> At first, you know, before I got locked up me and her we had our disagreements and arguments while we were together. When I got locked up, it was like she started to slip away. At first, she held on for about almost a year. But then after that she just barely came around anyway but she always wrote me. She always said that she was going to be here for me. And then all of a sudden it just started going the opposite way.

When Benito was released, he was hurt and angry, and right away went to his son's house.

> So, when I came home the first night and I went over to her house to get my son, she was wondering why I wasn't saying nothing to her, why I'm not talking to her. Because I don't got nothing to say to her. I just came, got my son and kept it moving. That's how it was going to be.

For 19-year-old Kevin, not only did the relationship dissolve, but things turned ugly. He said that his partner terminated his parental rights.

> I didn't know that. I just found out the other day. Because now she is trying to change the kid's name to this other guy and he wants to adopt her and he's saying it's his kid. . . . I am going to bring that up to the judge too, saying, "Now I want a paternity test and I want her to pay for it."

Incarceration places strains on relationships financially and emotionally.

In a few cases, however, the fathers said that their relationships with mothers improved during their incarcerations.[28] Fathers often described this time as a test of the relationship, placing the burden of fidelity on their partners. Loyalty might then result in a deeper emotional connection. Dante, a 20-year-old, African American father described a good relationship with the mother of his two-year-old-daughter. He was present at the delivery of her birth, which he described as a highlight in his life. Returning home from his incarceration, he was planning to marry his partner.

RON: You are about to get married?
DANTE: Yeah.
RON: When?
DANTE: Soon. I am going to do the things with the Justice of the Peace, just to get it done so we married. And then a year or two later have a big wedding.
RON: Why you getting married, man?
DANTE: I'm ready for it. I don't want to play no games, man. My girl, man, she is a winner. I won't feel like I'll find anything like her. She's stuck with me. Even when I went to jail. Kept it real with me.
RON: All the way?
DANTE: All the way, man. When I was in jail other people be talking like "Oh my girl out doing this and that."
RON: It happens, man.
DANTE: My girl, while I'm in jail, she won't look your way, she will only look this way.

Upon his release, Dante's commitment to his daughter and partner seemed to have deepened as a result of his incarceration.

Jamal, 19, also described how his relationship "actually got stronger" during his nine-month sentence for drug dealing. He said, "She started showing more feelings, like a lot of things started coming out like what she did in the past. It just brought us together. It came to the point when I got so close to her I just woke up in the middle of the night and just write a letter to her."

Relationship trajectories during prison terms did not necessarily determine whether mothers brought children to see their fathers at the prison facility. Four mothers, for instance, who were not intimately involved brought children to see their fathers, while some mothers in relationships that were still intact did not have the transportation or resources to visit. In fact, among the twelve fathers who were receiving visits from their children, six mothers were still intimately involved, but two of them were dependent upon the paternal grandmother for transportation. Even in cases where the relationships with the mothers had ended badly, it seemed that most of the mothers would not have prevented fathers from seeing their children if family members were willing to transport them. Fathers were at the mercy of their resource networks, and the general impression was that if they had someone to bring their kid, they'd be getting visits. There were a few cases in which acrimonious relationships invoked maternal gatekeeping, but usually the explanation for growing distance between mothers and children concerned resources and transportation.

The fluidity of relationships with mothers and children that occurred around the interruption of prison was also apparent among the eight fathers who had been released at the time of the interview. One of the fathers, Bruce, received regular visits from the mother and child during his prison bid, even though he and the mother were not romantically involved. After his release, however, they had reconciled their intimate relationship. Another father, Martin, said that the mother of his child admitted cheating on him toward the end of his two-year term and that they had broken up. Nonetheless, after his release, he was seeing his child three to four times a week, even though he and the mother remained apart. Darius did not receive visits because he had no one to bring his child to the facility and he and the mother's relationship went "on hold" when he got locked up. After his release, they were back together and he was seeing both the mother and child regularly, even though they were not living together. Like Dante described earlier, when he said his relationship got better during prison and that he was preparing to marry the mother, Marshall said that his relationship stayed steady during his incarceration and that he was planning to marry the mother now that he had been released. And then there was Jose, who maintained his relationship with the mother during his four-year bid, even though the lack of resources prevented regular visits. Now that he was released, they were drifting apart, and the volatility that had characterized their relationship before his incarceration had returned and was threatening their future together. Finally, as we already saw, Benito said he went straight to his child's house upon release and ignored the mother, who had broken up with him. However, he saw the child less after this initial visit, even though he said he was paying child support.

The turbulence of life on the margins resulted in complicated formations of relating that took on different configurations over time, especially during and after episodes of incarceration.[29]

The Fluidity of Family Formation

Incarceration was certainly a key disruptive force in the lives of couples, but the mutability of relationships on the social and economic margins was apparent for several couples that did not involve incarceration. Our study at the end of the decade enabled us to observe the fluidity of family formation as we attempted to track fathers for at least a year. Field researchers witnessed a wide range of relationships, some of which seemed happy and yet ended before the final interview, and others that seemed rocky and yet endured.

Income problems were central to all of these relationships, including the ones that remained intact. Not surprisingly, income problems affected moods and arguments between the fathers and the mothers of their children, but fading romance in their relationships and, in some instances, infidelities, also affected relationship stability. In relationships that ended during the course of our study, romantic and interpersonal issues were often given as the reasons, even though separating these issues from income problems was not always so easy.

Ray, a 30-year-old white father, was dealing with embattled relationship issues of various sorts throughout the entire study, although not always with the recent mother of his child. He spent the majority of this time engaged in a custody battle with the mother of his first child, but had obtained joint custody by the fourth interview. However, after being with the mother of his recent child for the first 16 months of the study, he abruptly stated just three months after we had last seen him, "I split up from my ex-fiancé. I caught her cheating on me four times. Kicked her out." He then dropped the second bombshell, "And I am a married man now" with a woman, as it turns out, who was pregnant with what would be Ray's third child. Ray blamed the break-up on his fiancé's infidelities, but the abruptness of the marriage made us question his own faithfulness in the relationship.

Very few of the men admitted their own infidelities to us, although at times, they hinted at them. Instead, they were more likely to talk about their partner's infidelities, especially when relationships ended. Rex, a 23-year-old black father, came the closest to admitting his own infidelities and their consequences for his relationship. He described to us at the second interview that the mother of his child was mistrustful and blamed their relationship problems on her jealousy. But in a masculine performance for Sagacity, he maintained, "I don't hang out as much as I used to. But every once in a while, I still got to go out just to stretch my legs and see if I still got it with the ladies." He said, "My girl [is] finding numbers left and right." Rex worked hard to maintain his innocence to us, insisting that these girls were just friends "from back in the day." By the third interview, Rex had moved out. He maintained that his partner's suspicions were unfounded throughout the study, but off-hand comments he made to the interviewer suggested otherwise.

Eric's relationship ended over his unemployment and drug relapse. Eric was 21 years of age at the time of our first interview, with a 6-month-old daughter. The three of them were living with his parents in a white suburb. Eric remained unemployed for the first six months of the study and described his heroin relapse: "I guess, you know, me and like the baby's mother were fighting a little bit and I just wanted, I guess, [to] take the edge off or something stupid. And I remembered like I tried to think of the good times on drugs instead of the bad times. I wanted to just kind of block out everything so I just wanted to do it again." His partner demanded that he enroll in a long-term drug rehabilitation program, but then left him for another man when he was in the program.

Feeling chagrined about his relapse and about losing his relationship, Eric had nonetheless stayed clean since completing the program and was working at the time of his last interview, though still pining for reconciliation with the mother of his child. Looking back, Eric thought that the combination of unemployment and relationship stress had led to his relapse—his escape from his problems. We had noted his anxieties around both in our first interview with him. At the time of the final interview, he and his partner had amicably worked out a situation where they shared childcare responsibilities when each was away at work, while Eric continued to hope that this period would be just a "relationship suspension."[30]

Relationship break-ups, like Eric's, attempted to embrace the new package deal, but this is not easy to maintain, given the emotional turbulence that accompanies separation. Of course, this is true across race and social class, but resources allow for different strategies for managing the new package deal. Spouses in the professional classes, for example, may divorce, buy houses in close proximity to one another and co-parent, even as they re-marry and enter into new family arrangements. Emotional distress in these situations may be difficult to manage, but careers, resources, counseling, and decent medical care buffer the distress.[31]

Among the men in our study, class location limited the material resources available to manage blended families and, as a result, deepened intrafamily divisiveness and hostility. Feelings of betrayal, resentment, and lost oppor-tunities affected postseparation relationships between former partners, while paychecks didn't stretch far enough to sustain normative lifestyles across blended families. As this occurred, further estrangement or vitriol intensified, and sometimes ended in severing relationships between fathers and their children, or in causing problems in the contexts of newly formed families.

Donte, a 23-year-old African American father, articulated well the diffi-culties of managing break-ups. He emphasized the imperative that parents' relationships remain cordial for the sake of the child.

> Because even if they not together, say he lives with his mom and he goes to see his father on the weekends—three or four days out of the week or whatever it is—and he goes to the dad's house. His dad is talking all this type of stuff about his mother. "Oh, well, your mother ain't this" and "your mother ain't that." And then he goes back and tells his mother what the dad was saying. "Well, your father ain't this. Your father not that." That's not a good relationship because then the child is going to get confused. . . . I seen it happen!

Donte continued by describing the healthy, mature relationship.

> Whatever issues you all got, it's not too big where you all can't work it out, even if you all don't be together. It's not a problem that big where you can't just solve it, unless he done killed your family [laughter]. Or said he refused to take care of his child. . . . Like if he's telling you he not going to take care of his responsibilities, then, hey, whatever. There is no need for you to involve

yourself with that. But if he's doing what he got to do and you doing what you got to do as a mother, there is no need for you all to be arguing back and forth. Y'all should have a healthy relationship. . . . Y'all got a kid together and you all going to have to see each other regardless—no matter what, even when they older.

Donte maintained that his maternal grandparents had modeled this behavior for his 39-year-old mother, even though his own father had refused his part in Donte's own childhood.

Donte was outlining the vision that centers the new package deal, but there are few institutions outside of the family that recognize and attempt to support it. And when they do, they very often advance the prevailing notion that fathers are absent, irresponsible, immature, and indifferent toward their children—especially in the courts, welfare agencies, prisons, and even many community-based programs.[32]

Amid the emotional turmoil of break-ups, fathers may feel as if they are pushed out of their children's lives. As we have seen, child support is a more pertinent concern among the courts than visitation rights.[33] Further, the ambiguous nature of family roles and relationships leaves father involvement to negotiation, and because mothers and maternal kin usually provide full-time care of children, they are, as Abdill describes, "at the head of the negotiating table."[34] Martin, an 18-year-old African American father and one of the fathers released from prison discussed earlier, explained how these processes can lead to father withdrawal.

> You do have some deadbeat dads out there. But how they make it seem like everybody is deadbeat dads, everybody is not deadbeat dads. There are some situations where the father and his baby's mother just ain't getting along and the baby's mother won't let him see him. So then when the father say, "All right, forget it. I'm not going to even stress it no more." And now they want to come on in and say, "Well, now you ain't doing what you supposed to do." But she just told me that she didn't want me to come around. So I took her advice and I ain't come around. In some situations that's how it is.

Martin insisted, "So all that deadbeat dad stuff is not all on the father!"

Martin said that he was involved in his child's life, seeing her several times throughout the week, even though he and the mother were not romantically involved. His comments were, instead, a general defense of fathers. However, these are complex issues. Fathers may use the mother's rejections and resistance to justify their absence or lack of effort to see their children. Or there may be good reasons for mothers to exercise gatekeeping practices, if, for instance, fathers are street involved, drug addicted, or violent.[35] Moreover, fathers may not be as involved as they could be, and they may take advantage of informal and ambiguous arrangements to take credit for occasional drive-by fathering, without putting in the hard, persistent work of parenting.[36]

As partners move on to new relationships, family formations become more complex, which places more strain on resources and requires new partners to be cooperative with child visitation and tolerant of ongoing relationships with ex-partners.[37] Research has shown that, for blacks and Latinos, father involvement decreases significantly when *mothers* get involved in a subsequent intimate relationship, and for whites, it decreases when *fathers* repartner.[38] New relationships redirect emotional and financial commitments, and change the boundaries of relationships, especially when children are born to subsequent intimate partners. But even without new births, fathers may become more involved with nonbiological children in new relationships than with their biological children, even though some research suggests relationships with biological children may be rekindled as the children age.[39]

It is in this complexity that the role of kin is particularly relevant. Kin help to regulate father engagement and disengagement over time, which is something that the snapshots of father involvement do not capture. Relationships between partners often vary across time as disagreements get addressed, disappointments fade, or resource flows change.[40] Kin are especially important in poor urban neighborhoods where fathers' participation in the streets may restrict their mobility and therefore their presence in certain areas of the city in order to protect children, mothers, and themselves. Kevin Roy perceptively points out that fathers' concerns about "who's over there" is a form of managing risk that itself comprises kin work.[41]

What seems to emerge from the literature on father involvement is that, both, fathers are more involved than is commonly believed by the public— and that is certainly conveyed by the images of the deadbeat dad—and that father involvement decreases over time after intimate relationships dissolve for all racial groups, even though this is less so for black fathers.[42] In relationships where corrosive behaviors create the greatest risk to maintaining relationships, violence is the most apparent reason for disengagement.[43]

Toxic Masculinity

Many of the men in our study grew up in chaotic and violent households and neighborhoods. Masculinity was crafted through efforts to acquire control in households and neighborhoods that were out of control, to prepare bodies and minds for violence in homes, schools, the streets, and prisons, and to persevere in contexts that had criminalized, stigmatized, and marginalized them.[44] Without the resources and opportunities to perform masculine identities that are indicative of the normative and symbolic practices of manhood and patriarchy, more marginalized groups of men within the working class adopt protest or street masculinities that attempt to restore male power, domination, and control to situations that threaten their gendered status.[45] As R. W. Connell explains, "Protest masculinities is a marginalized masculinity, which picks up themes of hegemonic masculinity in the society at large but reworks them in a context of poverty."[46]

The recent exposures by the #MeToo movement help us see these dynamics at work. Marginalized men who engage in drug and alcohol abuse, violence, and infidelities in an effort to seek male solidarity, domination and control, and masculine validation have reworked the configurations of male entitlement that #MeToo has spotlighted among men with power and status. These men engage in their own forms of alcohol and drug excess, sexual assault and intimidation, and male fantasies of potency and pleasure. We do not know if these predatory groups are representative of the larger groups of men within their respective social classes, but they expose the institutionally embedded cultural configurations of gender that incentivize and normalize male indulgence and entitlement, and sanction varying expressions of power, status, and desire.

Interpersonal violence is a derivative of power and domination that is organized through a matrix of race, class, and gender hierarchies. Hegemonic masculinity connotes male power and domination that is normalized and reproduced, and thereby seen as the natural order of social life. This cultural frame is internalized as men and women perform their gendered locations in meaningful and directed ways. However, as Gail Garfield explains, the daily exercise of interpersonal forms of power invokes frustration, irritation, and anger, which can produce resistance and challenges to the "natural order" of gender relations, and can subsequently invoke male violence as a manner of restoring the social order.[47] For men at the bottom of the racial and class hierarchy, the indignities suffered from joblessness, underemployment, police

brutality, or the "systematic disvaluing" of men's lives can lead to a more compelling need to express power and domination in spaces where it is still available.[48] Moreover, when we consider the destabilizing effects of the neoliberal
era, the casualization of relationships, the ambiguity of family roles, the loss
of place for men in the patriarchal family, and the (re)negotiation of con-
stantly changing social order and family formations, the use of violence by
lower income black, brown, and white men to challenge or reassert gendered
relationships of power and domination can create a harmful situation that
engenders expressions of toxic masculinity. As Mary Patrice Erdmans and
Timothy Black put it:

> Victims become victimizers as households are disrupted by misplaced vi-
> olence, and expressions of intimacy and vulnerability become intertwined
> in a destructive trajectory of verbal humiliations, physical violence, and
> contorted, self-preserving justifications. The insidious narratives of male
> dominance, integral to conventional expressions of manhood, get plowed
> into subplots of destructive masculinity and family instability.[49]

Searching for a place in which to drive their stakes of masculine status
and potency within precarious worlds of emasculating economic and cultural transition, the men in our study provided varying forms of masculine
expressions and practices. The worst looked like desperate efforts to retain
power and domination through violence and control within the household. Alberto described his controlling presence in his relationship with his
partner.

> She lies because she knows I'm going to get pissed off if she tells me the
> truth. But honesty is the best policy. Don't sit there and hide something
> when it's going to come out later down the road and it's going to piss me
> more off. I tell her, "Let's try to work with it. Deal with the problem before
> it comes and bites you in your ass." Because it's going to bite you in your
> ass. . . . I got to talk to her and make her sit down and . . . listen, just keep her
> mouth shut and make sure I talk to her and make sure that everything stick
> in her head. Because when I talk to her, she listens and everything I tell her
> is true.

Alberto was unapologetic about his dominance in his relationship, whereas
Ray told us he made efforts to rectify his violent dispositions:

I try to really hold my temper. I mean honest to God I try to hold my temper. Because of what I've seen, it's a little old switch in my head to where I won't hit a female. I put several holes in a wall because of it. But I will never hit a female. . . . I have three things that usually calm me down—one of which is talking to my mom. Another one is I go for walks. And I actually yell at myself in my head. "I am going to make her feel this way if I say this. What if I say this? What did I do wrong to add to the situation?" And the next one, I have a song that I listen to over and over.

We do not know how effective Ray's routines were, but he seemed committed to them, even if unaware of how punching holes in the wall was also a form of power and domination over his partner. Ray's own father and brother had both spent time in jail on multiple domestic violence charges. Ray acknowledged that people like himself need help, but that help was not easy to acquire. He said that there is not a lot of domestic violence or relationship counseling available, "especially with the poor. People that have money," he continued, "they can afford counseling. They can afford for someone else to mediate for them. They can afford different coping mechanisms. But around here," Ray declared, "it seems to be people don't go to counseling unless they are mandatoried [mandated] by probation. Or they don't get into anger management unless they are ordered to by probation."

In our study, 13 percent of the men had been arrested for domestic violence—10 percent from the Couples Study, 16 percent from the Father Initiative Study, and 9 percent from the NFN Study. When we explored this, most of the men described their conflicts with the mothers as verbal arguments, although a few acknowledged to us that their fights had escalated to physical violence. "Hitting a woman" was generally seen as unacceptable, or even a sign of weakness. If they were perpetrators of physical violence, they were not inclined to share this with us, and when they did, they tended to minimize the violence, describing how they were attacked by their partners and were simply restraining them, which caused bruises and resulted in arrests. A few fathers, like 29-year-old Todd, admitted to their brute violence. Todd described three violent incidents with three women in his past, one of whom had stabbed him with a knife. He asserted that he had adopted his grandmother's dictum, "If they're big enough to hit you, they big enough to get hit back." From the men's stories, we find that some minimized their violence, some described situations in which they exercised domination and control through intimidation, some admitted to extreme jealousy that led to emotional abuse and regular surveillance of their partners, and some depicted incidents of police intervention and arrest.

Fathers also demonstrated varying degrees of understanding of their violence. Some had been exposed to anger management programs and articulated some of the more salient lessons learned in these programs. Twenty-seven-year-old Felix had been incarcerated several times for domestic violence and had learned from prison anger management programs that intimate partner violence was a form of power and domination. He was trying to apply this to his life.

> I was controlling like my dad. I controlled not only the money [but] the relationship, even to sex. Controlled everything. As opposed to now, "You are the boss. Here is the money. Whatever I make is here is your money." I can balance money and I can write out bills and stuff like that [but] I let [my fiancé] do it because it makes her feel, you know, more of a woman than [if] I control everything. . . . It's like who wants a woman to fear him, you know? Especially when you have to go lay down with that person. You really want your wife to fear you, even in the bedroom? I mean that's not cool.

Felix described his efforts to share power in the relationship.

> The [relationship] balance, like the power, I still make executive decisions but she makes more executive decisions than I do. It's leaning more towards she has all the control [laughs] and she doesn't know it! . . . As opposed to my other relationships, I mean I started this whole relationship with I am going to do completely the opposite of what I was doing before. And completely the opposite has been nothing but good to me.

The irony in Felix's quote is that he conveys how he is in control of giving up control—to the extent that his fiancé doesn't even know it. Giving up controlling needs and routines is a long-term project and, while learning the underlying dynamics of intimate partner violence is a necessary first step, it does not mean that change will ensue easily or consistently. Later in the interview, Felix described an incident that occurred at a laundromat, where he and his fiancé were doing their laundry together. Here, we see the crack in Felix's resolve as he becomes agitated by how comfortable he believes his fiancé has become sitting and watching him load and unload the laundry. He described:

So when we got home, I told her "I think you are mistaken. You are really seriously mistaken. I don't know how comfortable you've gotten that you actually let me do this by myself." I was like "I am fine. I am not stressing it. But are you really that comfortable. We are not married now. So, when we are married, what's going to happen when we are married?" I had to like talk to her about it. . . . Here I do most of the cleaning and the housework, the cooking. She helps me out cleaning up, but I would rather her relax. So it doesn't hurt me to wash a plate. It doesn't hurt me to dust. It doesn't hurt me to clean up. My dad wouldn't do it. . . . So, it's like "I don't know how comfortable you've gotten." I am definitely not going to start a war over it, but, you know, it's how comfortable can you actually be? I was like "I don't know what train you think you hopped on. I don't know what plane you are taking, but you really have to share."

Felix appeared to be making efforts to change deeply embedded, destructive patterns of behavior, but he clearly had much more work to do. He was trying to find his place in the family that was performed differently from his father, and he was struggling with his masculinity. He wanted to become something he had not been prepared to be, and the sneers of emasculation taunted him.

Felix was not alone in his efforts to penetrate his embodied disposition to violence and the generational echoes of manhood, but lifetimes of violence and childhood humiliation made these changes difficult. Nearly 60 percent of fathers in our study grew up in physically violent homes perpetrated by fathers or stepfathers. Two-thirds of white and Puerto Rican fathers reported this to us, and one-third of black fathers.

Doing multiple interviews in the NFN Study enabled us to discuss a broader range of issues, including a focused discussion on the multiple forms of violence in the lives of men. Approximately one-half of these fathers shared painful stories of physical abuse in their homes growing up. In some two-parent homes, their fathers were physically abusive toward their mothers, but several respondents recalled fist fights they had with their mothers' live-in boyfriends. Several respondents described feelings of helplessness as they recounted some of their earliest, most prominent memories of family violence, while some were still struggling with anger that stemmed from witnessing brutal violence directed toward their mothers. Javi, a 19-year-old father, spoke with sobering pain, "Mainly it was abuse, physical abuse. . . . When my mother was pregnant, my father actually came one day and he actually grabbed my mother by the neck and put her on the wall and tried to lift her up. And I guess he hit a couple of punches and all that, but I was right on the couch looking at that. And that [gave] me a lot of flashbacks about him." Some of the men described how their fathers' or stepfathers' rage was (mis)directed at them. Physical and emotional abuse often coincided. Jack recalled, "My dad would always beat my ass, beat my ass, beat my ass . . . verbal abuse. He just curse a lot—'Fuck you! You fucking son of a bitch. I regret you are my fucking son,' all that bullshit."

While fathers often told us about the physical violence they experienced, they were less likely to consider the emotional consequences. Occasionally, they would drop derisive or sarcastic comments, or they would describe memories of violence with little affect, avoiding deep-seated and rarely verbalized emotions connected with these past events. Steven's willingness to share his story about his father's abuse and neglect provided a glimpse into emotional turmoil that stemmed from intimate partner violence.

> I remember when I was a little, little baby. I still remember them two [his parents] arguing and me standing in between them crying because I kept trying to tell them to stop and they just wouldn't stop. They just kept fighting and fighting. I remember my mom walking out the door. Like I got some shitty memories repressed that like I think of once in a while. And it's like "Damn, that's why I hate [my father] so much."

After his parents split up, Steven recalled a fight when he was visiting his father:

> [He] chased me down the stairs and he said, "What?" I said, "I want to go home." By the time I got down the stairs I turned around and he just back-handed me. And he split my lip and I just looked at him and I was like "What the hell is wrong with you?" And he didn't expect that coming from a kid. So he kind of went upstairs and thought about it and he came back down and he was like "I am sorry. I didn't mean to do that. I don't know what got over me." I was like "I want to go fuckin' home. There is no way I am staying here." I wanted to go home. I just walked past him and I called my mom and I told her. I hadn't seen him for about two months after that. He didn't even try to contact me. Nothing.

Steven described the sting of his father's rejection and ambivalent feelings that he harbored toward his father. "[My father] hasn't done anything for me . . . When I was a kid I always told myself, 'Don't fall for his tricks. Don't fall for his tricks. When he calls you don't bother. Don't listen to him.' But I ended up trying to give him a chance. . . . And that's the way it was my whole life. He never came through with anything."

Of course, we don't know much about these abusive parents, their own tales of poverty, victimization, despair, anger, humiliation—the types of historical injuries that can subjectively turn loved ones into "unworthy and disobedient others."[50] Our story starts with the fathers—their memories, thoughts, feelings, and struggles to be partners and parents. And we don't know much about their partners either. However, several of the mothers whom we do know about—either through our interviews with them or through the fathers' descriptions—also experienced abusive and neglectful childhoods and abusive intimate relationships. They, too, had embodied life histories of violence and had lived in chaotic households. Often these men and women were coming together to explore the prospects for intimacy and parenthood, stirred by the deep recesses of painful memories accumulated across social spaces—in homes, schools, neighborhoods, and prisons— and often living in places marred by poverty, unemployment, state retrenchment, and overcrowded, inadequate housing. Within these complex personal histories and daunting social circumstances, the added expectations of being a nurturing, engaged father created another layer of responsibility that these men had not been prepared for in their childhoods.

Violence disrupts intimacy and ends relationships. Moreover, violent fathers rarely make good parents, but tend to be controlling, authoritarian, and often abusive toward children as well.[51] After these break-ups, mothers often exert more protective gatekeeping, which may include protective orders against fathers or require supervised paternal visits, which often leads to father disengagement with children.[52] And yet there were relationships hatched within grueling histories of personal violence that appeared to be finding their way, at least for the moment. Focusing on these achievements is a reminder that these violent histories are not determinative, and that they can inspire compassion and sensitivity as well. Abran and Jackie illustrate.

Abran and Jackie

Abran vividly recalled when he was thirteen and his father hit him so hard he flipped him over the hood of a car, while his friends stood and watched.

Dad was violent—toward his mother and his siblings, but Abran felt like he got it more than his two brothers. He said he developed a "nervous condition" as a result of the physical abuse and that he was unable to sit quietly and concentrate in school. He did not appear to be angry at his father and said he still respected his father, whom he described as a quick-tempered, high school dropout, who washed dishes for a living in Brooklyn, New York. Abran said his father used violence as a form of protective parenting to keep Abran and his siblings from "hanging out with the wrong crowd." In fact, as he aged into adolescence and ran afoul of the law, the local police officers, who were friends with his father, would simply turn him over to his father when they apprehended him and leave the punishment to him. Abran reported that he suffered "flashbacks" due to his father's abuse. Abran's mother also did not finish high school and had worked in a factory in New York before she left Abran's father and moved to Hartford.

Abran changed schools in New York City regularly due to fighting and never advanced his education to a level of basic literacy. Unable to read, he had limited job opportunities; but more deeply, his illiteracy, combined with childhood trauma and depression, had become an affliction that led to self-destructive behavior, including cutting himself and one attempted suicide. He had received SSI for about eight years, since he was 18 years old, and had seen a therapist, although he had discontinued his psychiatric treatment because he did not think it was necessary any longer.

Ron and Tim interviewed Abran in a second-floor apartment of a house located in a low-income Puerto Rican neighborhood in New Britain. He was soft spoken, but forthcoming with us, while being attentive to twin infants lying in their cribs in an adjacent room. The apartment belonged to the mother of his twins, Jackie, and her father. Abran was on probation at the time for selling crack cocaine to an undercover agent in New York City. He had received a four-year probation sentence in lieu of prison, and his probation had been transferred to Connecticut.

Jackie had grown up in a chaotic household in New Britain. Her father, who was born in Puerto Rico, had a seventh-grade education, received SSI for a mental disability, was a womanizer, and had been arrested on numerous occasions for domestic violence. Jackie described both her father and her brother as having "clinical anger" problems that included "blackouts." She described her mother, who was white, as "never home" and instead out "drinking and drugging." Her mother had dropped out of high school in the

10th grade and had been unemployed most of her life, before obtaining her GED and going to work as a nurse assistant.

Jackie started using alcohol and marijuana at age 13. She was arrested and sent to a juvenile detention facility three times between ages 13 and 15. While home from detention, at age 14, an uncle came by to take her on a few shopping trips, which ended with attempted rape. After her third detention, she and a friend hitchhiked to stay with an acquaintance of her friend's in the Bronx. The home was the location of heavy drug use, and the men started pimping Jackie and her friend to support their drug use. This lasted for four months, before Jackie returned to Connecticut. Relieved to be back home, she nevertheless was arrested again for drugs and put on house arrest. Jackie boasted that the courts were unable to restrain her, as she cut the ankle monitor off, not once, but twice. At his wits' end, the judge sent Jackie to a "wilderness program" for juveniles for 30 days, but after six days, Jackie and three other girls escaped and were picked up shortly after hitchhiking. Jackie said that what "straightened her up," however, was a car accident that critically injured a friend, and left her with multiple cuts, bruises, and injuries. "I thought if I don't stop doing this now, I'm gonna die," she told us.

Both Abran and Jackie were from chaotic, violent homes, but they found in their relationship a warm place of mutual empathy and companionship. They met when Jackie was 16 and "we instantly clicked." They were happy to conceive, though a bit overwhelmed when the ultrasound revealed twins. Jackie said that she was amazed that Abran not only stayed with her through the pregnancy, but took care of her, attended all of her doctor appointments, went shopping with her in anticipation of the newborns, and helped choose names. Jackie resumed working at Burger King shortly after she delivered, had been there for a year and a half, and worked between 32 and 40 hours a week, taking home about $200 per week. She also received food stamps ($137 a month), Medicaid, and WIC.

The pregnancy had mended the relationship with her mother, who had been through rehab for her alcohol and drug problems. Jackie was still on probation, but she considered her probation officer "a second mom to me." And her home visitor was a weekly presence in the home who worked with both Jackie and Abran on child development issues. Her father had found a job at a convenience store and basically stayed to himself in the house.

Meanwhile, Abran was taking care of the twins each day while Jackie was at work. He said he had stopped drinking and smoking weed since he was on probation and regularly urine tested. This was not difficult since Jackie did not drink. He was 26 years old at the time of the interview, eight years older than Jackie. Abran expressed he was "happy to settle down," stating "I always wanted a kid, always." Interestingly, Abran saw family as an alternative to jail and had distanced himself from his street friends. He described Jackie as his "whole world" and an antidote to his illiteracy—she is "smart and intelligent," he said, "not like me." Abran was also happy to work with the home visitor, who had taught him how to "swaddle the babies," to "sit and play" with the twins, to work on motor skills by learning to "move their hands" and by "picking up objects." He was learning about child development from the home visitor, even though he could not read. The home visitor told us he was the only father she worked with and praised his determination to be a good dad.

Abran said that he and Jackie were never violent with one another, that they never argued in front of the babies, that he might yell at her and walk away in an argument, but that he had learned how to sit down and talk it out, and to apologize. He was against any form of corporal punishment, because of his violent past, even though Jackie thought that controlled spanking might be necessary as their sons aged.

This snapshot in Abran and Jackie's lives was hopeful. They both embraced a "starting-over" opportunity organized around a deep empathetic understanding of one another's chaotic and violent background, a chance to mend relationships and to heal, and a chance to find value in their lives and overcome the narratives that described them as delinquents, criminals, or as illiterate. Abran fantasized that his children would go to college and that they would "have what job they want." Jackie imagined that they "don't go to jail, get a good job, um, have a family and be with one girl, that's it."

Of course, we do not know how things worked out for Abran and Jackie, but we can see that the same chaotic and violent backgrounds that can inhibit intimacy and stability can also provide the motivations to transform people's lives, to seek spaces for healing, to pursue lives of social value grounded in parenthood, and to deepen understanding. But this does not happen easily within the social structures and institutions that govern social life. Abran and Jackie did receive some state support—SSI, Food Stamps, Medicaid, WIC, and support from the home visitor program and a probation officer. These programs were essential to their survival. But they suffered from low wages, poor educations, criminal records, a segregated neighborhood, unsubsidized market rent, crowded housing, and violent histories. Raising twins created a new fulcrum in their lives to negotiate the spaces they occupied and the institutions that governed their lives, and it demonstrated the power of starting-over narratives—and, for Abran, the transformative potential of fatherhood.

Starting-over narratives were even more apparent among the older fathers in our study. Several had children when they were younger and were disengaged; but as older fathers, they embraced fatherhood differently.

Two-Generation Fathers

The older fathers in our NFN Study had children when they were younger and were not involved in their children's lives, but they were involved with their children from a later and more current relationship. In other words, they had learned to be fathers the second time around, what Aasha Abdill refers to as "two-generation fathers." Abdill contrasts this with what Kathryn Edin and Timothy Nelson refer to as serial fatherhood, in which fathers exit relationships when they are unable to live up to the expectations of being a father and enter new relationships, only to repeat the pattern. Based on episodic father failure, the new pregnancy is described by Edin and Nelson as "an opportunity to snatch victory from the jaws of defeat."[53] In this construction, serial fatherhood becomes a pathological cycle of failed fatherhood. Instead, Abdill found that fathers in subsequent relationships had matured and settled into fathering in ways they were incapable of doing at younger ages. Some of the older fathers in our study were examples of two-generation fathers and, in one case, a three-generation father. Their stories not only illustrate the men's maturation and reconstructions of their lives; they locate fatherhood within biographies that help us to understand the processes through which personal transformation occurs and to see some of the institutional and cultural forces that they must confront. We will profile one of these fathers to illustrate.

James's Story

James, whom we have heard from regularly throughout this book, was a 40-year-old white father of two children at the time of our first interview. James had no relationship with his daughter who was grown and had been raised in James's hometown in upstate New York. He also had a 9-month-old son whom he was co-parenting with his son's 25-year-old mother in Willimantic. James explained that he did not know he had a daughter until she was two, and that early efforts to contact the mother were rebuffed. James declared that he was an alcoholic and that the mother's father, who was black, "really didn't care for me. I got his older daughter pregnant and that's basically not what he wanted for her in life. He just couldn't stand me from the day we met." These tensions, along with heavy drinking and a lengthy prison term, made it easy to give up trying to reach her. It was not a serious relationship to begin with, he claimed, but rather a short-term relationship with an older woman when he was a teenager. At 40, though, James took responsibility for his absence: "I was kind of too much into partying, so it wasn't like I was trying to be a father figure, you know what I mean?"

James grew up with an abusive, alcoholic mother. "The kind of life I grew up," he said, "was going to get my mother out of a bar room." James never knew his father, which he said was his mother's decision. He described his mother as a "violent drunk" who "fuckin' hit us with shit—a belt, bat, a stick, a switch, anything. Anything you could [get] your hands on, or get out one of these fists" [raising his clenched hand in the air]. James had one particularly painful, angry exchange with his mother etched in his memory, when she told him, "I never wanted you. I didn't want to have no kids." He recalled responding, "Well, why the hell did you have me in the first place? It's not my fault I was born. I didn't ask to come in this world." Later, his mother achieved sobriety and tried to apologize. "She has basically said there were a lot of things that she should have done different in life and maybe a lot of us wouldn't have turned out, maybe, I don't know, the way we did or the way we are." But James was unforgiving: "Like I said to her, it's too late for that."

At 40, as a former member of the street gang Los Solidos, and with twelve years of prison time behind him, James took a while to warm up to Sky. His initial demeanor was stoic and resolute; his statements were often punctuated with a silent, cold stare. After Sky mentioned a few names of people James had been locked up with, he relaxed and was more forthcoming, even cracking jokes with Sky. He regretted his heavily tattooed face and neck, and especially the teardrop inked on his cheek, and felt that they not only hindered job opportunities but also contributed to state surveillance from both the police and child protection services. James attended AA meetings, where he met his wife. When she became pregnant, he "manned up. I married the girl," he said proudly. He bonded with their landlord, who was also a recovering alcoholic and became a mother figure to James. This was his family—wife, son, and landlord—whom he said changed his life. He expressed unequivocally, "I love being a dad. I love being married. There is no regrets ever having him."

James was figuring out how to be a father. He changed diapers and read to his son. He said, "I take him for walks. I like to watch TV with him. He is into Blues Clues. I like educational things that I was never taught. I just would like to be the kind of person that he can look up to and trust and love and know that he's safe and he can live in a safe home and I guess grow up." James was trying to give as much as he could to his son now, because "by the time he gets around 20 or 30, I'll be dead. I'm in my 40s now. Who knows if I'll be alive by then." James was receiving treatments for Hepatitis C and was concerned that his past would not provide for longevity.

By our last interview with James, his son had turned two years old. He and his wife were struggling financially in the aftermath of the Great Recession. James said that he worried about his inability to provide for his family. When we asked if making money was part of being a man, James said, "Well, I think everybody thinks that. You have to make money. You have to." James reflected on his own situation and his masculinity. "It's rough," he said. "I mean. I don't know," he stammered. "It's hard to even answer that one because it's real hard," he said considering his own part-time custodial job. "You have to," he said again, as his thinking began to crystallize. "But then I guess it don't have to be like that. It's hard to even really answer that one [but] it's not everything. Because caring about your child, loving your child and being there, that's being a man and being a father," James concluded.

James was straddling generational expectations of fatherhood, as he struggled to articulate a new version of masculinity that extended beyond the provider role. Even though he deeply loved his wife, he advanced an understanding of the new package deal. A good father, he said, "takes responsibility. He's in that child's life no matter if he's in the mother's life, but he's in the child's life. He takes care of them—buys his food, clothe him, feed him, make sure he has a roof over his head. Puts him number one, even in front of his self. Because that's what I do." This was, however, a blind spot for James, whose passionate claim applied to his recent son, but not his daughter.

Like other fathers, James also was struggling with how to discipline his son. He was certain that it would not be like he was disciplined. "You know, you sit down and talk to your kid," he said. "You ain't got to put your hand on a kid. . . . I'd rather sit down with my child and have my child know that I love him; I care about him enough where he can come to me for any reason or anything." At age 40, fatherhood had become a form of redemption for James.

> I believe you mature as you get older. Because I know I have. I know when I was younger, I was not mature. I made so many mistakes in my life. You just can't turn back time. You can't. It just, the clock will never stop on your life. *Maybe like, after I am dead and gone, my son will grow up and know that like, "Hey, he had a rough life, but look how I turned out. He did a good job. . . . He was a good person, even though [he trails off into thought, before saying] I still think he was a good dad."*

James concluded with a statement about being a two-generation father, "I guess it comes with maturing and growing up in life, knowing that you are only going to live once. It's time to do something in the world."

And yet James was not in his daughter's life, contradicting his earlier declaration "no matter what." James told us that his daughter had searched for and contacted his sister. Moreover, she gave his sister her phone number and asked her to pass it along to James. She was married and had a daughter of her own. James expressed a strong desire to contact her and to see her, but he was paralyzed with shame and lacked confidence in knowing how to handle it. "I'd love to have a relationship with her, but it's where do you start? What do you do?" he asked. Someone with more resources could explore such a question with professionals and maybe build the skills and confidence needed, but James, through the fourth and last interview, had not made the call.

James was a second-generation father. Fatherhood and family were providing purpose and relative stability. He was struggling in the folds of rapid change—in jobs that did not pay enough, in vigilant institutions that emphasized surveillance over support, and in homes where the norms and expectations for fathering were altered and unsupported by any exposure to a parental role model. James represented a form of aging into fatherhood that was redemptive, validating, and socially respectable, but not easily arrived at or sustained. Traumatic childhoods, violence, and unstable social and economic conditions do not provide easy paths to healthy relating, nor healthy parenting. He was nonetheless finding his way as a second-generation father, even though he had not yet found the courage to contact his older daughter. Abdill's use of the term was applied to black fathers, but, in our study, it applied to black, brown, and white fathers.

Conclusion

The typical formulation of the coveted two-parent family and the single-mother family, as represented for instance by the U.S. Census, fails to capture the fluid and dynamic family formations that occur in between these categories.[54] There is not a single narrative that can be driven through the varying configurations of familial relationships that can tell the story of the 21st-century family. Clearly, there is much going on within the networks of relationships and changing households among lower income populations that may forbid or enhance father involvement. But as Jennifer Hamer pointed out more than 20 years ago, state and legal institutions have failed to adjust to these complexities and in many instances have undermined them.[55] In this chapter, we have attempted to identify how relating occurs amid social and economic instability.

The fault lines for father disengagement cut and crisscross through multiple domains—economic insecurity, extended families and multiple households, crowded housing, paternalistic state intervention, neighborhood and family violence, incarceration, drug and alcohol addictions, protest and street masculinities, and the emotional vicissitudes of repartnering. Fathering across these fault lines also occurs, but not without forging new paths for relating: where neotraditional family forms are constructed; where the casualization of family life and the new package deal engender shifting kin networks of caregiving, liminal fatherhood, relationship suspensions and renewals, and second-chance relationships; where lives saturated in family and neighborhood violence reproduce violence, disrupt intimacy, shape fathering dispositions, inform parenting capital but also provide the prospects for compassion and healing; where second-generation fathering takes shape; and where the prospects for starting over continue to paper over the endemic forces generating uncertainty. Low-income fatherhood is located within the interstices of structural dynamics that have made the impermanent, permanent.

But how do fathers make sense of fatherhood? What are their perspectives, their identities, their constructions of themselves as fathers? What resources and experiences do they draw on to locate themselves and understand their lives as fathers amid these larger forces of change? These are the questions we turn to in our final chapter, and it is here that the "setup" becomes most apparent.

8

Fathers Making Sense of It All

Now, they always talking about we people be on the street. All right. Give us some more jobs. You all won't even give nobody no jobs. "Oh, we'll call you, let you know." Your word ain't going to pay up, put no food on the table.

—Maurice

She's been collecting state . . . just because she collecting state they treat you like obviously you haven't been doing your job so you are a deadbeat dad. It's not true at all. Maybe for some people it is. But don't treat everybody like that.

—Rayshawn

I just want to be able to provide. It's beautiful. I love it. I am with her all the time, besides when I go to work. I come back and I am with her all the time. Feed her. Change her. I love it.

—Danny

In this last chapter, we examine the cultural frames and narratives fathers used to represent themselves, tell a coherent story about their lives, and project an identity of themselves into their futures. Perhaps unsurprising, it is rare that their frames and narratives convey an understanding of the systemic class, racial, and ethnic inequalities and barriers that confront them. Any systemic critique tended to reflect "a culture of gender distrust" perspective, which blamed women and a governmental system that the men felt was biased toward women. More generally, fathers were reactive to moralistic discourses that cast them as irresponsible, unreliable, negligent, deadbeat dads. They attempted to derive socially valued identities along a range of symbolic boundaries that included distinguishing themselves from fathers who relied on welfare, from fathers uninvolved in their children's lives, and,

It's a Setup. Timothy Black and Sky Keyes, Oxford University Press (2021). © Timothy Black and Sky Keyes.
DOI: 10.1093/oso/9780190062217.003.0008

most of all, from their own irresponsible, absent fathers. They adopted individualistic narratives about taking responsibility, "manning up," and making
fatherhood central to their lives. For the more marginalized, these narratives
usually followed the script of getting a job, going to school, and staying away
from negative things. And for some, this included a resilience narrative in
which they articulated past and current struggles that needed to be overcome
or managed, such as growing up in abusive, negligent, violent households
in poor and violent neighborhoods, living with disabilities, managing drug
and alcohol addictions, and atoning for past mistakes when associating with
"wrong crowds." The men imagined themselves doing better, and, in nearly
all cases, being engaged fathers was at the center of these projected, hopeful
constructions.

Working the Boundaries

For fathers who are unlikely to acquire much status from their ability to be
family providers, they derive moral value from "boundary work."[1] Working
and contributing to one's family provides a valued moral identity, from
which one acquires respect and dignity. However, the era of precarious work
creates challenges to these status claims, as the prospects of working-class respectability fade and the economic foundation for family stability crumbles.
Men live in this gray zone, and they derive moral status through boundary
work in which they compare themselves to others. In our study, fathers derived their moral value as fathers along three symbolic boundaries: by comparing themselves to their own fathers, by distinguishing themselves from
welfare dependent families, and by demonstrating that, irrespective of their
circumstances, they were not deadbeat dads.

Father Echoes

To talk about themselves as fathers almost always invoked talking about their
own fathers. Comparisons were unavoidable, comprising their measuring
stick, their moral standard, and very often their efforts to derive self-worth.
Frequently, these comparisons carried deep emotional intensity. For some,
like Robert, who took over his father's job mixing and pouring concrete,

maturation had deepened his understanding and respect for his father, and enabled him to see his father through a different lens.

> When you are a kid, you'll be at a store and the poor guy is walking around with three kids. "We want that. We want that." And, you know, our dad is like "No, I ain't got the money for that." Then we get all pissed off. And now I look back and I am like "Man, I should have shut my fuckin' mouth."

As a father himself and provider for his family, Robert acquired an empathetic understanding of his father's life. He identified with his father's angst, his familial commitments, and his identity as the household provider. His self-repudiation was also a claim to his own working-class respectability—finding place and status within an intergenerationally reproduced white nuclear family.

However, we calculated that two-thirds of the men in our study described their fathers as not present in their lives when they were growing up. Being present meant that they stayed regularly involved with them throughout their childhood and adolescence, but it did not require that their fathers live in the home. Many of these men were angry at their fathers for their absence and their financial and emotional neglect. When we asked Rio, whom we heard from in the last chapter, if being a father changed his view of his own father, he responded:

> I still think he's a coward. I still think he's a bitch-ass. Like, nigga, you avoided this. Why did you avoid it? . . . Why were you scared? Now you getting older and you don't have us around when you could have had us around. . . . Like, nigga, you 40-something years old and you still living with your mom. You can't show nothing for it.

Like Rio, others described their fathers as "sperm donors," embraced the popular notion that their lives would have been better if their fathers had been involved, felt strongly about rejecting the rejecter, or even wanted to punish their fathers by preventing their children from ever seeing their grandfathers.

Father absence often leads to father shame, as we saw in James's story in the prior chapter, and reconnecting with fathers after years of absence can be charged with intense emotions. In some instances, it works out—forgiveness occurs and relationships are (re)established. But efforts to reconnect also can result in disappointment. Hector illustrates:

> He was like a stranger. I don't even remember calling him papi or daddy. I don't even remember him picking me up. . . . I didn't know him like that. I knew he was my father, but I didn't have no love for him. The only thing I know about him, that he was a drug dealer and he is an addict now. That's it. I know where he live at. . . . I sent my girl with my older daughter so he could meet his granddaughter. And he hid. He didn't even open up—and my older brother went, too. They invited me. I didn't want to go see him. He don't want to know me. We tried to see him. So I feel the same way he feel. I don't care. I don't even stress it. I sayin' [getting more animated] I see programs, I see kids wanting to find their fathers and stuff. But when you try to look for somebody and that person doesn't want nothing to do with you, I am not going to look for him. I'm straight. My mother is my father.

Coming to the door required more emotional solidity than apparently Hector's father could manage, while Hector's claim of not caring was betrayed by his emotions that surfaced when he talked about his father.

Jermaine yearned for the opportunity to reject his father and described how father absence was a topic of conversation among his friends.

> It's like today, it's like I sat there and I was daydreaming. If my father were to roll up on me today and talk about "get in the truck," I wouldn't get in. That's the way I feel. I would look like "Why are you here? It's been so long and you ain't never do nothing for me. So might as well just leave and go on about your business." I used to just call him a sperm donor. You know, time to time, depending on the mood I am, somebody would ask me and I'd be like "Man, fuck that sperm donor." Excuse my language, but that's how I be, that's how I feel. I just don't feel no other type of way [than] rankin' on my father. They be like "You need to have more respect for your father than that." Why? He's not around. He's not in my life, so why should I? Even like me and a couple of my friends, we all been through the same. So like, their fathers not there, my father's not there. So we all sit down and we talk about it. Some of them say they have feelings for their father but they feel their father did them dirty. And I am like "I feel you. [But] I don't have no feelings."

While Jermaine insisted that he did not have feelings for his father, he was nonetheless fantasizing about the opportunity to reject the man who rejected him. Indeed, father absence was interpreted as rejection, and efforts to suggest that their fathers' rejections did not matter to them often communicated just the opposite. Underlying Rio, Hector, Jermaine, and others' anger concerning their fathers' absence and rejection was the question, Why? Why did he reject me? Explanations ranged from "He like to make money" and "didn't want to live our life"; "He was a drug dealer and he is an addict now"; "He is a loser"; or more painfully, "He didn't want to know me."

In some instances, as we have seen, fathers left their children and moved on to have other families, and here the feelings of rejection could be particularly harsh. Alberto lamented the loss of his father.

RON: Some people say that in order to be a good father you need to be living with the mother and the children. Is that true?

ALBERTO: Yeah.

RON: You need to be living there?

ALBERTO: Yeah.

RON: And you can't be a father and have another wife and still . . .

ALBERTO: It's going to have the kid's head confused like mines. I thought my father . . . after he got hitched with that other girl, I thought he didn't love me no more. That's how it feels. It feels like you don't got no more love. That's how I still feel.

RON: You still feel that way?

ALBERTO: I still feel that way. I cry about that because I am like "Damn. You had me spoiled. You gave me whatever I wanted. When you got hitched with this chick, it was like fuck us. It was like fuck me and my sister. Your world revolved around us and now you just saying, Hell no!" That's what bothered me. After he got hitched with her it was just . . . that's why I am trying to be there for my daughter. I don't care whatever the hell happens between her [mother and me]. She goes on and has sex with somebody else or do something crazy, I just got to forgive her and move on with it because I got to do it for my daughter.

Like Alberto, fathers' feelings of rejection shaped their desires to be there for their own children. Ironically, however, their anger at their fathers was often associated with their own struggles in their lives. It seemed that the more marginalized they were, the angrier they were at their fathers. In other words, their fathers provided a narrative of blame that was consistent with the dominant narrative about father absence—if only their fathers had been there, their lives would be different.

Many of the fathers in our study made it clear that, above all else, they did not want to be like their fathers, who had abandoned them, their mothers, and their siblings. They conveyed considerable emotion when they expressed this and embraced the moral status of being an involved father. Some of them appeared to be accomplishing this. We calculated that about one-third of study participants whose fathers were not present in their own lives had reversed this status and were involved fathers with their own children—at least at the time of the interview. For instance, 20-year-old Maurice was angry at his father because "he ain't been in my life" and also because he "put my mother on them drugs." Both of his parents had struggled with drug dependency, and Maurice asserted that the crack cocaine years of the 1980s had "fucked up their life." Maurice said growing up in these circumstances provided the motivation to "get things you never had." He had worked since age 14 because he "wanted something in this life." At the time of the interview, he was a present father, had a state job, was cohabiting with the mother of his children, and was determined not to be his father.

Maurice is a young father and we do not know if his determination would win out over a lifetime. Nearly one-half of study participants who had absent fathers had reproduced this status in their own families—they, too, were not regularly involved in their own children's lives. Of course, the large percentage of incarcerated fathers contributed to this calculation. Close to another fifth of the men in our study were present in at least one of their children's lives, but not involved with other children. In other words, despite their deep desires to not be like their fathers, many of these men at young ages had already become like their fathers. The more their lives seemed to replicate their fathers' lives, the more animosity they expressed toward them. As Tyler put it, "I don't want to be nothing like my father, but it hurts cuz I am."

Indeed, Tyler's life did look much like his father's. Tyler, a white father living in Norwich, was 24 years old when we interviewed him. He was one of the most down-and-out fathers that we interviewed. He had three children with three different mothers and was $9,000 in arrears for child support. Like his father, he had spent time in prison, been absent in his children's lives, and had been a heavy drug user. At the time of the interview, he was unemployed, homeless, looking for work, and eating at soup kitchens. Ashamed of himself, Tyler's anger was directed at the child support system and at his father.

Like I told you, I wanted to murder them over there at one time because I couldn't understand what they were doing to me. I just couldn't understand it, man. You want child support for this kid? Go after my father. He still owes me for 18 years. You know what I mean? Go get it from him. . . . I ain't even working and you are going to lock me up and keep me there until I can pay? How the fuck am I gonna pay when I am locked up? I don't have a problem paying when I'm working, I really don't.

There is more to Tyler's reproduction of his father's life than gets expressed by his shame and his loathing for his father. Tyler's unstable home life was punctuated by child abuse and neglect, where his resentment toward his parents began. He, in turn, joined a street gang at an early age and sold and used drugs. Living on the streets, he fathered three children. Tyler lacked the capacity to navigate effectively his current situation, marked largely by poverty, unemployment, child support arrearage, and his daily struggle with sobriety. He had been recently evicted from his apartment when we met him and lived with his cousin, who also ate at the local soup kitchen. Besides pointing to the absurdity of child support enforcement policies, Tyler's only defense that he could muster was to point his finger at his father, whom he regarded as the origin of his errant ways.

Gerard, who described the agony of seeing his son through the looking glass in Chapter 6, was incarcerated when we interviewed him. At 19 years of age, he had a solid plan to become a custodial and present father once he was released. Gerard was representative of other young, incarcerated fathers who had not been involved in their children's lives, but inside prison were reaching out and making plans to change this. He too was angry and resentful toward his own father, who left his life when Gerard was two years old. Gerard's father was also incarcerated and sent Gerard letters—from prison to prison—but Gerard did not respond.

Gerard said his family was ashamed of his imprisonment and lied about it to others. At the prison facility, he cleaned a correction officer's (CO) office, a prime job, and he reported that the CO was getting him a job upon his release. Gerard said that his mother was actively involved in his life and would also assist him in securing employment when he was released. Gerard planned on living with his mother in a large house with his child and the child's mother. Unlike Tyler, Gerard's networks, inside and outside of the prison, reflected some of his racial advantages—what we referred to earlier as his "complexion connections." Gerard was angry and ashamed, and appeared to have the connections to make changes in his life—at the core though was his anger at his father for not being there for him and a deep desire to not become his father.

Donte was a 23-year-old African American from Hartford, who did not have Gerard's social networks and could not seem to catch a break in his search for work. He was struggling to get by, but he was a present father to a three-month-old infant. Donte's own father had not been in his life since Donte was three years old. He was exposed to two stepfathers while he was growing up, but did not develop good relationships with either of them. Donte's father was incarcerated at the time of the interview and Donte reflected, "I mean I have some type of love for him just because without him I wouldn't be here and I love my life, but I call him my sperm donor—he's not a father, he was never around." Donte was struggling financially due to his unemployment but nonetheless derived moral status vis-à-vis his father, a victory that was underscored through his public protestations toward his father.

Whether it was explaining their marginalization or providing motivation to change, father absence and rejection anchored these fathers' narratives. And the more they appeared to be headed down the same path as their absent fathers, the harsher the narrative of blame appeared to be.

The other one-third of our study participants grew up in families with present fathers. Among these 50 fathers, a little less than one-half (21) of them were present fathers to their own children at the time of the interviews—or, in others words, had reproduced their father's status. The same number were less present than their own fathers, though not entirely absent, whom we classified as partially involved.

Present fathers were often just-getting-by, working-class men, like Elijah, who was working, providing, and struggling in a more traditional nuclear family much like his own father. A Puerto Rican high school graduate, Elijah worked between 40 and 60 hours a week at a casino earning $9.60 an hour to support his family, while the mother of his children managed the home and took care of their children. Similarly, Raleigh, another Puerto Rican father, struggled to pay the bills as a barber. His father was a forklift driver and both were present in-home parents. We classified Red, an African American father from the PT Barnum Projects in Bridgeport, as a present father, even though he did not live with one of his children, but had an informal visitation arrangement, saw the child regularly, and expressed his determination to remain a regular part of his son's life. Red had grown up in a two-parent home.

His parents were still together. He asserted, "I ain't like the average kid when parents split up and go through all sorts of problems." His mother worked "in nutrition" while his father worked intermittently, suffering long periods of unemployment. Red resembled his father in both his struggle with employment and in being a present father.

In reviewing these stories, though, we see that being present in the home was not always the best alternative, which the overly simplistic argument that attributes a large range of social problems to father absence seems to minimize, if not overlook entirely. When fathers in the home are violent and abusive, households are chaotic, and break-ups occur as a welcome relief. For some of the men in our study, they were struggling with not only staying involved with children but with the emotional residues—and sometimes trauma—of growing up in violent homes. As we saw in the last chapter, their struggles included trying to break these destructive patterns; in which case, not being like their fathers took on different meaning.

Tony grew up with his father in the home, but this young white father had reproduced nearly everything about his father, including his father's controlling and violent forms of masculinity. Tony and his wife, Violet, considered it an improvement that Tony now allowed her to see her friends, as long as he drove her there and picked her up. He said he would slap a woman if she cheated on him, was afraid to be alone with his daughter because of his violent tendencies, and admitted that he had punched holes in the upstairs door multiple times. Similarly, Greg, a white father from a Hartford suburb, had become much like his alcohol-dependent, white, working-class father and described to us prior incidents of control and intimidation exhibited toward the mother of his children. These fathers were present in the home, but they created toxic environments for mothers and children.

Other white fathers who grew up in similar conditions emphasized how they were attempting to break these patterns. Raymond, 32, was a present and hard-working provider, like his father, but stated emphatically that he would not abuse his kids like his father had and would never discipline them by "going beyond spanking." Chad, a 29-year-old white father, grew up with and was victimized by an alcoholic father who was physically and sexually abusive. Chad admitted that he had been physically abusive toward the mother of his first child and was himself a recovering alcoholic. He described current efforts to stay clean and to manage his anger in his second family, while his first child was living with his own mother, providing an opportunity for him to sustain a relationship with him.

Of course, managing violent expressions of masculinity in the home and disrupting intergenerational family patterns were not limited to white families; in fact, Michelle Fine and Lois Weiss show that domestic violence in black and brown families is more likely to be publicly exposed than in white households.[2] Jack had a present father who had been a member of the Latin Kings and was physically abusive toward Jack. We interviewed Jack four times, and in the beginning of our interactions with him he was a present, cohabitating father; but in our last interaction with him, he was mostly absent due to his break-up with the mother. Putting an ironic twist on the narrative of father absence, Jack's involvement with his children was attenuated after the break-up, making the comparison with his own father's presence less favorable, even though Jack gave no indication of reproducing his father's abusive behaviors toward his children or their mother while in the relationship.

The men who grew up without fathers and those who grew up with violent fathers were shadow boxing when they talked about their own fatherhood. Their narratives were shaped by their personal experiences and by the dominant narratives about father absence. Explaining their own struggles, whether unemployment, substance abuse, incarceration, or violence, they often directed their narratives at their fathers. There were no structural understandings to complement these narratives, just blame that landed on wayward fathers amid their own struggles with marginalization.

Assessing involvement in children's lives among the population of incarcerated fathers was difficult, as we explored in Chapter 6. Some of these men had grown up with fathers who had been present in the home. Narratives about their own fathering, in these instances, did not compare favorably to their fathers, but their redemption narratives and motivations for change often appeared to be grounded in their own experiences of having involved fathers in their lives growing up. Damien, a 19-year-old African American father from New Haven, like Gerard, was taking advantage of the reflective space provided in prison to map out concrete plans to be more involved in his children's lives upon release.

Fatherhood programs in prison encourage this process, which involves making amends with mothers and children, writing letters, establishing visits, exploring the exigencies of manhood and fatherhood, and preparing for a more involved life with their children when they return to the community.[3] Of course, these plans are challenged when the situational contingencies of their lives become apparent upon release, but they do provide both a cognitive and practical process for involvement. Damien engaged this process in prison and was receiving visits from his two children and making plans to be involved in their lives in a significant way upon his release. His involvement did not compare favorably to his own father, who worked as a schoolteacher and taught Sunday school, and lived in the home with his wife and eight children in a Bridgeport housing project. But these memories did provide a model for change.

Richard, a 33-year-old African American father from Bridgeport, was totally absent during his eldest daughter's childhood, and as he says, painfully, "she blames me for it." He had made his living on the streets and had been incarcerated. Not unlike many men in similar straits, he did not want his children to visit him when he was locked up. Richard was street-oriented and far different from his own father, who worked two jobs and was present in the home. At the time of the interview, Richard was in a nonconfining alternative incarceration program and involved in the lives of his younger children.

The deeply emotional formations of father–son relationships produced long shadows in the lives of our men as they discussed their own experiences with fathering and their prospects for fathering in the future. The more they were struggling with life circumstances, the more they blamed their fathers and the more they attempted to squeeze some modicum of moral status from these comparisons. Dominant narratives concerning father absence nourished their understandings of theirs and their fathers' lives. The intensity of these interpersonal dynamics did not provide any space for reflecting on how larger social structures and processes may have impeded fatherhood, the family, or the communities in which their families resided. These forces remain largely invisible and poorly developed by the media and public discourse. As the forces of social reproduction channeled fathers into similar racial and social class grooves that their fathers had traveled, their explanations for their own marginalized struggles searched within the webs of relationships with their fathers.

Those Deadbeat Dads and Welfare Frauds

Boundary work also involved fathers distinguishing themselves from "deadbeat dads" and "welfare frauds," both of whom gave them a bad name. They were different, they insisted, as they worked to establish a symbolic boundary through which they could derive a moral status. We already saw in Chapter 4 the fury that many of the men expressed toward child support enforcement policies and practices, when they were labeled deadbeat dads and treated with contempt by court magistrates. This thick layer of institutional and cultural typecasting created the symbolic boundary by which fathers' consciousness took shape.

Rayshawn is the father that we profiled in Chapter 4, whose children had been taken into state custody while he was incarcerated for trafficking cocaine and who had been brought before the courts just after his release because his child support arrearage had accumulated during his incarceration. Magistrate Aronowitz had threatened to invoke Rayshawn's six-year suspended sentence if he did not return to court with a substantial payment toward his arrearage. This 22-year-old African American father from Bridgeport was struggling to get custody of his children, to get a job, and to pay down his arrearage. He felt that being cast as a "deadbeat dad" was unfair and misguided, given his circumstances, and he engaged in boundary work to distinguish himself from the "real deadbeat dads." He explained:

> A lot of fathers—I don't want to say "all," but a lot of these, especially the fathers of the cities in these type of circumstances, do not do their job basically. And they make it bad for people like me or fathers like me. There are some of them that just don't care. Because there are some, it makes it bad for all of us. So, let's say me, for circumstances, I be taking care of my son, but the state doesn't know that. I don't feel like I have to report to the state everything I do for my son. But that's the way they treat me because they don't know I been taking care of my son. She's been collecting state . . . just because she collecting state they treat you like obviously you haven't been doing your job so you are a deadbeat dad. It's not true at all. Maybe for some people it is. But don't treat everybody like that.

For Rayshawn, the deadbeat dad is the generalized other—there are no names, no faces, no stories, just the symbolic edge along which an identity is formed in the image of a photographic negative.

Other fathers, many also profiled in Chapter 4, were enraged by being labeled and treated like a deadbeat dad by the courts. They felt misunderstood, stigmatized, and discriminated against. Like Rayshawn, many of them defended themselves against this moral campaign by acknowledging that there were deadbeat dads out there, but they were not one of them. Their anger at the courts was about the magistrates' inability to know the difference.

Jadzia's struggle with the moral symbolism of the deadbeat dad was located within a different state institution—the Department of Children and Families (DCF) child protection services. In his case, being a "deadbeat dad" was not simply about not paying child support, but carried an even heavier charge of neglecting his children altogether. He, too, felt that his circumstances had been twisted by state officials based on their predisposed perceptions of poor Puerto Ricans.

Jadzia, 26, married the mother of his two-year-old daughter after the child's birth. They had known one another since the third grade. She had a child from a prior relationship, and Jadzia considered himself the father of both. He and his wife lived with his wife's mother and Jadzia said that when he took a job at one of Connecticut's casinos, things took a turn for the worst in the household. His wife started using drugs and alcohol and her mother blamed Jadzia because he was working long hours on third shift and was never around. With the burden of child care falling more on her shoulders, his mother-in-law called DCF and reported the situation. She said that they were both using drugs and alcohol, and that the children were being neglected. DCF removed the children and placed the oldest with her biological father and prevented Jadzia access, since the child was not truly his. They placed his biological daughter in foster care and mandated that he complete several programs before reunification, including the Father Initiative Program (FIP), individual counseling, and a program that supervised and evaluated visits with his daughter twice a week.

Jadzia said that he was evaluated for alcohol and drug use, but that all of the tests came back negative. He said he did not drink or use drugs, and that his mother-in-law had fabricated the story. The consequences of DCF involvement were severe. Jadzia lost his job at the casino because of mandated time requirements, he painfully lost total contact with his nonbiological child, and he had not seen his wife or her mother since the ordeal began. Further, even though he was a high school graduate, had a respectable work history, had no child support arrears, had never been arrested, and had accepted responsibility as a father to both daughters, he felt as if DCF was treating him like a deadbeat dad who had neglected his children. He described how humiliating it was to have a staff member, paid to evaluate his interactions with his daughter, sit at a table and type her observations while he played and interacted with his daughter. He considered DCF's perception of him to be discriminatory and talked about it in social class terms.

Actually, the only discrimination I can see is me being a low-class person.... I see how certain parents are with their kids and how I was with my kids. And I see people that have money it's not a big issue with DCF. It's never a big issue because as long as they got the money to shell out for a good lawyer, it's over in a matter of months. Me being low class, it's a struggle. It's always been a struggle with DCF. That's how I see it. I don't have a good lawyer so they can pick on me and try to suck all my life out of me just to give up my daughter. And to me, my daughter is the only thing that has me with my head up and just dealing with things. That's how I see it. [crying] When you broke and you don't have no money, and not a good lawyer, that's the only person that leeches can actually attack. That's how I see DCF, it's just a big-ass leech.

At the time of the interview, Jadzia had moved into a one-bedroom apartment. He was working at Taco Bell. He was preparing for reunification with his daughter in six months by looking for a better job and by fixing up the bedroom for her, while he planned to sleep on the couch. He considered himself to be in a reactive or defensive position—he had to comply with DCF's mandates and accept their interpretations of him in order to get one of his children back. By the time of reunification, his daughter would have spent more time in foster care than with him. His involvement with DCF made him very sensitive to being labeled a deadbeat dad. "A deadbeat dad," he exclaimed, "is a pathetic person that can't control his kids or won't be there for his kids. He doesn't want to be there for his kids." His voice rising, he stressed, "A deadbeat dad I will never be." Not unlike other fathers struggling with the state's scrutiny of being neglectful of their children, Jadzia was engaged in the symbolic struggle of defining himself as different from the "deadbeat dad"— he was not "a pathetic person" and defensively worked the boundaries to squeeze dignity and status as an engaged father. He concluded: "Right now, I just live day to day and struggle to get my daughter back."

The other symbolic boundary along which fathers attempted to derive dignity and respect concerned reliance on social welfare. As we discussed in Chapter 3, dependence on state assistance was largely viewed as a failure of a father to provide for his family, and a threat to his masculinity. Some of the men split off state welfare along gender lines—welfare was something that their partners used and managed, while they found other sources of income, whether from on- or off-the-books jobs or from the streets. We quoted Steven, who made it clear that he would go to the streets before he would rely on the state, underscoring his masculine efficacy. Men distinguished themselves and families from the welfare leeches, as Ray put it. They widely embraced welfare-to-work programs to get parents off their butts and into the workforce. They worked the symbolic boundary represented by the lazy, welfare dad, while they failed to see how other forms of state support, like the Earned Income Tax Credit, Supplemental Security Income, and Unemployment Insurance were also forms of state welfare.

When fathers were working, the symbolic boundary from which they derived their moral identity as a working father directed scorn at the unemployed, welfare-reliant father. When we asked Hayden, a 19-year-old Puerto Rican father, his perspective on the welfare-to-work program, he asserted, "Long overdue." Hayden elaborated:

> I don't like it [welfare], personally, cuz I work very hard, and then when I see my check, Uncle Sam took most of it cuz I gotta support somebody else's kid because they're not working, so I don't like it. I'm not a welfare person. I disagree with it. I think it's not a good idea period to be on welfare, cuz I think you should learn the hard way. You made a kid; you go and work. Welfare is just a easy way out. That's the way it looks to me. It's a cop-out. It's the easiest way out. Cuz you don't have to worry cuz you know welfare is gonna pay for it.

As we pointed out in Chapter 3, however, many of the men's responses to public assistance were contradictory. Some lived in communities where state welfare was necessary to survival, and yet they still felt the need to invoke this symbolic boundary—to construct their own identity in relation to the welfare reliant.

Bobby, a 27-year-old African American father, married to the mother of his child, had relied on public assistance around the time of their five-year-old son's birth. Their income placed them close to the welfare cliff; so, while they qualified for food stamps and WIC, they had too much reported income to qualify for cash assistance or public housing, and relied on a food pantry to get through the month. Reflecting on that period of time, Bobby commented, "I didn't really like the state thing. It just makes me feel like I'm not doing enough and I'm not working hard enough." Like others, the actual interactions with public assistance staff were left to his wife. "I didn't do too much of the talking," Bobby said. Instead, he observed from a distance as his wife "did most of the talking and, yes, they were a pain, either they were a pain or she was getting frustrated, one or the other, but either way it wasn't looking out to our benefit."

At the time of the interview with Bobby, he had acquired a decent-paying job with benefits at a paper mill, while his wife worked two under-the-table, part-time jobs. As their household income shifted, so apparently did Bobby's attitude toward welfare.

When discussing the implementation of time limits for cash assistance, Bobby's critique was softened somewhat, perhaps because of his own involvement with state welfare, but he nonetheless distinguished himself from the welfare reliant to accentuate his own moral status.

> I think they shortened the term of welfare, too. They're gonna make you work and I think that's excellent. I don't know. If you get rid of it, then, people who actually need help are gonna be suffering in the long run and you might have more problems in the long run, but if you shorten it even more, then, that might be the fire under their tails that they need to get into doing the work that they're supposed to be doing. They should go out and find a job and that's that. I don't care if it's at McDonalds. Like I tell everybody, I had to work at Burger King before. I know what it's like working at Burger King. . . . Even though it's hard to find a place to live now because the rent has gone up, the cost of living has gone up, there's places that you can work your way into. All you gotta do is look. I know it gets tiring and tiring and frustrating and, you know, it sucks most of the time, looking for a job and looking for an apartment to live and you got kids and stuff.

At 27 years of age, Bobby had achieved working-class respectability, but he conceptualized this along the symbolic boundary that distinguished him from those who relied on state assistance and therefore were not working hard enough on behalf of their children.

Maurice, the biracial father described earlier, who was angry at his father for introducing his mother to drugs, grew up with his grandmother in the Charter Oak Housing development in Hartford. The father of four-month-old twins, Maurice graduated from high school and was working for the state processing tax forms. He, too, was supportive of time limits and the welfare-to-work program.

> Well, taking them off welfare and putting them to work? Yeah, because that way people will be more motivated instead of looking for a handout. . . .

[Welfare] is depending on something, then you're never going to want to do nothing for yourself. That's why we've got so many parents who—I mean with their hand out now—telling them they want this, they need that . . . how do you expect to get help when you can't help yourself? That's how I feel.

Growing up in in a poor housing project, however, Maurice also understood the challenges facing street youth. Earlier in the interview, he defended street hustlers: "Now, they always talking about we people be on the street. All right. Give us some more jobs. You all won't even give nobody no jobs. 'Oh, we'll call you, let you know.' Your word ain't going to pay up, put no food on the table." Building up steam, Maurice articulated a familiar perspective on the street that drugs were brought into poor neighborhoods by the government that street hustlers had learned to use to their advantages.

They say, "Oh, we out there thugging and all this." We ain't dumb. You brought the thing in that's going to kill us all and it just backfired on them. We just started making money out of it. We're just natural born hustlers and the only way you all try to kill us, well, we're going to sell it back to you all. If it ain't going to change, something going to happen bad—another riot. Better stop fucking with us.

Maurice was both sympathetic and critical of those he grew up with. He was a champion of self-reliance and supportive of street youth who made something from the circumstances in which they lived. At the same time, he was critical of those reliant on state welfare. He wanted the state and employers to provide jobs and opportunities, instead of cash and food stamps.

Maurice crafted his own identity in relation to these symbolic boundaries—he was the self-reliant youth who had worked the streets and was now working in formal employment, and he derived status and respectability within a cultural context that valued individual resilience over state reliance. He was critical of the government for bringing drugs into his community and for nurturing state dependence, and he was critical of those around him who passively accepted these conditions. Maurice was a survivor and was actively creating a life with the circumstances he was given, merging defiance and self-reliance.

Working the symbolic boundaries provided fathers with narratives of self-worth. Whether distinguishing themselves from their own neglectful fathers, from welfare-reliant, unemployed fathers, or from the popular trope, the deadbeat dad, these fathers were navigating the boundaries where they could claim dignity and respect. Missing from these constructions was an understanding of structural subjugation.

Systemic Inequality

It was rare that fathers described to us their life circumstances and struggles in terms of racial or class inequality. This is not surprising since these frames are not readily available to them; certainly not within the institutions that govern their lives but also, it would appear, not much within their own social spheres either. The hegemony of cultural individualism and meritocracy shaped the men's perspectives and, like Maurice earlier, even those with street histories were more likely to adopt a defiant individualism, in which they valued their self-efficacy and masculine prowess within difficult circumstances. However, there was some systemic critique, akin to what Jay MacLeod, in his classic, *Ain't No Making It*, referred to as a partial penetration of the dominant meritocratic ideology. Of course, it is possible that the men possessed a more critical consciousness that they did not share with us in the interviews—perhaps forms of "hidden transcripts" that were more likely to be shared in safe spaces, removed from the agents of dominant culture.[4] Even if this were the case, it is hard for us to imagine that a broader, coherent social critique was possible without vibrant cultural and political institutions that could nurture such a perspective. As MacLeod eloquently explained, given the hegemony of cultural individualism, critical views may be penetrating, "but insightful opinions are of little use in isolation; their needs to be an ideological perspective and cultural context in which their insights can be applied that leads to positive and potentially transformative rituals, symbols, territories, and political strategies."[5]

There were insights expressed to us that revealed some structural thought. Robert, the 31-year-old white father whose bombastic quotes are sprinkled throughout the book, conveyed social class anger and a class perspective on raising his son.

> Rich people got it made because you are with the right people. . . . You damn well know the president's kids someday are going to be mayors and shit because they are already in the clique. You got normal people that live normal

lives like that average American, pretty much you are stuck working in a factory and shit. . . . All I make is $35,000. How the fuck am I going to put my kid in college? The best way to go is the military.

Robert, his father, and his brother had all been in the Navy, but none of them had attended college after their military service. Robert saw the military as a practical option for his son to acquire dignity without sacrificing working-class humility.

> I don't want him to be a bum on the street. . . . I don't want him to be really wealthy [either]. I mean if he is just making ends meet when he has a family, that's fine, if it don't bother him. I would rather him have a little more money than the average American, but I don't want him to be rich. Because I don't like rich people because they are all snobs. . . . If he graduates school and he can't find a job, I am going to pressure the issue—join the military. It's guaranteed work and you won't get fired.

Robert wanted his son to embody working-class respectability, as distinct from the moral and social immoderations characteristic of elites.

In our interview with Hector, a 35-year-old Puerto Rican father of three children, he sardonically provided insight into social class dynamics when distinguishing between a good and bad father. When we asked Hector about his plans for his children's futures, he laughed. "I ain't going to make no plans." Hector quickly added, "Oh, I'll try my best [but] I can't do nothing," again laughing at the question. Perplexed by his response, we then asked, what makes a good father. Hector replied:

> Nothing makes a good father. What makes you a good father is if your kid goes off to college somewhere and that's when somebody look at you as a good father. If your kid is a dropout, to other eyes you are not a good father. But they don't know because they don't live under your household. . . . In my eyes? Look, man, I been with kids they been three or four years in college that are addicts and messed up, locked up, robbery background with college degrees. So I don't believe in that shit. I am saying a kid could drop out of college and find that, I don't know, get a girl pregnant, get married, find a job, and take care of his. That doesn't mean you are a bad father if you drop out of school. You got somebody pregnant and you taking care of his. Hey, you learn something!

Hector went on to distinguish between a good father and a bad father by saying, "To me a bad father is who abuses his kids. That's what a bad father is." A good father, he continued, "He try to raise them the right way." Hector concluded his thoughts by reflecting on the limited influence that a father can have within a stratified class system. He remarked, "It's a few percentage who makes it nowadays, that go all the way. So I know the steps that I got to take. It's for them to use them tools and see if they work in their life." Beyond that, Hector said, "I can't do nothing." Hector was pessimistically pragmatic in his response. He was not dismissing his role as a father and was attempting to elevate the significance of working-class dignity. Further, he was dispelling what he considered to be commonly held perceptions about the good and bad father, while acknowledging the poor prospects for social class mobility.

We also heard descriptions of racial discrimination. Earlier in the book, Nathan felt that he was denied work in the fast food industry as a young man because of his dreadlocks. Alford made a similar comment about racially discriminatory attitudes toward his appearance:

> It's a color thing. Some people out there see I got a couple tattoos or whatever . . . [they think] I am a drug dealer and stuff, but they don't even try to find out first. That's the first thing that come to their head. So I guess that probably has something to do with it too, my appearance. I don't know. But I think that's wrong because you can't base a person by their appearance.

Racial prejudice came up in other contexts as well, but usually when men were talking about institutional authorities who directly impinged upon their lives. Engagement with court magistrates, welfare and child protection professionals, police, and corrections officers generated some insight into the structural organization of power. Bernard, a 19-year-old Nicaraguan father, described racial dynamics in the juvenile detention system.

BERNARD: Ever since I been in juvenile, I never had a chance. . . . You know what fucked me up though? I do the pettiest stuff. They handcuffed [me] and I never get out of that police station. Never! I see white boys do a lot of crazy shit, stealing cars, doing this. And I just broke one rule and they hit me up with the maximum. And I see these little mother fuckers going home. What the fuck? The judge never gave me a chance. Never.

RON: You think it's because, like discrimination?

BERNARD: I think so. Back then there was a lot there. Because if you was a judge you see like this, you see a nice white family coming in there, little kid, he looking innocent. And now you see me and I come and then I live in the projects. And they say "Oh, look at this knucklehead." All right. [And then], "Let's give this family a chance because I know he is [nice]." That's the way they are looking at it. But "let's lock this dude up. Let's show him what's going on with this."

Bernard believed that he was a victim of racism within the juvenile system that gave breaks to white youth, but not to young men of color, like himself.

Given the large number of men incarcerated in our study, it was not surprising to find some structural insights derived from their experiences in prison. Tyler observed that prisons facilitated violence and destruction. He said it this way: "I'm going tell you, you keep hitting a dog in the head he's going to bite you. You keep throwing me in Level Five prisons and putting me with murderers when I only got 90 days, I'm going to bite you. I'm going to eventually start biting. And I don't want to." For Tyler, prisons were contributing to the very problems they ostensibly were intended to rectify.

Bruce directed his comments to the structural problem of prison release and "reintegration."

They don't have a place to go. They don't have food in their stomach. They don't have clothes on their back. They don't have anybody that cares. They don't have no one that loves them. So they just, "All right, nobody cares . . . so I am going to go out there and do the same thing." Employment is a big key because if you have money in your pocket you feel like a man. You have self-esteem and you don't want to go back to jail because you keep wanting to get that legal money staying out of jail.

Bruce's observations about the challenges of citizen reentry from prison are affirmed in high recidivism rates.[6]

It is not surprising given the criminalization of the poor that men would develop critical insights into racial and class dynamics from their encounters with these institutions. As we saw in Chapter 6, several described discriminatory behaviors among police officers. Their involvement in other institutions governing their lives also produced flashes of systemic understandings. As we recall, Jorge referred to state child protection services as a "big-ass leech" that preyed on poor families; fathers felt racial and class opprobrium when they encountered welfare bureaucrats; and they especially felt discriminated against in child support courts.

Standing before child support magistrates following periods of incarceration, they felt the injustice of accumulating child support arrears, especially when they were facing poor job prospects. More often, however, they interpreted these dynamics as gender discrimination. They believed that they were victims of state systems that were organized to take care of mothers and children, and that neglected their struggles and life circumstances. White fathers, angered by declining wage opportunities and divorce, felt humiliated and victimized by the courts, and wanted to press their rights in the court. "They've got to hear the guy's side of it," Stanley insisted. "Don't just thrive on the woman's take." A participant in a mostly black FIP, Stanley also directed some of his rage at black fathers, referring to them as "bums" and "lazy," while snapping at our black interviewer on several occasions. Following up on his comments about race, Ron asked him if he was a victim of racial discrimination in the courts. Stanley became indignant. "Why would you say that?" he exclaimed. "I am a victim of a woman's point of view, how's that? Yeah, because everybody always tends to give to the woman."

Among black and brown fathers, feelings of gender discrimination in the courts were no less apparent. They, too, were struggling with the moralistic symbolism of the deadbeat dad and felt victimized by the courts. But black and brown communities have historically been victimized by the courts. Fathers like Cordero were less likely to want to express their rights in the courts and more likely to want to avoid them altogether. He reflected:

> All in all, I think the individual, me as myself, gets intimidated and gets fearful when you are in front of people who come down with a ruling or decision that devastate and change your life. And when it comes to your own personal family, that's really devastating. They don't have no idea how much I have lived and done for many years. And then all of a sudden they get into our lives within a couple of months, a month or whatever. They make this type of decision which is really traumatizing.

Getting more demonstrative, Cordero stressed, "We love our children. But the politicians make it seem like they care, but they really don't. It's all about the money." FIPs were important in encouraging fathers to show up to court hearings and in providing advocacy for fathers like Cordero.

Further, it appeared that black and brown fathers were more likely to want to resolve family issues informally, which is understandable since, as Jennifer Hamer and Maureen Waller have each demonstrated, child support enforcement and state welfare have never been organized to support the structure of black and brown families in low-income communities.[7] However, informal dynamics foster considerable gender distrust in communities where resources are lacking, intimate relationships are casual, and childrearing relies on broader kin networks. The dynamics of structural unemployment and precarious work, state welfare retrenchment, negotiated resource networks, and the changing expectations of father involvement deepen gender distrust.[8] Political and economic forces become less visible in these situations as mothers and fathers point fingers at one another to explain their struggles for survival. Deprivation creates harsher voices.

In these contexts, street income becomes even more valued and a source of power, grandmothers yield more authority in providing and negotiating care and in defining the roles of parenting, and father involvement becomes episodic.[9] In the worst scenarios, state and economic resource constriction and deprivation places so much stress on these informal networks that destructive tendencies flourish. Nineteen-year-old Lorenzo tried to make sense of this with Ron.

LORENZO: I feel most guys feel they ain't a man because they know that they messed up in a certain situation and due to their financial position, it weakens their mind. It limits them. They get lazy, man. They get weary. They get emotional. They get violent now. They get critical now. Desperate now. And that's what it leads to. Now they are incarcerated. Now they are doing time. Now they are confined. Now they are taking drugs. They are limiting their actions because they are too obsessive and it just weakens the heart and it weakens the mind of the man. And then that weakens the woman. Because after a while all the men is not going to be around. They are going to be incarcerated. And then what?

RON: Yeah, it affects the children.

LORENZO: So now what? Now if he's a deadbeat dad and it's a thousand more in that deadbeat dad category that leaves the women messed up.

RON: Because the men aren't around to help them?

LORENZO: Right. And they feel like they need a man at a certain point to keep that stabilized household.

RON: Yeah, that's true.

LORENZO: But then what about the women? They begin to get emotional. Some of them hit the kids because they are upset for no reason. Mostly these kids get abused by these men and deadbeat dads, these women and deadbeat moms. They get abused, man, over nothing. These innocent lives get abused over something that's dealing with deadbeat issues. And then you wonder why DCF is involved. For any guy out there, don't feel like you ain't a man because you are not able to take care of your responsibility at that moment. Everything takes time. It took nine months to come out the woman. Trust me, it takes time to reach this potential.

Lorenzo is trying to articulate how structural forces are affecting poor black families. He identifies processes of structural unemployment, symbolic violence, emasculation, self-destruction, and familial violence. He was defensive, without being dismissive, of the criticisms directed at fathers; and he wanted to place more blame on mothers' participation in family dissolution without ignoring structural forces. In the end, he, too, entered into the realm of gender war in the inner city from a defensive male perspective, while struggling to see how larger systemic issues were at play.

Perspectives on structural oppression are difficult to develop and sustain. Structural understandings get little to no support within the institutions where low-income communities are located, while a political-cultural context that would validate and help to develop structural insights into coherent ideological perspectives is virtually nonexistent. Consequently, these insights become largely irrelevant, or viewed as impractical. They are seen as making excuses or else as ideas that are not useful to the immediacy of marginalized lives.

Moreover, systemic insights often become misguided when racial and class oppression gets channeled into gender distrust and hostility. The consequences of growing inequality, social and economic marginalization, and resource deprivation land on families, where distress and despair result in finger pointing between fathers and mothers. Paternal absence, irresponsibility, and undependability get channeled on one side, while maternal greed, gatekeeping, and disloyalty get channeled on the other. Examining the declining conditions that fail to support and sustain marriage or cohabitation, childrearing, or the basic foundation for preparing the next generation to be productive workers and part of a citizenry gives way to mounting animosity directed at those intimately entwined in the situation.

Low-income fathers are likely to respond to these scenarios in one of two ways. They may embrace a father's rights narrative that is supported by varying movements.[10] In this regard, they insist that they be treated fairly by the courts and get access to their children, and they counter the dominant narrative about father indifference. When we gave reports on our research in 2010, we were followed by a group of men who were angry and were patrolling the narratives about fathers that were being publicly articulated. Inevitably, we were cornered afterward and challenged on several comments that we made. More extreme instances of this strategy, however, that blame women for the fears and uncertainties that haunt white men in the 21st-century political economy can fuel misogynistic perspectives that are central to male and white supremacy narratives. The mass shooting at a Florida yoga studio in June 2019 by Scott Paul Beierle is a tragic example.[11]

The more common way that fathers understand and attempt to resolve the problems stemming from deepening inequality, state and corporate retrenchment, and the dissolution of the family is to take matters into their own hands and attempt to make changes themselves. These efforts are consistent with the institutional messages that these men are regularly exposed to, which emphasize that only they can change their lives by making better decisions—or to use prison lingo to "start thinking for a change"—and ultimately become responsible, involved fathers. Consistent with American individualism, and deepened by an era of neoliberal reason, many of the fathers expressed their determination to remake themselves, to make fatherhood the center of their lives, and to get their shit together.

Getting Your Shit Together

The men in our study expressed a great deal of emotion and determination in making smart decisions, atoning for their mistakes, changing their lives, and making fatherhood central to new life directions. These narratives generally fell into two categories: (1) *therapeutic* narratives in which they were focused on healing from past suffering associated with family violence, substance abuse, and prison, and in creating new identities that emphasized reformed dispositions and new self-conceptions; and (2) *life-course transitional* narratives that underscored adult responsibility for their families and children, in which finding work, moving out of unsafe areas, saving money for a house, staying away from crime and the streets, and being engaged fathers were articulated.

Therapeutic Narratives

In Jennifer Silva's book *Coming Up Short*, based on interviews with young working-class men and women, she examined connections between neoliberal economic restructuring and cultural articulations. She explains this as the reworking of adult identities "along new cultural logics and new structural constraints," in which, broader economic and political dynamics penetrate "a lived system of meanings and values in the emotional sphere."[12] Silva expressed surprise to find that most of her respondents "were absolutely fluent in the language of therapeutic needs, desires, emotional suffering and self-growth."[13] Confronting early experiences of trauma was key to this process, especially emotional anguish stemming from substance abuse and family violence. While fatherhood is not the focus of her book, Silva does explain how precarious work and the increasing demands on the family to navigate an uncertain world have made intimacy and marital commitment risky and fraught with tensions, fears, and resentments. She maintains that the "hidden injuries of risk" foster fear, mistrust, and isolation among the working class and shows how happiness and risk have become privatized, while narratives of personal redemption and transformation have become predominant.

In our study, we found similar patterns among many of the men. Living amid social and economic marginalization often took the form of addressing past traumas and seeking personal transformation. As we saw in the last chapter, many of the men grew up with domestic abuse, and some with extreme violence that was haunting as they transitioned into adulthood, intimate relationships, and fatherhood. For some like 22-year-old Demitri, early trauma was turned into determination. He described how the worst memories of his father were "when he mistreated my mother, when he would hit her, he would beat her, those are the worst." He disassociated from his father: "For me [my father] wasn't any good. He wasn't. For me, he wasn't and never will be my father." Demitri harvested the lessons from early trauma.

I know what I suffered and I know that I'm not going to make him [son] go through something like that because what I felt when I was living what

I was living, like when my father beat my mother, the way he treated me, well I know that I couldn't do that because I suffered, understand? And I wouldn't want him to suffer what I had suffered. You know, so in that case it helped me a lot.

For others, though, they modeled their fathers' abusive behaviors and were now learning to undo these destructive patterns. They were "reformed abusers" whose exposure to domestic violence prevention and anger management programs provided a language through which to better understand these intergenerational dynamics.

We profiled Felix in the last chapter who was struggling to undo embodied dispositions to intimate partner violence. Growing up with an abusive father, he said, "I was very abusive. I picked that up. You can say I picked that up. And I didn't ever see anything wrong with it. It's like, you know, it was something that came with the territory. You know, a man does this." Exposed to domestic violence programs in prison, Felix lamented that "basically the kids saw what I saw, you know like the controlling, the slamming of doors, the domestic violence, coming home late." Felix was trying to adopt a new self-narrative, and he told us proudly that he had not been arrested for five years, and that he had lived with the mother of his most recent child for three years. He also saw two of his children from a prior relationship every weekend, but he did not have access to the children from his first relationship, despite attempting to prove to the judge he had changed .

Shane, a 28-year-old white father, related growing up in an abusive home with an alcoholic mother to his own psychological make-up. After Shane's father was hospitalized with schizophrenia, his parents divorced and his mother remarried. Shane's stepfather was regularly violent toward his mother and so they broke up and reunited several times, never with better outcomes. Shane explained that the way he grew up:

affected me in a lot of different ways; I didn't even realize how I was affected until these last couple of years. . . . When I was in school, I wasn't close to a lot of people. And I didn't like getting close to people. I've learned not to really trust many people. I trust certain people to a certain extent, but I have boundaries when it comes to everybody. I noticed when it comes to my relationships, I am very skeptical. When it comes to my girlfriends, I am very overprotective towards everybody in my life, more overprotective of them than myself. I notice I always try to run from any type of problems. I'd rather stay enclosed because of what I've seen.

Shane was working two jobs, both in food service, for a total of 55 hours per week. He lived with his girlfriend, their son, and her son from a rape. He took medication for anxiety and was ambivalent about marrying his girlfriend, and dreamed of someday being a counselor. Felix received disability benefits, worked sporadically, and lived with the mother of his most recent three-year-old son. Both Shane and Felix were just getting by, struggling with income and housing, but they turned inward to deal with the violence and trauma in their lives. They were expressive about this—Felix focused on reworking his masculinity and Shane on trust, boundaries, and overprotectiveness—and they both appeared dedicated to healing and charting a different course than their parental role models.

In a similar way that violence disrupted households, so did alcohol and drug abuse, and many of the men struggled with their own addictions. They attended AA/NA programs and committed to their recoveries. Their lives were informed by these therapeutic narratives. Saulo confessed, "This ain't my first time. This ain't my second time. This ain't my third time I relapsed. [sighs] So now I know I got a sickness which I got to deal with for the rest of my life." He asserted, "You got to want to help yourself. You know? Because if you don't help yourself, there is nobody that's going to help you."

Daniel agreed. "It ain't too late," he said. He explained that he never pursued recovery for himself in the past and, consequently, failed repeatedly. He explained:

Every time I go in before it was for my moms. My mom used to drive up and down Park Street looking for me and shit like that. Or my girl would be like "If you don't go, I ain't going to be with you no more." So always was for somebody, not for me. And I always cheated, man. I was running dope through the detox.

Daniel explained that he has now embraced the journey to recovery. "This time I'm straight now," he insisted, as he intended to clean up the damage done. He said his oldest daughter "is playing it sideways right now and I don't blame her for that one."

Ted explained his commitment to the AA program: "I have a sponsor now, you know. One person helps the others, that's how the program works, one alcoholic helping another to stay sober one day at a time." Others, like Greg, rejected AA, but found other ways to pursue a sober life. Greg said, "I went to (AA) once. I listened to people talk about relapsing and during the break I just walked out, got in my truck and left because right then and there I didn't need people talking about relapsing." Greg instead relied on his intimate partner: "I rely on her to keep me on track." He said he had been sober for five years. Like Greg, others talked about being "saved" by intimate partners. We heard that if it was not for their relationships, "I'd be lost," "I don't care if I live or die," "I'd probably be in jail right now," or "I'd be out at the strip joints and bars."

These fathers represented a different masculinity than their fathers' generation. They were not stoically suffering the indignities of poor educations and precarious jobs, the damaged grandeur of masculine self-determination, or the racial and class dynamics of marginalization through inebriated barroom brawls and household terror. Instead, they were emerging from the dark corners of repressed and controlled identities and crafting expressive selves that embraced a therapeutic language of self-transformation. This turn inward to confront one's demons was projected outward as a therapeutic self. It focused on healing emotional suffering, but not on the social and economic contexts in which emotional suffering was concentrated. As Ramon simply put it: "I'm trying to change my life and stuff."

Manning Up

While several of the fathers were preoccupied with how to cure the maladies of their pasts, most advanced a forward-looking individualistic narrative about sacrifice, responsibility, and determination. Because so many were young, they expressed a commitment to making life course transitions to adult responsibility—to find work or be a provider, to save for a home and a car, to take care of their children, and to stay away from crime and bad influences. They described this as a form of masculinity—of manning up. They knew what they had to do; now it was time to do it.

Many sounded like Rex when he said, "If I can walk, talk, I can find a job. I still don't expect nothing from nobody." Despite considerable hardship, Marcus told us that he never gets depressed.

So I have to stay strong, I have to stay strong because I have my kids here. . . . If I can't help myself, I can't help them. See, I go down, [I'm] never going to be able to help my mother. She need my help. So I have to stay strong. I have to stay on my feet, no matter what I receive. This is what make me go on strong and have the determination to keep going. Because by now I would have killed myself a long time ago.

Marcus was formerly incarcerated, unemployed, and fighting with the courts over his child support arrearage at the time of the interview.

Lorenzo, whom we quoted earlier on the dissolution of the family in poor neighborhoods, imagined his future in his interview with Ron.

LORENZO: All right, enrolling in some type of employment activity, gaining my financial necessities. Hopefully pursuing my education. . . . After my education I want to invest in my own business, which would probably be the music thing or maybe a clothes fashion.
RON: And so what are you going to have to do to make that happen?
LORENZO: I am going to have to sacrifice. I am going to have to take my time and really focus on the setbacks that's going to happen and how to overcome that. Also, I have to be more educated.
RON: And how are you going to get that education?
LORENZO: Hopefully a student loan, something. Something, man. Some kind of sacrifice. I don't care if I go to the library and read books. As long as I get the knowledge that I need for what I am going for, I'll be all right. In five years, I'll be all right.

Lorenzo was unemployed and in an employment training program at the time.

Chris was also focused on his education. "I am just trying to go to school for the education in my mind to get a better job for me and my son," he said. "That's what I'm going to need anyway. Some kind of degree. Associate's, bachelor's, whatever. A higher degree. I need to further my horizons." Later he lamented, "There ain't no jobs nowhere. There's jobs out there, but a man with no transportation, with no car or nothing. What am I going to do? Jog? Ride a bike to the next three towns?" Determined, he continued, "When I find a job, that come next. School or whatever will come next. . . . Once I get that job, I can get people off my back. Then I get to school."

Victor's quest was similar to many of the marginalized men in the study. He said confidently that in five years he will have a "steady job, my own home, my own car." At the time, he was working on his GED and had a seasonal job at a party rental place. Or like Mark, even when the men were locked up, they would frequently say, "Got to be a man now. Got to be there for my daughter . . . I wasn't doing the right thing. I am going to get a job, go to school. And stay away from them negative things."

These fathers expressed determination to change their lives, and to do it for themselves and their families. Their frame was familiar and reinforced in state institutions. In welfare offices, the message was clear, get a job and take care of your families. In child support enforcement courts, get a job, pay off your debts, and be an involved father. In prisons, stay away from your old playgrounds, stop making excuses, man-up, get a job, and turn your life around. In cognitive-behavioral programs, pause before you react to tense situations, place your index finger to your temple, and think differently for a change. In AA/NA programs, nobody can do it for you, you must be ready to change, to accept your mistakes, to find personal strength in a higher power, and to manage your disease. In anger management programs, acknowledge that your anger is a problem, recognize the triggers, and learn new routines to manage these swells of emotions. In fatherhood programs, be financially responsible and emotionally available for your children, confront estrangement, reconceptualize manhood, and make sacrifices for your kids.

Fathers had internalized these messages, and they espoused the language of individualism and neoliberal reason. In the former, they asserted that they were the captains of their own ships, had made bad decisions, done "stupid shit," and now it was time to man-up, get a job, make sacrifices, and then enjoy the spoils of working-class responsibility—buy a car and a home, move into better neighborhoods, get more schooling, dress their children better, and embody the American dream.

In the era of neoliberalism, a new form of reason has merged with 20th-century American individualism. Wendy Brown describes neoliberal reason as a governing rationality that extends a "specific formulation of economic values, practices, and metrics to every dimension of human life."[14] In this way, neoliberalism does not only reorganize the relationship between the state and economy; it also restructures how we conduct ourselves and relate to one another. In part, this is done through the institutional absorption of economic rationality, where this rationality becomes an organizing force within every institution governing our lives—school, health, government, family, workplace, prisons, social welfare services, and so on. Subsequently, individuals are transformed into entrepreneurs, whose focus is on acquiring the skills and the mentality necessary to speculate on their own individual investments within a precarious economy. Here we see where poverty governance intersects, as the institutions through which poverty is managed adopt a governing rationality that promotes entrepreneurialism as the central tenet for individual reform and salvation to overcome the entrapments of poverty. This is all done with good intentions as the prevailing rationality shapes the poor and those who provide services to the poor into mutually entrained actors working toward sustenance, inclusion, and transcendence.[15]

Fathers less attached to the labor market are particularly exposed to these messages from myriad institutions. Social workers, counselors, therapists, sponsors, magistrates, probation officers, and a whole layer of paraprofessionals recruited from the ranks of the indigent carry out this mission with exuberance, passion, and determination to teach the misguided, errant populations how they can transform themselves and maximize their own interests. Colleges and universities, professional conferences and workshops have trained professionals and semiprofessionals how to perform these vital institutional functions and to adopt the most effective strategies— or the "best practices"—for saving the poor and marginalized, and integrating them into this vibrant neoliberal world.

Many of the fathers in our study, as we have seen, have embraced this powerful cocktail of American individualist and neoliberal ideologies. Many have done so, despite being unemployed or working in precarious, poorly paying jobs, living with family members in crowded conditions in deprived neighborhoods, coming out of prison with criminal records, being thousands of dollars in child support and court debt, or having no other revenue streams except the street economy. They hope to make something out of nothing through determination. And they intend to be engaged fathers.

Fathering as Central

As we saw in earlier chapters, men expressed considerable desires to be engaged fathers. The father identity gave them social status, meaning, and the prospects for change. When men imagined their futures, their motivations to "do the right thing" were usually related to taking care of children and being a father whom their children would respect. Some men were doing the work of fatherhood—changing diapers, playing with children on the floor, walking them to school; some were fighting in the courts for the right to see their children; some were attempting to reconnect with children after absences; some were trying to figure out how to father in unsafe neighborhoods and schools; some were in prison daydreaming about their children; some were charting out new directions in their lives around fatherhood; some were trying to be like the fathers that their fathers were not; and some were aging into fatherhood as second-generation fathers.

More than anything else, the men typically wanted to talk about themselves as fathers. Some, like Moises, provided moving testimonials about being fathers. For Moises things had come together. "My daughter is with me. So I don't even care. Nothing matters. This is the happiest point of my life. This is the highest point of my entire life. This is it." Ron affirmed the comment, "So you are making progress?" "Progress," Moises laughed. "More than progress."

> This year has been the ultimate. It was a very bad year, but the outcome of it was just the ultimate. I got my daughter, my own place, I'm single, got a good job. I get paid five a week. Can't nobody touch that. I got good friends. In my opinion I have a good view on how shit should be. I think I'm on top of my game right now. . . . My daughter is happy. Every time you see her, she's smiling. You know what I'm saying? I'm good.

Moises escaped from an extremely cruel and abusive home life when he was 10 years of age. He bounced around at different households between Brooklyn, New York, and Groton, Connecticut. Moises joined a gang at 10, sold drugs, and experienced bouts of homelessness. He wore a lengthy scar over one eye sustained by a fellow gang member, which led him to sever ties with the gang. He had never been incarcerated. Moises never made it beyond eighth grade, but he learned math from hustling on the streets and was accepted into a training program to learn how to run a craps table for a casino. At 23, he was working at the casino, had a car, a two-bedroom apartment, and his music, which he said had therapeutically sustained him during his chaotic adolescent years. His child was born to a white woman, whom he had been with for three years, but had split up with before the birth because, according to him, of her infidelities. A DNA test determined that the child was his and so, with the assistance of the FIP, he obtained joint custody in the courts. Due to some serious indiscretions on the part of the mother, the court also granted his apartment as his two-year-old daughter's primary residence. His life goal was to be a record producer, but he clarified, "My life's goal is to be the best father in the world, and then a record producer."

Likewise, things were starting to work out for Danny, also a 23-year-old Puerto Rican father, who had not finished high school. He described being a father of a two-month-old:

> I just got the job at the barber shop so everything is starting to fall in place right now. It's helping out a lot. I was just scared not being able to take care of her. That was my main concern. You know what I'm sayin? Right now I am living with my mom. Soon I'll have my own apartment, you know? So that's all I want. I just want to be able to provide. It's beautiful. I love it. I am with her all the time, besides when I go to work. I come back and I am with her all the time. Feed her. Change her. I love it.

Danny's job at the barber shop became his anchor for the possible.

Demitri, who we described earlier as growing up with an abusive father, found work after he was released from prison. First, he worked for a company that closed down, and then he worked as a temp for three months, but the company did not hire him on permanently. He expressed similar joy in being a father to his three-month-old son: "Now that I have my son, well, I feel happy. . . . You know, it's something beautiful, you understand, something that you, there's no words to describe it." Demitri was elated about being a father, but struggling with precarious employment.

Gary, a 27-year-old white father of three who didn't live with his children, talked about the pain of being separated from them each day.

> I mean I wake up every day and my girls aren't with me and I know that it's a week before I see [them] again [and] it gets me down. . . . I love them with all my heart and I'd do anything I could to be with them. . . . And I want to make sure that they know who I am and that I would do anything that I could for them. That's my main goal is to make sure that they know, yes, they are loved. Period. Whether I have to walk through hell or I don't care what it takes. I will go to the ends of the earth and I will not quit until they

know that. I see so many guys that walk away from their kids. And that's okay for them but that's a part of me. That's a living, breathing, walking part of me, literally. And to turn my back on them would be to turn my back on myself.

Gary never knew his own father, had a difficult time getting along with women, had three children with three mothers, but was married at the time of the interview to a woman with whom he did not have children. Gary was a limousine driver, who reported some emotional problems and a drinking problem. He was angry at the courts and relied on the FIP to provide legal advocacy. For Gary, his kids comprised a meaningful place in a turbulent existence.

This was true for even Tyler, homeless and eating at a soup kitchen. Tyler insisted, amid his own life turbulence, "It's like, this is the first time in my life I feel good that I want to see my kids. I want to make a difference. I want to get a good job. I want to go back to school. I do. I want to get a trade." For Tyler, his children were a lifeline, something to keep him afloat—inspiring perhaps a fantasy, but the chance to stumble forward nonetheless.

We have already seen how fatherhood provides motivation for men preparing to leave prison. "I'll be damned if I ever come back here again," 19-year-old Gerard insisted. "I am severing all ties with all people when I get out. All I need is my family," he said. Gerard told us that as a young father, "I didn't think about me having the baby. I tried blocking that out of my life. But now that I see him and everything . . . I am so happy that I have him now. That's what straightened out my life." Vincent, also 19, put it this way:

> Everything I've done in here—GED classes, parenting and drug and alcohol classes, anger management—I've done for him. I want him to look back and be proud of me even though I did this. I want him to look back at me and be like "Yeah, my Daddy went through that but he did this, this and this." I don't want him to look back and be like "My Daddy fucked up back then." . . . Jail is probably going to bring me closer to him because I realize what I lost when I was in here.

Even 20-year-old Alford, profiled in Chapter 6, who went to prison after he shot a man in a dice game, and who explicitly had rejected the low-wage workforce for the drug trade, asserted:

I am going to distance myself from the people I used to chill with. Try even harder on the job. And now it ain't about just me no more. It's about my daughter. So I am surviving for her. I am trying to live for her and make her life as best as possible. Make her life just real good, man. It's going to be a lot different.

Alford's imagination was inspired by a 9-month-old daughter he had never touched and a rapidly approaching release date.

Daniel, an older African American father, talked about getting to know his daughter after his release from prison:

Me and her talking more. I am telling you it's getting better, man, with my little daughter. Even though my little daughter be like "That's my dad. That's my dad." I always been her dad, but I always ain't been right, right? But now I'm right, man. It's getting better, man.

For men whose lives have been defined by prison and the streets, being a father provided them with a second chance to "make something of themselves," as Joshua said, through their children. He explained: "And as far as my kids, they brighten my life up, man. They make everything, like it make me emotional right now because they give me something to live for. They make me feel like at least if I don't become something, I am going to try to make something out of them." Fatherhood provided an imagined path forward among men with narrowing horizons—a reset button for marginalized youth.

Finally, as we have seen, nothing provided more fuel for the fire than being better fathers than their own absent fathers had been. "Oh, [I'm] a thousand times better already," Justin said, laughing. "I've been fighting for three, maybe four years to be involved in my son's life and I've been paying child support. Two things right there that my father never did." This 33-year-old father continued, "And now that I am getting to see my son and talk to him everyday, I make a point of doing it, even if I take off somewhere, I make sure I have my cell phone so I can call him." Ray said, "Me not having a father growing up and I wanted to make sure that never happened to my kids, no matter what happened." And Patrick said, "It's something I never had [and] always craved. . . . I don't want to be anything like my father. I want to make a difference in my child's life. I want my child[ren] to be able to say [they] graduated because of me or they are successful because of the love I gave them. That's what I want."

Fathering was central to most of the men in our study. It provided a key conceptual frame through which they measured themselves, imagined their futures, held on to lives of dignity and respect, staked their masculinity, and searched for meaning in their lives. This was channeled through a deeply internalized culture of individualism, as they articulated their quest to man up, be the man their fathers were not, get a job, keep their children safe, and achieve the markers of success—a car, a home, and even marriage. Whether these men were just-getting-by working-class or the more economically and socially marginalized; white, black, or brown; or men with criminal pasts; their articulated visions of themselves converged around this narrative. In fact, the more marginalized they were, the more likely they appeared to adopt a father-as-central, individualistic perspective. But then, why wouldn't they? Virtually every institution through which their consciousness was being shaped and their lives managed was reinforcing these cultural messages.

The main problem with this formulation is that with the exception of the superdads, who manage to transcend barriers—work two or three jobs, pay off their child support debt, remain crime-free, become involved fathers— the majority are likely to see this as but a mirage. But then maybe a mirage is not a bad thing, when the prospects for structural change that would address the racial and class hierarchies that press down on these fathers is not likely to change. As MacLeod suggested, "The American Dream may be but a mirage. Still, it provides a vision toward which the thirsty may stumble."[16] And yet what happens when things don't work out—living wage jobs don't materialize, child support debt accumulates, court magistrates bear down, tensions rise in relationships, mothers prevent fathers from seeing their children, the streets become the only reliable revenue source, depression sets in, drug and alcohol medicates pain and disappointment, men get violated by probation officers for missing meetings, failing a drug test, or driving with a suspended license? What happens then—especially when the men have adopted the father-as-central, individualistic perspective that they can change their lives, that they can do it alone? Who, then, is to blame when it doesn't work out or, even worse, when some of them realize they are becoming their fathers?

Conclusion

Most of the fathers in our study were born at the cusp of the transition to a neoliberal political economy that has reshaped the labor force and opportunity structure. For those households located at the bottom of the labor force, these changes have been brutal, producing precarious jobs for many, while pushing others into the straits of structural unemployment. At the same time, state resources for these households have been retrenched, privatizing the burdens of caring for children in the 21st century. In other words, as the share of income for the bottom quintile of the labor force has fallen, state resources that might help to buffer these losses have also decreased, leaving families to fend more for themselves.

In this political-economic context, the state has attempted to force poor men and women to comply with declining labor force conditions, by replacing welfare with precarious, low-wage work and through incarceration.[17] This state paternalism is legitimated as a moralistic endeavor to strengthen families by promoting, if not coercing, dual-earner, low-income households, father responsibility, and resilient individualism. In this scenario, the market economy is seen as a force that is external to the workings of democratic state institutions and social life. The role of the state is to smooth out the crisis tendencies of the market, reset the economy when recessions occur, secure the global advantages of nationally based corporations, and augment public compliance to the needs and outcomes of globally competitive markets. In others words, the precarious economy and austerity politics are seen as the immutable, natural outcomes of our current historical period.

Structures are lived and, as such, we are left to make sense out of our own lives amid theses structural forces and transitions. In sociological terms that means we attempt to subjectively understand the objective conditions that structure our lives. As we listen to the men in our study, it is clear that they rarely see how these larger structural dynamics are relevant to them. There are insights into the systemic processes through which intersecting hierarchies of race and social class create advantages and disadvantages, but insights are not likely to get developed into coherent worldviews without political and cultural institutions and organizations that can help to sustain and enact them in meaningful ways. Without this, structural insights give way, largely, to an individualist hegemony.

Fathers in our study attempted to make sense out of their life circumstances along symbolic boundaries that had been established by moralistic public narratives directed at them. They wrestled with the narratives of father absence, state dependence, and father irresponsibility by comparing themselves favorably to their own neglectful fathers, to welfare frauds, and to deadbeat dads. It did not matter how marginalized these men were; these were the symbolic boundaries that preoccupied them and along which they attempted to construct narratives of dignity and respect.

When fathers conveyed their future orientations and strategies to create meaningful lives, they advanced personal narratives that took two different forms: therapeutic narratives and life course transition narratives. In the former, they adopted language that focused their gaze inward and backward to conceptualize trauma and emotional suffering, often stemming from familial violence and substance abuse. This was a language of healing and coping that rarely, if ever, made connections between systemic inequalities and emotional distress. Instead, this was construed as a personal journey to come to terms with one's own demons, embedded in interfamilial webs of pain.

In the latter, fathers intended to change their life course—to man-up, get jobs, take care of children, to get their "shit together." Almost invariably, whether they were wrestling with demons of the past, or manning up to meet their responsibilities, or both, fatherhood was at the center of these projections. They wanted to be engaged fathers, as they had internalized the messages emanating from myriad institutions governing their lives.

Without broad systemic change to truly address the intersecting racial and class hierarchies that create and reproduce inequality, fathers are being set up. Some will find a way to succeed—they will be superdads or they will draw on a reserve of family resources or they will claw together the lifestyle of the just-getting-by working class and manage to keep their relationships intact or they will age into some form of fatherhood as second-generation fathers. However, this group of fathers will be vulnerable to any crisis that may occur that will shatter their fragile stability. Nonetheless, we will herald the successes and the personal resilience of this group.

But what about the others? We suspect, that given the social and economic conditions in which the fathers' hopeful narratives are erected, that most will fall short of their visions. They may want to do it alone, but they cannot. Their passionate narratives about manning up and financial and emotional involvement with their children are not enough. And when they fail, what then? What are the consequences—for them, their children, the mothers, the larger society?

Suppose that we took their desires seriously. In other words, what if we took seriously the voices of these fathers? What if we reversed the process and rather than expecting families to conform to the harrowing conditions of the market at the bottom of the labor force, we created an economy that met the needs of families—all types of families? An economy that took seriously the needs of social reproduction; the longing for emotional connection; and the development of human potential? What if family became a location for self-discovery, democratic decision making, citizen preparation, and for the exploration of love and kindness?

9

Conclusion

> I think hard times are coming when we will be wanting the voices
> of writers who can see alternatives to how we live now, and can see
> through our fear-stricken society and its obsessive technologies,
> to other ways of being, and even imagine some real grounds for
> hope.... We live in an era of capitalism; its power seems inescapable.
> So, did the divine rights of kings. Any human power can be resisted
> and changed by human beings. Resistance and change very often
> begin ... in the art of words.
>
> —Ursula Le Guin[1]

The rapidity of political-economic change and the shifts in cultural norms and expectations concerning families and fathers have been breathtaking—occurring in a period of one to two generations. The institutions that at one time provided some stability and continuity in the life course have eroded—particularly work, family, education, marriage, religion, and civic organization. State strategies to compress income inequality, distribute resources, regulate the economy, support employment and idle labor, and invest in education, leisure, and civil order have given way to a historical wave of privatization, financialization, individualization, excessive competition, corporate malfeasance, and public indifference. This is take-the-gloves-off capitalism at its worst—something that conservative pundits like David Brooks, or even Tucker Carlson, and liberals like Joseph Stiglitz and Paul Krugman can all agree on. These structural transformations articulate lives, and they do so differently depending upon where one is located within intersecting hierarchies of power and domination.

We might consider the families represented in this book, those at the bottom of the labor force—from the just-getting-by working class to the economically redundant—as the canary in the mine. The instability that

It's a Setup. Timothy Black and Sky Keyes, Oxford University Press (2021). © Timothy Black and Sky Keyes.
DOI: 10.1093/oso/9780190062217.003.0009

neoliberal capitalism has sewn into the social fabric reaches across social classes, but its most incendiary effects reach deep into the communities, families, and relationships of the dispossessed. It is here where marriage has nearly ceased to exist, where fatherhood has become transitory, where poverty governance is most paternalistic, where punishment and debt are searing, and where idleness and restlessness smoulder in the cracks of structural unemployment. Our focus on vulnerable fathers in this book is one lens through which to examine these dynamics and to see the instability that market-based politics and culture generate across society.

Depending upon the extent of racial and class marginalization, fragile fathers are caught in a web of contradictions. As we have seen, they are forced to conform to the marketplace in an era of precarity and uncertainty, while they are held financially accountable to their children. They are often dependent upon declining forms of state assistance, while they attempt to preserve a sense of masculine self-reliance. They are demanded to pay current and accumulated child support despite unemployment or underemployment, while they also try to stay away from illicit income opportunities. They are expected to be engaged, nurturing fathers, amid their concerns about how to prepare and protect children living in poor, violent neighborhoods, or how to discipline their children so they learn working-class values. Further, they are expected to be engaged, nurturing fathers, with little to no preparation for practicing it, and, in some cases, despite the traumatizing, and often untreated, consequences of violent and abusive biographies. Finally, they are told by myriad institutional authorities that they can change their lives through entrepreneurial thinking, better decision making, and determination, which belies the need for social change to make this possible.

These contradictions are not just confounding; they also can be immobilizing and paralyzing, and lead to self-repudiation when things do not work out, deepening the men's experiences of social and familial dislocation. When enough low-income fathers find themselves lost in familiar places, then being lost becomes the "new normal," uncertainty becomes the only certainty, and figuring it out as you go may be the best they can do. Consider, for instance, the expectations placed on socially and economically marginalized fathers today to enact fluid masculinities. In the course of a day, these fathers might need to act subservient to a range of authorities—in workplaces, courts, probation and welfare offices, service programs, or prisons; to move through the informal hypermasculine spaces of the streets, peer groups, or cell blocks; and to engage in nurturing behaviors with children and disquieting decision making with mothers. Fathers must learn to code-switch across these spaces and to craft fluid forms of masculinity, and every switch can be an abrupt turn in one's day. Further, there are not a lot of opportunities for processing these daily encounters; instead, fathers are largely expected to figure it out on their own.

Nonetheless, throughout our book, we noted that fathers expressed deep desires to be involved fathers, and many described the ways they were doing so with their young children. They were learning how to be nurturing—how to play, change diapers, feed toddlers, give baths, and take care of crying babies in the middle of the night—and figuring out how to discipline children differently from their parents' generation in accordance with contemporary state and working-class standards. They expressed a number of motivations for being engaged fathers—to do it differently than their own fathers; to ac-quire social status, especially when other avenues were restricted; to atone for past mistakes and to convert past street experiences into parenting capital; to be closer to the mothers of their children and to increase their prospects for long-term relationships, and eventually marriage; to leave something of themselves behind that has social value, especially for those who have lived marginalized lives; and to fulfill their images of manhood. We also suspect that the expressions of masculinity that nurturing encouraged opened fa-thers to emotional connections to children that enhanced their feelings of love and empathy, and that allowed them to explore parts of themselves that may have been closed off by a more hardened masculinity sculpted on the streets or in violent social and institutional spaces. We suspect this because of the ways some of the men talked about fatherhood, including their out-pouring of affection, their tears, their guilt, their determination, their hopes, and their dreams. Fatherhood was often at the center of their constructions about current and future lives.

However, we also saw that the social conditions in which they lived were not likely to help them realize these desires, stabilize and maintain these relationships, prepare them to be engaged fathers, nor provide them with lives of dignity and respect. We saw that neoliberalism and austerity politics in the 21st century were doing just the opposite—they were laying the burden of fatherhood largely on theirs and their family's shoulders, while economic and state support receded and punishment, debt, market conformity, and a culture of individualism prevailed. For some of the men, they were finding their way—as low-wage breadwinners, as transitory fathers, or as second-generation fathers. For others, fatherhood was fuel for a starting-over fantasy that allowed them to edge forward in their lives, even when the opportunity structure was illusory.

***

For vulnerable families, the decline in state support is evident. The casualization of work and family has not been supported with state resources that would complement these altered configurations of gender, work, and family. This is most apparent in the changing paradigm of state welfare and child support enforcement. Reflecting the neoliberal ethos, public assistance is no longer provided as resources intended to support families for whom the market fails to provide, but instead as delimited resources for individuals who fail to provide for themselves in the marketplace. And this has occurred as the market has become less likely to provide steady, living wage jobs for many.

This paradigmatic shift justifies reductions in welfare spending. Further, it emboldens states to aggressively enact child support enforcement policies that view public assistance to children to be a loan that parents are expected to pay back to the state. In this regard, state policies have usurped a mechanism that could reasonably distribute family resources across multiple households and supplement those resources with state assistance where necessary, to one that has increased incarceration, exacted resources from poor families, institutionalized gender distrust, and increased child support debt to obscene levels.

Any discussion concerning policy reform to support fatherhood and low-income families must start here. First and foremost, the *state portion* of child support debt should be forgiven across all states. As we saw in Chapter 4, the extraordinary increase in child support debt, well over $100 billion, most of which is owed by indigent fathers, is obscene. It should be clear by now that this debt cannot be reduced by punitive state efforts. This policy slaps a lifetime of debt on poor fathers who have no labor force opportunities to pay off these arrearages, while it institutionalizes the symbolic power of the state's classifying and stratifying role.[2]

In their book *Failing Our Fathers*, Ronald Mincy and his colleagues, Monique Jethwani and Serena Klempin, provide a comprehensive overview of child support reforms that would rectify some of the issues confronting indigent fathers. Most importantly, they demonstrate that many states have implemented arrear abatement programs for fathers who demonstrate they can stay current on their child support orders. As they point out, states have been willing to cancel arrears as an incentive for fathers to make child support payments because states can retain more in child support payments under these conditions. In other words, there has been no shift in the state's ideology that governs child support, but rather an understanding that the state can acquire more money from fathers with these policies. Nor have states forgiven these debts for all indigent fathers. Mincy and his colleagues raise the question whether these abatement programs should also be applied to the mother's portion of the arrears, if it would increase the likelihood of fathers making their current payments.

Other policy proposals the authors advocate—and some states have adopted—include making changes to how child support orders are determined, by, one, allowing fathers a basic level of income, or a self-support reserve, before determining the amount of the order; two, basing orders on the actual income of fathers, rather than imputing the amount of their income based on wage earning assumptions; and three, eliminating retroactive orders when fathers can show that they were unaware of the order. They also point to reforms that would reduce sanctions, such as driver license revocation and incarceration, would eliminate interests and penalties on arrears, and would extend the Earned Income Tax Credit to nonresidential fathers who have remained current on their payments during the year.[3]

Mincy and his colleagues use a runaway train as a metaphor for the process of proposing and passing these reforms. They explain that the train's passengers include fathers in arrears, that the number of passengers swelled considerably during the Great Recession, and that, since the 1996 Welfare Reform Act was passed, the train has been running out of control down the tracks, with child support arrears spiraling into the stratosphere. Many good policy proposals remain in the caboose of the train, and the authors suggest it will take an act of near superheroism to get these proposals to the engine. Doing so will depend on rigorous research, consensus among policymakers, leadership, and, most of all, money.[4] Without federal legislation and resources, states are left alone to fund these innovations, and few have the funds to do so, the authors declare, even when the research has shown positive outcomes.

We appreciate these policy recommendations, the role of policy research, and the outlines of a process by which reforms are passed. But we might phrase this a little differently. In an era of neoliberalism and austerity politics, it is unlikely that states will adopt these policies, unless they can be shown to save the states money, and even then, passing this legislation is likely to be uneven across states. As we pointed out in Chapter 4, the Deficit Reduction Act of 2005 provided the states with the option of passing through all of the child support money it collected to families. In effect, this could have turned the child support program into a government subsidy program by passing along the state's portion of the payment to families. However, in 2016, only five states passed through the entire payment, while one-half of states had no pass through whatsoever.

In other words, in an era of neoliberal austerity, child support reforms are not likely to get very far through research and leadership, or by advancing a policy agenda and process. In states that have created strong policy and research organizations, good legislative leadership, and a robust lobbying presence in the state capital—like in Connecticut—the chances for progressive reform are indeed much greater than in other states. Nonetheless, the past decade in Connecticut also demonstrates that, in the end, austerity wins out. Confronting a $5 billion state deficit in 2017 and then a $4 billion one in 2019, Connecticut drew considerable attention across the media. The *Wall Street Journal* wrote, "What's the Matter with Connecticut"; the *Atlantic* increased the pitch, "What on Earth Is Wrong with Connecticut"; *Slate* wondered, "What happened to the country's richest state?" in their article entitled "Trouble in America's Country Club"; while the finance writer for *Governing* summed it up with "How did America's Richest State Become Such a Fiscal Mess?" The general consensus was that tax revenues were collapsing as corporations, their highly paid "knowledge workers," and wealthy residents were leaving the state, in part to escape the state's tax burden but also to escape the deteriorating conditions and fiscal burdens of Connecticut's poor cities. This of course led to the state doubling down on their own tax breaks and subsidies to try to keep them. Basically, this left the well-oiled policy organizations that lobby at the statehouse for low-income populations to negotiate with legislative leaders about where, when, and how much the cuts to social service programs and resource transfers should be. This is what austerity looks like, and in this context, the policies and programs that are certified with the ringing endorsement of "best practices" by policy researchers will have to take a back seat—or remain in the caboose.

Nevertheless, broadening the spectrum to include other reforms that would stabilize low-income families and support fatherhood, our chapters provide an outline for the scope of what *needs* to be done. And here we lend our voices to yet another range of reform initiatives. They include increasing the minimum wage to $15, universal health care, food stamp expansion, early education investment, progressive and enforceable taxation, guaranteed family income, affordable housing, baby bonds, universal child care, expanded earned income tax credit, a federal works program . . . an exhausting list, perhaps, but not an exhausted one—we could go on. But again, this looks more like a wish list in an era of neoliberalism and austerity politics, especially when we consider some of the postrecession outcomes.

We might have thought that the Great Recession would have been a wake-up call that would lead to economic restructuring, a radical change in course, or at least an effort to roll-back neoliberal polices. Instead, we see more of the same. Inequality increased between 2009 and 2015, with income for the top 1 percent growing more rapidly than income for the remaining 99 percent in almost every state. More shocking, in Connecticut during this period, all of the income growth went to the top 1 percent, while income decreased for everyone else.[5] Wage inequality in the state is currently the third highest in the country.[6]

In addition, the federal minimum wage has not been increased for 10 years, and while median household income has inched up as unemployment has decreased, these increases are not occurring because of wage growth, but because workers are working more hours.[7] In Connecticut, wages have largely stagnated since the Great Recession. Between 2007 and 2014, the lowest decile of wage earners lost, on average, 1 percent of their wages each year. This was reversed in 2014 when a state minimum wage increase went into effect, to be followed with subsequent annual increases through 2017.[8] Finally, the future does not look so good either. Job projections by the Bureau of Labor Statistics indicate that, nationally, the fastest growing jobs over the next 10 years will be low-income jobs.[9]

As this book goes to press, there is perhaps no better example of the "more of the same" argument than the conditions that have led to the United Auto Workers strike. The continuing divide between profits and wages, as well as the use of temp workers to institutionalize a contingency workforce—both discussed in Chapter 2—are central to the strike. Despite the public bailout of the industry during the recession and the wage and benefits sacrificed by workers, General Motors has been unwilling to share the more than $14 billion in profits it made in 2018 and has instead closed large auto production plants in the United States, while they continue to build plants in Mexico.[10] The two-tiered wage structure that characterized the pay structure in the industry has now given way to a fully entrenched three-tiered structure, in which an older generation of workers is paid the highest wages, a younger generation a lower wage, with now another layer of temp workers paid a yet lower wage. The permatemps, referred to in Chapter 2, are now a permanent fixture in the auto industry, with workers laboring for years before they are considered for the second-tier of lower paid company-vested workers.[11]

Turning to the issues of state welfare and housing, clearly the suffering of workers and families during the Great Recession and its aftermath did not produce any challenges to austerity politics, nor any expansions to public assistance. Instead, we see perennial efforts among Congress to cut food stamps benefits and to add work requirements to both food stamps and Medicaid recipients, as well as state refusals to accept Medicaid expansions that would extend health care to low-income families.[12] The effects of the Great Recession on housing have also been well documented. Not only were large territories of household wealth wiped out in black and brown urban areas where predatory lending was focused,[13] but bank loan modification programs for underwater homeowners were grossly underfunded and un-evenly implemented, while bankers walked away from the mess without criminal indictment.[14] Further, despite the widespread attention that Matthew Desmond brought to affordable housing in his book *Evicted*, and the conversations that ensued throughout the nation after the publication of the book, still only 1 in 4 households who qualify for housing assistance receives it due to funding limitations, while more than eight million low-income households pay more than one-half of their income for rent or settle for living in substandard, dilapidated housing.[15]

Finally, there is a drop of good news—there has been progress in decreasing the incarceration rate in the United States, dropping by more than 13 per-cent in federal and state prisons, and by 12 percent in jails between 2007 and 2017. Still, in 2017, there were more than 2.2 million people in prisons or jails, and another 6.6 million under correctional supervision, numbers that dreadfully exceed our peer countries.[16] There also have been more resources put into community reentry programs for returning citizens, but as we have seen, the thrust of these programs, inside and outside of the prison, has been on individual rather than systemic change—on substance abuse, mental health, anger management, and cognitive-behavioral programs, rather than housing, living wage jobs, higher education, and public assistance.[17]

In other words, the conditions in which families at the bottom of the labor force are established and sustained have not improved since the decade that we focus on in this book; instead, they have worsened on a wide range of measures. Despite the devastation created by the Great Recession, we have gotten more of the same. This would seem to us to suggest that we can no longer respond in the same way—that is, by simply lending our voices to the chorus of liberal reformers that tell us the policies that we *need* to adopt to support low-income families and, for us, fatherhood.

***

We need a movement-based political solution, as much, if not more than we need policy research solutions. Policy research does not create change— regardless of how many great policies are in Mincy's and others' cabooses. Instead, change will require a political solution that goes beyond these tech- nocratic presumptions and reform efforts, and that projects a different vision of the economy, the state, and the family.

Several sociologists have written about the "stalled revolution," where the movement toward gender equality in the home and workplace has fallen short of reaching its objective of truly shared responsibility for acquiring income, organizing and managing the home, and providing care for chil- dren and others in the household. However, they point out that the revolu- tion has not stalled because of a lack of desire for change, but rather because the institutions that would support these changes are lacking. For instance, Kathleen Gerson found in her study of young adults that four-fifths of women and two-thirds of men expressed a desire for equal partnerships in both paid work and care work. Without institutional support, however, the default drive is to establish neotraditional families that bend toward equality but maintain gendered roles in the family to meet household needs within constraining opportunities, or else to eschew relationship commitments al- together in order to maximize personal freedoms and minimize the stress that relating in resource-deprived households creates.[18]

This research importantly shows that gender equality cannot be achieved without significant institutional change. Certainly, in the United States, where, compared to other advanced capitalist countries, policies that sup- port work and family are abysmal, there is much room for change that could be addressed through policy reforms. Even so, policies for paid family leave, universal child care, gender wage equity, to name just a few, go into the ca- boose along with other good policy reforms, unlikely to see the front of the train in an era of neoliberal capitalism and austerity politics.

When we turn our lens to those at the bottom of the social and economic hierarchies, the need for movement-based political strategies looms larger. In areas where market and state resources have been systemically drained, and where social and economic marginalization are inscribed on bodies and minds, the interpersonal struggle for survival, dignity, love, and compassion is severely challenged. In the immediacy of this drama, mutual blame and the lines demarcating a gendered order are (re)constituted. At times, fathers turn their anger and hostility toward mothers and what they see as a biased system against them. In the worst-case scenarios, they seek to exercise male power in the spaces still available to them—including the home. Mothers turn to resource networks, often family members, creating what Abdill refers to as the maternal garden to define and regulate the participation of fathers.[19] Lacking in this formulation, however, are the class and racial forces of marginalization that are shaping the lives of both low-income fathers and mothers and that intensify gender distrust and mutual blame. The language of political elites that characterizes mothers as welfare queens and fathers as deadbeat dads falls like daggers in these communities as mothers and fathers wrestle with this symbolic violence and direct this painful rhetoric at one another. Meanwhile, this same political discourse directs the public's attention to the stereotypic surface, while it mystifies the deeper manifestations of class and racial marginalization.

In our study, fathers expressed their desires for engaged fatherhood—for developing their repertoires for raising children and doing carework. What would it take to support these desires for engaged fatherhood, or to move our society toward gender equality across all institutions, including both work and family? It is here where the support for social movements working toward social and economic transformation is vital, and where a new vision of the state, economy, and family is needed. As this book is going to publication, the movements for racial justice advanced by the uprisings over the brutal murders of George Floyd, Breonna Taylor, and Ahmaud Arbery provide a context for the critical examination, reimagination, and reorganization of state institutions, like the police, prisons, schools, and mental health and substance abuse facilities. Consequently, a vibrant public discourse advocating the defunding of the police and prison abolition is gaining traction. The same critical reflections and processes are need for advancing the transformation of work and family. Here, we take our inspiration and guidance from feminist scholars and activists. We do so in two respects.

First, second-wave feminists of the 1960s and 1970s deviated from liberal feminists by asserting that the dispositions, sensitivities, practices, routines, and ways of being, shaped by the experiences and social location of women, should not only be socially valued and embraced but central to transforming the institutions that govern society.[20] We do not need simply to replace men with women in male-constructed and male-dominated institutions; we need to change the institutions themselves. We need, especially, to embrace and value the relational qualities and competencies of women that have been largely cultivated through caretaking roles, social reproduction needs, community work, and kitchen-table resistance, and to recognize the democratic potential that these human capacities contribute toward a more humane social world. In this sense, true gender equality across institutional and social spaces requires that men share in the social reproduction practices that have been socially devalued and relegated to the women's sphere in order to expand their own human capacities and to help transform themselves and the social world as well. In other words, gender equality is not about how much housework and carework men do when they come home from work, but how they learn to internalize and enact the nurturing and relational qualities that these practices engender, and how the reconstitution of masculinity and femininity in these and similar social spaces will then contribute to institutional transformation and social change. True father nurturing and engagement, as part of a new gendered order that constitutes equality across all institutions, require it.

Second, we also draw on the social reproduction feminists and their analysis of the current crisis of care that has been exacerbated by neoliberalism. Nancy Fraser explains that the well-being of any society requires the systematic and institutional development of its social capacities "for birthing and raising children, caring for friends and family members, maintaining households and broader communities, and sustaining connections more generally." Fraser asserts, "Without it there can be no culture, no economy, no political organization."[21] Further, she explains that capital accumulation has always relied on this, while at the same time the economic need for expansion and accumulation has undermined it. The privatization of social reproduction means that the withdrawal of public support for these social capacities increases the burdens on families and households. This is apparent in the stress and anxiety that exist among higher income groups to balance family needs and work, which has increased the use of exploited immigrant household labor, as well as the demand for marital therapy. Families at the bottom of the labor force, however, have, once again, become the canary in the mine, directing attention to the looming disaster that Fraser warns us about. "No society," she writes, "that systematically undermines social reproduction can endure for long."[22]

Social reproduction is a feminist issue because the role of social reproduction has been mostly relegated to women, but as the authors of the manifesto, *Feminism for the 99 Percent*, point out, it is "also shot through at every point by the fault lines of class, race, sexuality and nation."[23] Written by social reproduction theorists, the manifesto asserts that the response to the crisis in care needs to be anti-capitalist and to draw broadly on a range of social movements that are addressing inextricably interrelated issues. For the crisis of care is derivative of a "crisis of society as whole," including the "economy, ecology, politics and care"—a crisis of "the entire formation of society," "a crisis of capitalism."[24] As such, these are not just women's issues, but issues for all who are "exploited, dominated and oppressed."[25] The authors propose that as scholars, we too need to "join with every movement that fights for the 99 percent, whether by struggling for environmental justice, free high-quality education, generous public services, low-cost housing, labor rights, free universal health or a world without racism or war."[26] Accordingly, movements need to center the "making of people" in resistance movements and in their vision for change—in contrast to the primacy placed on the "making of profits"—and need to raise the question, what kind of people do we want to develop—what kind of labor, what kind of citizenry, what kind of human being?[27]

Fathering from the margins needs to be seen in this light—within the scope of this larger narrative and these political movements. The increase in hours worked by all members of households, the uncertainty that the precarious nature of these jobs creates, the retrenchment of public assistance, the increase in punishment and debt, and the processes by which all of this is conveyed as the natural order of things have had multiplicative effects on a crisis of care. Expecting marginalized fathers to adopt the "new fatherhood" as engaged, involved fathers in this mix, and to do it largely on their own, constitutes a setup.

Throughout this book, we have focused our gaze mostly on low-income fathers. It is our point of entry, but it is not intended to minimize the struggles of low-income mothers, who, for all intents and purposes, have been victimized by similar forces and who are left largely to themselves to find their way forward, too often, without the support of men—especially men who are incarcerated, sick, enraged, lost, or demoralized. But we take the approach outlined by David McNally, who writes that "truth resides in the processes of critical thinking, which can only move through the partial and one-sided understandings toward richer and more comprehensive ones."[28] We work our way through the experiences of low-income fathers to see more broadly the forces of oppression and marginalization at work. In doing so, we also see the basis for gender distrust and the intensive anger and blame that mothers and fathers direct at one another. To ease the gender wars in these areas, we need a new discourse through which marginalized mothers and fathers can reframe their own experiences and that integrates class, racial, and gender dynamics. We need a discourse that makes class and racial (as well as sexual) marginalization visible in our understandings of family, and we need for this discourse to be accessible to these populations, through symbols, rituals, strategies, and practices that valorize parenting on the margins.

Neither the fathers in our study, nor parents and couples anywhere, will be able to achieve true gender equality in the rich sense that second-generation and social reproduction feminists have advanced without social and economic transformation that places as much social and moral value on work in the home and community as work in the labor force, and that recognizes and cultivates the human capacities for carrying out this work.[29] Certainly, true gender equality cannot be created in the current system of neoliberal capitalism and austerity politics, but neither do we believe it can be created in any form of capitalism where "the making of profits" is put before "the making of people."

Notes

Preface

1. Black (2010).

Chapter 1

1. See Erdmans and Black (2015).
2. Lorber (2012).
3. Gerson (2011); Coontz (2013); Stone (2007).
4. Swinth (2018); Fraser (2013); Nicholson (1997).
5. In addition to sources cited in note 4, see Bhattachayra (2017); Epstein (2001); Williams (2001); and Ehrenreich (1976).
6. Willrich (2000).
7. Teachman and Paasch (1994).
8. Haney and March (2003).
9. For a survey of this literature, see McLanahan, Tach, and Schneider (2013).
10. Gans (1995); Katz (1989).
11. Soss, Fording, and Schram (2011).
12. Katz (1989).
13. On intersectionality among black feminists, see Taylor (2017); also see Collins (2004). On expanding gender analysis to include race and class in work-family studies, see Williams (2001, 2010) and Gerstel and Sarkisian (2006).
14. Mills (1959).
15. Krugman (2009).
16. Serwer (2009).
17. U.S. Department of Commerce (2010).
18. This is based on cities with a population of 100,000 or more. See U.S. Census Bureau (2000). On millionaires, see http://www.netstate.com/states/tables/state_millionaires.htm
19. Connecticut Voices for Children (2012).
20. Hall and Geballe (2002).
21. Hero, Hall, and Geballe (2007).
22. Levy, Rodriquez, and Villimez (2004).
23. These calculations are based on data are taken from 2000 US Census data compiled as Census CD (New Brunswick, NJ: Geolytics Inc.) and reported in Black et al. (2006).
24. Hall and Geballe (2006, 3); Hall (2005, 9).

25. Mauer and King (2007).
26. Erdmans and Black (2015).
27. Seven fathers were removed because we did not have interviews with their partners. The interviews were semistructured and covered a range of topics, including family background, school, intimate relationships, pregnancy, parenting, work, availability of resources, and experiences with state welfare services, law enforcement officers, and home visitors.
28. Stephen Markson was Tim's coinvestigator on the study and supervised Ron's work.
29. All men gave written consent and, with the exception of the incarcerated men, received a stipend of $35 at the conclusion of their interview.
30. Sites were selected to create a racially, ethnically, and geographically diverse sample. Participants gave consent to participate and were paid $20 for each interview in this study.
31. For those with multiple interviews, we included them as working full-time if they achieved this at anytime during the interview period.

Chapter 2

1. Smeeding et al. (2011, 101).
2. Greider (1987).
3. Panitch and Gindin (2012); McCarthy (2016).
4. Kotz (2015).
5. Uchitelle (2006).
6. Uchitelle (2006, 11).
7. Kalleberg (2011, 28).
8. Kenworthy (2014).
9. Financial sector debt increased from 20 percent of GDP in 1979 to 118 percent in 2007. Kotz (2015, 129).
10. Black (2016).
11. Kotz (2015).
12. Kotz (2015, 97, 165).
13. Moody (2017, 18).
14. Kalleberg (2011, 36).
15. Fletcher (2012).
16. Moody (2017).
17. Logan (2002). On tactics used by employers to undermine unions, see Fletcher (2012) and Fletcher and Gapasin (2008).
18. *Union Members-2010* (2011).
19. Stiglitz (2012, 28).
20. Kalleberg (2011, 106).
21. Kalleberg (2011, 117).
22. These data included men who had no earnings. See Sum et al. (2011).
23. Kalleberg (2011, 44–45).
24. Farber (2015).

25. Pew Research Center (2010). Cited in Mincy, Jethwani, and Klempin (2015, 19).

26. Western (2006); Western and Pettit (2010).

27. Kalleberg (2011, 44–48).

28. Cherlin (2014, 148–149).

29. Cherlin (2014, 149).

30. These data are taken from the National Survey of Family Growth. Mincy, Jethwani, and Klempin (2015, 8).

31. Stiglitz (2012, 16). Also see Edin and Shaefer (2015).

32. Hero, Rodriguez, and Siegel (2010).

33. Pearce (2005).

34. The child poverty rate in Hartford in 2005 was 44.5 percent.

35. In 2014, Connecticut became the first state to pass legislation to raise its minimum wage to over $10, phasing in increases from $8.70 per hour in June 2014 to $10.10 in January 2017. Although Connecticut may have been the first to announce increasing its minimum wage to over $10 an hour, by the time it was phased-in in 2017, they had the fourth highest rate, behind Massachusetts ($11), Washington ($11), and California ($10.50 for workplaces with 26 or more employees). See Labor Law Center (2017).

36. These comparisons were made between workers in the lowest decile of the labor force across states. See Hero, Rodriquez, and Siegel (2010). We are indebted to the Connecticut Voices for Children, whose superb and prolific reporting on the economic and social conditions of low-income households across several decades has been a major source of information for us.

37. Wages dropped 7 percent for those at the bottom decile of labor force from 2001 to 2006 in Connecticut, and 9 percent for those at the bottom quintile, from $11.17 an hour to $10.14. See Hero, Hall, Geballe (2007).

38. Hero, Hall, and Geballe (2007).

39. Hero, Hall, and Geballe (2007).

40. By the mid-2000s, the top quintile of wage earners in Connecticut were taking home a little less than one-half (45 percent) of all income in the state, while the bottom quintile was taking home 6 percent, and the bottom two quintiles, 17 percent. Hall and Geballe (2008).

41. Hero, Hall, and Geballe (2007).

42. Hero, Hall, and Geballe (2007).

43. Santacrose and Rodriquez (2011, 5).

44. Santacrose and Rodriguez (2011).

45. Bell, Biston, and Lee (2011).

46. Hero, Rodriquez, and Siegel (2010).

47. Bell, Gibson, and Lee (2011).

48. See Campbell (2010).

49. Santacrose and Rodriguez (2011).

50. Cherlin (2014, 128).

51. Santacrose and Rodriguez (2011).

52. Hero, Rodriguez, and Siegel (2010).

53. Allgretto et al. (2013).
54. On the franchise model, see Weil (2014).

The Puzder nomination exposed additional disturbing facts about fast food restaurants. Bloomberg News reported that, in 2016, CKE Restaurants, in which Andrew Puzder is CEO, controlled 3,729 Hardees, Carl's Jr., Red Burrito, and Green Burrito restaurants See http://www.bloomberg.com/research/stocks/private/snap-shot.asp?privcapid=282503. The primary business model is the franchise, in which CKE outsources its restaurants to franchisees to operate in return for a portion of the profits and reduced liabilities. At several of the Hardees restaurants, franchise owners had run afoul of the law, which included such offenses as paying subminimum wages, requiring workers to clock out during slow periods at the restaurant, refusing over-time pay, denying employees breaks during long work shifts, and requiring workers to pay for their own uniforms. See Jamieson (2017). There were also multiple charges of sexual harassment at CKE restaurants. Puzder tried to sidestep the charges by minimizing, if not disclaiming, the "joint employer" legal definition of the franchise model. Most likely, Puzder would have continued through the confirmation process if had not been for allegations of domestic violence made by his wife and televised on an earlier episode of *The Oprah Winfrey Show* that forced his resignation. The violations of the Fair Labor Standards Act (FLSA) reported in these stories directed media at-tention to the fast food industry. The Bloomberg Bureau of National Affairs followed with a story that showed that the Department of Labor (DOL) under the Obama administration had conducted around 4,000 investigations into FLSA violations at the 20 largest fast food brands. Reviews of the DOL's Wage and Hour Division investigations revealed more than 68,000 violations and close to $14 million in back pay that had been ordered to compensate some 57,000 employees. At least one viola-tion had been found at three-quarters of investigated restaurants. See Penn (2016). In other words, FLSA violations were found to be a systemic problem of the franchise model, in which franchise owners engage in shady practices to squeeze profits in a highly competitive industry, while franchisers, like CKE, distance themselves from these charges and rake in profits. Employees, with few places to turn for protection—especially without union representation—suffered the costs of these shady practices. Further, media investigations into the Puzder nomination also revealed that Puzder, like other leaders of restaurant businesses, are influential members of the National Restaurant Association, which spent $4.3 million in 2015 and $3.9 million in 2016 to lobby against minimum wage increases, joint employer recognition, and health care employer mandates, to name a few basic issues. See Balcerzak (2017).

55. Allgretto et al. (2013).
56. Temple (2013).
57. Jacobs, Perry, and MacGillvary (2015).
58. Allgretto et al. (2013). More broadly, since the Great Recession, the demographics of fast food workers in the United States have changed from previous eras. While teens and older retirees were once overrepresented in fast food, today's fast food worker is older (median age of 29) and many are raising children (26 percent). See Feuer (2013).

59. Newman (1999).

60. In 2012, McDonalds alone cost taxpayers an estimated $1.2 billion in public benefits provided to their employees for health care, food, and other necessities, despite making $5.46 billion in profits and paying CEO Donald Thompson a salary of $13.7 million. See Temple (2013).

61. Hatton (2011); Gonos (2000); Smith and Neuwirth (2008).

62. See Gonos (1997) for an excellent sociolegal history of how the definition of employer shifted from the "right of control test," in which the employer was assumed to be the organization that furnished and managed the work, to the employer "who hands him his paycheck."

63. Bluestone and Harrison (1982); Gonos (1997, 100).

64. Gonos (1997, 100).

65. Hatton (2011); also see Smith and Neuwirth (2008). For an excellent analysis of the role that the THI played in restructuring work in Cleveland, Ohio, see Kerr (2011).

66. Hatton (2011).

67. Gonos (2001).

68. Hatton (2011).

69. "Vendor on premises" provided supervisory temp workers to manage other temp workers at the worksite; "in-house outsourcing" turned over entire departments at the worksite to the temp agency; "day labor" supplied workers to employers based on a day-to-day, as-needed basis; and "master vendor contracts" identified the temp agency as the sole or preferred suppliers of temp workers. Hatton (2011, 108, 115).

70. During the 1981–1983 economic recession, the temp industry grew 9 percent each year. In the first year of the recovery, national employment grew less than 1 percent, but temp jobs grew 17.5 percent. Similar growth occurred throughout the decade, tripling the numbers of temp employees, while estimates of the number of agencies grew from an estimated 2,500 to 5,000 in 1980 to more than 10,000 agencies, by some accounts, at the end of the decade (Hatton 2001, 85).

71. Hatton (2011, 13); Katz and Krueger (1999).

72. Benner, Leete, and Pastor (2007, 4). In the first half of the 1990s, the temp industry grew, on average, 17 percent each year, but it was reduced to 8 percent in the second half of the decade as foreign competition took its toll and the industry began to ossify into monopolies through mergers and acquisitions (Hatton 2011, 116–117). Between 1979 and 1995, the THI grew at an annual rate of 11 percent, which was more than five times the rate of growth for all other nonagricultural employment (Autor 2003; Benner, Leete, and Pastor 2007).

73. Gonos (1997).

74. Hatton (2011).

75. Freeman and Gonos (2011, 9).

76. Freeman and Gonos (2011, 9).

77. Hatton (2011, 108).

78. We do not have an accurate account of the percent of fathers who were working for temp agencies, because we did not ask the question directly. Later we realized that

many of the places of work that the men had identified were placements from temp agencies.

79. Gonos (2000, 15).
80. Gonos (2001, 605).
81. Gonos, personal communication.
82. Ditsler and Fisher (2006).
83. In 1985, blue-collar temp jobs accounted for only about 6 percent of temp jobs, but this increased to around 30 percent in 1997. In 2006, of the six largest occupational categories employing temp workers, manufacturing and production jobs accounted for one-third of temp workers (Freeman and Gonos 2011, 10).
84. Sennett (1998, 31).

Chapter 3

1. Piven and Cloward (1971).
2. Connell (1995); Orloff and Monson (2002).
3. Orloff and Monson (2002).
4. Orloff and Monson (2002); Curran and Abrams (2000).
5. Haney and March (2003).
6. Orloff and Monson (2002); Curran and Abrams (2000).
7. O'Connor (2010); Soss, Fording, and Schram (2008).
8. O'Connor (2010, 708).
9. O'Connor (2001, 22–23).
10. Orloff and Monson (2002); Fraser (2017).
11. Orloff and Monson (2002).
12. Coontz (1992).
13. Brown (2015); Foucault (2010).
14. O'Connor (1998).
15. Quadagno (1994); Abramovitz (1996); Neubeck and Cazenave (2001).
16. Hacker and Pierson (2010, 275); see also Piven (2004).
17. Hacker and Pierson (2010); Abramovitz (1996).
18. Soss, Fording, and Schram (2011).
19. Fathers' ages ranged from 17 to 44 with an average age of 25 (median of 23), while mothers ranged from 14 to 41, with an average and median age of 21.
20. O'Connor (2000).
21. For families still receiving cash assistance, eligibility was 75 percent of the State Median Income. See Palermino (2003). Due to fiscal crisis in 2016, eligibility for former TANF recipients and for working families was closed.
22. Hillman and Oppenheimer (2011).
23. HUSKY stands for Health Care for Uninsured Kids and Youth.
24. Bethany told us that Pablo was ineligible for these benefits because he was not the biological father and for some reason did not meet the state's definition of a "caregiver relative," even though they were married.

25. By federal law, recipients can qualify if their net income is below 130 percent of the FPL, which includes some SNAP accepted deductions in the calculations. See Center on Budget and Policy Priorities (2018).

26. One study showed that one-half to two-thirds of recipients who left the rolls in New Jersey and Illinois reported times during the month when their incomes were insufficient to feed their families (Burnham 2002, 47).

27. The formal name for WIC is the Special Supplemental Nutrition Program for Women, Infants, and Children.

28. Burnham (2002).

29. The act required AFDC recipients with children over three (with the option for states to lower the age to one) to work or else enroll in education or job training programs provided by the states, and it contributed funds for childcare, transportation, work-related expenses, and Medicaid for a year while mothers were transitioning from AFDC to the workforce. The centerpiece of the $6.8 billion policy was the Job Opportunities and Basic Skills (JOBS) program, which began in October 1990 (Pavetti 2001).

30. Pavetti (2001).

31. The new paternalism, advanced by conservative welfare scholars, like Lawrence Mead and Charles Murray, carried a thinly veiled line of coercion as it increased states' autonomy in tying benefits to behavior that states defined as normative. Soss, Fording, and Schram (2011).

32. Schram and Soss (2002); Goldberg and Schott (2000).

33. Soss, Fording, and Schram (2011, 263–264) report that the national decrease, measured from two years before the law took effect in 1994 to 2008, was 72 percent. In Connecticut, the decrease in numbers was from 55,000 families in 1996 to 20,965 in 2005 (McNichol 2005).

34. Soss, Fording, and Schram (2011, 95–96); Pavetti (2001).

35. It should be noted that families had been combining cash assistance and wages or other sources of income for many years. Because benefits were so low, families often had to find ways to circumvent the rules to create a survival family wage. This was well documented in Edin and Lein's 1990s study, and it only got worse as cash benefits continued to fall behind annual inflation rates and as eligibility criteria narrowed. See Edin and Lein (1997); also see Deparle (2004).

36. The state allowed for two six-month extensions. However, these extensions were not automatic; they were granted based on a family's extenuating circumstances. Additional time could be granted in cases in which there were two or more serious barriers to employment: the family was experiencing domestic violence, the family's income was below the amount of cash assistance they were eligible for, or disability in the family either prevented the adult from working full-time or required a family member to be cared for. Nonetheless, even with extensions, families still were limited to five years of cash assistance in their lifetimes by federal legislation. See McNichol (2005).

37. Burnham (2002).

38. The underemployment rate includes the unemployed, involuntary part-time workers looking for full-time work, discouraged workers no longer looking for work, and the much smaller population who want to work but are facing barriers like transportation or childcare. See Hall and Geballe (2003).
39. Fine and Weiss (1998); Levine (2013).
40. Van Horn (2014, 5).
41. The increase was from a low of 82,500 in 2000 to 224,000 in 2010. These calculations were based on information taken from the website of the U.S. Department of Agriculture. See U.S. Department of Agriculture (2017a).
42. These data are provided in a US Congressional Research Center report, Table B-5, published in 2019. According to this report, national rates increased during this same time period by 11 percent. See Congressional Research Service (2019).
43. Hillman and Oppenheimer (2011).
44. In total, from 1990 to 2010, taxes collected from corporations in Connecticut fell 73 percent compared to personal income tax collections. Connecticut Voices for Children attributed this to a combination of corporate tax cuts, expanded loopholes, and tax avoidance by businesses. See Hero, Rodriguez, and Geballe (2010); also see Gibson (2012). Gibson cited two studies completed in 2015, the first by University of Connecticut Center of Economic Analysis (CCEA) and the second by the state's Program Review and Investigation committee. The first reported that 14 of the 24 corporate tax credit programs actually resulted in net job losses. The latter study concluded that 16 of the 26 business tax credits "appear of little benefit to the state's economy, and should be eliminated" (3).
45. Schram (1998).
46. Government Accountability Office (2017).
47. Hacker (2004). The effect of UI reform was profound, as the amount spent on an un-employed worker dropped from its peak of $12,000 in 1973 to $4,000 in 2000. See Massey (2007, 169).
48. Pierson (1994); Soss, Fording, and Schram (2011). By the fall of 1984, only one-fourth of unemployed workers received benefits compared to four-fifths of unemployed workers in the 1973–1975 recession. See Ferguson and Rogers (1986, 137).
49. Work requirements had already been in place extending back to 1971 amendments to the Food Stamp program. To qualify, recipients had to register for work, could not quit a job unless for "good cause," and were required to accept employment when offered. There were a number of exemptions, however, that could be applied. The federal government set minimum penalties for failure to comply with the work requirements—one-month disqualification for the first offense, three months for the second, and six months for the third—but allowed states to extend these periods if it chose. It also allowed states to determine if the penalty would be extended to all members of the household. Connecticut's disqualification policies are among the harshest in the country. It is one of three states to extend disqualification periods be-yond the minimum and to penalize all family members when the head of the house-hold failed to comply with work requirements, joining Virginia and Louisiana. See U.S. Department of Agriculture (2017b).

50. Only six states have left the ban in place. See McCarty et al. (2016).

51. While EITC can be traced back to 1975, its major reforms occurred in 1986, 1990, and 1993. The 1986 reform increased tax benefits to compensate for inflationary erosion of benefits, and it tied future increases to inflation. The 1990 and 1993 revisions increased the credit for families with two or more children, while a small credit was added for low-income childless tax filers in 1994. Both Presidents Clinton and Obama significantly expanded the program. In 2011, it raised 3.1 million children above the poverty line and decreased the child poverty rate in the United States by four percentage points. See Sarah Halpern-Meekin et al. (2015, 5, 62–63).

52. Garfinkel, McLanahan, and Thomas (1998); Mincy, Jethwani, and Klempin (2015).

53. SSI is an income-tested program that provides cash assistance and health care to the aged, the blind, and the disabled. Men in our study applied through the disability provision.

54. Hanson, Bourgois, and Drucker (2014)

55. As we might expect, applications for SSI have increased considerably during the period of neoliberalism—for adults 18–64, applications increased 125 percent between 1980 and 2009. As applications have increased, however, the approval rate has declined. For all applicants, the approval rate declined from 47 to 33 percent between 1992 and 2009. For historical data on SSI, see Social Security Administration (2017, 119, 145). https://www.ssa.gov/policy/docs/statcomps/ssi_asr/). Furthermore, the assessment process is long. The average time for receiving a decision on the first application is four months, and for a subsequent application, it takes on average of two years (Duggan, Kearney, and Rennane 2015). If an adult receives SSI, there is a limit on how much income one can earn, and their benefits are reduced accordingly. For people who have recurring illnesses, or move through the cycles of relapse and recovery from drug addiction, making decisions about whether to work and give up SSI benefits or remain on SSI and work a limited number of hours is difficult. See Campbell, Baumohl, and Hunt (2003).

56. In Connecticut, the program is called State-Administered General Assistance (SAGA). In the past, General Assistance had been a cash program for poor, single adults. This program never paid much, but it has declined considerably since 1996, when the federal government transferred total control of the program to the states. Only about one-half of states provide any form of GA (Uccello and Gallagher 1997).

57. There is a small eligibility window for poor adults with specific, nonmedical reasons, which include being over age 55 with a limited work history, over age 65, or needed in the home to care for an incapacitated spouse. See Connecticut Department of Social Services (2018).

58. New York, however, is an exception. In 2006, it became the first state to offer adult fathers living outside of the home a tax credit on earnings up to $33,995, if they were working and were current on their child support payments (Mincy, Jethwani, and Klempin 2015, 11).

59. Hungerford and Thiess (2013).

60. Massey and Denton (1993).

61. Connecticut Voices for Children (2010).

62. Hero (2009); Bell, Gibson, and Lee (2011); Hero, Rogriguez, and Siegel (2010); Santacroce and Rodriguez (2011); Mauer and King (2007). Mauer and King reported that in 2005, Connecticut had the highest incarceration disparity rate between Latinos and whites in the nation and the fourth highest between blacks and whites.

63. It is also the case that when fathers failed to appear for a child support hearing, and a bench warrant was issued for their arrest, their identities would subsequently come to the attention of the police if they ran their names in the police database. Given the extent to which police surveillance occurs in poor black and brown communities, racial minorities are therefore disproportionately likely to be arrested for an outstanding warrant (Orloff and Monson 2002).

64. Haney and March (2003).

65. Sennett (2006, 3).

Chapter 4

1. As with the fathers, we also use pseudonyms for judges and all other public officials.

2. Fineman (1991); also see Smock et al. (1999).

3. After declining in the 1990s, it would return to 34 percent in 2010 after the Great Recession. See U.S. Census Bureau (2018).

4. Meyer and Bartfield (1996). Additionally, Edin, Lein, and Nelson (2002, 128) reported that only 37 percent of nonmarried fathers from the National Longitudinal Survey of Youth (NLSY) said they paid child support in 1985.

5. Edin, Lein, and Nelson (2002, 128).

6. Center for Disease Control and Prevention: National Center for Health Statistics. 2018. *Health, United States, 2016—Individual Charts and Tables: Spreadsheet, PDF, and PowerPoint files*, Table 4. https://www.cdc.gov/nchs/hus/contents2016.htm#004. These data are tricky. The rate of unmarried births is calculated based on the number of births per 1,000 unmarried women ages 15–44. For nonmarried, non-Hispanic white women, the rate increased from 24 to 28 between 1990 and 2000, and then to 33 in 2010. For nonmarried black women the rate decreased from 90 to 70 between 1990 and 2000, and then to 65 in 2010. This rate is not provided for Puerto Ricans, but for nonmarried Hispanics, the rate decreased from 90 to 87 between 1990 and 2000, and then to 81 in 2010. For Hispanics, however, the rate decreased precipitously between 2010 and 2015, when it declined to 67. The percent of nonmarried births is calculated relative to the rate of married births. So despite the rapid decline in births to nonmarried black mothers, the percent of births to nonmarried non-Hispanic black mothers relative to married births still increased from 67 percent in 1990 to 72 percent in 2010. The percent of births to non-Hispanic white mothers increased from 17 to 29 percent between 1990 and 2010, and for nonmarried Puerto Ricans mothers from 56 to 65 percent.

7. A 1976 law extended the surveillance nexus to state employment agencies, who were required to provide addresses of noncustodial fathers, information regarding their unemployment benefits, and any refusals of employment offers. See U.S. House of Representatives (2012).

8. The 1977 legislation also authorized the federal government to garnish the wages of federal noncustodial workers. It also encouraged states to collect from fathers on behalf of other states. See U.S. House of Representatives (2012).

9. U.S. Department of Health and Human Services.

10. Neubeck and Cazenave (2001, 121).

11. Piven and Cloward (1971); Schram and Turbett (1983); Fording (1997).

12. Welfare rights groups across the nation formed the National Coordinating Committee of Welfare Groups in 1966, which gave birth to the NWRO. Quadagno (1994, 120); also see Piven and Cloward (1971).

13. Piven and Cloward (1971).

14. Soss, Fording, and Schram (2011, 94).

15. Massey (2007, 172–173).

16. Neubeck and Cazenave (2001).

17. Garfinkel, Meyer, and McLanahan (2001, 23–24).

18. The 1981 Omnibus Reconciliation Act (OBRA) also required state CSE agencies to collect spousal support for AFDC families and fees for delinquent support, as well as a proportion of unemployment compensation to apply to arrearages, and exempted arrearages from bankruptcy proceedings (which had first been implemented in 1975 and then repealed in 1978, before being reinstated with the 1981 legislation). See U.S. House of Representatives (2012).

19. Solomon-Fears (2012).

20. Efforts were also made to strengthen state efforts to collect child support from nonwelfare families, even though the incentives were less, since this money was passed along to the custodial parent, minus the fees.

21. The 1986 OBRA was the first effort to provide some relief to fathers, but it was a back-handed reprieve. The law required states to modify child support orders for fathers who had a change in their income, but it prohibited retroactive modification. This became important because fathers who went to prison and were not informed of their rights or provided assistance to modify their orders while they were incarcerated often accumulated very large arrearages while they were locked up, which according to the 1986 bill could not be retroactively modified. See U.S. House of Representatives (2012).

22. We should also note that the Family Support Act of 1988 further strengthened the infrastructure to facilitate immediate wage withholding and made information exchange more fluid between agencies and states by requiring parents to provide Social Security numbers when birth certificates were issued. It also increased the pressure on states to establish paternity of children born out of wedlock and required states to provide genetic testing in disputed cases. More importantly, it required states to create mandatory child support guidelines to be revised every four years, and it directed judges who departed from these guidelines to provide a written rationale for doing so. A subsequent 1994 amendment tightened up reporting expectations and procedures to credit reporting agencies and made men with arrearages ineligible for small business loans. See U.S. House of Representatives (2012).

23. Early drafts of Clinton's proposal were based on David Ellwood's reform agenda, which would have required the government to subsidize poor mothers when fathers could not pay support. But this provision had been dropped long before the bill reached the floor of the House or Senate. See DeParle (2004, 104–105).

24. Solomon-Fears explains, however, that after October, 2000, the rules changed and more of the child support payment was passed along to families *after* they left the welfare rolls. See Solomon-Fears (2012).

25. The 1998 Child Support Performance and Incentive Act "distributed incentive funds to states on a competitive basis, depending on how well they performed on five measures: (1) paternity establishment, (2) establishment of support orders, (3) collections on current support, (4) collections on arrears, and (5) cost effectiveness." Mincy, Jethwani, and Klempin (2015, 118).

26. Haney and March (2003).

27. See Erdmans and Black (2015, 16–23).

28. For an excellent analysis of this, see Haney (2018).

29. Garfinkel et al. (1998). Also see Gibson (2012).

30. United States Department of Health and Human Resources (2007).

31. Wheaton and Sorenson (2007).

32. McLanahan and Carlson (2002).

33. Wheaton and Sorensen (2007).

34. In 2005, the amount of money recovered had dropped to $2.2 billion, with a recovery rate of 22 percent, and by the end of the decade to $1.8 billion, with an 18 percent recovery rate. See Solomon-Fears (2012).

35. Haney (2018).

36. Sorensen, Sousa, and Schaner (2007); U.S. Department of Health and Human Services (2008).

37. Nationally, the amount of money collected from welfare-assisted families decreased by 21 percent between 1999 and 2009. This figures include collections on behalf of welfare-assisted and foster care families. See Solomon-Fears (2012, table A-4, 34).

38. All of these data are taken from Solomon-Fears (2012). Collections from non-welfare-assisted families reached $211 million in Connecticut in 2009, which meant that money collected from welfare-assisted families as a percent of total collections fell in Connecticut from 31 percent in 1999 to 16 percent in 2009.

39. Solomon-Fears (2012).

40. Harris (2016).

41. See Bourdieu (1979); Bourdieu (1984). Also see Wacquant (2010).

42. U.S. Bureau of Justice Statistics (2007).

43. See Wacquant (2009).

44. Garfinkel et al. (1998); U.S. House of Representatives (2012).

45. Edin and Nelson (2013); Mincy, Jethwani, and Klempin (2015).

46. Will (1986). Quoted in Edin and Nelson (2013, 3).

47. Blankenhorn (1995).

48. Quoted in Mincy, Jethwani, and Klempin (2015, 2).

49. This quote was taken from a YouTube clip of Mathis's television program *Judge Mathis*. See YouTube.com. 2009.
50. For the text of Obama's speech, see "Obama's Father's Day Remarks" (2008).
51. Soss, Fording, Schram (2011).
52. Haney (2018).
53. Amato, Meyers, and, Emery (2009); Furstenberg et al. (1983); Juby et al. (2007).
54. See Roy (2014).
55. Edin and Nelson (2013).
56. See Johnson, Levine, and Doolittle (1999)
57. Black et al. (2003).
58. See Katzenstein and Waller (2015).
59. Solomon-Fears (2012).
60. The report indicated that 30 percent of nonoffending fathers paid their support in full versus 11 percent of offending fathers. Meanwhile, 51 percent of offending fathers paid nothing compared to 23 percent of the nonoffending sample. The report was shared with us by CSE.
61. These dollar amounts are reported in 2009 dollars. Wheaton and Sorenson (2010). Taken from Mincy, Jethwani, and Klempin (2015, 43–44).
62. Wheaton and Sorensen (2007).
63. In Connecticut, in 2008, if a child support payment exceeded the TANF benefit by $50, then the state passed through the entire amount of the payment and the payment was counted toward income in figuring state assistance.
64. Ganow (2001).
65. The 2008 data were taken from Vinson and Turetsky (2009). For 2016 data, see National Conference of State Legislatures (2017). States vary considerably in terms of child support policies. Mincy, Jethwali, and Klempin provide an overview of these policies. They point out, for instance, that some states consider a father's ability to pay when determining a child support order that includes a "self-support reserve" or a "low-income standard" that allows for the father to meet basic needs, while other states place the child's needs above the father's ability to pay. See Mincy, Jethwani, Klempin (2015, 119).
66. U.S. Government Accountability Office (2011).
67. The shortcomings of these policies are further revealed from studies that have focused on noncustodial fathers less attached to the labor force, poorly educated, and formerly incarcerated. A 2008 Urban Studies report summarized the lessons gleaned from several evaluation studies of programs targeting this population, including Young Unwed Fathers Project, Parent' Fair Share, Welfare-to-Work Grants, Responsible Fatherhood Programs, and Partners for Fragile Families. See Martinson and Nightingale (2008).
68. For an excellent description of the culture of the criminal courts and the processes through which racial and class hierarchies are reproduced, see Gonzalez Van Cleve (2017).
69. Curran and Abrams (2000).

Chapter 5

1. Rierden (1993).
2. Madden (1988).
3. Rierden (1993).
4. Radcliffe (1998, 6).
5. Beauregard (2002, 103–105).
6. Logan and Harvey (1987); Judd and Hinze (2018).
7. Hirsch (1983); Massey and Denton (1993).
8. Desmond (2016, 302).
9. Desmond (2016, 252).
10. Wacquant (2009); Western (2018).
11. City-Data.com (2015).
12. Radcliffe (1998, 8–10).
13. These companies would be Colt, United Aircraft, and Pratt and Whitney. By the end of 1941, 1,300 members of the armed forces would be stationed in Hartford to protect these industries against foreign attack. See Radcliffe (1998, 21, 24).
14. Beauregard (2002, 103–105); Hirsch (1983).
15. Radcliffe (1998).
16. Radcliffe (1998, 41).
17. Massey and Denton (1993).
18. From 1956 to 1976, 2,214 units of low-income housing were built in New Haven, but 7,850 units were demolished, leaving a net loss of 5,636 units (Weibgen 2013). Also see Kerr (2011) for how this occurred in Cleveland.
19. Radcliffe (1998, 67).
20. Quadagno (1994, 114). In 1974, Nixon decreased spending further by rolling urban renewal initiatives into block grants to the states and expanding states' discretion, and by creating the housing voucher program. This resulted in the Community Development Block Grant and the Section 8 Housing programs. The bill, the Housing and Community Development Act, was actually signed into law by President Ford 13 days after Nixon resigned.
21. The fiscal crisis that rocked 1970s New York City is emblematic of the priorities of neoliberal urban development. As Kim Phillips-Fein shows in her history of neoliberal reorganization in New York, austerity was imposed on the poor and working class while city politicians tirelessly worked toward creating opportunities for the urban elite. It was in this emerging neoliberal policy environment that "disaster capitalists" like Donald Trump were given free reign to amass fortunes while skirting tax responsibilities. See Phillips-Fein (2017). On "disaster capitalism," see Klein (2007).
22. Radcliffe (1998, 68–69).
23. In many ways, the West Rock public housing development in New Haven encapsulates the story of the promise and the demise of public housing in the United States. For an excellent discussion of this, see Wolkoff (2006). Elm Haven, a downtown public housing high rise in New Haven that stacked apartments on top of one another in a

modern design, particularly suffered the federal and local neglect of public housing in the 1970s. See Weiner (2011).

24. Rierden (1993).
25. Lavoie (1994); Burgeson (2011).
26. Madden (1988).
27. Katz (1989, 189–190).
28. Weiner (2010).
29. Rierden (1993).
30. Locally, few would recognize housing developments in New Haven by their formal names, but would identify themselves as living in the Ville, the island, the G, the Hill, the Jungle, or the Tre. Street gangs were named accordingly as the Jungle Boys, the Island Brothers, the Tribe, and the Kensington Street International, or KSI, which was part of the Tre. See Weiner (2010).
31. Weiner (2010).
32. Radcliffe (1998, 64, 78).
33. Radcliffe (1998, 90).
34. Carlesso (2014).
35. RICO refers to the Racketeer Influenced and Corrupt Organizations Act. See Parenti (2008).
36. Chaskins and Joseph (2015).
37. Weber (2002); Coleman (2004).
38. On "sneaking thrills" and the "seduction of crime," see Katz (1988).
39. Bourgois (1989, 619–649); Contreras (2012).
40. Of course, the illicit drug trade reaches far beyond the pockets of urban poverty. The United Nations estimated the value of the illicit global drug trade at $322 billion in 2003 (United Nations Office on Drugs and Crime 2005, 127), while Global Financial Integrity updated the estimates to between $426 and $652 billion in 2014 (May 2017, 3). US cities provide organizing nodes for the part of the drug trade that services the country that spends the most on illicit recreational drugs in the world. Together, the United States (44 percent) and Europe (33 percent) accounted for three-quarters of all revenue from retail drug sales at the turn of the new millennium. Urban networks extend into their respective regions, providing drugs to suburban and rural areas, to satisfy the leisure preferences of individuals from all social classes and racial and ethnic groups. See United Nations Office on Drugs and Crime (2005).
41. Davis (1990); Bourgois (1995); Hoffer (2006).
42. Contreras (2012).
43. Black (2010); Bourgois (1995); Venkatesh (2000).
44. See Anderson (1999).
45. Katz (1988); Fagan and Wilkinson (1998).
46. Anderson (1999); Venkatesh (2009).
47. See Paulle (2013).
48. See Patterson and Fosse (2016); Newman (1999).
49. Collins (2009); Paulle (2013).

50. Ng-Mak et al. (2004).

51. Macmillan (2004); Western (2018).

52. Netherland and Hansen (2016).

53. Victor (2018); Tucker and Borchardt (2019).

54. Freudenberg (2001); Jensen, Gerber, and Mosher (2004).

55. For an extensive account of the consequences of violence for mothers in these same neighborhoods, see Erdmans and Black (2015).

56. Grant (2004).

57. In 2010, 48 percent of children in Hartford, 41 percent in New Haven, and 40 percent in Bridgeport were poor. See Connecticut Voices for Children (2012).

58. Wacquant (2000); Wacquant (2001). For more on the Puerto Rican version of this story, see Black (2010).

Chapter 6

1. Reinhart (2010).

2. Mauer and King (2007).

3. Gottschalk (2015).

4. Pettit (2012, 83–84, 87).

5. Wakefield and Wildeman (2014).

6. Contreras (2012).

7. Anderson (1999, 9, 34).

8. Massey (2001).

9. Wacquant (2000); Wacquant (2001).

10. Wacquant (2000); Wacquant (2001); Wacquant (2009). Wacquant also emphasized that this intrepid prison culture emanated from behind the wall into popular culture in the form of gangsta rap, language, dress, tattoo art, graffiti—certainly embraced within the ghetto but also beyond through commodifying and commercial exploits.

11. Gibbons and Katzenbach (2006). Also for a classic work on prison life and the role of violence, see Sykes (1958).

12. Wacquant (2000); Wacquant (2001).

13. In 1925, the *Detroit Independent* described "repeated assaults on Negroes. Fifty-five blacks had been shot by policeman in the first half of the year alone. A few of them had been executed—there was no other word for it." See Boyle (2007), quoted in Taylor (2016).

14. Massey and Denton (1993); Taylor (2016).

15. Taylor (2016).

16. See Hall and Hubbard (1996); Short (2006).

17. See Davis (1990); Sullivan (1992); Herbert and Brown (2006); Soss, Fording, and Schram (2011).

18. Thomas (1997); Bourgois (1995); Black (2010). Also see Contreras (2012) for a similar study in a Dominican neighborhood in New York.

19. Rios (2011).

20. See Muhammad (2010).
21. What Nathan is saying resonates with some of the literature on social networks in sociology. See, for instance, Sinan and Van Alstyne (2011).
22. Marcus and Martin's quotes reflect what some ethnographers refer to as the moral economy. See Karandinos et al. (2014); also see Bourgois and Schonberg (2009).
23. Collins (2009).
24. Paulle (2013). On embodied performance, also see Khan (2012).
25. For an excellent ethnographic study of the "puglisitic habitus," see Wacquant (2006).
26. This phrase is taken from Fine and Weiss (1999).
27. The exceptions were designated only for men who were in the Father Initiative Program who *earned* contact visits with their children.
28. Curtis (2019, 155).
29. See Roy and Dyson (2005).
30. Curtis (2019, 160).
31. For an excellent study from the standpoint of mothers about relationships between fathers and their children's mothers when fathers are incarcerated, and about their discussions concerning their futures together, see Comfort (2008).
32. MacLeod (1995).
33. Roy and Dyson (2010).

Chapter 7

1. Cherlin (2014).
2. Laub and Sampson (2006).
3. Roy (2006).
4. It is important to note, however, that this is only one path to teen motherhood. See Erdmans and Black (2015).
5. Fine and Weiss (1998).
6. See Pittman (2015). On black grandmothers' role in fostering and maintaining community in the midst of neoliberal urban reform, gentrification, and resident displacement, see Pittman and Oakley (2018).
7. Abdill (2018).
8. On the privatization of risk, see Hacker (2006). On entrepreneurial reason, see Brown (2015).
9. Gerson (2011, 215).
10. See Roy and Dyson (2010); Randles (2017); and Mincy and Pouncy (2002). The program mission stated by the Fatherhood Initiative Program in Connecticut was to "assist non-custodial fathers to assume their full emotional, educational, legal and financial roles in the lives of their children."
11. Personal communication. Also see Fingarson et al. (2019); Adamsbaum et al. (2019).
12. Williams (2001).
13. Gerson (2011).

14. The quality of the relationships was coded using a four-point Likert scale from 1 (none), 2 (poor), 3 (fair), to 4 (good) and was determined by the men's characterization of the quality of their relationships, as well as their regular involvement with mothers and children.
15. On this issue, also see Edin and Nelson (2013).
16. On this topic, see Lareau (2003).
17. In 2003, *60 Minutes* ran a story on Willimantic as "heroin town." See CBS News (2003).
18. See Furstenberg and Cherlin (1991); Townsend (2002); Edin, Tach, and Mincy (2009); Abdill (2018); and Edin and Nelson (2013).
19. Edin, Tach, and Mincy (2009); Abdill (2018).
20. Waller and Swisher (2006).
21. See Nelson, Clampet-Lundquist, and Edin (2002); Roy and Burton (2007); and Edin, Nelson, and Paranal (2004).
22. Carlson and McLanahan (2002); Edin, Tach, and Mincy (2009).
23. Stack and Burton (1993); Roy and Burton (2007); Roy, Buckmiller and McDowell (2008); Jarrett, Roy, and Burton (2002); Roy and Lucas (2006).
24. Roy and Vesely (2009); Roy and Burton (2007).
25. Abdill (2018).
26. Abdill (2018, 116–117).
27. Three incarcerated fathers were expecting fathers and one case was not clear enough for us to make a confident determination, so four fathers were removed from these calculations.
28. For a good analysis of how prison can bring couples closer together from the standpoint of women who visit their male partners in prison, see Comfort (2008).
29. For a good discussion of relationships after release from prison, see McKay et al. (2019).
30. Roy, Buckmiller and McDowell (2008).
31. Wheaton and Clarke (2003).
32. Abdill (2018); Curtis (2019); Mincy, Jethwani, and Klempin (2015); Haney (2018).
33. Mincy, Jethwani, and Klempin (2015).
34. Abdill (2018, 168).
35. Waller and Swisher (2006); Nelson, Clampet-Lundquist, and Edin (2002).
36. Edin and Nelson (2013).
37. Edin, Tach, and Mincy (2009).
38. Edin, Tach, and Mincy (2009).
39. Eggebeen (2002).
40. Roy, Buckmiller, and McDowell (2008).
41. Roy (2004).
42. Edin, Tach, and Mincy (2009).
43. Waller and Swisher (2006).
44. See Garfield (2010); and Rios (2017).
45. Roy and Dyson (2010).
46. Connell (2005, 114).

47. Garfield (2010).
48. Garfield (2010, 9).
49. Erdmans and Black (2015).
50. Bourgois (2009, 37).
51. Bancroft, Lundy, and Silverman (2002).
52. Waller and Swisher (2006).
53. Edin and Nelson (2013).
54. Abdill (2018).
55. Hamer (2001).

Chapter 8

1. Lamont (1992, 2002).
2. Fine and Weiss (1998).
3. Roy and Dyson (2010); Randles (2017).
4. Scott (1990).
5. MacLeod (1995, 249).
6. Gottschalk (2015).
7. Hamer (2001); Waller (2002).
8. Furstenberg (2001).
9. Roy and Lucas (2006).
10. For more on this, see Williams (2001).
11. See Hendrix (2019).
12. Silva (2013, 9, 98).
13. Silva (2013, 21).
14. Brown (2015, 30).
15. Soss et al. (2011).
16. MacLeod (1995, 259).
17. Wacquant (2009).

Chapter 9

1. This was taken from Le Guin's acceptance speech when receiving the National Book Foundation's Medal for Distinguished Contributions to American Letters in 2014.
2. Wacquant (2010).
3. See chapter 6 (113–145) for a full discussion of their reforms in Mincy, Jethwani, and Klempin (2015).
4. Mincy et al. (2015, 116).
5. Sommeiller and Price (2018).
6. Mills and Silberman (2018).
7. Cassidy (2018); Fontenot, Semega, and Kollar (2018).
8. Mills and Silberman (2018).
9. Bureau of Labor Statistics (2019); Cassidy (2018).

10. Macrotrends.net (2019).
11. Slaughter and Brooks (2019).
12. On proposed food stamp cuts, see Rosenbaum and Keith-Jennings (2016). For a description of the states that accepted and refused the Medicaid expansion, see the Kaiser Family Foundation (2019). On added work requirements for SNAP and Medicaid benefits, see Goodwin (2018) and Dewey (2018).
13. See Steil et al. (2017); Rugh, Albright, and Massey (2015).
14. McCoy (2013, 26).
15. Douglas (2019).
16. Federal and state numbers were recorded in the middle of the year 2017—jail numbers at the end of the year and supervision numbers at the beginning of the year. The jail figure also includes people who are being held but were unconvicted. All figures were taken from the Bureau of Justice Statistics (n.d.).
17. See James (2015).
18. Gerson (2011). On the stalled revolution, also see Coontz (2013).
19. Abdill (2018) actually refers to the "black maternal garden." We are applying the concept more broadly.
20. Swinth (2018).
21. Fraser (2016, 99); also see Fraser (2013).
22. Fraser (2016, 99).
23. Arruzza, Bhattacharya, and Fraser (2019, 22).
24. Arruzza, Bhattacharya, and Fraser (2019, 16).
25. Arruzza, Bhattacharya, and Fraser (2019, 5).
26. Arruzza, Bhattacharya, and Fraser (2019, 15).
27. Arruzza, Bhattacharya, and Fraser (2019, 21).
28. McNally (2017, 95).
29. Similarly, see Williams (2001) on what she refers to as "reconstructive feminism."

References

Abdill, Aasha M. 2018. *Fathering from the Margins: An Intimate Examination of Black Fatherhood*. New York: Columbia University.

Abramovitz, Mimi. 1996. *Regulating the Lives of Women: Social Welfare Policy from Colonial Times to the Present*. Boston: South End Press.

Adamsbaum, Catherine, Paul De Boissieu, Jean Paul Teglas, and Caroline Rey-Salmon. 2019. "Classic Metaphyseal Lesions Among Victims of Abuse." *Journal of Pediatrics* 209: 154–159.

Allgretto, Sylvia, Marc Doussard, Dave Graham-Squire, Ken Jacobs, Dan Thompson, and Jeremy Thompson. 2013. *Fast Food, Poverty Wages: The Public Costs of Low-Wage Jobs in the Fast-Food Industry*. Berkeley: UC Berkeley Labor Center. October 15. http://laborcenter.berkeley.edu/pdf/2013/fast_food_poverty_wages.pdf.

Amato, Paul R., Catherine E. Meyers, and Robert E. Emery. 2009. "Changes in Nonresident Father-Child Contact from 1976 to 2002." *Family Relations* 58, no. 1: 41–53.

Anderson, Elijah. 1999. *Code of the Street: Decency, Violence, and the Moral Life of the Inner City*. New York: W. W. Norton & Company.

Aral, Sinan, and Marshall Van Alstyne. 2011. "The Diversity-Bandwidth Trade-Off." *American Journal of Sociology* 117, no. 1: 90–171.

Arruzza, Cinzia, Tithi Bhattacharya, and Nancy Fraser. 2019. *Feminism for the 99 Percent: A Manifesto*. New York: Verso.

Autor, David H. 2003. "Outsourcing at Will: The Contribution of Unjust Dismissal Doctrine to the Growth of Employment Outsourcing." *Journal of Labor Economics* 2, no. 1: 1–42.

Balcerzak, Ashley. 2017. "Puzder out; Acosta in. Here's Who Cares Most About Labor." *The Huffington Post*. February 16. Retrieved March 3, 2017. http://www.huffingtonpost.com/entry/puzder-out-acosta-in-heres-who-cares-most-about_us_58a6268fe4b026a89a7a2896.

Bancroft, Lundy, and Jay G. Silverman. 2002. *The Batterer as Parent: Addressing the Impact of Domestic Violence on Family Dynamics*. Thousand Oaks, CA: Sage.

Beauregard, Robert A. 2002. *Voices of Decline: The Postwar Fate of U.S. Cities*. London: Routledge.

Bell, Jamie, Wade Gibson, and Mary Alice Lee. 2011. *Poverty Rising and Income Falling in Connecticut, Census Data Indicate*. New Haven: Connecticut Voices for Children. http://www.ctvoices.org/sites/default/files/files/econ12censuspovertyacsrelsum2.pdf.

Benner, Chris, Laura Leete, and Manuel Pastor. 2007. *Staircases or Treadmills? Labor Market Intermediaries and Economic Opportunity in a Changing Economy*. New York: Russell Sage Foundation.

Bhattachayra, Tithi. 2017. *Social Reproduction Theory: Remapping Class, Recentering Oppression*. London: Pluto Press.

Black, Shannon. 2016. "How Stanley Black and Decker Came to be." *Market Realist.* April 1. http://marketrealist.com/2016/04/stanley-black-decker-came/

Black, Timothy. 2010. *When a Heart Turns Rock Solid: The Lives of Three Puerto Rican Brothers on and off the Streets.* New York: Vintage.

Black, Timothy, Meredith C. Damboise, Madelyn Figueroa, Dawn Fuller-Ball, Kevin Lamkins, and Mary Erdmans. 2006. *Nurturing Families Network 2006 Annual Evaluation Report.* West Hartford, CT: Center for Social Research, University of Hartford.

Black, Timothy, Stephen L. Markson, Ronald Albert, and Christine Woolley. 2003. *Father Involvement Study: Final Report.* West Hartford, CT: Center for Social Research, University of Hartford.

Blankenhorn, David. 1995. *Fatherless America: Confronting Our Most Urgent Social Problem.* New York: Harper.

Bluestone, Barry, and Bennett Harrison. 1992. *The Deindustrialization of America: Plant Closings, Community Abandonment, and the Dismantling of Basic Industry.* New York: Basic.

Bourdieu, Pierre. 1979. "Symbolic Power." *Critique of Anthropology* 4, no. 13–14: 77–85.

Bourdieu, Pierre. 1984. *Distinction: A Social Critique of the Judgement of Taste.* Cambridge, MA: Harvard University Press.

Bourgois, Philippe. 1989. "In Search of Horatio Alger: Culture and Ideology in the Crack Economy." *Contemporary Drug Problems* 16: 619–649.

Bourgois, Philippe. 1995. *In Search of Respect: Selling Crack in El Barrio.* Cambridge: Cambridge University Press.

Bourgois, Philippe. 2009. "Recognizing Invisible Violence: A Thirty-Year Ethnographic Retrospective." In *Global Health in Times of Violence* (pp. 18–40). Edited by Linda Whiteford and Paul Farmer. Santa Fe, NM: School of Advanced Research Press.

Bourgois, Philippe, and Jeffrey Schonberg. 2009. *Righteous Dopefiend.* Berkeley: University of California Press.

Boyle, Ken. 2007. *Arc of Justice: A Saga of Race, Civil Rights, and Murder in the Jazz Age.* New York: McMilllan.

Brown, Wendy. 2015. *Undoing the Demos: Neoliberalism's Stealth Revolution.* New York: Zone Books.

Bureau of Justice Statistics. N.d. "Total Correctional Population." Bureau of Justice Statistics. Retrieved September 26, 2017. https://www.bjs.gov/index.cfm?ty=tp&tid=11.

Bureau of Justice Statistics. 2019. "Employment Projections: 2018–2028 Summary." Washington, DC: Bureau of Labor Statistics. September 4. Retrieved September 22, 2019. https://www.bls.gov/news.release/ecopro.nr0.htm.

Burgeson, John. 2011. "Waiting List for Public Housing over 2000 Deep." *Connecticut Post.* December 20. Retrieved on April 23, 2015. http://www.ctpost.com/local/article/Waiting-list-for-public-housing-over-2-000-deep-2410050.php.

Burnham, Linda. 2002. "Welfare Reform, Family Hardship, and Women of Color." In *Lost Ground* (pp. 43–56). Edited by Randy Albelda and Ann Withorn. Cambridge, MA: South End Press.

Burton, Linda M., Andrew Cherlin, Donna-Marie Winn, Angela Estacion, and Clara Holder-Taylor. 2009. "The Role of Trust in Low-Income Mothers' Intimate Unions." *Journal of Marriage and Family* 71, no. 5: 1107–1124.

Campbell, Kevin, Jim Baumohl, and Sharon R. Hunt. 2003. "The Bottom Line: Employment and Barriers to Work Among Former SSI DA&A Beneficiaries." *Contemporary Drug Problems* 30, no. 1–2: 195–240.

Campbell, Susan. 2010. "Searching Out the Hard-Core Homeless." *Hartford Courant*. December 5. https://www.courant.com/hc-xpm-2010-12-05-hc-campbell-homeless-1205-20101205-story,amp.html.

Carlesso, Jenna. 2014. "20 Years Ago, Shooting Death Drove City's War on Gang Violence." *Hartford Courant*. October 28. https://www.courant.com/courant-250/moments-in-history/hc-250-hartford-gangs-20141027-story.html.

Carlson, Marcia, and Sarah McLanahan. 2002. "Fragile Families, Father Involvement, and Public Policy." In *Handbook of Father Involvement: Multidisciplinary Perspectives* (pp. 461–488). Edited by Catherine S. Tamis-LeMonda and Natasha Cabrera. Mahwah, NJ: Lawrence Erlbaum.

Carlson, Marsha J., and Frank F. Furstenberg, Jr. 2006. "The Prevalence and Correlates of Multipartnered Fertility Urban U.S. Parents." *Journal of Marriage and Family* 68: 718–732.

Cassidy, John. 2018. "Ten Years After the Great Recession, Middle-Class Incomes are only Just Catching Up." *The New Yorker*. September 13. Retrieved September 23, 2019. https://www.newyorker.com/news/our-columnists/ten-years-after-the-start-of-the-great-recession-middle-class-incomes-are-only-just-catching-up.

CBS News. 2003. "Heroin Town: A Drug War in a Small Town." *60 Minutes*. June 10. https://www.cbsnews.com/news/heroin-town/.

Center on Budget and Policy Priorities. 2018. "A Quick Guide to SNAP Eligibility and Benefits." Washington, DC: Center on Budget and Policy Priorities. https://www.cbpp.org/sites/default/files/atoms/files/11-18-08fa.pdf.

Centers for Disease Control and Prevention. 2018. "Health, United States, 2016—Individual Charts and Tables: Spreadsheet, PDF, and PowerPoint Files," Table 4. https://www.cdc.gov/nchs/hus/contents2016.htm#004.

Chaskins, Robert J., and Mark L. Joseph. 2015. *Integrating the Inner City: The Promise and Perils of Mixed-Income Public Housing Transformation*. Chicago: Chicago University Press.

Cherlin, Andrew J. 2014. *Labor's Love Lost: The Rise and Fall of the Working-Class Family in America*. New York: Russell Sage Foundation.

City-Data.com. 2015. "Bridgeport History." Retrieved May 18, 2015. http://www.city-data.com/us-cities/The-Northeast/Bridgeport-History.html.

Coleman, Roy. 2004. "Images from a Neoliberal City: The State, Surveillance and Social Control." *Critical Criminology* 12, no. 1: 21–42.

Collins, Patricia Hill. 2004. *Black Sexual Politics: African Americans, Gender and the New Racism*. New York: Routledge.

Collins, Randall. 2009. *Violence: A Micro-Sociological Theory*. Princeton, NJ: Princeton University Press.

Comfort, Megan. 2008. *Doing Time Together: Love and Family in the Shadow of the Prison*. Chicago: University of Chicago Press.

Congressional Research Service. 2019. *The Temporary Assistance for Needy Families (TANF) Block Grant: Responses to Frequently Asked Questions*. Washington, DC. https://fas.org/sgp/crs/misc/RL32760.pdf.

Connecticut Department of Social Services. 2018. "State Administered General Assistance (Cash Assistance)." Fact Sheet. https://portal.ct.gov/-/media/Departments-and-Agencies/DSS/Economic-Security/SAGA_CASH_FactSheet.pdf.

Connecticut Voices for Children. 2010. "Child Well-Being Data by Town: 2010." http://www.ctvoices.org/sites/default/files/well10augtowndata.pdf.

Connecticut Voices for Children. 2012. "Poverty, Median Income, and Health Insurance in Connecticut: Summary of 2011 American Community Survey Census Data." http://www.ctvoices.org/sites/default/files/econ12censuspovertyacs.pdf.

Connell, R.W. 2005. *Masculinities*. Berkeley: University of California Press.

Contreras, Randol. 2012. *The Stick-Up Kids: Race, Drugs, Violence, and the American Dream*. Berkeley: University of California Press.

Coontz, Stephanie. 1992. *The Way We Never Were: American Families and the Nostalgia Trap*. New York: Basic Books.

Coontz, Stephanie. 2013. "Why Gender Equality Stalled." *The New York Times*. February 26. https://www.nytimes.com/2013/02/17/opinion/sunday/why-gender-equality-stalled.html.

Curran, Laura, and Laura S. Abrams. 2000. "Making Men into Dads: Fatherhood, the State, and Welfare Reform." *Gender and Society* 14, no. 5: 662–678.

Curtis, Anna. 2019. *Dangerous Masculinity: Fatherhood, Race, and Security Inside America's Prisons*. New Brunswick, NJ: Rutgers University Press.

Davis, Mike. 1990. *City of Quartz: Excavating the Future of Los Angeles*. New York: Verso.

DeParle, Jason. 2004. *American Dream: Three Women, Ten Kids, and a Nation's Drive to End Welfare*. New York: Viking.

Desmond, Matthew. 2016. *Evicted: Poverty and Profit in an American City*. New York: Crown.

Dewey, Caitlin. 2018. "The GOP Plan to Tighten Food Stamp Work Requirements Is Advancing—Without a Single Democrat's Vote." *Washington Post*. April 18. Retrieved September 26, 2019. https://www.washingtonpost.com/news/wonk/wp/2018/04/18/the-republican-plan-to-tighten-food-stamp-work-requirements-is-advancing-without-a-single-democrats-vote/.

Ditsler, Elaine, and Peter Fisher. 2006. "Nonstandard Jobs, Substandard Benefits: A 2005 Update." Iowa City: The Iowa Policy Project. https://www.iowapolicyproject.org/2006docs/060929-nonstd_full.pdf.

Duggan, Mark, Melissa S. Kearney, and Stephanie Rennane. 2015. "The Supplemental Security Income (SSI) Program." Working paper. Washington, DC: National Bureau of Economic Research. https://www.nber.org/papers/w2109.pdf.

Edin, Kathryn, and Laura Lein. 1997. *Making Ends Meet: How Single Mothers Survive Welfare and Low-Wage Work*. New York: Russell Sage.

Edin, Kathryn, and Timothy J. Nelson. 2013. *Doing the Best I Can: Fatherhood in the Inner City*. Berkeley: University of California Press.

Edin, Kathryn J., and H. Luke Shaefer. 2015. *$2.00 a Day: Living on Almost Nothing in America*. Boston: Houghton, Mifflin, and Harcourt.

Edin, Kathryn, Laura Lein, and Timothy Nelson. 2002. "Taking Care of Business: The Economic Survival Strategies of Low-Income, Noncustodial Fathers." In *Laboring Below the Line: The New Ethnography of Poverty, Low-Wage Work, and Survival in the Global Economy* (pp. 125–147). Edited by Frank Munger. New York: Russell Sage.

Edin, Kathryn, Timothy J. Nelson, and Rechelle Paranal. 2004. "Fatherhood and Incarceration as Potential Turning Points in the Criminal Careers of Unskilled Men."

In *Imprisoning America: The Social Effects of Mass Incarceration*. Edited by Mary Patillo, David Weiman, and Bruce Western. New York: Russell Sage Foundation.

Edin, Kathyrn, Laura Tach, and Ronald B. Mincy. 2009. "Claiming Fatherhood: Race and the Dynamics of Paternal Involvement Among Unmarried Men." *Annals of the Academy of Political and Social Science* 621, no. 1: 149–177.

Eggebeen, David J. 2002. "The Changing Course of Fatherhood: Men's Experience with Children in Demographic Perspective." *Journal of Family Issues* 23, no. 4: 486–506.

Ehrenreich, Barbara. 1976. "What Is Socialist Feminism?" *WIN Magazine*. Retrieved September 29, 2019. https://www.marxists.org/subject/women/authors/ehrenreich-barbara/socialist-feminism.htm.

Epstein, Barbara. 2001. "What Happened to the Women's Movement?" *Monthly Review* 53, no. 1. Retrieved September 9, 2019. https://monthlyreview.org/2001/05/01/what-happened-to-the-womens-movement/

Erdmans, Mary Patrice, and Timothy Black. 2015. *On Becoming a Teen Mom: Life Before Pregnancy*. Berkeley: University of California Press.

Fagan, Jeffrey, and Deanna L. Wilkinson. 1998. "Guns, Youth Violence, and Social Identity in Inner-Cities." *Crime and Justice* 24: 105–188.

Farber, Henry S. 2015. "Job Loss in the Great Recession and Its Aftermath: U.S. Evidence from the Displaced Workers Survey." NBER working paper #21216. Washington, DC: National Bureau of Economic Research. https://www.nber.org/papers/w21216.Ferguson, Thomas, and Joel Rogers. 1986. *Right Turn: The Decline of the Democrats and the Future of American Politics*. New York: Hill & Wang.

Feuer, Alan. "Life on $7.25 an Hour." *New York Times*. November 28. https://www.nytimes.com/2013/12/01/nyregion/older-workers-are-increasingly-entering-fast-food-industry.html.

Fine, Michelle, and Lois Weiss. 1998. *Unknown City: The Lives of Poor and Working-Class Young Adults*. Boston: Beacon.

Fineman, Martha Albertson. 1991. *The Illusion of Equality: The Rhetoric and Reality of Divorce Reform*. Chicago: University of Chicago Press.

Fingarson, Amanda K., Mary Clyde Pierce, Douglas J. Lorenz, Kim Kaczor, Berkeley Bennett, Rachel Berger, Melissa Currie, Sandy Herr, Sheila Hickey, Julia Magana, Kathi Makoroff, Marcia Williams, Audrey Young, and Noel Zuckerbraun. 2019. "Who's Watching the Children? Caregiver Features Associated with Physical Child Abuse versus Accidental Injury." *Journal of Pediatrics* 212: 180–187.

Fletcher Jr., Bill. 2012. *They're Bankrupting Us: And 20 Other Myths About Unions*. Boston: Beacon Press.

Fletcher Jr., Bill, and Fernando Gapasin. 2008. *Solidarity Divided: The Crisis in Organized Labor and a New Path toward Social Justice*. Berkeley: University of California Press.

Fontenot, Kayla, Jessica Semega, and Melissa Kollar. 2018. *Income and Poverty in the United States: 2017. Current Population Reports*. Washington, DC: US Census Bureau. Retrieved September 23, 2019. https://www.census.gov/content/dam/Census/library/publications/2018/demo/p60-263.pdf.

Fording, Richard C. 1997. "The Conditional Effect of Violence as a Political Tactic: Mass Insurgency, Welfare Generosity, and Electoral Context in the American States." *American Journal of Political Science* 41, no. 1: 1–29.

Foucault, Michel. 2010. *The Birth of Biopolitics: Lectures at the College de France, 1978–1979*. New York: Picador.

Fraser, Nancy. 2013. *Fortunes of Feminism: From State Managed Capitalism to Neoliberal Crisis*. New York: Verso.

Fraser, Nancy. 2016. "Contradictions of Capital and Care." *New Left Review* 100: 99–117.

Fraser, Nancy. 2017. "Crisis of Care? On the Social-Reproductive Contradictions of Capitalism." In *Social Reproduction Theory* (pp. 21–36). Edited by Tithi Bhattacharya. New York: Pluto Press.

Freeman, Harris, and George Gonos. 2011. "The Challenge of Temporary Work in Twenty-First Century Labor Markets: Flexibility with Fairness for the Low-Wage Temporary Workforce." Western New England University School of Law. Legal Studies Research Paper, no. 11-7. https://digitalcommons.law.wne.edu/cgi/viewcontent.cgi?article=1160&context=facschol.

Freudenberg, Nicholas. 2001. "Jails, Prisons, and the Health of Urban Populations." *Journal of Urban Health* 78, no. 2: 214–235.

Furstenberg, Frank. 2001. "The Fading Dream: Prospects of Marriage in the Inner-City." In *Problem of the Century: Racial Stratification in the United States* (pp. 224–246). Edited by Elijah Anderson and Douglas S. Massey. New York: Russell Sage Foundation.

Furstenberg, Frank F. Jr., and Andrew J. Cherlin. 1991. *Divided Families: What Happens to Children When Parents Part.* Cambridge, MA: Harvard University Press.

Furstenberg, Frank F., Christine Winquist Nord, James L. Peterson, and Nicholas Zill. 1983. "The Life Course of Children of Divorce: Marital Disruption and Parental Contact." *American Sociological Review* 48, no. 5: 656–668.

Ganow, Michelle. 2001. "New Challenges for States in Financing Child Support." *Welfare Information Network Issue Notes* 5, no. 7. Washington, DC: Welfare Information Network.

Gans, Herbert J. 1995. *The War Against the Poor: The Underclass and Antipoverty Policy.* New York: Basic Books.

Garfield, Gail. 2010. *Through Our Eyes: African American Men's Experiences with Race, Gender, and Violence.* New Brunswick, NJ: Rutgers University Press.

Garfinkel, Irwin, Sara S. McLanahan, and Thomas L. Hanson. 1998. "A Patchwork Portrait of Nonresident Fathers." In *Fathers Under Fire: The Revolution in Child Support Enforcement* (pp. 31–60). Edited by Irwin Garfinkel et al. New York: Russell Sage Foundation.

Garfinkel, Irwin, Daniel R. Meyer, and Sara S. McLanahan. 2001. "A Brief History of Child Support Policies in the United States." In *Fathers Under Fire: The Revolution in Child Support Enforcement* (pp. 14–30). Edited by Irwin Garfinkel, Sara S. McLanahan, Daniel R. Meyer, and Judith A. Seltzer. New York: Russell Sage.

Garfinkel, Irwin, Cynthia Miller, Sara S. McLanahan, and Thomas L. Hanson. 1998. "Deadbeat Dads or Inept States? A Comparison of Child Support Enforcement Systems." *Evaluation Review* 22, no. 6: 717–750.

Gerson, Kathleen. 2011. *The Unfinished Revolution: Coming of Age in the Era of Work, Family and Gender.* New York: Oxford University Press.

Gerstel, Naomi, and Natalia Sarkisian. 2006. "Sociological Perspectives on Families and Work: The Import of Gender, Class, and Race." In *The Work and Family handbook: Multi-disciplinary Perspectives and Approaches* (pp. 237–265). Edited by Marcie Pitt-Catsouphes, Ellen Ernst Kossek, and Stephen Sweet. Mahwah, NJ: Lawrence Erlbaum.

Gibbons, John J., and Nicholas deBelleville Katzenbach. 2006. *Confronting Confinement: A Report on Safety and Abuse in America's Prisons.* New York: Vera Institute of Justice. https://storage.googleapis.com/vera-web-assets/downloads/Publications/confronting-confinement/legacy_downloads/Confronting_Confinement.pdf.

Gibson, Wade. 2012. *Taking Stock: Four Decades of State Revenues, Expenditures and Deficits*. New Haven: Connecticut Voices for Children. http://www.ctvoices.org/publications/taking-stock-four-decades-state-revenues-expenditures-and-deficits.

Goldberg, Heidi, and Liz Schott. 2000. "A Compliance-Oriented Approach to Sanctions in State and County TANF Programs." Washington, DC: Center on Budget and Policy Priorities. https://www.cbpp.org/archives/10-1-00sliip.htm.

Gonos, George. 1997. "The Contest over Employer Status in the Postwar United States: The Case of Temporary Help Firms." *Law & Society Review* 31, no. 1: 81–110.

Gonos, George. 2000. "'Never a Fee!' The Miracle of the Postmodern Temporary Help and Staffing Agency." *WorkingUSA* 4, no. 3: 9–36.

Gonos, George. 2001. "'Fee-Splitting' Revisited: Concealing Surplus Value in the Temporary Employment Relationship." *Politics & Society* 29, no. 4: 589–611.

Gonzalez Van Cleve, Nicole. 2017. *Crook County: Racism and Injustice in America's Largest Criminal Court*. Stanford: Stanford University Press.

Goodwin, Liz. 2018. "Trump and House GOP Push for Stricter Work Requirements for Welfare." *The Boston Globe*. February 12. Retrieved Septebmer 25, 2019. https://www.bostonglobe.com/news/nation/2018/02/12/trump-and-house-gop-push-for-stricter-work-requirements-for-welfare/yyZgEmuINUIpCCwQ1sOzrN/story.html.

Gottschalk, Marie. 2015. *Caught: The Prison State and the Lockdown of American Politics*. Princeton, NJ: Princeton University Press.

Government Accountability Office. 2017. *Unemployment Insurance: Receipt of Benefits Has Declined, with Continued Disparities for Low-Wage and Part-Time Workers*. Washington, DC: Government Accountability Office. September 19. https://www.gao.gov/assets/120/117747.pdf.

Greider, William. 1987. *Secrets of the Temple: How the Federal Reserve Runs the Country*. New York: Simon and Schuster.

Hacker, Jacob. 2004. "Privatizing Risk Without Privatizing the Welfare State: The Hidden Politics of Social Policy Retrenchment in the United States." *American Political Science Review* 98, no. 2: 243–260.

Hacker, Jacob S. 2006. *The Great Risk Shift: The New Economic Security and the Decline of the American Dream*. New York: Oxford University.

Hacker, Jacob S., and Paul Pierson. 2010. *Winner-Take-All Politics: How Washington Made the Rich Richer—and Turned Its Back on the Middle Class*. New York: Simon & Schuster.

Hall, Douglas. 2005. *Child Well-Being Data by Town*. New Haven: Connecticut Voices for Children. June. http://www.ctvoices.org/publications/child-well-being-data-town.

Hall, Douglas J., and Shelley Geballe. 2003. *The State of Working Connecticut, 2003*. New Haven: Connecticut Voices for Children. http://www.ctvoices.org/sites/default/files/econ03workingct09.pdf.

Hall, Douglas, and Shelley Geballe. 2002. *Pulling Apart in Connecticut: An Analysis of Trends in Family Income*. New Haven: Connecticut Voices for Children. April. http://www.ctvoices.org/sites/default/files/econ02CtInequRpt04.pdf.

Hall, Douglas, and Shelley Geballe. 2006. *The State of Working Connecticut, 2006*. September. New Haven: Connecticut Voices for Children. http://www.ctvoices.org/sites/default/files/SWCT2006fullreport.pdf.

Hall, Douglas, and Shelley Geballe. 2008. *Pulling Apart in Connecticut: An Analysis of Trends in Family Income*. New Haven: Connecticut Voices for Children. http://www.ctvoices.org/sites/default/files/econ08pullingapart.pdf.

Hall, Tim, and Phil Hubbard. 1996. "The Entrepreneurial City: New Urban Politics, New Urban Geographies?" *Progress in Human Geography* 20, no. 2: 153–174.

Halpern-Meekin, Sarah, Kathryn Edin, Laura Tach, and Jennifer Sykes. 2015. *It's Not Like I'm Poor: How Working Families Make Ends Meet in a Post-Welfare World.* Berkeley: University of California Press.

Hamer, Jennifer. 2001. *What it Means To Be Daddy.* New York: Columbia University Press.

Haney, Lynne. 2018. "Incarcerated Fatherhood: The Entanglements of Child Support Debt and Mass Imprisonment." *American Journal of Sociology* 124, no. 1: 1–48.

Haney, Lynne, and Miranda March. 2003. "Married Fathers and Caring Daddies: Welfare Reform and the Discursive Politics of Paternity." *Social Problems* 50, no. 4: 461–481.

Hansen, Helena, Philippe Bourgois, and Ernest Drucker. 2014. "Pathologizing Poverty: New Forms of Diagnosis, Disability, and Structural Stigma Under Welfare Reform." *Social Science & Medicine* 103: 76–83.

Harris, Alexes. 2016. *A Pound of Flesh: Monetary Sanctions as Punishment for the Poor.* New York: Russell Sage Foundation.

Hatton, Erin. 2011. *The Temp Economy: From Kelly Girls to Permatemps in Postwar America.* Philadelphia, PA: Temple University Press.

Hendrix, Steve. 2019. "He Always Hated Women. Then He Decided to Kill Them." *The Washington Post.* June 7. https://www.washingtonpost.com/graphics/2019/local/yoga-shooting-incel-attack-fueled-by-male-supremacy/?utm_term=.c2169d51600a.

Herbert, Steve, and Elizabeth Brown. 2006. "Conceptions of Space and Crime in the Punitive Neoliberal City." *Antipode* 38, no. 4: 755–777.

Hero, Joachim. 2009. *Connecticut Family Asset and Opportunity Scorecard, 2009.* New Haven: Connecticut Voices for Children. http://www.ctvoices.org/sites/default/files/econ09assetscorecard.pdf.

Hero, Joachim, Douglas J. Hall, and Shelley Geballe. 2007. *State of Working Connecticut, 2007.* New Haven: Connecticut Voices for Children. September. http://www.ctvoices.org/sites/default/files/SOWCT2007fullreport.pdf.

Hero, Joachim, Orlando Rodriguez, and Shelley Geballe. 2010. *Time for Connecticut to Re-examine Its Business Tax Credits.* New Haven: Connecticut Voices for Children. http://www.ctvoices.org/sites/default/files/bud10taxcreditrevision.pdf.

Hero, Joachim, Orlando Rodriguez, and Jacob Siegel. 2010. *State of Working Connecticut, 2010.* New Haven: Connecticut Voices for Children. September. http://www.ctvoices.org/sites/default/files/econ10sowctfull.pdf.

Hillman, Annemarie, and Cyd Oppenheimer. 2011. *Connecticut Early Care & Education Progress Report, 2010.* New Haven: Connecticut Voices for Children. http://www.ctvoices.org/sites/default/files/ece11progressreport.pdf.

Hirsch, Arnold R. 1983.*The Making of the Second Ghetto: Race and Housing in Chicago, 1940–1960.* Cambridge, UK: Cambridge University Press.

Hoffer, Lee D. 2006. *Junkie Business: The Evolution and Operation of a Heroin Dealing Network.* Belmont, CA: Thomson/Wadsworth.

Hungerford, Thomas L. and Rebecca Thiess. 2013. "The Earned Income Tax Credit and the Child Tax Credit." September 25. Issue Brief #370. Washington, DC: Economic Policy Institute. http://www.epi.org/publication/ib370-earned-income-tax-credit-and-the-child-tax-credit-history-purpose-goals-and-effectiveness.

Jacobs, Ken, Ian Perry, and Jenifer MacGillvary. 2015. *The High Public Cost of Low Wages.* Berkeley: UC Berkeley Labor Center. Retrieved March 3, 2017. http://laborcenter.berkeley.edu/the-high-public-cost-of-low-wages/.

James, Nathan. 2015. *Offender Reentry: Correctional Statistics, Reintegration into the Community, and Recidivism*. Washington, DC: Congressional Research Service. Retrieved September 26, 2019. https://fas.org/sgp/crs/misc/RL34287.pdf.

Jamieson, Dave. 2017. "How the Fast-Food Chain Led by Trump's Labor Nominee Stiffed Workers Again and Again." *The Huffington Post*. February 2. https://www.huffingtonpost.com/entry/andy-puzder-hardees-labor-law-violations_us_5893b7ade4b09bd304ba7f14.

Jarrett, Robin L., Kevin M. Roy, and Linda M. Burton. 2002. "Fathers in the 'Hood': Insights from Qualitative Research on Low-Income African-American Men." In *Handbook of Father Involvement: Multidisciplinary Perspectives* (pp. 211–248). Edited by Catherine S. Tamis-LeMonda and Natasha Cabrera. Mahwah, NJ: Lawrence Erlbaum.

Jensen, Eric L., Jurg Gerber, and Clayton Mosher. 2004. "Social Consequences of the War on Drugs: The Legacy of Failed Policy." *Criminal Justice Policy Review* 15, no. 1: 100–121.

Johnson, Earl S., Ann Levine, and Fred C. Doolittle. 1999. *Fathers' Fair Share: Helping Poor Men Manage Child Support and Fatherhood*. New York: Russell Sage Foundation.

Juby, Heather, Billette, Jean-Michel Billette, Benoit Laplante, and Celine Le Bourdais. 2007. "Nonresident Fathers and Children: Parents' New Unions and Frequency of Contact." *Journal of Family Issues* 28: 1220–1245.

Judd, Dennis R., and Annika M. Hinze. 2018. *City Politics: The Political Economy of Urban America*. London: Routledge.

Kaiser Family Foundation. 2019. "Status of State Medicaid Expansion Decisions: Interactive Map." Retrieved September 25, 2019. https://www.kff.org/medicaid/issue-brief/status-of-state-medicaid-expansion-decisions-interactive-map/

Kalleberg, Arne L. 2011. *Good Jobs, Bad Jobs: The Rise of Polarized and Precarious Employment Systems in the United States*. New York: Russell Sage Foundation.

Karandinos, George, Laurie Kain Hart, Fernando Montero Castrillo, and Philippe Bourgois. 2014. "The Moral Economy of Violence in the US Inner City." *Current Anthropology* 55, no. 1: 1–22.

Katz, Jack. 1988. *Seduction of Crime: Moral and Sensual Attractions in Doing Evil*. New York: Basic.

Katz, Lawrence, and Alan Kreuger. 1999. "The High Pressure U.S. Labor Market of the 1990s." *Brookings Papers on Economic Activity* 1, no. 1: 1–65. https://www.brookings.edu/bpea-articles/the-high-pressure-u-s-labor-market-of-the-1990s/

Katz, Michael B. 1989. *The Undeserving Poor: From the War on Poverty to the War on Welfare*. New York: Pantheon.

Katzenstein, Mary Fainsod, and Maureen Waller. 2015. "Taxing the Poor: Incarceration, Poverty Governance, and the Seizure of Family Resources." *Perspectives on Politics* 13, no. 3: 638–656.

Kenworthy, Lane. 2014. *Social Democratic America*. New York: Oxford University Press.

Kerr, Daniel. 2011. *Derelict Paradise: Homelessness and Urban Development in Cleveland, Ohio*. Amherst: University of Massachusetts Press.

Khan, Shamus. 2012. *Privilege: The Making of an Adolescent Elite at St. Paul's School*. Princeton, NJ: Princeton University.

Klein, Naomi. 2007. *The Shock Doctrine: The Rise of Disaster Capitalism*. New York: Metropolitan.

Kotz, David. M. 2015. *The Rise and Fall of Neoliberal Capitalism*. Cambridge, MA: Harvard University Press.

Krugman, Paul. 2009. "The Big Zero." *New York Times*. December 29. https://www.nytimes.com/2009/12/28/opinion/28krugman.html.

Labor Law Center. 2017. "State & Federal Minimum Wage Rates." Retrieved February 22, 2017. http://www.selfsufficiencystandard.org/docs/Connecticut%202005.pdf.

Lamont, Michele. l992. *Money, Morals, and Manners: The Culture of the French and American Upper-Middle Class*. Chicago: University of Chicago Press.

Lamont, Michele. 2002. *The Dignity of Working Men: Morality and the Boundaries of Race, Class, and Immigration*. Cambridge, MA: Harvard University Press.

Lamont, Michele, and Virag Molnar. 2002. "The Study of Boundaries in the Social Sciences." *Annual Review of Sociology* 28: 167–195.

Lareau, Annette. 2003. *Unequal Childhoods: Class, Race and Family Life*. Berkeley: University of California Press.

Laub, John H., and Robert J. Sampson. 2006. *Shared Beginnings, Divergent Lives: Delinquent Boys to Age 70*. Cambridge, MA: Harvard university Press.

Lavoie, Denise. 1994. "Father Panik Village Now a Criminals' Paradise." *Los Angeles Times*. January 9.

Levine, Judith A. 2013. *Ain't No Trust: How Bosses. Boyfriends, and Bureaucrats Fail Low-Income Mothers and Why It Matters*. Berkeley: University of California Press.

Levy, Don, Orlando Rodriguez, and Wayne Villemez. 2004. *The Changing Demographics of Connecticut, 1990 to 2000. Part 2: The Five Connecticuts*. May. Storrs: University of Connecticut, Connecticut State Data Center.

Logan, John. 2002. "Consultants, Lawyers, and the 'Union Free' Movement in the USA Since the 1970s." *Industrial Relations Journal* 33, no. 3: 197–214.

Logan, John R., and Harvey L. Molotch. 1987. *Urban Fortunes: The Political Economy of Place*. Berkeley: University of California Press.

Lorber, Judith. 2012. *Gender Inequality: Feminist Theories and Politics*, 5th ed. New York: Oxford University.

MacLeod, Jay. 1995. *Ain't No Makin' It: Aspirations and Attainment in a Low-Income Neighborhood*, 2nd ed. Boulder, CO: Westview Press.

Macmillan, Ross. 2004. "Violence and the Life Course: The Consequences of Victimization for Personal and Social Development." *Annual Review of Sociology* 27: 1–22.

Macrotrends.net. 2019. "General Motors Gross Profit 2009-2019." Retrieved September 27, 2019. https://www.macrotrends.net/stocks/charts/GM/general-motors/gross-profit.

Madden, Richard L. 1988. "Bridgeport Starts to Scale Down and Remodel Its 'Model Housing' Complex." *New York Times*. July 16.

Martinson, Karin, and Demetra S. Nightingale. 2008. *Ten Key Findings from Responsible Fatherhood Programs*. Washington, DC: Urban Institute. https://www.urban.org/sites/default/files/publication/31516/411623-Ten-Key-Findings-from-Responsible-Fatherhood-Initiatives.PDF.

Massey, Douglas S. 2001. "Segregation and Violent Crime in Urban America." In *Problem of the Century: Racial Stratification in the United States* (pp. 317–344). Edited by Elijah Anderson and Douglas S. Massey. New York: Ray Sage Foundation.

Massey, Douglas S. 2007. *Categorically Unequal: The American Stratification System*. New York: Russell Sage.

Massey, Douglas S, and Nancy A. Denton. 1993. *American Apartheid: Segregation and the Making of the Underclass*. Cambridge, MA: Harvard University Press.

Mauer, Marc, and Ryan King. 2007. "Uneven Justice: State Rates of Incarceration by Race and Ethnicity." Washington, DC: Sentencing Project. July 1. https://www.sentencingproject.org/publications/uneven-justice-state-rates-of-incarceration-by-race-and-ethnicity/.

May, Channing. 2017. *Transnational Crime and the Developing World*. March. Washington, DC: Global Financial Integrity.

McCarthy, Michael A. 2016. "The Monetary Hawks." *Jacobin*. August 3. Retrieved on January 28, 2019. https://www.jacobinmag.com/2016/08/paul-volcker-ronald-reagan-fed-shock-inflation-unions/

McCarty, Maggie, Gene Falk, Randy Alison Aussenberg, and David H. Carpenter. 2016. *Drug Testing and Crime-Related Restrictions in TANF, SNAP, and Housing Assistance*. Washington, DC: Congressional Research Service. https://fas.org/sgp/crs/misc/R42394.pdf.

McCoy, Patricia A. 2013. *The Home Mortgage Foreclosure Crisis: Lessons Learned. Joint Center for Housing* Studies. Cambridge, MA: Harvard University. https://www.jchs.harvard.edu/sites/default/files/hbtl-01_0.pdf.

McKay, Tasseli, Megan Comfort, Christine Lindquist, and Anupa Bir. 2019. *Holding On: Family and Fatherhood During Incarceration and Reentry*. Berkeley: University of California Press.

McLanahan Sara S., and Marcia J. Carlson. 2002. "Welfare Reform, Fertility and Father Involvement." *The Future of Children: Children and Welfare Reform* 12, no. 1: 147–165.

McLanahan, Sara, Laura Tach, and Daniel Schneider. 2013. "The Causal Effects of Father Absence." *Annual Review of Sociology* 39: 399–427.

McNally, David. 2017. "Intersections and Dialectics: Critical Reconstructions in Social Reproduction Theory." In *Social Reproduction Theory*. Edited by Tithi Bhattacharya. London: Pluto Press.

McNichol, Jane. 2005. *The Betrayal of Welfare for Working Families*. Hartford, CT: Legal Assistance Resource Center of Connecticut.

Meyer, Daniel R., and Judi Bartfield. 1996. "Compliance with Child Support Orders in Divorce Cases." *Journal of Marriage and the Family* 58, no. 1: 201–212.

Mills, C. Wright. 1959. *The Sociological Imagination*. New York: Oxford University Press.

Mills, Jamie, and Rachel Silberman. 2018. *The State of Working Connecticut: Wages Stagnant for Working Families*. New Haven: Connecticut Voices for Children. August.

Mincy, Ronald, Monique Jethwani, and Serena Klempin. 2015. *Failing Our Fathers: Confronting the Crisis of Economically Vulnerable Nonresident Fathers*. New York: Oxford University Press.

Mincy, Ronald M., and Hillard Pouncy. 2002. "The Responsible Fatherhood Field: Evolution and Goals." In *Handbook of Father Involvement: Multidisciplinary Perspectives* (pp. 555–597). Edited by Catherine S. Tamis-LeMonda and Natasha Cabrera. Mahwah, NJ: Lawrence Erlbaum.

Moody, Kim. 2017. *On New Terrain: How Capital Is Reshaping the Battleground of Class War*. Chicago: Haymarket.

Muhammad, Khail Gibran. 2010. *The Condemnation of Blackness: Race, Crime, and the Making of Modern Urban America*. Cambridge, MA: Harvard University Press.

National Conference of State Legislatures. 2017. *Child Support Pass-Through and Disregard Policies for Public Assistance Recipients*. Washington, DC: National Conference of State Legislatures. July 18. http://www.ncsl.org/research/human-services/state-policy-pass-through-disregard-child-support.aspx.

Nelson, Timothy J., Susan Clampet-Lundquist, and Kathyrn Edin. 2002. "Sustaining Fragile Fatherhood: Father Involvement Among Low-Income, Noncustodial African-American Fathers in Philadelphia." In *Handbook of Father Involvement: Multidisciplinary Perspectives* (pp. 525–553). Edited by Catherine S. Tamis-LeMonda and Natasha Cabrera. Mahwah, NJ: Lawrence Erlbaum.

Netherland, Julie, and Helena B. Hansen. 2016. "The War on Drugs That Wasn't: Wasted Whiteness, 'Dirty Doctors,' and Race in Media Coverage of Prescription Opioid Misuse." *Culture, Medicine, and Psychiatry* 40, no. 4: 664–686.

Neubeck, Kenneth J., and Noel A. Cazenave. 2001. *Welfare Racism: Playing the Race Card Against America's Poor*. London: Routledge.

Newman, Katherine S. 1999. *No Shame in My Game: The Working Poor in the Inner City*. New York: Knopf.

Ng-Mak, Daisy S., Suzanne Salzinger, Richard S. Feldman, and C. Ann Stueve. 2004. "Pathologic Adaptation to Community Violence Among Inner-City Youth." *American Journal of Orthopsychiatry* 74, no. 2: 196–208.

Nicholson, Linda. 1997. *The Second Wave: A Reader in Feminist Theory*. New York: Routledge.

"Obama's Father's Day Remarks." 2008. *New York Times*. June 15. https://www.nytimes.com/2008/06/15/us/politics/15text-obama.html.

O'Connor, Alice. 2000. "Poverty Research and Policy for the Post-Welfare Era." *Annual Review of Sociology* 26: 547–562.

O'Connor, James. 2001. *The Fiscal Crisis of the State*. New York: Transaction.

O'Connor, John. 1998. "US Social Welfare Policy: The Reagan Record and Legacy." *Journal of Social Policy* 27, no. 1: 37–61.

O'Connor, John. 2010. "Marxism and the Three Movements of Neoliberalism." *Critical Sociology* 36, no. 5: 691–715.

Orloff, Ann S., and Renee Monson. 2002. "Citizens, Workers or Fathers? Men in the History of U.S. Social Policy." In *Making Men into Fathers* (pp. 61–91). Edited by Barbara Hobson. Cambridge, UK: Cambridge University Press.

Palermino, Peter. 2003. "Income Eligibility Changes for PG 1D and PG 2." Department of Social Services. Hartford, CT. Retrieved April 24, 2017. http://www.ct.gov/oec/lib/oec/earlycare/c4k/transmittals/6_prioritization/e-incomeeligibilitychangesforpg1dandpg2-03-11-2003.pdf.

Panitch, Leo, and Sam Gindin. 2012. *The Making of Global Capitalism: The Political Economy of American Empire*. New York: Verso.

Parenti, Christian. 2008. *Lockdown America: Police and Prisons in the Age of Crisis*. New York: Verso.

Patterson, Orlando, and Ethan Fosse. 2016. "Introduction." In Orlando Patterson and Ethan Fosse (pp. 1–25), *The Cultural Matrix*. Cambridge, MA: Harvard University Press.

Paulle, Bowen. 2013. *Toxic Schools: High-Poverty Education in New York and Amsterdam*. Chicago: University of Chicago Press.

Pavetti, Ladonna A. 2001. "Welfare Policy in Transition: Redefining the Social Contract for Poor Citizen Families with Children and for Immigrants." In *Understanding Poverty* (pp. 229–271). Edited by Sheldon H. Danzinger and Robert H. Haveman. New York: Russell Sage.

Pearce, Diane. 2005. *The Real Cost of Living in 2005: The Self-Sufficiency Standard in Connecticut*. Hartford: Office of Workforce Competitiveness, State of Connecticut. Retrieved on June 28, 2014. http://www.selfsufficiencystandard.org/docs/Connecticut%202005.pdf.

Penn, Ben. 2016. "Is Franchise Model a Recipe for Fast-Food Wage Violations." *Bloomberg Bureau of National Affairs*. September 13. https://www.bna.com/franchise-model-recipe-n57982076930/.

Pettit, Becky. 2012. *Invisible Men: Mass Incarceration and the Myth of Black Progress*. New York: Russell Sage Foundation.

Pew Research Center. 2010. *A Balance Sheet at 30 Months: How the Great Recession Has Changed Life in America*. Washington, DC: Pew Research Center. https://www.pewsocialtrends.org/2010/06/30/how-the-great-recession-has-changed-life-in-america/.

Phillips-Fein, Kim. 2017. *Fear City: New York's Fiscal Crisis and the Rise of Austerity Politics*. New York: Metropolitan.

Pierce, Diana M. 2015. *The Self-Sufficiency Standard for Connecticut 2015*. The Permanent Commission on the Status of Women. Hartford, CT. Retrieved August 3, 2019. http://selfsufficiencystandard.org/sites/default/files/selfsuff/docs/CT2015_SSS.pdf.

Pierson, Paul. 1994. *Dismantling the Welfare State? Reagan, Thatcher, and the Politics of Retrenchment*. Cambridge: Cambridge University Press.

Pittman, LaShawnDa. 2015. "How Well Does the Safety Net Work for Family Safety Nets? Economic Survival Strategies Among Grandmother Caregivers in Severe Deprivation." *The Russell Sage Foundation Journal of the Social Sciences* 1, no. 1: 78–97.

Pittman, LaShawnDa, and Deirdre Oakley. 2018. "'It Was All Love in the Buildings They Tore Down': How Caregiving Grandmothers Create and Experience a Sense of Community in Chicago Public Housing." *City & Community* 17, no. 2: 461–484.

Piven, Frances Fox. 2004. *The War At Home: The Domestic Costs of Bush's Militarism*. New York: New Press.

Piven, Frances Fox, and Richard A. Cloward. 1971. *Regulating the Poor: The Functions of Public Welfare*. New York: Random House.

Quadagno, Jill. 1994. *The Color of Welfare: How Racism Undermined the War on Poverty*. New York: Oxford University Press.

Radcliffe, David. 1998. *Charter Oak Terrace: Life, Death and Rebirth of a Public Housing Project*. Hartford, CT: Southside Media.

Randles, Jennifer M. 2017. *Proposing Prosperity?: Marriage Education Policy and Inequality in America*. New York: Columbia University.

Reinhart, Christopher. 2010. "Connecticut Prison Population Statistics." Connecticut General Assembly. OLR Research Report. Hartford, CT. January 15. Retrieved January 1, 2017. https://www.cga.ct.gov/jud/related/20100119_January%2019,%202010%20-%20Oversight%20Hearing%20on%202008%20Criminal%20Justice%20Reforms/20100119/Connecticut%20Prison%20Population%20Statistics.pdf.

Rierden, Andi. 1993. "The Last Farewell to Father Panik Village." *New York Times*. October 17.

Rios, Victor M. 2011. *Punished: Policing the Lives of Black and Latino Boys*. New York: New York University Press.

Rios, Victor. 2017. *Human Targets: School, Police and the Criminalization of Latino Youth*. Chicago: University of Chicago Press.

Rosenbaum, Dottie, and Brynne Keith-Jennings. 2016. "House 2017 Budget Plan Would Slash SNAP by More Than $150 Billion over Ten Years." Washington, DC: Center on Budget and Policy Priorities. Retrieved September 25, 2019. https://www.cbpp.org/research/food-assistance/house-2017-budget-plan-would-slash-snap-by-more-than-150-billion-over-ten.

Roy, Kevin. 2004. "Three-Block Fathers: Spatial Perceptions and Kin-Work in Low-Income African American Neighborhoods." *Social Problems* 51, no. 4: 528–548.

Roy, Kevin M. 2006. "Father Stories: A Life Course Examination of Father Paternal Identity Among Low-Income African American Men." *Journal of Family Issues* 27, no. 1: 31–54.

Roy, Kevin. 2014. "Fathering from the Long View: Framing Personal and Social Change Through Life Course Theory." *Journal of Family Theory & Review* 6, no. 4: 319–335.

Roy, Kevin, and Linda Burton. 2007. "Mothering Through Recruitment: Kinscription of Nonresidential Fathers and Father Figures in Low-Income Families." *Family Relations: An Interdisciplinary Journal of Applied Family Studies* 56, no. 1: 24–39.

Roy, Kevin M., and Omari L. Dyson. 2005. "Gatekeeping in Context: Babymama Drama and the Involvement of Incarcerated Fathers." *Fathering: A Journal of Theory, Research and Practice About Men as Fathers* 3, no. 3: 289–310.

Roy, Kevin M., and Omari Dyson. 2010. "Making Daddies into Fathers: Community-Based Fatherhood Programs and the Construction of Masculinity for Low-Income African American Men." *American Journal of Community Psychology* 45: 139–154.

Roy, Kevin M., and Kristen Lucas. 2006. "Generativity as Second Chance: Low-Income Fathers and Transformation of the Difficult Past." *Research in Human Development* 3, no. 2–3: 139–159.

Roy, Kevin M., and Colleen K. Vesely. 2009. "Caring for 'the Family's Child': Social Capital and Kin Networks of Young Low-Income African American Fathers." In *The Myth of the Missing Black Father* (pp. 215–240). Edited by Roberta L. Coles and Charles Green. New York: Columbia University Press.

Roy, Kevin M., Nicolle Buckmiller, and April McDowell. 2008. "Together but Not 'Together': Trajectories of Relationship Suspension for Low-Income Unmarried Parents." *Family Relations* 57: 198–210.

Rugh, Jacob S., Len Albright, and Douglas S. Massey. 2015. "Race, Space, and Cumulative Disadvantage: A Case Study of the Subprime Lending Collapse." *Social Problems* 62: 186–218.

Santacroce, Matt, and Orlando Rodriguez. 2011. *State of Working Connecticut, 2011: Jobs, Unemployment, and the Great Recession*. New Haven: Connecticut Voices for Children. http://www.ctvoices.org/sites/default/files/econ11sowctfull.pdf.

Schram, Sanford F. 1998. "Introduction Welfare Reform: A Race to the Bottom?" *Publius* 28, no. 3: 1–7.

Schram, Sanford F., and Joe Soss. 2002. "Success Stories: Welfare Reform, Policy Discourse, and the Politics of Research." In *Lost Ground: Welfare Reform, Poverty and Beyond* (pp. 57–78). Edited by Randy Albelda and Ann Withorn. Cambridge, MA: South End Press.

Schram, Sanford S., and J. Patrick Turbett. 1983. "Civil Disorder and the Welfare Explosion: A Two-Step Process." *American Sociological Review* 48, no. 3: 408–414.

Scott, James C. 1990. *Domination and the Arts of Resistance: Hidden Transcripts*. New Haven, CT: Yale University Press.

Sennett, Richard. 1998. *The Corrosion of Character: The Personal Consequences of Work in the New Capitalism*. New York: W.W. Norton.

Sennett, Richard. 2006. *The Culture of the New Capitalism*. New Haven, CT: Yale University Press.

Serwer, Andy. 2009. "The '00's: Good Bye at Last to the Decade from Hell." *Time*. November 24. http://content.time.com/time/subscriber/article/0,33009,1942973-7,00.html.

Short, John Rennie. 2006. *Urban Theory: New Critical Perspectives*. New York: Palgrave MacMillan.

Silva. Jennifer M. 2013. *Coming Up Short: Working-Class Adulthood in an Age of Uncertainty*. New York: Oxford University Press.

Slaughter, Jane, and Chris Brooks. 2019. "GM Strikers Say 'No More Tiers'!" *Labor Notes*. September 18. Retrieved September 27, 2019. https://labornotes.org/2019/09/gm-strikers-say-no-more-tiers.

Smeeding, Timothy M., Jeffrey P. Thompson, Asaf Levanon, and Ersa Burak. 2011. "Poverty and Income Inequality in the Early Stages of the Great Recession." In *The Great Recession*. Edited by David B. Grusky, Bruce Western, and Christopher Wimer. New York: Russell Sage Foundation.

Smith, Vicki, and Esther B. Neuwirth. 2008. *The Good Temp*. Ithaca, NY: Cornell University Press.

Smock, Pamela J., Wendy D. Manning, and Sanjiv Gupta. 1999. "The Effect of Marriage and Divorce on Women's Economic Well-Being." *American Sociological Review* 64, no. 6: 794–812.

Social Security Administration. 2017. *SSI Annual Statistical Report, 2017*. Office of Retirement and Disability Policy; Office of Research, Evaluation, and Statistics. Washington, DC. https://www.ssa.gov/policy/docs/statcomps/ssi_asr/2017/ssi_asr17.pdf.

Solomon-Fears, Carmen. 2012. *Analysis of Federal-State Financing of the Child Support Enforcement Program*. Washington, DC: Congressional Research Service. July 19. Retrieved July 15, 2018. https://greenbook-waysandmeans.house.gov/sites/greenbook.waysandmeans.house.gov/files/2012/documents/RL33422_gb.pdf.

Sommeiller, Estelle, and Mark Price. 2018. "The New Gilded Age: Income Inequality in the U.S. by State, Metropolitan Area, and County." Washington, DC: Economic Policy Institute.

Sorensen, Elaine, Lilliana Sousa, and Simon Schaner. 2007. *Assessing Child Support Arrears in Nine Large States and the Nation*. Washington, DC: The Urban Institute. https://www.urban.org/sites/default/files/publication/29736/1001242-Assessing-Child-Support-Arrears-in-Nine-Large-States-and-the-Nation.PDF.

Soss, Joe, Richard C. Fording, and Sanford F. Schram. 2008. "The Color of Devolution: Race, Federalism, and the Politics of Social Control." *American Journal of Political Science* 52, no. 3: 536–553.

Soss, Joe, Richard C. Fording, and Sanford S. Schram. 2011. *Disciplining the Poor: Neoliberal Paternalism and the Persistent Power of Race*. Chicago: University of Chicago Press.

Stack, Carol B., and Linda M. Burton. 1993. "Kinscripts." *Journal of Comparative Family Studies* 24, no. 2: 157–170.

Steil, Justin P., Len Albright, Jacob S. Rugh, and Douglas S. Massey. 2017. "The Social Structure of Mortgage Discrimination." *Housing Studies* 33, no. 4: 1–18.

Stiglitz, Joseph E. 2012. *The Price of Inequality: How Today's Divided Society Endangers Our Future*. New York: W.W. Norton.

Stone, Pamela. 2007. *Opting Out: Why Women Really Quit Careers and Head Home*. Berkeley: University of California Press.

Sullivan, Mercer. 1992. "Crime and the Social Fabric." In *Dual City: Restructuring New York* (pp. 225–244). Edited by John H. Mollenkopf and Manuel Castells. New York: Russell Sage Foundation.

Sum, Andew, Ishwar Khatiwada, Joseph McLaughlin, and Sheila Palma. 2011. "No Country for Young Men: Deteriorating Labor Market Prospects for Low-Skilled Men in the United States." *The Annals of the American Academy of Political and Social Science* 635, no. 1: 24–55.

Swinth, Kirsten. 2018. *Feminism's Forgotten Fight: The Unfinished Struggle for Work and Family.* Cambridge, MA: Harvard University Press.

Sykes, Gresham M. 1958. *The Society of Captives: A Study of a Maximum Security Prison.* Princeton, NJ: Princeton University Press.

Taylor, Keeanga-Yamhatta. 2016. *From #BLACKLIVESMATTER to Black Liberation.* Chicago: Haymarket Books.

Taylor, Keenanga-Yamahtta. 2017. *How We Get Free: Black Feminism and the Combahee River Collective.* Chicago: Haymarket Books.

Teachman, Jay D., and Kathleen M. Paasch. 1994. "Financial Impact of Divorce on Children and Their Families." *The Future of Children* 4, no. 1: 63–83.

Temple, Jack. *Super Sizing Public Costs: How Low Wages at Top Fast-Food Chains Leave Taxpayers Footing the Bill.* New York: National Employment Law Project. http://www.nelp.org/content/uploads/2015/03/NELP-Super-Sizing-Public-Costs-Fast-Food-Report.pdf.

Thomas, Piri. 1997. *Down These Mean Streets.* New York: Vintage Books.

Townsend, Nick. 2002. *The Package Deal: Marriage, Work, and Fatherhood in Men's Lives.* Philadelphia, PA: Temple University Press.

Tucker, Randy, and Jackie Borchardt. 2019. "John Boehner to Chair New National Cannabis Lobbying Group." *Cincinnati Enquirer.* February 8. https://eu.cincinnati.com/story/money/2019/02/08/cannabis-former-house-speaker-john-boehner-chair-new-lobbying-group/2810644002/

Uccello, Cori E., and L. Jerome Gallagher. 1997. "General Assistance Programs: The State-Based Part of the Safety Net." *New Federalism: Issues and Options for States.* Washington, DC: Urban Institute. https://www.urban.org/sites/default/files/publication/70346/307036-General-Assistance-Programs.PDF.

Uchitelle, Louis. 2006. *The Disposable American: Layoffs and their Consequences.* New York: Knopf.

Union Members-2010, 2011. Bureau of Labor Statistics News Release. Washington, DC: U.S. Department of Labor. January 21. Retrieved March 11, 2017. https://www.bls.gov/news.release/archives/union2_01212011.pdf

United Nations Office on Drugs and Crime. 2005. *World Drug Report, 2005.* Vienna, Austria. https://www.unodc.org/pdf/WDR_2005/volume_1_web.pdf.

U.S. Bureau of Justice Statistics. 2007. *Key Facts at a Glance, Correctional Populations.* December. Washington, DC: Office of Justice Programs. https://www.bjs.gov/glance_redirect.cfm.

U.S. Census Bureau. 2000. "Census 2000 Summary File 3." Washington, DC.

U.S. Census Bureau. 2018. "Historical Poverty Tables: People and Families," Table 2. https://www.census.gov/data/tables/time-series/demo/income-poverty/historical-poverty-people.html.

U.S. Department of Agriculture. 2017a. "SNAP Data Tables." Food and Nutrition Service. Washington, DC. Retrieved May 30, 2017. https://www.fns.usda.gov/pd/supplemental-nutrition-assistance-program-snap.

U.S. Department of Agriculture. 2017b. *State Options Report: Supplemental Nutrition Assistance Program.* Food and Nutrition Service. Washington, DC. Retrieved

January 29, 2019. https://fns-prod.azureedge.net/sites/default/files/snap/13-State_Options-revised.pdf.

U.S. Department of Commerce. 2010. Table prepared by Bureau of Business and Economic Research, University of New Mexico. Bureau of Economic Analysis. Retrieved June 25, 2010. http://bber.unm.edu/econ/us-pci.htm.

U.S. Department of Health and Human Services. "Trends in the AFDC Caseloads Since 1962." Table 2.1. Washington, DC: Office of the Assistant Secretary for Planning and Evaluation. https://aspe.hhs.gov/system/files/pdf/167036/2caseload.pdf.

U.S. Department of Health and Human Resources. 2007. *FY 2007 Budget in Brief.* Washington, DC: Administration for Children and Families. https://wayback.archive-it.org/3920/20130927185702/http://archive.hhs.gov/budget/07budget/.

U.S. Department of Health and Human Services. 2008. *Story Behind the Numbers: Who Owes Child Support Debt.* 2004. Washington, DC: Office of Child Support Enforcement. https://www.acf.hhs.gov/sites/default/files/ocse/im_08_05a.pdf.

U.S. Government Accountability Office. 2011. *Departures from Long-Term Trends in Sources of Collections and Caseloads Reflect Recent Economic Conditions.* GAO-11-196. Washington, DC: Child Support Enforcement. January 2011. https://www.gao.gov/assets/320/314589.pdf.

U.S. House of Representatives. 2012. "Child Support Enforcement Legislative History." Washington, DC: U.S. House of Representatives, Committee on Ways and Means. Retrieved December 19, 2016. http://greenbook.waysandmeans.house.gov/2012-green-book/child-support-enforcement-cover-page/legislative-history.

Van Horn, Carl E. 2014. *Working Scared (Or Not at All): The Lost Decade, Great Recession, and Restoring the Shattered American Dream.* New York: Rowman and Littlefield.

Venkatesh, Sudhir. 2000. *American Project: The Rise and Fall of a Modern Ghetto.* Cambridge, MA: Harvard University Press.

Venkatesh, Sudhir. 2009. *Off the Books: The Underground Economy of the Urban Poor.* Cambridge, MA: Harvard University Press.

Victor, Daniel. 2018. "John Boehner's Marijuana Reversal: 'My Thinking Has Evolved.'" *New York Times.* April 18. https://www.nytimes.com/2018/04/11/us/politics/boehner-cannabis-marijuana.html.

Vinson, Michelle, and Vicki Turetsky. 2009. State Child Support Pass-Through Policies. Washington, DC: Center for Law and Social Policy. June 12. https://www.clasp.org/sites/default/files/public/docs/PassThroughFinal061209.pdf.

Wacquant, Loïc. 2000. "The New 'Peculiar Institution': On the Prison as Surrogate Ghetto." *Theoretical Criminology* 4, no. 3: 377–389.

Wacquant, Loïc. 2001. "Deadly Symbiosis: When Ghetto and Prison Meet and Mesh." *Punishment & Society* 3, no. 1: 95–133.

Wacquant, Loïc. 2006. *Body and Soul: Notes from an Apprentice Boxer.* New York: Oxford University Press.

Wacquant, Loïc. 2009. *Punishing the Poor: The Neoliberal Government of Social Insecurity.* Durham, NC: Duke University.

Wacquant, Loïc. 2010. "Prisoner Reentry as Myth and Ceremony." *Dialectical Anthropology* 34: 605–620.

Wakefield, Sara, and Christopher Wildeman. 2014. *Children of the Prison Boom: Mass Incarceration and the Future of American Inequality.* New York: Oxford University Press.

Waller, Maureen. 2002. *My Baby's Father: Unmarried Parents and Paternal Responsibility.* Ithaca, NY: Cornell University Press.

Waller, Maureen R., and Raymond Swisher. 2006. "Father's Risk Factors in Fragile Families: Implications for 'Healthy' Relationships and Father Involvement." *Social Problems* 53, no. 3: 392–420.

Weber, Rachel. 2002. "Extracting Value from the City: Neoliberalism and Urban Redevelopment." *Antipode* 34, no. 3: 519–540.

Weibgen, Adrien A. 2013. "There Goes the Neighborhood: Slums, Social Uplift and the Remaking of Wooster Square." *Yale Law School Student Scholarship Repository*. Paper 24. https://digitalcommons.law.yale.edu/cgi/viewcontent.cgi?article=1024&context=student_legal_history_papers.

Weil, David. 2014. *The Fissured Workplace: Why Work Because So Bad for So Many and What Can Be Done to Improve It*. Cambridge, MA: Harvard University Press.

Weiner, Ali. 2010. "Pledging Allegiance." *The New Journal*. October 24. http://www.thenewjournalatyale.com/2010/10/pledging-allegiance/

Western, Bruce. 2006. *Punishment and Inequality in America*. New York: Russell Sage Foundation.

Western, Bruce, and Becky Pettit. 2010. *Collateral Costs: Incarceration's Effect on Economic Mobility*. Washington, DC: Pew Charitable Trusts. https://www.pewtrusts.org/~/media/legacy/uploadedfiles/pcs_assets/2010/collateralcosts1pdf.pdf.

Western, Bruce. 2018. *Homeward: Life in the Year After Prison*. New York: Russell Sage Foundation.

Wheaton, Blair, and Philippa Clarke. 2003. "Space Meets Time: Integrating Temporal and Contextual Influences on Mental Health in Early Adulthood." *American Sociological Review* 68: 680–706.

Wheaton, Laura, and Elaine Sorenson. 2007. *The Potential Impact of Increasing Child Support Payments to TANF Families*. Washington, DC: The Urban Institute, Brief 5. December. https://www.urban.org/research/publication/potential-impact-increasing-child-support-payments-tanf-families.

Wheaton, Laura, and Elaine Sorenson. 2010. "Extending the EITC to Noncustodial: Potential Impact and Design Characteristics." *Journal of Policy Analysis and Management* 29, no. 4: 749–768.

Will, George F. 1986. "Voting Rights Won't Fix It." *Washington Post*. January 23.

Williams, Joan C. 2001. *Unbending Gender: Why Family and Work Conflict and What To Do About It*. New York: Oxford University Press.

Williams, Joan C. 2010. *Reshaping the Work-Family Debate: Why Men and Class Matter*. Cambridge, MA: Harvard University Press.

Williams, Rhys. 2001. *Promise Keepers and the New Masculinity: Private Lives and Public Morality*. Lanham, MD: Lexington Press.

Willrich, Michael. 2000. "Home Slackers: Men, the State, and Welfare in Modern America." *Journal of American History* 87, no. 2: 460–489.

Wolkoff, Adam. 2006. "Creating a Suburban Ghetto: Public Housing at New Haven's West Rock, 1945–1979." *Connecticut History Review* 45, no. 1: 56–96.

YouTube.com. 2009. "Judge Mathis on the Downfall of Black Society." Accessed April 8, 2018. https://www.youtube.com/watch?v=Uodt40rTq5E.

Index

For the benefit of digital users, indexed terms that span two pages (e.g., 52–53) may, on occasion, appear on only one of those pages.

Figure and tables are indicated by *f* and *t* following the page number.